VAGABOND OF VERSE

ROBERT SERVICE

— a biography —

Vagabond of Verse

JAMES MACKAY

MAINSTREAM
PUBLISHING
EDINBURGH AND LONDON

First published in Great Britain in 1995 by
MAINSTREAM PUBLISHING COMPANY (EDINBURGH) LTD
7 Albany Street
Edinburgh EH1 3UG

ISBN 1 85158 704 7

A catalogue record for this book is available from the British Library

Subsidised by THE SCOTTISH ARTS COUNCIL

Typeset in 11pt Bembo by Saxon Graphics Ltd, Derby
Printed and bound in Great Britain by
Butler & Tanner Ltd, Frome and London

For Renate

(ONTENT$

ACKNOWLEDGMENTS

IN WRITING THIS BOOK I HAVE HAD CONSIDERABLE HELP from many disparate sources. First and foremost I must thank Jack Ramsay of Irvine for prodding me into tackling a project which rapidly developed into a labour of love. Jack put me in touch with people in Kilwinning with an intimate knowledge of local history in general and the Service family in particular. In this regard I am heavily indebted to Roy Lauchlan MBE who supplied me with a great deal of information and conducted me round the places of interest connected with the poet. MacIan Service of Glasgow and Anne Millar of Bearsden drew on their incomparable knowledge of Service genealogy, while Helen Dick and J.J. McCreadie of Largs also supplied information on Service family connections in Ayrshire. In pursuit of the authorship of 'Eskimo Nell' I must thank Mary Leggatt, Robert Cogan and Professor Emeritus G. Ross Roy. Judith McColm and Janis Thorn of the Kilwinning Public Library were most helpful in numerous ways.

For details of the poet's antecedents in Preston I have to thank the staff of the Lancashire County Records Office. Roger Schultz of the reference section of the Preston District Library was unfailingly courteous in ferreting out local directories, files of nineteenth-century newspapers and the 1871 Census returns. I am grateful to Reeds & Rains, estate agents, who enabled me to examine one of the terraced houses in Christian Road, then on the market, which was identical to the one in which the poet was born. Maggie Mulholland helped me in a number of ways, from pointing me in the direction of the Preston records to organising my travels abroad in quest of Service.

The Glasgow period ought to have been the easiest to cover, but many of the greatest mysteries of the poet's life belong to the '80s and '90s of the last century and, despite a very great deal of tedious searching of directories,

Census returns and files of old newspapers and periodicals, some of them remain to be solved. For example, identifying 'Silverman', the poet's best friend, when no such name occurred in the Glasgow directories of the period, might have been well-nigh impossible without the help of Dr Ben Braber of the Garnethill Jewish Archives; in this regard, the interest of Drs Jack Miller, Jacob Shapiro and Kenneth Collins was also most helpful. Inevitably the Mitchell Library was my main source of information, notably the Glasgow Room, the History and Topography Department and the Language and Literature Department. Tracking down the Corpse in the Cooling Room entailed weary weeks of peering at microfilms of the *Glasgow Herald* and other newspapers of the 1880s; at other times, however, the answers to seemingly insoluble problems simply dropped into my lap, thanks to the encyclopaedic knowledge of the librarians. To the hard-pressed staff of the Mitchell Library I owe a very great debt indeed. Singling out individuals is invidious, but I must pay tribute to Hamish Whyte, himself a poet of renown, for making the task of sifting through the mass of material in the papers deposited by the late Arthur Stewart more manageable. Dr Irene O'Brien of Strathclyde Regional Archives supplied me with information on school log-books as well as shipping records of 1896. I am grateful to the staff of the Library and Archives at the University of Glasgow, for access to the Jimmy Logan collection of theatrical memorabilia and the records of the University Court. To my good friend James L. Hempstead of Dumbarton I owe an apology for the time he expended in the fruitless search through local newspapers for any details regarding the Renton footballer who lost his legs in a railway accident in Canada.

Farther afield I have had invaluable assistance from the staff of Dumbarton District Library, Levenford House, the Librarian of the House of Commons, the staffs of the National Library of Scotland, the British Library, Bloomsbury and the Newspaper Library, Colindale, London, the Archivists of the Royal Bank of Scotland and the Canadian Imperial Bank of Commerce, the staff of the Yukon Department of Tourism, Heritage and Cultural Resources, the Yukon Library and Archives in Whitehorse, the Libraries of Victoria and Vancouver, particularly Lynne Macdonald of the Language and Literature Division in the last-named, the McPherson Library of the University of Victoria, Alan H. MacDonald of the Library of the University of Calgary and the staff of the Calgary City Library, Peter L. Freeman of the University of Alberta Library, Edmonton, the Curator of the Robert Service Museum, Carcross, British Columbia, the Librarian, Duncan Public Library, Vancouver Island, the staff of the Los Angeles Public Library, the Librarian and Archivist of the General Sikorski Institute in London, David Mattison of the British Columbia Archives in Victoria, and the friendly Canadian-Scottish staff of Dawson Museum and Historical Society. My thanks are especially due to Lynn Pecknold, principal of the Robert Service School in Dawson, and also Dr

Helen Henley for supplying me with invaluable reminiscences of the Corfield family. To the staff of Canadian National Archives in Ottawa I am indebted for details of Robert Service's work in connection with his survey of Canadian forces serving in France in 1918. Shannon Service of Toronto, Ruth Service of Barrie, Ontario, Patricia Service of Vancouver and Kelvin Service of Niagara on the Lake have greatly assisted me in filling in the gaps concerning the Service family in Canada. Greg Gatenby of Toronto very generously put at my disposal his own notes and cuttings file on Robert Service and made a number of helpful suggestions.

For the period spanning forty-five years in which the poet lived in France I must thank Marie Dagorne and Jean Vallée of Lancieux and Loïc-René Vilbert of Dinan, all of whom went out of their way to be extremely helpful. Indeed, their enthusiasm for the Canadian-Scot who settled in Brittany was singularly impressive. For information on the German commandant who took over Robert's villa in Brittany I am indebted to Inge and Tom Meredith of Johannesburg.

The search for the real Robert Service has taken me to three continents, from Alaska to Tahiti. These pilgrimages, of course, were undertaken over a period of years; but in connection with the immediate legwork required for this book I am grateful to the Scottish Arts Council for a travel grant, without which a great deal of the research would not have been possible.

I am, however, immensely indebted to the poet's daughter, Iris Service Davies, who has taken a very keen interest in this project from the outset and who has permitted me to quote freely from her father's works, in prose and verse. We have corresponded frequently, and I have also had the privilege of her gracious hospitality in Monte Carlo and Brittany. She has not only given generously of her time, but allowed me the wholehearted and unrestrained use of family memorabilia, photographs, press-cuttings and manuscript material, as well as lending me copies of her father's novels which were difficult to get access to otherwise. Robert W. Service had an ambivalent attitude towards fame: he deplored the inconvenience of the limelight for most of his life, but towards the end he feared that he might be forgotten. I have found, however, that the merest mention of this project was enough to start even the most casual of acquaintances reciting their Service favourites at great length. There must be countless thousands of people around the world who retain a warm affection for the Vagabond of Verse. It is Iris Davies's fervent hope that this study of her father's life will kindle fresh interest in him and his works.

James Mackay
Glasgow
July 1994

PREFACE

I FIRST BECAME ACQUAINTED WITH THE WORKS OF Robert W. Service at the age of seven. I well remember the small volume bound in dark maroon, with the gold lettering BALLADS OF A BOHEMIAN on the spine, which lay on a bookshelf at home. It was my introduction to poetry of any sort, and the rhymes seemed so artless that I was soon tempted to imitate them. My mother, an unsentimental woman, destroyed my childish efforts in rhyme so none of this juvenilia will ever rise up to haunt me.

Two years later *Ploughman of the Moon* was published. Two uncles (younger brothers of my mother) and a cousin read this racy autobiography with immense relish and I could hardly wait to get my hands on it. Certain passages made such an impression on me that, forty-five years later, when I re-read this book, I had the feeling of coming upon an old friend. In one sense I was disappointed. It was common knowledge at my school that Robert Service was one of our most distinguished old boys; but although the book contained vivid — indeed, often painful — descriptions of his schooldays, the school was not mentioned by name, nor were any of the schoolmasters and fellow pupils. This exasperating indifference to names and dates characterised his autobiographical writing; it was poetic licence at its most unlicensed.

Robert William Service brought the magic of the Klondike Gold Rush to countless millions of readers all over the world. Although best remembered for his rollicking ballads 'The Shooting of Dan McGrew' and 'The Cremation of Sam McGee', published in 1907 in a slim volume entitled *Songs of a Sourdough* (later retitled, for American readers, as *The Spell of the Yukon*), Service was the author of a dozen other books of verse, from *Ballads of a Cheechako* (1909) to *Rhymes for My Rags* (1956). In addition, he produced three collected volumes, six novels, two autobiographies, a song-book and a keep-fit manual which contained a great deal of his own homespun philosophy of life. He was still composing verse right up to the time of his death in September 1958 and some of this subsequently appeared in *Later Collected Verse* (1960). During his long and exceedingly diverse career, he was also a journalist and war correspondent, and it is a matter for regret that his talent for descriptive writing was never channelled into travel books.

Born in England and raised in Scotland, Service spent the greater part of his long life abroad. He emigrated to Canada at the age of twenty-two, and because he made his reputation in the far North-West he is widely regarded as a Canadian poet — 'the Canadian Kipling' and 'the Bard of the Yukon' are epithets still applied to him. But he settled in France in 1913 and, apart from a wartime interlude in Hollywood and Vancouver (1940–45), he spent the rest of his life in that country, alternating between winters in Nice or Monte Carlo and summers at Lancieux in Brittany where he died.

All his life, Service was afflicted by a restlessness and wanderlust which was to take him to the ends of the earth. As an emigrant to British Columbia, with a mere five dollars in his pocket, he wandered all over the Pacific coast, from Alaska to Mexico, taking a wide variety of jobs in rapid succession. As a bank clerk, he was sent to Whitehorse and Dawson in the Yukon and was a keen observer of the Gold Rush days which he chronicled so vividly in his verse. Service never considered himself a poet; he was a versifier, a rhymester, a balladeer who wrote in simple language which was readily understood by the common man. Therein lay his appeal, and his phenomenal success. Half a century later, Service reckoned that Dan McGrew alone had netted him more than half a million dollars. *Songs of a Sourdough* had sold over three million copies by 1940, and, indeed, it continues to sell well to this day, with new editions appearing regularly.

Service, in fact, became the most successful poet of the twentieth century in material terms. Other poets, perhaps more worthy of that appellation, received honours and recognition; he at least had the consolation of fortune if not fame. Much of his verse of the 1920s, and several of his novels, dealt with the low-life of Paris, conveying the impression that he moved in the Bohemian circles of the Latin Quarter. In truth, although he lived for a time in Montparnasse, Service could afford a villa in Monte Carlo and two houses in Brittany. Having written about roughnecks, bums and hobos, Service was assumed to be one of them; but he was an acute observer rather than an active participant. 'I was not my type,' he was later to declare simply.

Had he written nothing more than *Songs of a Sourdough* his reputation would have been assured. In fact, it is probable that he would enjoy a higher literary standing today had he rested on his laurels. Although his subsequent work enjoyed substantial success, his autobiographies (1945–48) have long been out of print, while his novels are today unread. Yet they had a considerable vogue at the time and several of them were filmed. Service had published over eight hundred poems by the time he reached the age of eighty and it was his stated ambition to live to a hundred and write at least a thousand poems. He achieved the latter, but died in his eighty-fifth year.

The public image of the reckless gold-seeker, the man of action and the rugged outdoor type was only partially true. The bank clerk who rhymed for fun probably obtained more from the Klondike than most of the gold prospectors, but his nuggets were in verse. In two conflicts (the Second Balkan War and the First World War) Service was an observer rather than an active participant, but, as an ambulance-driver and later as an Intelligence officer in the Canadian Army, he came close enough to the suffering to be able to chronicle it graphically in many of the poignant verses which later appeared in *Rhymes of a Red Cross Man* and *Ballads of a Bohemian*, earning him the epithet of 'Bard of the BEF' (British Expeditionary Force).

There was a certain ambivalence about his love of the great outdoors. As he put it himself, he 'had a pedestrian lifestyle supported by an automobile income'. He could have afforded to travel the world in style and luxury. Instead, he would take his wife on long bicycling jaunts through France. He once set out to walk from New York to Florida but gave up when he got to Philadelphia; but he also made a 2,000-mile trip by canoe along the Mackenzie and Yukon Rivers which ranks as one of the epic journeys of the Canadian Arctic.

At the same time, Service was an essentially private man. He married relatively late in life, at the age of thirty-nine, but he remained happily wed to his French wife, Germaine, for forty-five years. Twin girls were born in 1917 but one died a year later, devastating Service who assuaged his grief in a tender and poignant poem. Over the years, he came to loathe his most famous creations Dan McGrew and Sam McGee, and was intensely embarrassed by the persona which they conveyed. For years he was nagged by his American publisher to write his life story. In the end, he relented, but produced a volume that is a masterpiece of obfuscation. *Ploughman of the Moon*, subtitled 'An Adventure into Memory', is remarkably deficient in hard facts, and the vast majority of the personal names mentioned therein are completely fictional. He did not mention that he was born in England, far less naming the town of his birth, leading many to suppose that he was Scottish through and through. The town of his early upbringing (Kilwinning) is described only as the Long Grey Town while Glasgow, where he spent his later boyhood and his first seven years as a bank clerk, is referred to only as 'the city'. He was the eldest of a family of ten (seven sons and three daughters) but his siblings are rarely mentioned. His father is discussed, usually disparagingly, but his mother hardly referred to at all. Incidents at school are described in considerable detail but neither teachers nor classmates are given their names, or are disguised behind fictional ones.

So, too, with the period of manhood in North America which takes up the rest of the first autobiographical volume. The second volume, *Harper of Heaven* (1948), dealt with Service's life from the age of forty to seventy, but is even less revealing than its predecessor, being largely a chronicle of travels from the South Pacific to Soviet Russia. Indeed, the raw material which was so profligately expended in this volume could more profitably (for his readers) have been expanded to fill several travel books. His experiences during two prolonged sojourns in the Soviet Union in the 1930s, for example, would have had much more impact had they been distilled into a separate volume.

Previous biographers — Carl Klinck (1976) and Wallace Lockhart (1991) — set out with the avowed attention of stripping away the false trails, the pseudonyms and the deliberately misleading statements in order to get at the true man, but in both cases they soon gave up the struggle, or fell into the trap of accepting what Service had to say at face value. My approach, however, has been to apply the techniques of investigative journalism and analysis of a very diverse range of primary sources to get at the truth. The results have produced a much more fully rounded and illuminating picture of one of the literary giants of the twentieth century, a man who preferred reticence to the limelight and who developed self-deprecation to a high art. Here at last is a biography which I hope truly does justice to one of the literary enigmas of our time.

CHAPTER 1

THE WRONG SIDE OF THE TRACKS

For I am cast of common clay,
And from a ditch I fought my way,
  And that is why
The while the poet scans the skies,
My gaze is grimly gutterwise,
  Earthy am I.

'Sympathy', in *Rhymes for my Rags* (1956)

THE LANCASHIRE TOWN OF PRESTON WAS AN EXCITING place to be in 1868. In that year the Lancashire historian and globe-trotter James Bryce returned to his native county and was amazed to find that it had taken a sudden leap out of one age into another:

The speed with which this region has increased in wealth and population finds no parallel except in America or Australia, and the phenomena which have accompanied its growth are exactly those which are observed at this moment in our newest colonies. Towns have risen so fast as hardly to have yet become aware of their own existence; they are straggling and irregularly built, handsome piles mixed with hovels, public buildings extemporised in odd corners, big rambling shops in which, as in a backwoods store, everything is sold, from silks and notepaper at one counter to herrings and potatoes at the other. They are, in short, overgrown villages of 60,000 or 70,000 people.[1]

The population of England and Wales multiplied three and a half times in the course of the nineteenth century, but that of Lancashire grew at almost twice that rate, from 673,486 in 1801 to 4,406,409 in 1901. At the same time, there was a significant move from the county districts into the mushrooming towns. Preston had been a thriving market town of about 12,000 inhabitants at the beginning of the century. By 1831 it had more than doubled, to 33,000, but in the ensuing twenty years it more than doubled again, to 68,000 in 1851. Although the rate of growth slowed down thereafter, it was still pretty substantial. By 1871 Preston had a population of 85,427. The reason for this phenomenal growth was cotton. The Horrocks brothers erected their Yellow Factory for the spinning of cotton thread in Stanley Street in 1791, and within a decade they had opened four more. They were only the most enterprising and successful of the cotton-spinners whose factories sprang up all over the town in the ensuing decades. By the 1860s the town boasted 32 mills with a total of 490,102 spindles employing 511 spinners, all men.

The weaving of cotton, however, lagged behind and continued to rely mainly on hand-loom weavers until the middle of the century. Power looms had been introduced in the 1820s but their operators were under-capitalised and most went bankrupt within a few years. Preston benefited from the railway mania of the 1840s; between 1838 and 1849 lines were opened that radiated from Preston to Wigan, Lancaster, Fleetwood, Bolton, Manchester, Blackburn and Liverpool. The town's position at the head of the Ribble estuary encouraged the development of a port which, by 1845, could admit sea-going schooners. Three years later the first 300-ton vessel arrived from New Orleans laden with cotton and corn. Steam-powered looms and jennies, combined with the dramatic development of communications, triggered off Preston's great industrial boom.

The transition from hand-loom weaving, carried on as a cottage industry, to the vast factories employing thousands of hands, had a marked effect on the type of housing thrown up in the 1850s and 1860s. The bustling, burgeoning Preston of that period was a town of strange contrasts. The magnificent new Town Hall and impressive shops on the Fishergate were fronted by gutters down which flowed uncertainly the slops and raw sewage thrown out of houses. Channels of urine drifted sluggishly out of the narrow alleyways and ran, open and unprotected, across the pavement in broad streams.[2] In the High Street a huge uncompleted sewer discharged its contents down the centre of the street. In the Plungington district new mills were built without roads.

The Queen's Mill, newly built [1861] on this moor, has neither roads nor drains; and the rain and waste steam have formed lakes around it of coal-ash mud, which the operatives must ford to enter the mill. A landowner here provided his houses with drainage and water closets; but, unfortunately, the want of playground obliges the children to play where they may, and the closets soon got out of order; and this pioneer movement was abandoned, and the reign of the cesspool resumed.[3]

And along New Hall Lane to the east of the town,

More mills, and more mud; a row of houses, with a man weaving in a cellar of one of them; a great stagnant swamp, with a brick-yard in it, and a square dung-heap; an isolated row of houses in Skeffington road, with pools of drainage before them; more mills, more mud, more dwellings propped up while building.[4]

The most apt local comment on this collision between the old world and the new was, 'Preston is a hundred years in arrear of the steady and somewhat surprising progress of its own manufactures'.[5] Although written in 1844, this was still fair comment thirty years later. Despite the slump caused by the American Civil War (which temporarily cut off the town from its raw supplies) Preston continued to expand, and the cotton industry reached its zenith in the 1880s when about a third of the population was directly employed in the 73 mills.

During the third quarter of the nineteenth century the pattern of industry changed. The number of firms engaged solely in cotton-spinning grew at a much slower rate, and those which concentrated on weaving outnumbered them by two to one. Power-loom weaving was women's work and female labour was much cheaper than male. This pattern continued to grow right down to the turn of the century. Although cotton-spinning was beginning to decline in importance, there was still money to be made from it. About 1868 James Parker, who had enjoyed a fair measure of success as a wholesale grocer, diversified by acquiring a controlling interest in a spinning mill at Kirkham to the west of the town. He continued to ply his trade as a grocer, but liked to be thought of mainly as a cotton-spinner.

Like most citizens of Preston, James and his wife were incomers. James had been born at Clitheroe in the year of Waterloo, the eldest son of Thomas Parker and Alice Heaton who had married at Croston, their ancestral village, in September 1802. James Parker met his wife-to-be at the Wesleyan Methodist Chapel in Clitheroe. Ann Hodgson, daughter of James and Agnes Hodgson, hailed from Liverpool and had been raised in the Particular Baptist faith. She was nineteen months older than her future husband, a not unusual custom for that time. They were married in the Methodist chapel on 9 September 1835, a fortnight before James's twentieth birthday.[6] Although his parents and siblings were content to remain in Clitheroe, James Parker was attracted to the rapidly growing town of Preston. He and his wife managed to delay starting a family until after their move to the town about 1838. A son, baptised Thomas Whitehead Parker, was born there in February 1839, followed at comparatively wide-spaced intervals by John Clince (1843), Mary Jane (January 1846), Joseph Adam (January 1849) and Sarah Emily (September 1854).[7]

By 1871 James Parker was a prosperous wholesale grocer and tea merchant with impressive premises at 131 Church Street and an even more imposing Georgian mansion in Preston's most fashionable thoroughfare, Winckley Square, overlooking a beautiful park. By that date both Thomas and Mary Jane (commonly known as Jane) were married and had left the parental home. John was twenty-eight but unmarried and still living at home. In the census of that year he was described as a cotton-spinner and seems to have attended to the Kirkham side of the family business. The youngest of the family was Sarah Emily, familiarly known as Emily. In 1871 she was sixteen years of age, petite and vivacious; although she would never be a striking beauty, she had an attractive personality and a rather happy-go-lucky temperament.

At the 1871 census James Parker was described as fifty-six which was accurate enough, but Ann had managed to deduct two years from her age — something that her grandson was to do on a number of occasions throughout his life. For all the impressiveness of their mansion, the Parkers lived cannily, with only two servants, Sarah Tudor and Mary Fell.

The Parkers moved in the best circles. For many years James had been a Conservative councillor, representing the prestigious St John's Ward since November 1853. His occupation of that seat was uninterrupted until the election of November 1874 when he and his colleague Miles Dent were unseated by the Hawkins brothers. 'Mr Parker, who felt his defeat keenly — as was but natural in one who assumed to have the ward at his feet — was not long without a seat,' reported the *Preston Guardian*. The elevation of Councillor Hayhurst to become an alderman left a convenient vacancy in St John's and Parker obtained re-election with little difficulty, through the warm support of his friends on the Council. The same newspaper recorded that James Parker, though one of the safest votes in the Town Council, never rose above common councillor. At one point he did apply for the alderman's gown but his application was tossed aside 'with a sarcastic, not to say contemptuous, laugh'.[8] So, too, withered any aspirations he may have had to the mayoralty.

Ann Parker died early in 1872. The removal of a mother's wise guidance may well explain what happened next, for Emily formed an emotional attachment with one of the clerks employed by the Preston Bank in the Fishergate.

She was seventeen, a very attractive girl by all accounts. Why she should fall for Robert Service seems a mystery, for he was decidedly on the plump side, red of face and already bald. At thirty-five, he was twice her age — not quite old enough, perhaps, to have been her father, though what used to be called a confirmed bachelor, set in his ways. But Emily's father, though only fifty-seven, was already an old man,[9] and in fact Emily's eldest brother Thomas was only three years younger than Robert. Emily, who had grown up in a family where she was very much the baby, would not have found the eighteen years difference in age so very startling.

What is even more surprising is that Emily, who could have had the pick of Preston's eligible young men, should have fallen in love with the portly, balding Scotsman.[10] As a banker's clerk, Robert Service commanded a salary of only a hundred pounds a year. Although his son would later describe him as a banker, or even as the manager of the Preston Bank, Robert Senior was fairly low down the pecking order. He had entered this profession straight from school at the age of fourteen and after serving his apprenticeship with the Commercial Bank of Scotland in Glasgow, he had obtained a clerkship in the same organisation. After eighteen years with the Commercial Bank, with little prospect of advancement, he had headed south and obtained a similar position in Preston where the spectacular recovery of the cotton trade after the American Civil War promised rapid promotion. The Preston Bank had been established in 1844 and the handsome new building at 39 Fishergate was opened twelve years later.

Preston, however, soon proved to be little different from Glasgow where the prospects of promotion were concerned. In 1873 the manager of the bank was George B. Dalby and the cashier or sub-manager was George T. Tully.[11] Robert Service was not important enough to feature on the list of the bank's officials given in the local directory. Robert settled to the monotony of totting figures in ledgers, and lived in a boarding house at 15 Syers Street, not far from the bank, along with other bachelor clerks, often many years his junior.

Emily Parker was undoubtedly the best thing that ever happened to the rather solitary, diffident bank clerk. It is hardly surprising that their unlikely but whirlwind courtship was not regarded favourably by the girl's father. In the end, the couple eloped — not to Gretna Green which had the merit, for runaways, of being the nearest point across the border in Scotland where a girl under the age of twenty-one did not require the consent of her parents or guardian, but to much more prosaic Ormskirk, a mere twenty miles to the south. There, on 21 October 1872, Robert and Emily were wed.[12] At the time, Emily was living with her sister Mary Jane at 18 Leyland Road, Southport, some eighteen miles south-west of Preston, but it was in the parish church of North Meols in the neighbouring town of Ormskirk that she was married.

The witnesses to the marriage were her sister and William Service, younger brother of the groom and then a twenty-four-year-old schoolmaster who appears to have come south from Scotland for the occasion.

Such a marriage, once solemnised, was perfectly valid, with or without parental consent, and in due course the runaway couple returned to face the music. It appears that James at first would have nothing to do with his wayward daughter. This would explain why no dowry was settled on her which might have enabled the newly-weds to enjoy a measure of comfort not far removed from that to which she had been accustomed.

Instead, Robert brought his child bride to a new house barely two hundred yards from her father's mansion; but the contrast could scarcely have been greater. Christian Road was a dead-end running off Fishergatehill, parallel with the line of the London and North Western Railway. It consisted of thirty dwellings, in two facing terraced rows of fifteen terminating in the railway goods yard. Widening of the railway tracks in recent years has led to the demolition not only of Charles Street, which lay between Christian Road and the railway, but of the east side of Christian Road itself, so that only the terrace on the west side remains. But some idea of how very congested this development was in its heyday can be obtained from the fact that the remaining houses back on to the backs of the terraced houses in Stanley Place. Christian Road and Stanley Place, despite their rather grand names, were mean terraces in the classic northern back-to-back tradition.

Between each group of three houses is a narrow passageway leading to a lane of minuscule proportions, parallel to the streets and providing the only gap between them. This lane, barely a metre broad, was wide enough only to permit the scavengers to remove the noisome pails from the tiny brick privies at the rear of each dwelling. There were no back courts where children might play or housewives dry their washing. Instead, lines were strung across the streets from house to house so that the family laundry had to contend with the pollution of chimney-stacks and the smuts from the passing locomotives.

The houses in Christian Road were identical. Each had a front door and a downstairs window set in red brick with painted stucco facings. Upstairs were two windows, one for each of the front bedrooms. Despite their unprepossessing appearance, these houses were solidly built and surprisingly commodious. Rising damp was kept at bay by a deep coal-cellar. On the ground floor there was a front parlour, with the obligatory aspidistra in the window presenting an image of defiant gentility to the world. Beyond was the kitchen cum dining-room cum main living-room of the household. In many cases this room also served as a bedroom to the parents, with a wall-recess bed and perhaps even a truckle bed (little more than a board on wheels) pulled out from under it at night to accommodate the youngest member of the family.

Nowadays this room has become elevated to the dining-room, with the original scullery upgraded to a kitchenette.

Upstairs there were four bedrooms, two facing the front and two looking out on to the back of the houses in Stanley Place. The houses remaining in Christian Road have been upgraded and gentrified in recent years. Loft conversions have provided a fifth bedroom as well as a bathroom, but it is extremely unlikely that such facilities existed in the early 1870s when the road was being developed. Then the womenfolk drew their water from a communal standpipe. Indoor plumbing, far less hot water and central heating or electricity, would not be installed till many years later. Indeed, it is remarkable that Christian Road and Stanley Place survived the wholesale destruction of older dwellings which took place in the 1960s and 1970s. Rather late in the day, the local authorities began to realise that the slums of the inner urban areas could have been refurbished, and that basically they were of sound construction despite the haste in which they were erected in the first place.

The houses in Christian Road were built as artisans' dwelling-houses — hardly what one would expect of a bank official, far less the 'manager of the Preston Bank' as Robert Junior was later to claim in his autobiography. Nor is it the sort of house one would imagine any self-respecting mill-owner allowing his daughter to occupy under normal circumstances. The relations between old James and Emily must remain a matter for speculation, but it is probably significant that none of the seven boys born to Robert and Emily was named after her father.

Christian Road was still under construction when Robert and Emily moved in at Number 4. It does not feature at all in the 1869 directory, and at the time of the 1871 census only 1 to 8 had been built, 3 and 4 being as yet unoccupied. Their neighbours at Number 2 in 1873 were thirty-four-year-old David Bostock, a school inspector's assistant, with his wife Dinah aged twenty-eight and their two daughters, Clara (six) and Lilian (eleven months). Interestingly, they had a Welsh maid, twenty-four-year-old Mary Griffiths from Denbighshire. Across the street, at Number 5, lived Lawrence Smith, a thirty-four-year-old tailor, with wife Mary (twenty-eight), son William (three) and three lodgers: John Birdsall, a railway clearing-house clerk, Thomas Drury, a pawnbroker's assistant, and George Drury, his elder brother, a commercial traveller in tea.[13] The lodgings of these three young men, in fact, were not dissimilar to those which Robert Service had occupied but a short time before.

Ironically, Christian Road these days is something of a misnomer, as many of its inhabitants are of the Muslim faith, probably the proprietors or at least the employees of Ram's newsagent, Rahmani's, Kazee Saris and other small shops just around the corner on Fishergatehill. Christian Road may superficially be much as it was in the 1870s, but in fact it has changed very considerably. Privatisation is evident in the fine new front doors of different patterns, and in the antique bull's-eye window panes at Number 2.

Number 4 even has a splendid teak door, but the brass numeral 4 has been screwed on upside-down, perhaps by an occupant not too familiar with western numerals. No circular blue plaque nor bronze tablet adorn its red-brick façade to draw attention to the fact that it was here, on 16 January 1874, that Preston's most famous son came into the world.

Emily was barely nineteen when she gave birth to her eldest son, the first in a family of seven boys and three girls. Defying hallowed Scottish tradition, the baby was not named after his father's father; instead he was named for his own father, but Robert added a middle name — William, after the brother who had witnessed his marriage. This precedent was followed little more than a year later when a second was born, and named John Alexander after Robert Senior's elder brother Alexander (who had died in August 1874), as well as his father and his youngest brother John (who was actually the same age as Emily).

There was something rather fey about Robert Senior, who let almost six weeks elapse before he got around to registering young Robert's birth.[14] This betokens an other-worldliness and irresponsibility which were to be character-istics noted in later years by his famous son, sometimes critically but at other times with sneaking admiration. By describing himself as a 'bank cashier', Robert Senior was undoubtedly gilding the lily. In the contemporary Preston directory he was described more accurately as a banker's clerk (which had also appeared under the heading of Rank or Profession on his marriage certificate).

At some point, probably after the birth of John Alexander, James Parker was reconciled with his younger daughter. By now he was far from well and he began preparing for death by drawing up a new will on 1 November 1875.[15] He continued to carry out his public duties for two weeks, and then took to his bed, dying of cancer at half past three on Monday morning, 24 November.

The *Preston Guardian* in its somewhat left-handed obituary,[16] concluded that 'it is stated that he leaves a large fortune — variously estimated at £50,000 to £100,000 and even more'. Certainly the myth that James Parker had left a large fortune was one perpetuated by Robert Service in his autobiography, claiming that

> Mama's father was a wise man who owned cotton mills. He left her
> about ten thousand pounds, with instructions that it was to be invested
> in Government securities, and that she was only to have the life interest.
> This was providential because if Papa had been able to get his hands on
> the principal, I hate to think what would have happened to our little
> brood.[17]

In point of fact, however, James Parker's wealth had been greatly exaggerated. His will, proved at Lancaster on 14 January 1876 by his brother Jonathan as chief trustee, indicated a net worth of less than £18,000.[18] Of this, the surprisingly substantial sum of £4,000 was left to his housekeeper, Hannah Woodcock. She was described quaintly as a 'Singlewoman' and was clearly a recent addition to the household as she was not in James's employment at the time of the 1871 Census. Indeed, it would not be stretching the imagination to suppose that the thirty-year-old housekeeper and young Emily did not get along, and her sudden advancement in the old man's affections may even have induced the daughter to leave home.

£2,000 was left outright to James's eldest son Thomas and £300 to his younger surviving son Joseph. From this it appears that John, who would then have been about thirty-two, may have predeceased his father. Out of the residue, the trustees were to invest the money and grant the life-rent to the two sons and two daughters. The income from two-fifths went to Thomas, and from one-fifth each to the other children — Mary Jane (who had married Henry Pemberton in 1868), Joseph Adam and Sarah Emily. After deducting the outright legacies it would appear that the most Emily could have inherited from her father was the life-rent on a sum of about £2,300 — less than a quarter of the sum declared in the family legend. According to James's will, the capital sum reverted to the trustees (his brother Jonathan and elder son Thomas) on the death of any of the other beneficiaries.

According to Robert Junior, the income from Emily's legacy gave her the handsome sum of two hundred pounds a year. In an era when interest rates were low, it seems unlikely that a capital sum of £2,300 would yield more than seventy or eighty pounds a year, no matter how prudently it was invested. At any rate it was a windfall sufficiently large to induce Robert Senior to resign from the bank. He did not, as his son would later maintain, become entirely a gentleman of leisure living off the proceeds from his wife's legacy; but with the security offered by this slender income he set up in business on his own account as a general commission and insurance agent. With his new-found status he moved his family to a rather more salubrious neighbourhood, on the other side of the railway, at 27 Latham Street, a terrace of twenty-nine houses running off Avenham Lane and not so far from the Parker residence in Winckley Square. Nowadays an area of decayed gentility, it was in the late 1870s a street occupied by the respectable upper working class or lower middle class.

In *Ploughman of the Moon*, the first of his two autobiographical volumes, Robert does not refer to Preston at all. If he had any infant memories of his birthplace he never mentioned them. His father soon discovered that being self-employed was much more arduous and requiring of self-discipline than working in a bank. The opportunities to gain commissions or sell insurance appear to have been rather limited, for in 1877, following the birth of his third son Thomas, he decided to return to Scotland. He would go back to Glasgow where the opportunities were infinitely greater than in Preston. In the spring of 1878 the family packed their worldly goods and took the train north. By May of that year the Services were installed in a small rented flat at 29 Lansdowne Crescent where Robert Senior hoped to make a go of it as a commission agent.[19] This was in quite a select neighbourhood, off Great Western Road in Glasgow's West End.

To this brief interlude belongs young Robert's earliest memory. Typically, in the account which follows, he omits to identify either Kilwinning or Glasgow, although they are both referred to obliquely in one of the opening sentences:

It is interesting to discover one's first recollection. Mine is of *going to jail*. It was the year before I went to live in the Long Grey Town with my aunties, and I was then in the city with my parents. I was wearing my kilt for the first time. Perhaps that was what impressed the occasion on my memory. I was walking with my nurse. She lugged me along with one hand while with the other she pushed the pram with my baby brother. I hung back, wanting to look at the shops. A candy shop particularly excited me, but my nurse dragged me on. Then Romance entered her young life and she released my hand to surrender hers to a budding butcher. This was my chance. Always the Escapist I slipped away.

The sweetie shop was round the corner, and there I gave myself up to the joy of window-shopping. For half an hour I stood with my nose flattened against the pane; then I suddenly remembered my nurse. No sign of her. I was lost. It rather elated me. Forlornly I stood at the curb and a crowd collected. 'Oh, the puir wee laddie! He's wandert,' I heard them say, and I enjoyed their commiseration. The crowd increased. Suddenly a stalwart policeman parted the people and loomed over me. He had a long black beard, but I looked up at him without awe.

'Where d'ye live?' he asked.

'Half past four,' I answered. No doubt this was because nurse had been told to get home by half past four, and that was all I could remember. But again he asked me, and again I answered: 'Half past four.' I still recall how the crowd laughed, while I wondered why they should.

Then the officer took me by the hand and conducted me to the police station. It is difficult for a bobby to maintain his dignity holding a tiny tot by the hand. He must have felt this, for he walked in a stately way and loftily ignored me, while the people we passed gave me glances of pity. But I trotted along cheerfully, enjoying it all. The station waiting-room consisted of bare walls and benches garnished with squalid-looking people. They gave me the same commiseration. The 'wee callant wi' his braw kilts' held the centre of the scene. Then a blousy matron arrived and clasped me to her bosom. I resisted — till she brought me tea and buns and tempted me to sit on her knee. I was enjoying myself when Mama blew in. She was frantic and ran to grab me; but I was having a gorgeous feed and, with my mouth full of bun, I refused to leave the matron. Kicking and howling I was dragged from the police station; and (though I have no doubt I richly deserved it), I take this occasion to state I have never been in one since.[20]

Service does not identify the 'jail' to which he was taken, but as the nearest police station at that period was the headquarters of the Hillhead Burgh Constabulary near the top end of Byres Road, it seems likely that this was where he was temporarily confined. Interestingly, though never far above the poverty line, the Service family kept up middle-class pretensions and always employed at least one servant. When the census was taken in 1881 the occupants of 29 Lansdowne Crescent consisted of Robert Service, aged forty-five, described as 'Bank Clerk (Unemployed)' and his wife Sarah Emily, aged twenty-seven. They had three sons living with them at the time: four-year-old Thomas, two-year-old Joseph, and Peter, an infant of only three weeks. Florenda Jamieson was described as a 'General Domestic Servant', but Ellen Bean, who hailed from Brechin, was the 'Ladies Nurse', and presumably the girl who had led little Robert astray.

It will be noted that neither Robert nor John featured in this list; they had been taken to their father's birthplace, probably in the summer or autumn of 1878 within months of the move to Glasgow, there to be brought up by John Service and his family. Why the eldest sons had been offloaded in this manner is a complete mystery and Robert provides no clue in his autobiography. It seems likely that, as Emily was expecting another baby (Joseph) at the time, it made sense to get the elder boys out of the way. Doubtless this was intended as a temporary measure but, in fact, it was to be four years before Robert and John were re-united with their parents.

CHAPTER 2

KILWINNING, 1878-83

Only a rhymer, — just a chiel
Spewed from the land of Burns,

'L'Envoi' in *Rhymes for my Rags* (1956)

ROBERT SERVICE'S AUTOBIOGRAPHY BEGINS WITH A CHAPTER dealing with his early life in the Long Grey Town. Nowhere is it actually named, but this set the tone for the rest of the book which was remarkably short on names of places and people and entirely bereft of dates.

In point of fact, the Long Grey Town was Kilwinning, a small burgh and market town of some five thousand souls, situated on the right bank of the River Garnock in north Ayrshire, about twenty-four miles south-west of Glasgow. In the eighth century a saintly hermit named Winning had had his cell there and the town was named after him. In 1140 an abbey was founded by Hugh de Morville, Lord of Cunninghame, for Tyronensian monks of the Benedictine order, and in its heyday it was one of the richest monastic establishments in Scotland. At the Reformation in 1560–61 this beautiful example of Early English ecclesiastical architecture was the target of the fanatical vandals; what they failed to destroy, the stonemasons of the eighteenth century completed as they removed stone for the villas then springing up on the outskirts. Sufficient of the ruined building survives, however, to give some idea of its magnificence. The Continental architects and stonemasons who came in the twelfth century to build the great abbey founded a lodge which, in time, became the birthplace of Scottish freemasonry and hence the Scottish rites which spread all over the world. The royal company of archers of Kilwinning was another venerable institution, dating back to 1488. As late as the nineteenth century the archers met every July to shoot at the popinjay, a painted wooden parrot.

An account of Kilwinning in 1851 dismisses it as comprising 'one street, a few lanes and a square called the Green'.[1] Although it grew considerably in the ensuing three decades the centre of the burgh retained its village character. The long street running west from the ruined abbey was known as the Howgate (derived from 'hie gait', the main road of the settlement) and along it lay the two-storey homes and business premises of the town's shopkeepers. Robert's description of Kilwinning as the Long Grey Town was particularly apt.

Kilwinning, like Preston, was an ancient ecclesiastical foundation which in secular times derived its prosperity from the agriculture of the surrounding district. It, too, felt the effects of industrialisation in the nineteenth century, but on a far more modest scale. By the late 1870s the iron, coal and fireclay works at Eglinton, together with engineering works and worsted spinning, gave employment to most of the inhabitants.[2]

Robert Service, who had absolutely no interest in his ancestry, once responded to an enquiry from a genealogist that in Kilwinning 'Services were as thick as fleas on a yellow dog'.[3] The surname was certainly of considerable antiquity, probably dating back to the twelfth century and the influx of foreigners connected with the building of the abbey. It is derived from the Norman-French *Cervoise* meaning a landlord or tavern-keeper, and, indeed, in the parochial registers of Kilwinning, some of the poet's ancestors are recorded as having kept hostelries. In his autobiography Robert betrayed a cavalier disregard for history, claiming that the hand-loom weavers (still active in the 1870s) were 'of Huguenot origin and responsible for the town's foundation',[4] blithely ignorant of the five-hundred-year gap between the Norman-French stonemasons and the Protestants forced out of their own country by the revocation of the Edict of Nantes in 1685.

Certainly, as far back as the records go, there were Services aplenty in Kilwinning. George Service, born early in the seventeenth century, and his wife Jean Young had three sons and two daughters. The second son, William (born in 1679), was twice married, having two sons and a daughter by Isobel Muir of Dalry whom he married in August 1709, and two sons and two daughters by Ann Thomson, a local girl, whom he wed in July 1724. The elder son of the first marriage was James Service, born in 1716, who married Marrion Ferguson on 27 April 1744. Their second son, John, was born on 6 August 1749 and, like his grandfather, was twice married. By his first wife,

Marrion Hanna whom he married on 15 September 1772, he had four daughters and two sons. Marrion Hanna died in 1783 and the following year John Service married again. His new wife was Jean Young, by whom he had a second family, including a son named John who was the grandfather of John Service, born in May 1851. This John Service qualified as a medical doctor and eventually settled in New South Wales where he died in 1913. In the latter part of his life, however, he was the author of four books, of which three — *The Recollections of Dr Duguid*, *The Remarkables of Robin Cummles* and *Laird Canticarl of Montgrynan* — were written in the Ayrshire vernacular and achieved a measure of fame at the time.

Robert Service, in his old age, vaguely recollected to his daughter Iris that he had a distant relative who had become an author in Australia, but he made no reference to this in either of his autobiographical works. The poet himself was a descendant of the first family of John Service. Alexander, born on 10 September 1780, married Agnes Cran in July 1808. A daughter, Isabel, was born in 1809 and the eldest of three sons on 27 October 1811. This was John Service, father of Robert the bank clerk and grandfather of Robert the poet.

One of John Service's tales, no doubt repeated so often that even he himself believed it, was that his father Alexander was a second cousin of Robert Burns, and that the two had been 'drouthy cronies' together. Wallace Lockhart[5] goes so far as to say that, according to family lore, Alexander Service 'achieved the distinction of getting drunk in Irvine with Robert Burns', and Service himself records:

> My great-grandfather had been a crony of Robert Burns and claimed him as a second cousin. One of our parlour chairs had often been warmed by the rump of the Bard; for, besides being a rhymester, my ancestor had been a toper; so I expect if that chair could have talked it could have told of wild nights with John Barleycorn. To my folks anything that rhymed was poetry, and Robbie Burns was their idol.[6]

This blithely ignores the fact that Alexander Service was barely a year old when Burns was in Irvine (1781–82). Even if the great-great-grandfather, John Service, was the subject of this legend, rather than his son, the story does not ring true. Apart from the fact that there is no link in the genealogies of Burns and Service, there is no record in the prose or verse of Burns to suggest that he ever visited Kilwinning[7] although, as an active freemason, it would have been natural for him to have made the short journey from Irvine to the neighbouring town. Burns himself became Depute Master in Lodge Kilwinning St James, at Tarbolton. Less likely, however, is the notion of Robert Burns the toper. At this period, and for some years thereafter, Burns could not afford to indulge in strong drink.[8] The legend smacks of a mid-nineteenth-century invention, at a time when Burns's reputation had been blackened and reached an all-time low in this respect.

John Service married a Paisley girl, Agnes Niven, who was two years his junior. Originally he kept a small store in the Howgate, but in 1861 he was appointed sub-postmaster of Kilwinning at a salary of fifteen pounds a year.[9] Seven years previously, as a result of the extension of the Registration Act to Scotland, he had been appointed Registrar for the parish. This had been a natural choice, as he had become Session Clerk of the parish church in 1852. John continued to perform his duties, both sacred and secular, until his death at the age of seventy-six. During the quarter century in which he ran the post office, the postal services expanded out of all recognition. He had only been in office a few months when Kilwinning was granted savings bank facilities (on 17 February 1862), which meant a modest increase in salary but a considerable boost in commission payments. In January 1870 came the most radical development, the telegraph, Kilwinning being assigned the call-sign KFA. For many years telegrams were sent and received by Morse code: 'Aunt Jennie jiggled a handle that in some inconceivable way sent off telegrams' is how Robert was to describe it later.[10]

In August 1883 the parcel post was instituted and, with the advent of postal orders two years later, the mail order business was born. These developments threw an enormous burden on the postmaster, especially at a time when Kilwinning was enjoying an industrial boom. In the 1880s the office opened for business at 7 a.m. and continued until 8 p.m. from Monday to Saturday. Till the late 1850s the post office was even open on Sundays, though closed during the hours of divine worship. The strong Sabbatarian movement of the mid-nineteenth century forced the post office to curtail Sunday working but, even so, Kilwinning, along with other post offices, was open on Sunday mornings between nine and ten o'clock so that letters could be handed over to callers. In 1886 John Service applied to have his establishment upgraded to the status of a head post office, but this was turned down and it was classified as a railway sub-office, signifying that it received and despatched mails direct by sealed bag via the railways.[11]

On 24 September 1976 a plaque on the wall of the old post office on the Main Street was unveiled by Iris Davies, the poet's daughter. The plaque states that Robert lived in Kilwinning between 1879 and 1883, but the first of these dates is probably incorrect. On his own account, Robert was living there before the age of five, at which point he was enrolled in the village school. This would therefore accord with the notion that he came to Kilwinning in the late summer or autumn of the previous year, not long after his parents left Preston and settled in Glasgow.

In his autobiography Robert Service devotes thirty-six pages to his time in Kilwinning. The impression he conveys is that he was an only child, raised by his grandfather and a gaggle of aunts. In fact his grandmother was alive throughout the entire period, dying on 3 October 1883, some time after Robert had been removed by his mother and taken back to Glasgow. Even more remarkable is the fact that Robert nowhere acknowledges the fact that throughout the Kilwinning period his brother John, barely a year younger, also lived at the post office. Indeed, throughout the autobiography his nine siblings are treated with the utmost casualness at the best of times, never actually named, and totally ignored for the most part.

John and Agnes Service lived above or behind the post office premises in the Howgate, together with their four daughters. Of their four sons, Alexander had died unmarried in 1874 at the age of thirty-four, Robert of course had pursued his uncertain career in banking, and only William (born 1848) and John, the baby of the family (born 1854), had made a success in their chosen professions of teaching and medicine respectively. At the Census of 1871 the eldest daughter Jeannie, then thirty-three, was a dressmaker while Isabella (twenty-five) was a milliner. Three of the family assisted their father with the post office. Alexander (a bachelor of thirty) was the village postman, while Agnes (twenty-eight) and Janet (twenty) were telegraphists. William (aged twenty-two) was then studying at Glasgow University for an Arts degree and John (aged eighteen) was a pupil teacher at the parish school. A decade later, William was the Classics master at Park School, Glasgow, while John, an MD of Glasgow University, was briefly in practice in Gibson Street, Hillhead, before going off to Bilbao in Spain.[12]

At the beginning of his autobiography Robert speaks of living with his grandfather and 'my three aunts', although a page or two later, almost as an afterthought, he introduces a fourth maiden aunt. The reason for the discrepancy is soon made clear. Aunt Agnes was consumptive and was isolated from the rest of the household in a tiny summer-house at the back of the garden, to the rear of the post office. She was the fourth child and second daughter of John Service and had been born in April 1843. 'I had another aunt who died when I was very young,' Robert wrote. 'She was little more than a girl, and I only remember her vaguely.' She was in fact in her thirty-eighth year when she expired on 14 November 1880. There is a possibility that Robert inherited his poetic inclinations from her.

> To me she was the loveliest of the family. She had such a waxen complexion and such pink cheeks. She never did any work and often sat apart, brooding sadly. In these moods she would repulse me when I tried to caress her; but I think it was more from a fear of infecting me

than from any irritation she felt. Sometimes, however, as if yielding to an uncontrollable tenderness, she would hug me to her, and once she brought out some delicately written poems and read them to me. She said they were her own and I thought them beautiful.[13]

Robert recalled later that he envied his aunt living out in the little summer-house. Catching the occasional glimpse of her haggard face at the window overhung with blackcurrant bushes, he felt drawn to her, but her door was kept locked. Towards the end of her life she was installed in the best bedroom of the house.

It had one of those stuffy enclosed beds; and there she sat, smoking some herbal cigarettes that were supposed to help her breathing. I laughed delightedly to see her smoking, but the others did not share my mirth. I recall the unearthly brightness of her eyes and the burning glow in her cheeks. She smoked her cigarettes like a real lady. Then, after a little, she asked if she might kiss me, and hugged me ever so tightly to her nightdress. And that night she died . . .

This was Robert's earliest experience of death. The memory of his dead aunt in her open coffin remained indelibly in his consciousness for the rest of his life. Before the lid was screwed down on the coffin, Grandfather John got up and put his hand on her waxen brow, saying 'Puir lassie . . . My wee Aggie . . . She's cauld, sae cauld.'

Of his other aunts, Robert says that all three were virgins. 'They might have married, but they were jealous of each other, and when a man came spierin one of them the others crabbed his style, so that the poor laddie gave up.' By 1878–79 the roles of these daughters had subtly changed. Jean Service, born in January 1838, had now abandoned dressmaking and, as the eldest, assumed the role of housekeeper. Isabella, born in June 1845, had likewise given up millinery and assisted her father in the post office, taking care of the rapidly increasing volume of counter-work, while Janet, born in March 1851, alone carried on as the telegraphist. When Robert and his little brother came to Kilwinning the sisters were aged forty, thirty-three and twenty-seven respectively, so Bella and Jennie would still be considered marriageable; but one can imagine Jeannie frightening off her sisters' would-be suitors.

Of Grannie Service, usually the sort of personality that an impressionable child would remember vividly, there is no mention at all. Nor does Robert mention the fact that his brother John, barely a year his junior, also lived at the post office. The impression conveyed in his auto-biography is of a rather solitary child raised in this strange household of the septuagenarian grandfather and the four embittered spinsters. Indeed, the tone of a rather joyless, Calvinistic childhood is set by the very opening words of the autobiography:

'Please, Aunt Jeannie, can I go out and look at the hens?'

Over her spectacles my aunt gazed at me suspiciously. 'Whit fur, Rubbert Wullie, do you want to look at the hens?'

'I don't know whit fur, I jist want to look at them.'

'You'd be faur better lookin' at yer bonnie Bible. Don't ye like yer wee Bible?'

'Ay, but I like the hens better.'

The stiff, forbidding nature of the Service household comes across vividly in Robert's description of the adults and the house in which they lived. The parlour, with its horsehair-padded furniture, antimacassars and woolwork picture of Moses in the Bulrushes, is almost stereotypical. The bookcase was grim with volumes of sermons, and the pendulum of the grandfather clock swung with relentless austerity. Under a glass bell was a collection of wax fruits — apples, pears, peaches and grapes. Robert had never tasted peaches or grapes and as he gazed at them his mouth watered. Could they be as delicious as they looked?

His aunts sat round the glowing fire reading works of a devotional or improving nature. They wore black silk skirts and in front of the fire they drew them up over their knees. 'I was supposed to be too young to notice, but the fatness of their legs disgusted me,' wrote Robert. Elsewhere he confessed:

I used to sleep with Aunt Jeannie, who cuddled me a lot. Every Saturday she would change her chemise and tell me not to look while she was doing it. But one night I dared to peep. What I saw made me duck my head under the blankets. 'If women are as ugly as that,' I pondered, 'I never want to get married.'[14]

As befitted the Session Clerk of the Established Church, John Service kept a Sabbatarian household:

For six days of the week I was happy, but the Sabbath was misery. We rose late. The house was hushed, the post office dark. Newspapers had been put away and whistling was forbidden. I asked Aunt Jeannie if I might whistle hymns, but she vetoed the idea. 'Ye don't know the tunes well enough to stick to them,' she objected. After breakfast of 'parrich and finnan haddie' came preparation for church. All of us went, except one of my aunts who stayed to prepare lunch. Happy was

I when I was sick enough to keep her company. Together we would stand behind the Nottingham lace curtains and watch the church-goers . . . About ten the bells began to ring, and from the far ends of the long town the worshippers formed into procession. It was a solemn march, everyone dressed in Sunday best, with face grave. Black was the dominant colour, and to show a bit of brightness was to shock convention.[15]

In the ensuing passage Robert vividly encapsulates the humbug and hypocrisy of the parishioners, the preoccupation with material trivia, the snide comments and malicious speculation about secret drinking and unwanted pregnancy. In view of his position, Grandfather went off to church half an hour before the rest of the family, dressed in a faded frock-coat and a ruffled top-hat that transformed the workaday postmaster into the leading elder of the Kirk. Grandfather carried a pocket flask of whisky to fortify him during the long and arduous service. On the rare occasion that he joined his family in their pew he would be chewing a clove.

According to Robert, the parish minister was a Mr Lamb. In point of fact the incumbent during this period was the Revd William Lee Ker who had been presented to the living by the fourteenth Earl of Eglinton in 1866 (the last clergyman to be selected in this aristocratic manner). He had served as assistant to the Revd Dr Archibald Campbell until his death in 1879, and was the parish minister from then until his own death in May 1902. Even as a relatively young assistant, Ker left his liberal mark on the parish. It was on his own initiative that a new pulpit was installed in 1867, and subsequently he expanded the accommodation for the burgeoning congregation by rearranging the pews. He was a young man of forceful personality but possessed of considerable charm and tact, for shortly after succeeding Campbell he had persuaded the congregation to accept organ music. To permit the Devil's 'kist o' whistles' in the kirk was a major achievement, but Ker even cajoled the congregation into singing the new-fangled hymns as well as psalms, and to stand up while singing. In this revolution he was aided and abetted by the Countess of Eglinton who presented a harmonium, replacing it a few years later in 1887 by a fine American organ. By now the congregation had the bit between its teeth, for it was the parishioners themselves who clubbed together to replace it by the present large pipe organ in 1896.[16]

Ker was not only an able and popular pastor but he took a keen interest in the history and antiquities of his parish. He wrote two books, on the abbey and the parish in general, and the latter volume is still the standard work on the subject. None of this, however, cut any ice with young Robert Service who only remembered the dreariness of the lengthy sermons: 'Usually his discourse was prosy, but in inspired moments his voice rose to a yowl. This would occur at least once in every sermon, and I awaited the moment with an expectant thrill.' The minister was highly regarded by his flock. When he preached a sermon fulminating against Darwin's theories about the descent of man and the origin of species, his congregation had it put into permanent form as a printed pamphlet.[17]

Returning from church was very different from the solemn parade on the way to divine worship. 'Duty grimly done, we walked joyously, heads high, eyes smiling. We formed groups, greeting, gossiping, even joking.' At lunch Grandfather was 'pawky and aromatic', while the aunts discussed the sermon with critical comments on the garments of the other women. 'They knew what bonnets were re-trimmed, what dresses dyed. Over the cold meat, rice and prunes, they tore their neighbours apart.' The respite was brief for it was soon time for the afternoon Sunday school, presided over by Aunt Jeannie.

> After Sunday school she usually suggested a walk to the cemetery. It
> was her idea of divertissement. There, hanging over tombs, she would
> sniffle and sigh. When at a certain point her handkerchief was
> produced, I hotly resented the dear departed; however, to her it was an
> orgy of sentiment she enjoyed to the last tear.[18]

The trauma of Aunt Aggie's premature death and those regular Sunday afternoon jaunts to the cemetery left Robert with a marked aversion to graveyards and funerals which he shunned most of his life, although, ironically, it was left to him to erect a granite obelisk in the cemetery recording the names and dates of his Kilwinning kinfolk.[19] Repelled by the pharisaical attitudes and zealotry of his early childhood, Robert acquired a distaste for church-going of any kind.

> Yet I approve of piety . . . for others. Oh, yes, I send my cheque to the
> vicar and applaud those who hold down the family pew, but I would
> rather worship in my own kale-yard. If I am not a pillar of the church,
> I am, at least, one of the pagan columns that support it from outside.[20]

On attaining his fifth birthday, shortly after the New Year holiday of 1879, Robert was enrolled in the burgh school. According to Robert, this was the only school in the parish but this was hardly the case. The Kilwinning School Board had been established in 1872, and three years later the first fruit of its enterprise was a splendid new board school, officially known as Kilwinning Public School. In addition, however, there was the Eglinton District School serving the landward area of the parish, and the Fergushill Public School which catered to the needs of the teeming colliery community on the outskirts of the town. But it would be true to say that the Kilwinning Public School was the only school in the town itself, so its pupils were drawn from all social classes except the very highest. A century earlier education had been truly classless, as Robert Burns recorded in his famous autobiographical letter to Dr Moore:

> It is not commonly at these green years that the young Noblesse and Gentry have a just sense of the immense distance between them and their ragged Playfellows. — It takes a few dashes into the world to give the young Great man that proper, decent, unnoticing disregard for the poor, insignificant, stupid devils, the mechanics and peasantry around him; who were perhaps born in the same village.[21]

By the 1870s, however, the young Noblesse and Gentry were away at their prep schools and boarding-schools. The local aristocrat was the Earl of Eglinton, a remote figure visible once a year at the district agricultural show. 'He and his family were spoken of with bated breath. They were seen only on the rarest of occasions and spent most of their time in London or Cannes. To them our town was almost non-existent.' Then came the Quality, the landed gentry who rode to hounds and treated their inferiors with disdain. Next in the pecking order were the doctors, bankers and lawyers who kept their distance from the shopkeepers and tradespeople who formed the lower middle classes to which John Service belonged. In turn, they looked down on the skilled artisans, the weavers and mechanics, who regarded the miners and ironworkers as 'a race apart'. Robert was aware of the class structure for it was often drummed into him—'Keep in your place and don't try to imitate your betters'.

> . . . about two miles out of town were the coal pits and iron works, but the colliers and furnacemen were regarded as beyond the pale. When they came into town on Saturday night, to drink their pay, they seemed a race apart. The pitmen, especially, were pallid, stunted creatures, and to me in my childish days a source of fear and repulsion.[22]

But in the classroom all class barriers were swept aside. Children of more or less the same age sat together, from the minister's son to Nellie Purdie whose mother was in the poorhouse. Robert vividly recalled one incident concerning the latter.

> She was a frail lass, with bare feet and ragged gown, but she had a mass of pale gold hair that I admired in spite of its untidiness. Then one day

the teacher stooped over her and said in a tone of disgust: 'Nellie, you're a dirty girl. You have beasties in your hair.'

Nellie hung her head and began to cry. I felt sorry for her, so I rose, holding up my hand.

'Please, Teacher, Auntie Jeannie caught ten in my head last night.'

The teacher said: 'No doubt you got them from Nellie.'

'Oh, no,' I said chivalrously, 'I'm sure she got them from me.'

Our teacher told me to hush and retired behind her desk to laugh chokingly. When I got home that night I told the family of the incident. Aunt Jeannie went as red as a beet, but the others laughed a lot . . [23]

It is important, at the outset, to note that not a single proper name given in the first autobiographical volume is real, with the exception of the four aunts. Other close relatives are merely referred to as Grandfather, Mama or Papa, with fleeting references to 'my brothers and sisters'. It is hardly surprising to discover that there was no one by the surname of Purdie in Kilwinning in the 1880s, nor Dougan (an Irish boyhood chum) either, for that matter, and at this remove in time it is impossible to identify those childhood companions. The only boy who can be identified with certainty was the minister's son and Robert's *bête noire*, whom he refers to as Willie Lamb, but who, in real life, was William Ker, named after his father.

Robert could not remember much more about his schooldays in Kilwinning, except that one day the headmaster stopped him in the playground and asked him what he was going to do when he grew up. Young Robert, who must have been all of eight at the time, said gravely that he intended to become a philosopher. The dominie laughed heartily and told the boy's family, confirming their belief in his originality. Years later Aunt Jeannie wrote to Robert: 'You did not become a philosopher, but you became a poet, which is much better.'

The headmaster, naturally, was not named. 'He was a bearded man, as all Heads were in those days,' was Robert's description of John Copeland who had been appointed parochial schoolmaster in 1853 at the age of twenty-nine, almost twenty years before the coming of the school board system. Indeed, he was one of the last parish dominies in Scotland and a man of considerable stature in educational circles. Not only did he edit the majority of the textbooks published by the Scottish School Book Association but he also wrote quite a number of his own. A native of Monymusk in Aberdeenshire and a confirmed bachelor, he held the headmastership for almost forty years. Ably assisted by William Blair, who eventually succeeded him, Copeland saw his fine new public school grow at an astonishing rate. Although it was regarded as one of the finest of its kind when it opened in 1876, it could not cope with the population explosion of the 1880s, when Kilwinning was at the height of its industrial boom. Within a decade, classes of seventy or eighty pupils were commonplace, as Her Majesty's Inspector noted with alarm in his annual reports. This dire situation was eased in 1908 when a higher grade school was erected on an adjoining site. As Kilwinning Junior Secondary, it continued until 1971 when it was destroyed by fire, and eventually replaced by the modern campus of Kilwinning Academy.[24]

On one occasion Robert overheard his grandfather commenting, 'Yon's a queer wee callant. He'd rather play by himsel' than wi' the other lads.' This was true enough; rather than join the other boys in the street, Robert would amuse himself alone in the garden inventing games and situations which stretched his imagination to the limit. He would be a hunter in the jungle of the raspberry canes, or an explorer in the dark forest of the shrubbery, or he would squat by his lonely campfire on the prairie — actually the family drying-green, all the time holding conversations with imaginary companions. No wonder his grandfather and aunts regarded him as something of an oddity beyond their comprehension.

Apart from the consumptive Aggie, the only aunt with intellectual pretensions was Jennie. While the others were content with newspapers, she alone read books and encouraged Robert to learn poetry from the school primers, excerpts from the works of Campbell and Longfellow. Robert not only learned the long, narrative poems so fashionable in the nineteenth century, but he was encouraged to recite them as well. Mounting a chair in the parlour he would declaim lines from 'The Wreck of the Hesperus' and other dramatic poems. 'The more I ranted and gestured, the more they applauded. In those days I was not troubled by an inferiority complex, and to outsiders must have been an egregious little pest.'

From learning and reciting the poetry of others it was a logical step to trying his hand at poems of his own composition. The sin of rhyme, as Burns put it, came upon young Robert one day in January 1880, at his sixth birthday party to be precise. The supper table was spread like a feast in his honour, with a large boiled ham as the centrepiece, surrounded by a variety of cakes and other delicacies. Grandfather was about to say grace when Robert piped up. Could he say grace on this occasion?

> All eyes turned to me, and I could see disapproval shaping in their faces. But I did not give them a chance to check me. Bowing my head reverently I began:
>
> God bless the cakes and bless the jam;
> Bless the cheese and the cold boiled ham;

Bless the scones Aunt Jeannie makes,
And save us all from belly-aches. Amen.

I remember their staring silence and my apprehension. I expected to be punished, but I need not have feared. There was a burst of appreciation that today seems to me incredibly naive. For years after they told the story of my grace till it ended enraging me.[25]

One can imagine his feelings were he to behold the plaque on the wall of the old post office which concludes with the line: 'Later in life he often referred to his happy childhood in Kilwinning. He composed his first poem here on his 6th birthday.' Although Robert wrote of this incident more than sixty years later with his customary self-deprecation, one may sense a subconscious pride in his first attempt in rhyme:

This was my first poetic flutter, and to my thinking it suggests tendencies in flights to come. First, it had to do with the table, and much of my work has been inspired by food and drink. Second, it was concrete in character, and I have always distrusted the abstract. Third, it had a tendency to be coarse, as witness the use of the word 'belly' when I might just as well have said 'stomach'. But I have always favoured an Anglo-Saxon word to a Latin one, and in my earthiness I have followed my kinsman Burns. So, you see, even in that first bit of doggerel there were foreshadowed defects of my later verse.[26]

So far as Robert had a boon companion at this early period, it was not Willie Ker, the rather namby-pamby son of the parish minister who appears in the autobiography as Willie Lamb, but Pat Dougan, son of the village chimney-sweep. This friendship outraged Robert's aunts, not only because he had transgressed the unwritten class laws, but because the Dougans (or whatever their real name) were Papists. Robert was told in no uncertain terms that, consorting with heathen like that, he would be burned in the Bad Fire himself. Robert, having once burned the tip of a finger on a hot stove, winced at the prospect, but Aunt Jeannie's dire threats of hell-fire did not diminish his hero-worship. Pat was a striking lad, three years older than Robert, with a broad, blunt face, clinched by a tight mouth and steel-grey eyes with a stormy stare. His widowed father was a devil-may-care character known as Three Fingered Frank. He had wandered the globe, been a soldier and a sailor and 'heaven knows what other disreputable character'. To the impressionable little boy, Frank Dougan was the most colourful of men. With his maimed right hand and roguish good looks, he looked every inch the reckless adventurer. Though he went on the binge in the pubs of Kilwinning most nights, he was a born raconteur with an endless fund of yarns. But it was this Irish chimney-sweep who first introduced Robert to Shakespeare:

> . . . he would get out a shabby Shakespeare and spout immortal lines. We thought he did it beautifully, and I felt little thrills go up my spine. He awoke in me a joy of Shakespeare I have never outgrown. For a desert island choice between the Bible and the Bard I would elect the latter . . . I think he must have spouted Shakespeare for the boys in the back room for one day I heard Jimmie Dunn, the blacksmith, remark: 'It's a sair pity to see a man that can out-rant a' the actors, soopin' lums for a livin'.'[27]

Jimmie Dunn was another boyhood hero, much admired for the size of his arms, out of all proportion to the rest of his body. Robert often hung around the village smithy, entranced by the strenuous business of shoeing horses. Once he recited 'Underneath the spreading chestnut tree' to him. 'At that age Longfellow was tops with me as a poet, except, of course, Burns.' This high regard for the Ayrshire poet is a recurring theme in the early chapters of Robert's autobiography. By the Third Reader he was extending his repertoire to include the martial patriotic ballads of Thomas Campbell and the exotica of Byron. 'Oh, how I loved the hackneyed lines and mouthed them mightily! But always I returned to Burns. Apart from his being in a way a family connection, I felt a spiritual kinship with him.'[28] He would often argue with Pat on the relative merits of Shakespeare and Burns, trying to convince the older boy that Burns was greater than the Bard of Avon. Pat liked those poems of Burns in standard English, but Robert preferred the vernacular poetry.

> It was the tongue of our town and every word was vital. But I savoured him at his saltiest, and read with gusto about *The Lass that made the bed for me* and the *Louse in the lady's bonnet*. I preferred humour to sentiment and liked it racy. Already I felt an urge to shock people.[29]

From Pat Dougan Robert also acquired a very early interest in drama. On one occasion Three Fingered Frank took his son to Glasgow to see Barry Sullivan, the red-haired Irish Hamlet, performing in *Richard the Third*. As a result, Pat was stage-struck and determined to become an actor. In 1896 Robert paid a flying visit to Kilwinning before emigrating to Canada and, quite by chance, bumped into a young man of twenty-five. The would-be actor was now a bricklayer's labourer, married, with one child and another one on the way. Robert inwardly pitied his old chum, trapped in a dead-end job with no prospects of advancement, far less the opportunity to realise his early ambition. He was invited into the tiny apartment in one of the labourers' rows of Fergushill, and out of politeness he assented.

> The single room was bare of ornament, yet a good fire blazed, for coal was cheap. A bairn cried in a cot and a little woman rose from soothing it. She would have been slight but she was heavy with another. She was pretty in a frail way, with a bunch of bright hair. She looked at me curiously as she poured tea though she said nothing. However, Pat gave her little chance. He talked as if my coming had roused him from despair. I could see hope kindling in his eyes. His wife looked at him with pathetic anxiety. She made a sympathetic appeal to me and I felt sure he would never do anything to hurt her.
>
> 'Remember to write,' he said. 'You're going to a grand country where a man's got a chance to find his own level. It's a Godsend you dropped by. Somehow I feel the luck's going to turn. Well, I'll do my damnedest to make it. So long, old boy . . .'
>
> As I walked home I felt depressed. Here was I, free, with all the promise of the future, and he going back to his sordid house and his hod. And I thought of his father . . . 'Wasted lives!' I sighed. 'Oh, there are so many like that. They never get a chance.' Then I thought of his little wife, and a light flashed in my mind. No wonder she looked at me in that peculiar way. I recognized her now. It was Nellie Purdie, the girl I had championed in the schoolroom.[30]

Robert's Canadian biographer, Carl Klinck, with an ignorance born of distance, thought that Kilwinning was on the edge of the West Highlands and that Aunt Jeannie had tried to make a hardy Hielandman of Robert by insisting on his wearing of the kilts (*sic*).[31] In point of fact, however, the wearing of the kilt, as we have seen, was initiated by Emily Service in the summer of 1878, shortly after the move north. It was not the wearing of the kilt, as such, which Aunt Jeannie advocated, but the wearing of the garment *sans culotte*. Robert infers that the self-same kilt was the garment which he wore at Kilwinning, by which time it had become not unlike the cutty sark worn by Nanie in 'Tam o Shanter'

> In longtitude tho sorely scanty,
> It was her best, and she was vauntie . . .

One of Robert's vivid memories was his first day at school, when Aunt Jeannie had sent him off in his Highland costume. By the late 1870s tartan in general and the kilt in particular had become fashionable among the middle classes, emulating the example of Queen Victoria and the late Prince Albert. But in Kilwinning such pretensions, especially for ordinary everyday wear, were regarded as ludicrous. The other boys had ragged little Robert, pulling up his kilt. One bully had gone so far as to pick the boy up and spank him across his bare rump, in front of the girls at that. Robert was hurt and humiliated and came home crying. Aunt Jeannie was for persevering, but Grandfather intervened. 'Gie wee Rubbert Wullie his troosers,' he ordained. Thereafter the kilt was confined to Sunday best.

One morning in 1883, however, Aunt Jeannie told the boy, 'Ye're wearin' yer kilt the day.' Robert protested that he was going to school.

'No, ye're no'. Yer father and mother are comin' to visit ye.'

This news filled the nine-year-old Robert with dismay. It had been a long time since he had seen his parents and he had almost forgotten their existence.

From time to time I had heard of the birth of new brothers but did not feel interested. So I donned my kilt, now too short for me. When my parents arrived I was so shy I hid in the wash-house and had to be routed out. I hung back as I was introduced to the authors of my being, and it was only by offering me sweets that my mother coaxed me on her knee. When she did, I remember a look of horror coming over her face. However, she said nothing — just then.

Apart from my diffidence, the visit was not a success. Aunt Jeannie objected to tobacco, and Papa was obliged to go outside to smoke. While he puffed his pipe moodily by the pump, Mama was having an argument with Aunt Jeannie by the hen-house.

'My word!' said Mama. 'I consider it shocking. To think that that poor boy has *nothing on* under his kilt — nothing. He's absolutely bare.'

'That's whit makes Hielandmen hardy,' said Aunt Jeannie. Mama was unconvinced. Then Aunt Jeannie stressed the handiness of the garment when it came to performing certain natural functions, and this Mama was obliged to admit though it evidently shocked her. 'Well, I don't approve of it,' she said, 'and I'm real vexed.' I think it was this matter of the kilt that made her finally retrieve me, although my aunts wanted to adopt me. However, Mama was anti-adoptionist to the core. If she had had a hundred children instead of a mere ten, I do not think she would have parted with one.[32]

Years later, Robert recalled this incident when he was inspired to write his ode to the national dress:

Imagine how it's braw and clean
As in the wind it flutters free;

And so conducive to hygiene
In its sublime simplicity.
No fool fly-buttons to adjust,
Wi shanks and maybe buttocks bare;
Oh Chiels, just take my word on trust,
A bonny kilt's the only wear.
True, I just wear one in my mind,
Since sent to school by Celtic aunts,
When girls would flip it up behind,
Until I begged for lowland pants.
But now none dare do that to me;
And so I sing with happy lilt —
How happier the world would be
If every male would wear a kilt!.[33]

The grandmother who was never mentioned died in October 1883. John Service did not remarry and, indeed, followed her to the grave less than four years later. Robert has left us an affectionate pen-portrait of the man who exerted the greatest influence on him in his formative years. He was a pawky Scot of the non-committal type. If you said it was a fine day, he would look thoughtfully at the sky and finally admit, 'Weel, I've seen waur.' He was fond of a sly joke and had a fund of kirk session stories; Robert cited as an example the story of the lassie who indignantly told her musical but over-ardent sweetheart that she would never fornicate with a man that whistled on the Sabbath. This betokens that penchant for Rabelaisian humour which is a recurring theme in Scotland and acted as a safety valve for the repression of natural feelings engendered by the extreme religiosity of the times.

He had two enthusiasms, the Scotch Kirk and Scotch whisky. Every morning he would stir into his porridge, which he took in a wooden bowl, a big wooden spoonful of Mountain Dew. But he also boasted that though he liked his wee dram he had never been the worse of liquor. He was canny in his cups.[34]

'When I left the Long Grey Town,' says Robert, 'I did not return for many years,' adding that this was on his farewell visit which would have taken place in 1896. Yet, in the preceding paragraphs, he infers that he was in Kilwinning one fateful day in May 1887:

Cold boiled ham was Grandfather's delectation, and the sight of it always makes me think of his death. We had a whole one for supper in honour of a lady visitor. Grandfather carved it with virtuosity and kept us in a simmer of merriment with his humorous remarks. Finally, the lady had to catch a train, and as she said her good-byes, she complimented Grandfather on the deliciousness of his ham. Immediately he carved a huge slice. 'Here, lassie, tak' this awa' wi' ye.'

'But how would I carry it?'

His answer was prompt. 'Pit it inside yer bunnit.' We all laughed at his sally, and he reached for his glass of water. I saw the glass tilt in his hand and the water spill down his beard. I thought it was because he was laughing so; then I saw the glass fall to the floor. Still laughing, he looked at his hand wonderingly. A look of childish surprise came over his face. There was no pain, no fear, just helpless bewilderment. Then he slumped over and was dead. So he enjoyed life to the last, and passed like a flash with a laugh in his eyes and a joke on his lips.[35]

The facts, however, belie this dramatic description. The brief obituary which appeared in the *Glasgow Herald* of 9 May 1887 stated: 'One of the oldest and most respected townsmen of Kilwinning, Mr John Service, died on Saturday morning, after a short illness, at the age of 76 years.' As it is very unlikely that Robert was actually present when John Service suffered the stroke that killed him, the embellishment of the story may be put down to that 'adventure into memory' which formed the subtitle to his autobiography.

John Service's will was proved at Ayr on 11 June 1887, confirmation being granted to his eldest son. The value of his estate was £182 14s 10d.[36] He was succeeded in the postmastership by Jeannie and she continued to run the office from the building in the Howgate but moved to much more commodious premises farther along the street on 5 July 1897. At that time she was handling an average of 116 parcels a week and 11,624 telegrams a year. In the previous year she had sold or encashed 6,532 postal orders, 1,754 money orders and 1,311 savings transactions.[37] She was assisted by her sisters Jennie and Bella till January 1913 when the latter died at the age of sixty-seven. Jeannie and Jennie then retired 'to a tiny cottage, living pinched and meagre days'. Later Robert would profoundly regret that he never sent them the odd hundred pounds. He would never have missed the money, but it would have made all the difference between scrimping and luxury to them. It is probably significant that although Isabella Service left £57 8s 3d[38] neither of her surviving sisters left any property worth mentioning.

Jeannie was the longest-lived of them all, dying on 31 May 1919 at the age of eighty-one. Janet survived her by little more than a year and a half, dying on 9 February 1921 at the age of sixty-eight.[39] The stark details were recorded on a rather thin marble tombstone which John Service had purchased shortly after his wife's death in 1883. Forty years later Robert was to return briefly to

Kilwinning and visit his old haunts. He was saddened to find that the family tombstone had been flattened and broken in a recent storm, and in its place he then erected a fine granite obelisk, surmounted by a veiled urn, with lettering picked out in lead. Nearby, among the jumbled disorder of broken tombstones long since discarded, the original marble stone, now thickly patinated with green lichen, can still be seen.[40]

CHAPTER 3

SCHOOLDAYS IN GLASGOW, 1883-88

At school I never gained a prize,
Proving myself the model ass;
Yet how I watched with wistful eyes,
And cheered my mates who topped the class.

'Dunce', in *Songs of a Sun-lover* (1949)

TOUCHINGLY, ROBERT SERVICE DEDICATED THE FIRST VOLUME
of his autobiography to the memory of his father, adding a couplet composed
specially for the occasion:

Full of rich earthiness, a Grand Old Guy,
With all his faults a better man than I.

Despite this, references to Robert Senior in the book itself were invariably
uncomplimentary. Apparently young Robert had not seen his father since the
day he had been dumped on his Kilwinning relatives. Following a philosophical aside about the Fourth Commandment, taking the view that he could
never see why parents should be honoured just because they were responsible
for our existence, he went on to record his first impression of his father, on
that fateful day in 1883 when his parents came to visit him:

I must confess that on his visit to me Papa failed to make a favourable impression. He had the reddest face I ever saw. His head was balder than that of Mister Lamb [the Revd William Lee Ker], but his mutton-chop whiskers were longer. In fact they looked like discouraged Dundrearies. But what most impressed me was his stomach, which ballooned a fancy waistcoat girt by a heavy gold chain. Although he carried his bay-window with dignity, I disliked it.

Of the many good things Papa did for me, not the least was to serve as a physical warning. My hair has faltered but never failed, while my girth has not got out of bounds. Of course we are not permitted to pick our parents; but I think every father should so conduct himself that his children would never want any other, even if they had the choice.[1]

The removal to Glasgow was a shock in more ways than one. Robert left the comparative tranquillity of a small town in a rustic setting for a sprawling metropolis whose population was fast approaching the million mark and the title of Second City of the Empire. Although the autobiography conveys the impression that Robert was raised as an only child, treated by adoring aunts as a boy-wonder, he was with his brother John all along. Nevertheless, the placid upbringing of these two boys in a household of adults was in marked contrast to the maelstrom of siblings into which they were now thrust so precipitately. By now Peter was a two-year-old toddler, but baby Stanley was on the scene, and Emily was pregnant again and in due course would give birth to her first daughter, Agnes Ann, named after the mothers of Robert and Emily respectively. Other children would be born at regular intervals: Jane in 1886, Janet Isabella in 1889 and Albert in 1891. Unusually for the period, all ten children grew to maturity, and most of them lived to a ripe old age.

Robert recorded his first impression of the move to the city:

First of all, I had to get acquainted with a swarm of brothers. I forget how many there were, but it was rather bewildering. At first they looked on me as a stranger and were inclined to resent me, especially as I tried to patronize them. But soon I fell into line, though I never quite recovered from the feeling that I was a *changeling*.[2]

Robert, brought up in an extremely religious, God-fearing household, had been accustomed to say his prayers, kneeling by his bedside. This performance earned him a pillow-buffeting on the first night in his new home, and ragging from a roomful of kid brothers. Mama intervened, telling them to follow his example, but as they had never been taught to say their prayers they found Robert's antics hilarious. Their attitude, however, hardened his resolve to carry on. 'Maybe I got a self-righteous kick out of it,' he added in his self-deprecating style. By and by, Robert compromised and began saying his prayers from the cosy confines of the bed itself, and then the custom tailed off as he fell asleep before his nightly devotions were completed. Filled with remorse the following morning, he would try to compensate by a prayer on awaking, resolving that the lapse should never recur. 'But it did, more and more often, till finally I lost the prayer habit,' though he was left with the sneaking feeling that he was letting God down. He recalled that he never knew either of his parents to attend church, although he and his brothers and sisters were sent off each Sunday to fill the pew for which Robert Senior paid a pound a year.

Technically, the Services did not live in Glasgow, but in Hillhead, then, and for many years thereafter, an independent burgh. In 1850 it had been a pleasant hamlet on the banks of the River Kelvin, separated from the city by green fields and pastures, forming the northermost portion of the great parish of Govan which straddled the Clyde and lay in the counties of Renfrew and Lanark. Both Glasgow and Govan grew at such a pace in the second half of the nineteenth century that they soon embraced each other, and then it was only a matter of time until the larger town swallowed up its neighbour. The question of annexation was first raised about the time young Robert left Kilwinning, and it would rage back and forward for three decades before Glasgow won the day and Govan parish, with its five burghs, was absorbed in 1912. By 1883, however, despite the independent status of Hillhead, the only thing that marked it out as separate from the city was the different street-lamps.

The removal of Robert and John from the care of their grandparents was not as spur-of-the-moment as Robert infers in his autobiography. It was not the spectacle of the little bare-arsed Highlander that induced Emily to retrieve her sons, but a calculated decision to reunite her family. At the time of the 1881 Census the family were still living at 29 Lansdowne Crescent, but soon afterwards they removed to a newly built terrace house in Kelvinside. In later years the name of this district was to become synonymous with refined speech in a rather affected accent. If Hillhead, as the West End of Glasgow, was regarded as a superior neighbourhood, then Kelvinside, as the west end of Hillhead, was the *crème de la crème*. Nowadays Kelvinside is regarded as the area north of Great Western Road, west of the River Kelvin and bounded by the Botanic Gardens, but in the 1880s it was specifically the district *south* of Great Western Road lying to the west of Byars or Byres Road. This thoroughfare runs almost due north from the Clyde at Partick Cross and terminates opposite the main gate of the Botanic Gardens. Then as now, it neatly bisects the Hillhead district; but, conscious of their superiority, the residents west of the road regarded themselves as a breed apart, hence the prevalence of Kelvinside rather than Hillhead in the addresses of the period.

In the 1870s this side of Byres Road was very sparsely populated. It was still an area of stately mansions and scattered farms, but at the end of the decade the land was bought by speculative developers, drained, streets laid out, lighting and sewers installed, and then huge tenement blocks were erected.

> Our home was in a four-storey block of flats called Roselea Terrace. Opposite it was a similar block called Ferndale Terrace. Their sole rustic suggestions were their names; for they were both grim and gloomy, and only in high summer did the sunshine gild our door-mat. But it was a highly respectable street, where we lived in genteel poverty. Our flat was number nineteen, the biggest and the last in the terrace.[3]

Previous biographers have taken these statements at their face value, though there is actually little truth or accuracy in them. By referring to his address as Roselea Terrace, Robert may have been guilty of a genuine lapse of memory, for its name was actually Roclea or Rocklea Terrace, both spellings occurring in maps and directories of the period, but from 1881 till 1889 the Services lived at Number 8, not Number 19. It was not till 1889, however, that they moved to the end of the terrace, occupying the main-door flat at Number 18. This flat was rather similar, but being 'end of terrace' it was indeed slightly larger. To complicate matters, the developers from the outset appear to have been divided regarding the name of this thoroughfare for it was also referred to almost from the beginning as Roxburgh Street, in line with the custom prevalent in Kelvinside of naming streets after the duchies and earldoms of the United Kingdom, perhaps to reinforce the aristocratic atmosphere of the district. But during the whole of Robert's childhood, far from being the last in the terrace, the Service flat was at the midway stage in the street, there being eight street numbers on either side. Ferndale Terrace was a complete fiction, as the houses on the opposite side of the street were merely the odd numbers in Roclea Terrace/Roxburgh Street. The pattern of tenements in this street was that alternate houses on both sides were main-door flats, the others having a common close-mouth giving access to six flats, two on each of three upper storeys. Number 8 was a main-door flat and therefore one of the bigger apartments, though no bigger than the other main-door flats in the street.

> It was on the ground floor and had a basement where there was an occasional rat, lots of mice and swarms of cockroaches. The latter were big glossy fellows that came out at night, so that we hated to venture into the kitchen after dark. They crunched horribly under the descending carpet slipper, and when the gas was lit they scuttled off in all directions. Often they got in the beds, and I always remember the screams of Mama when a big one dropped from her panties.[4]

By modern standards, the flat in Roxburgh Street was large and spacious, characterised by high ceilings and tall windows. The large front room on the ground floor overlooking the street was designated grandly as the drawing-room, but as the Service family continued to multiply it became yet another dormitory. Below it, in the basement, was another large room which was known as the nursery; here Robert slept with his brothers. He would sit till midnight reading adventure yarns when the house lay asleep. 'Then I would stumble to bed and know nothing more till awakened in the morning by Papa pulling the [bed]clothes off me. That was his way of making me get up.'

Memory played him false when Robert recollected that the terrace stopped at his house and gave on to a vacant lot which he called the Hollow. This was only true after the family moved to Number 18 in 1889. In 1883, however, only the houses as far as Number 16 had been erected and occupied. Number 18 was not added till 1885. Beyond the terrace, on the corner with Saltoun Street, there now stands a large sandstone villa which was not constructed till the 1890s. Its site must have been the Hollow, full of potholes and clothed with rank grass and nettles, that served as a playground.

> Board fences surrounded it, the crevices full of earwigs. It was priceless to us, as otherwise we would have been obliged to play in the streets. Although only a squalid wasteland, to our notion it was precious country where green things grew and the air was fresh. I have no doubt that sunken field did much to help our growth.[5]

Roxburgh Street was a place of young families in the 1880s, and Robert was part of a gang of about twenty boys. Beyond the intersection with Saltoun Street, the thoroughfare from Roxburgh Street continued up a slope. Robert refers to it as Sunnybrae Gardens on one page and Sunnybrae Crescent on another, though in truth this semi-circular street enclosing a private park is called Athole Gardens, using the archaic spelling of that ducal family. Here, the boys were of a superior breed.

> Their fathers were successful business men, and they went to private academies, not to plebeian board-schools like ourselves. We called them 'gentry pups' and sought fights with them. But down in Byars Road, which lay below us, was another class of small tradesmen, and their sons we called 'keelies'. With them, too, we were always at war. We were the middle-middle class, most bellicose of all, because we were better fed than the 'keelies', and less fastidious than the 'gentry pups'. In short, we were rather nasty little vulgarians.[6]

Doubtless one of the 'gentry pups' referred to was Robert Young, three years Robert's junior, who lived with his father John Young, a prosperous yarn merchant, at 8 Athole Gardens, though Robert Young would have been away at his expensive boarding-school in term-time. As 'Boss' Young, he came to be known to two generations of Glasgow youth, and it was in his house in Athole Gardens, exactly a quarter of a century later, that the First Glasgow Boy Scouts, the oldest official Scout troop in the world, met in January 1908. Back in 1883, however, another youth movement, the first of its kind anywhere, was being formed at Woodside on the eastern fringes of Hillhead and, as the Boys' Brigade, it flourishes worldwide to this day. In 1884–85 the new movement spread like wildfire and the newspapers carried lengthy reports of the spectacular displays of dummy-rifle drill and precision marching by the lads decked out in white belts and pill-box hats. But the Service brothers seem to have been impervious to the blandishments of the BB bugles.

Such discipline as Robert endured at this period was imposed by his school. In a chapter entitled 'Drab School', Robert described his first city school in jaundiced terms, being in 'a dubious region between slum-land and respectability. It was dingy, grey and shabby . . .' In fact Church Street Public School, like many of the tenements in the surrounding streets as well as the great municipal art galleries at Kelvingrove nearby, was constructed of a rich red sandstone, quarried at Locharbriggs in Dumfriesshire.

This school, standing in the triangle formed by Dumbarton Road, Church Street and the foot of Byres Road, was about half a mile away in the neighbouring burgh of Partick. It had started life grandly, in 1850, as Partick Academy, but when this august establishment was translated to larger premises in Peel Street near Partick Burgh Hall, the building was sold to the recently formed Govan Parish School Board and in September 1878 it reopened as Church Street Public School, with Edward Ellice Macdonald as headmaster and Margaret Russell as infant mistress. Initially it had 141 pupils but the number on the school roll rose rapidly and in the early 1880s averaged about four hundred pupils. The headmaster was often compelled to take classes himself, whenever any of his slender staff were absent for any reason. In the 1880s the teaching staff consisted of four men and two women graded as Assistants Second Class and four pupil teachers, usually girls little older than the most senior of the scholars. Teachers learned on the job, though the men were usually undergraduates of the nearby university, who required frequent time off to attend classes and sit exams. As if such disruption to the curriculum were not enough, the school was plagued by overcrowding. A frequent comment in the reports of HM Inspectors was that two classes were often taught in the same room, which was most distracting for pupils and teachers alike.

Macdonald and his senior assistant George Hally had both left Church Street before Robert Service began attending this school; in June 1882 they both went to Albert Road Public School in the burgh of Pollokshields which was also under the aegis of Govan Parish School Board. Instead, the headmaster in Robert's day was Archibald Macfie, who had previously been headmaster of Broomloan Road Public School, in the burgh of Govan itself, and he was ably assisted by Alex McDougall, lately of the Highlanders Academy in Greenock.

Robert, now past his ninth birthday, was in Standard III, under Albert Connor. Late in 1883 Connor resigned his post as he was emigrating to Argentina. Although he does not mention this fact, Robert was probably stirred by tales of the pampas and the young teacher's hopes and expectations in South America — something to be stored in the subconscious.

Robert remembered little about this school other than the punishment meted out to wayward and unruly pupils:

> The Masters wore shabby tail-coats and swung straps as they paced the floor. At my first school canes had been the instruments of discipline, but here thongs of leather were the symbols of authority. One can imagine the young Master going to the leather merchant and carefully selecting the tool of his trade. 'Let me have a nice supple one with tails that flick around the fingers.' . . . Or 'Maybe I'd better try one of those broad heavy fellows. Perhaps it would be more effective if I soaked it in brine. Let me swish it through the air to get the balance of it.' What would a Master be without his faithful strap.[7]

The whole of the ensuing page of the autobiography is devoted to the punishments which Robert himself sustained. One incident in particular rankled for

many years, though strangely Robert places this in Church Street, rather than
Hillhead, the secondary school he attended from 1885 to 1889. It concerned the
German master and as Church Street did not run to such an appointment it
places the event at a rather later date. Hillhead, on the other hand, had a nation-
wide reputation for modern languages; in 1893 a fifth of the honours passes in
the school certificate for modern languages in the whole of Scotland were taken
by this one school. The German master was the much-loved Dr Louis
Lubovius. One day he said something which set the class laughing uncontrollably, and Robert was singled out as a scapegoat. For such a serious misde-
meanour pupils were sent to the headmaster to be flogged.

Robert describes the headmaster as a bearded man in a frock-coat,
which confirms that the incident occurred at Hillhead. Archibald Macfie was
clean-shaven, but Edward Ellice Macdonald (by that time headmaster at
Hillhead) sported a heavy walrus moustache and in the 1880s also wore a
beard. In vain did Robert protest that the whole class had been laughing. 'I
cannot punish the whole class,' said Macdonald, 'so I will make an example
of you.'

> And he did. That was the only time I got six. But though my hands
> were numb he did not break my spirit. Towards the last I was feeling
> distinctly murderous. It was not so much what he did to me as the
> gusto with which he did it. I found myself eyeing a heavy ink-well on
> his desk and wondering what would happen if I hurled it at his head.
> It was red ink too. I believe another lash would have made me do it.
>
> One does not forgive and forget punishment that is severe and
> unjust. Years after, when I heard he had been drowned while bathing, I
> laughed for joy. Yet I have no doubt he gave no further thought to the
> matter and would have been profoundly surprised at my lasting
> resentment.[8]

Indeed, Edward Ellice Macdonald's brilliant career in education was tragically
cut short in a bathing accident at Cullen, Banffshire in the summer of 1912.[9]

Macdonald was one of the greatest Scottish headmasters at the turn of the
century, but he was aloof to the point of being difficult, respected by his staff
and feared by his pupils. When his great domed, bald head went bright red it
was a danger signal. A great walker and a powerful swimmer, he lived at
Bearsden, then a village several miles north-west of Glasgow, but he walked to
and from Hillhead every day. At examination times he would take a bundle of
exercise books home with him to mark. He would work till three or four in the
morning, then walk out along the Stockiemuir Road to the Whangie, a spectac-

ular hill north-west of the city, watch the sun rise, return for an invigorating cold bath and breakfast of porridge, then set out briskly for a day's work at school.

Colonel Charles Hepburn, a prominent Glasgow businessman who entered Hillhead in the 1890s, recounted an anecdote about Macdonald which paralleled Robert's experience:

> As Headmaster he made a regular practice of visiting classrooms in the afternoon. When he stumped along the concrete corridors the whole school shook. He burst into the English classroom one day when I was on my feet reciting Burns's 'Address to a Haggis'. I had just reached the lines, 'But mark the rustic, haggis-fed; the trembling earth resounds his tread,' when Mr Macdonald made his entrance. The timing was dramatic; the class roared with laughter. The Headmaster demanded to know what the joke was. Nobody had the courage to tell him. I was ordered to his room where I got six of the best. Ten years later when I was walking through the Lairig Ghru from Aviemore to the Pools of Dee I met Mr Macdonald about halfway, walking in the opposite direction. We sat down in the heather and had a chat while we ate our sandwiches. 'Do you remember,' he asked me, 'many years ago while you were at school, I visited the English class when there was an outburst of laughter. For years I've wondered what caused the hilarity.' I told him. 'Why did you not tell me at the time? It would have saved you six of the best.' I told him I was much too scared. He apologised and all was well.[10]

By his own admission, Robert acquired something of a reputation as a street tough during his sojourn at the 'drab school'. The catchment area for Church Street Public School included the congested tenements of the shipyard workers south of Dumbarton Road and resentment between the social classes frequently erupted in brawls in Torness Street, the short thoroughfare that ran parallel to Dumbarton Road, at the back of the school. Robert was often involved in playground showdowns that ended in fisticuffs after school. Sometimes the school janitor, John Nesbitt, would intervene. He was an ex-soldier, a veteran of the Egyptian campaign recently concluded. 'Fighting's a blackguardedly thing,' he would say as he marched the pugilists to their class teacher. 'You fought in the Army,' Robert riposted but the janitor would not argue the matter.

Of his companions at this school Robert recalled only one, and he was unforgettable. They shared a desk. He had a pale face and a big head. One day Robert observed his companion making drawings:

'It's the Fat Boy in Pickwick,' he told me gleefully. 'When he's not eating he sleeps.'

I admired the drawing, which was copied from Phiz. He had a lively sense of humour, and, though he did not shine at his lessons any more than I did, he was more avid and precocious. In fact, I was rather awe-struck to find that he had been able to absorb a *real novel*, as my reading was confined to penny dreadfuls and papers like *Ching Ching's Own*. My friend high-browed me, and sought to wean me away from Jack Harkaway and Deadwood Dick, but without success. *Eric, or Little by Little* gave me a pain in the neck, while *Tom Brown's School Days* repelled me by its moral platitudes. He tried to interest me in the *Boys' Own Paper*, known as the B.O.P., and endorsed by the public schools [in the English, rather than the Scottish sense]. No doubt it was *pukka*, but I was not. I liked stories by Manville Fenn and Talbot Baines Reed, but constructive articles such as *How to Rig a Model Yacht* or *How to Stuff Birds* left me cold. So my apostle of uplift failed in his effort.[11]

This was one of the few people whom Robert actually identified, although characteristically he was not specifically named.

I mention him because to-day he is known as Britain's Best Journalist. He is the London Editor of a famous daily newspaper and has published many books. Cabinet Minsters consult him, and mandarins of letters weigh his words. One of his brothers is a famous etcher who has been knighted; while another is skipper of a big Atlantic liner, and himself an author of note. I used to call him Jimmy but now I call him James. He still high-brows me and I love it. May he long live to drink the Scotch he enjoys so heartily.[12]

Jimmy was, in fact, James Bone (1872–1962), Editor of the Manchester *Guardian*. In 1947, the year after *Ploughman of the Moon* was published, he became a Companion of Honour. Here again, Robert's memory was somewhat faulty for Jimmy Bone was two years older than Robert and in one of the higher classes of the school. Oddly enough, Jimmy's brother David was in Robert's class, while Muirhead, the baby of the family, was in Miss Russell's Standard I. David Bone himself published a number of books, including novels and an autobiography *Landfall at Sunset* (1955). The latter is precise where Robert's autobiographical volumes were not, giving names, dates and exact locations throughout. The master mariner turned novelist was understandably reticent about his early board-school education and briefly mentioned the schools in Church Street and Hamilton Crescent: 'I have only vague recollection of the progress, or the lack of it, I registered at either of these establishments.'[13] On one point, however, he was silent: he makes no mention of the budding poet. Robert mentions a visit to the Bone brothers at their home in the grandly named Buckingham Terrace some years later, following a chance encounter with Jimmy in the street:

> It was a gloomy house in a dreary street, but his personality pervaded it till it was as gay as a pub. He revealed a new enthusiasm. He had just discovered the music-hall. He sang songs from the repertoires of Bessie Bellwood and Marie Lloyd and infected me with his enthusiasm. Then his brother, the artist, joined us. Although some years younger he high-browed us, but little did I think that one day he would receive a knighthood. In the background hovered twins, one of whom became captain of an Atlantic liner and an author of note. It was Jimmy who first mentioned the name of Kipling to me, quoting some of his verse . . .[14]

Muirhead was, indeed, the first of the Bone brothers to achieve fame and a title, being knighted in 1937. He was two years younger than Robert, having been born in Partick in March 1876. After school he had studied architecture and then art at evening classes in Glasgow School of Art under the redoubtable Charles Rennie Mackintosh and was inspired by the picturesque aspect of the buildings of Glasgow to execute drawings of them. As an etcher working in dry-point as well as a superb draughtsman with pencil, charcoal and sepia, he achieved an early reputation, publishing a portfolio of Glasgow etchings as early as 1899. Two years later he collaborated with his brother Jimmy to produce a book entitled *Glasgow in 1901* and later illustrated Jimmy's classic *London Perambulator* of 1926. David Bone, coeval with Robert, went to sea as a naval cadet, exciting Robert's envy for he, too, longed for the mariner's life. He was not just the skipper of a big Atlantic liner, however, but eventually became Commodore of the Anchor Line and was himself knighted the year before Jimmy became a Companion of Honour. Incidentally, there were no twins in the Bone family; perhaps Robert confused the eldest brother, Drummond Bone, and David although they were four years apart.

The 'slum-school' as Robert dismissed it, probably never had so many brilliant pupils at the same time, although Church Street was not as dismal as Robert would have us believe. The master shipbuilder Alexander Stephen instituted a bursary of a hundred pounds a year to enable the brightest boy in

Govan parish each year to go to Glasgow University. In 1882 the Stephen Bursary went to a pupil at Church Street but the following year Church Street took the top four places in this keenly fought scholastic competition.

It is a matter of conjecture whether Robert ever boasted of his supposed family connection with the National Bard, but in the Bone brothers he was confronted by a quartet who had an actual connection with Burns. The Bone boys were the sons of David Drummond Bone (born in March 1841), a master printer who gravitated towards radical journalism after leaving his native Ayrshire. The county connection, in itself, should have been a bond between Robert and his classmates, but whereas Robert's grandparents on both sides had been High Tories, the Bones were the grandsons of Robert Bone, a notorious Chartist forced to flee the county for his life after his printing press was smashed by a reactionary mob in the turbulent 1840s. Robert Bone had been born in Dalrymple parish in 1809, the son of William Bone, coachman at Newark House, and his second wife Anne Drummond. William Bone (born at Dalrymple in 1757) had two claims to fame: he had been a fellow-pupil, under John Murdoch, of Robert Burns; and his first wife had been Helen Kilpatrick, daughter of the Dalrymple blacksmith, and long regarded as the heroine of Burns's first song 'Handsome Nell'.[15] Although this attribution has since been shown to be incorrect, it was wholeheartedly believed for almost a century and a half, and there is no reason to suppose that the Bone brothers were unaware of it, though Sir David unaccountably omits any reference to it in his autobiography. Nor, modestly, does he mention the fact that the family was of Norman descent, from the De Bohuns, one of whose scions had the misfortune to come to grief before the Battle of Bannockburn when he was felled by the Bruce's battleaxe.

Overcrowding at Church Street forced Govan Parish School Board to open two schools on the north side of the Clyde in order to relieve the pressure and provide a better system of higher education. To this end a school was established in Hamilton Crescent to serve the needs of Partick and Partickhill, and the Bone brothers went there in 1885. On 1 April that year Archibald Macfie left Church Street to become headmaster of Albert Road Public School in Pollokshields, thus following in the footsteps of Edward Ellice Macdonald who was now promoted to the headship of a brand new school. A week later, Margaret Russell left Church Street to head the infants and junior primary department at the same school. On 20 April 1885 the new headmaster of Church Street, Simon Fraser, noted in the school log-book that 130 Hillhead children had left that day to go to the new school in Sardinia Terrace.

Hillhead Public School was formally opened on 13 April, Macdonald noting laconically in the school log-book, 'School opened'. If Church Street was apostrophised as the Drab School, Robert regarded Hillhead as the Dream School. Each day he and his brothers trooped off

> to what was then the Finest School in Scotland. There we were lucky, for it was brand-new and only five minutes from our house. It was a show school. The city fathers were proud of its beauty. It was equipped for science, art and domestic economy. Visitors were shown round *ad nauseam*. It made the swanking private academies look cheap. The Masters had University degrees and were hand-picked, while the Head wore a stove-pipe hat. It was a dream school dumped almost at our door.[16]

The new school was barely a quarter of a mile distant. Almost opposite the foot of Roxburgh Street, on the far side of Byres Road, is the foot of Great George Street, a steep hill up which the Service brothers would have toiled every morning. On the summit, Sardinia Terrace (later renamed Cecil Street) ran off to the left. Along this street, on the right-hand side, lay the new school. Over the ensuing century considerable ingenuity was shown in tacking on bits at the side, back and top, but it is still possible to imagine what an elegant and classically symmetrical building this was originally. The architecture, by H. and D. Barclay, was a triumph over a severely constricted and uncompromisingly steep site, and was widely regarded at the time as a great advance on anything previously attempted in school construction. Its most notable feature still is the pedimented centrepiece decorated with classical statuary, with Ionic columns above the pilastered entrance and caryatids, obviously influenced by the notable Glasgow architect Alexander 'Greek' Thomson. The flanking bays repeat the Ionic columns from the first floor and the façade is lavishly decorated with Grecian key patterns. Even the gateways carved BOYS and GIRLS are pedimented in the style of Greek temples. Inside, the large well-lit double staircase was handsomely decorated with full-size plaster copies of the Elgin Marbles which, the *Glasgow Herald* noted approvingly, were 'of a highly educative value'. The school was on three floors, the top one being known from the outset as 'the attics'. Under the skylights set in the sloping roof were the art studios, science laboratories and domestic science classrooms. As the reputation of the new school spread, the numbers of pupils rose sharply. Some two hundred pupils were enrolled on the opening day, but by the time the school broke up for the summer holidays at the end of June the number had risen to five hundred, and by the time Robert Service left the school roll had risen to over seven hundred.

Such was its prestige that it quickly came to be known as Hillhead High School, although that epithet was not added to the title officially till many years later. Today the tall building on Cecil Street is a primary school, the secondary departments having been relocated on a new site in nearby Oakfield Avenue in 1931. From the upper storeys, towering over the rooftops of the nearby houses, one gets a stunning panorama of Glasgow with splendid views of the hills that ring the city. Robert described his time at Hillhead:

> Here I remained until my final expulsion. I had the same teacher for three years and came to have a liking for him. He was a bantam of a man, with bandy legs and a big red moustache like a viking. To me he was a hero because he had been a famous football right-winger, and had won his international cap. That far outweighed any scholarship in my eyes. For a while I worshipped him.[17]

The teacher to whom Robert looked up with such veneration was James Watson. One Saturday night Robert saw him staggering out of a pub, very much the worse for drink. Once he pitched and fell, and picked himself up with difficulty. 'I shrank into a doorway. How thankful I was he had not turned my way! I was as hurt as if I had received a clout on the face.' No longer was he a hero in Robert's eyes.

The sketchy account he gives of his secondary schooling conveys the impression of a boy who took a delight in flouting convention. 'My chief failing was a pertness that amounted to impertinence,' he commented. Most of the narrative is occupied with lengthy and graphic accounts of the punishments he endured for cheeking his teachers. On many occasions his quick wit and ready tongue got him into trouble. For someone who was no stranger to the stout Lochgelly tawse brandished by the masters with such skill, Robert had to devise some sort of protection.

> I was always thinking out ways to cheat the Powers That Be and one of them was my patent palm-shield. I cut a sheet of transparent mica-like material to the shape of my hand and equipped it with an elastic band so that it lay flat on my palm. At a little distance it was invisible. The chaps were enthusiastic, so it was decided we must try it right away. We selected a Master who was short-sighted. We would have preferred him a little deaf, but one could not ask too much.
>
> I had some difficulty provoking him into punishing me, for he was a mild man who taught mathematics; but at last I succeeded in rousing

his wrath. He invited me to step onto the floor and produced a broad strap. All the chaps were agog with anticipation. Boldly I held out my right hand with its celluloid sheath. I saw his eyes glisten with satisfaction as he flung back the strap and swung it down with all his force. CLACK! It was a sound like a pistol-shot. The air between my palm and its shield was so violently expelled the crack made me jump. It also made the Master jump. I plunged my hand into my pocket, and there I left my protective device. Then taking out my hand I wrung it as if in pain. The boys rocked with laughter. The Master was puzzled. He examined his strap, then my hand, then told me to go to my place. After which he turned on the grinning class, singled out six and gave each a proper one.[18]

'When I was close to thirteen,' wrote Robert, 'we had a wonderful summer and I spent three glorious months by the sea.' This would have been from late June to early September 1886, when Hillhead broke up for the holidays. Where Robert spent his time at the seaside is not revealed, but as Uncle Henry and Aunt Jane Pemberton were still living in Southport it may be that it was to this rather genteel Lancashire resort that he went. At any rate, in this period he changed almost beyond recognition. He returned to Glasgow a head taller, with a cracked voice and the hint of a moustache. Physically he felt the equal of any schoolmaster and swaggered everywhere with a monumental chip on his shoulder. When a teacher growled, 'You deserve a proper thrashing,' Robert would glower back contemptuously as if to say, 'Just try it'.

Oh, I know I should have been ashamed of myself, taking advantage of my strength to bully my Masters. They could not have a brawl with me that would end in a fight. I put them in an awkward position and they knew it. A year ago they would have beaten me, now they left me alone. I am afraid I was not a very nice boy, but all my life I have resented authority . . . In most of my classes I was lazy, unambitious, and a dreamer.[19]

He found mathematics a bore, was fair at French and good at German. 'Grammar and spelling bored me, and all my life they have never seemed to matter much,' he confessed; and, indeed, his letters betray a disregard for orthography which seems oddly at variance with his craft as a writer. History kindled his imagination while geography brought dreams of far-off lands. The wanderlust which was to dog him all his adult life was incubating in those teenage years. 'In one class I was superlatively good — English Literature. Oh, how I adored it! There I shone like a star and astonished even the Master by my knowledge.'

Robert was a voracious, if somewhat indiscriminate, reader. He devoured any book that interested him, but chiefly fiction. He romped through the boys books of the period, especially anything by R.M. Ballantyne and Jules Verne. His first novel of a heavier calibre was *Ivanhoe*, but he confessed that it was the only one by Scott through which he struggled, dismissing the Waverley novels as 'boringly descriptive'. Harrison Ainsworth was more to his taste, and he read everything he ever wrote. His first Dickens novel was *Pickwick* which he enjoyed, later reading most of the others 'with delight'. The yarns of Captain Marryat were his prime favourite. 'I liked humour and character, but a lively story interest was my chief demand.'

Every Saturday his mother would give him a penny for a book at Miss Bell's Circulating Library in Byres Road, on condition that he got one for her. Miss Bell's emporium, in what was then grandly known as Victoria Buildings, stood next to the Gardens Café. The one was noted for the flavours of its ice-cream, while the other was like an Aladdin's cave to children. It had two large windows and an extensive interior, crammed with newspapers, periodicals, stationery, fancy goods and a fascinating range of colourful toys. But it also boasted one of the earliest circulating libraries and fulfilled a useful service before the advent of the public lending libraries.

Emily's favourite reading matter at that time was the romantic novels of Mrs Braddon and Mrs Henry Wood, though in her old age she developed a passion for detective novels and eventually nagged her son into writing a couple, *The Master of the Microbe* (1926) and *The House of Fear* (1927), specially for her delectation. If Emily regressed, Robert made rapid improvements, so that he came instinctively to recognise quality in writing and to appreciate characterisation and atmosphere. He even tried his hand at writing plays but was humiliated before the entire classroom when the master discovered the manuscript of a five-act historical tragedy in Robert's desk. 'We have among us a budding Ben Jonson or maybe a suckling Shakespeare,' the schoolmaster poked fun at him and the class roared with appreciative laughter. 'I was furious with the Master,' seethed Robert, 'and if one of the boys twitted me about it in the playground, I flared up and was ready to fight.'

Robert was also an habitué of the Mitchell Library, today one of Europe's leading reference libraries, and even in the 1880s one of Glasgow's great civic institutions, having been founded by the tobacco magnate Stephen Mitchell in the year of Robert's birth. Every month, the *Glasgow Herald* would publish the statistics of visitors and books borrowed, though nowhere was there mention made of the eleven-year-old schoolboy, arguably the

Robert Service (father of
the poet), *c.*1885

Emily Parker Service
(mother of the poet)

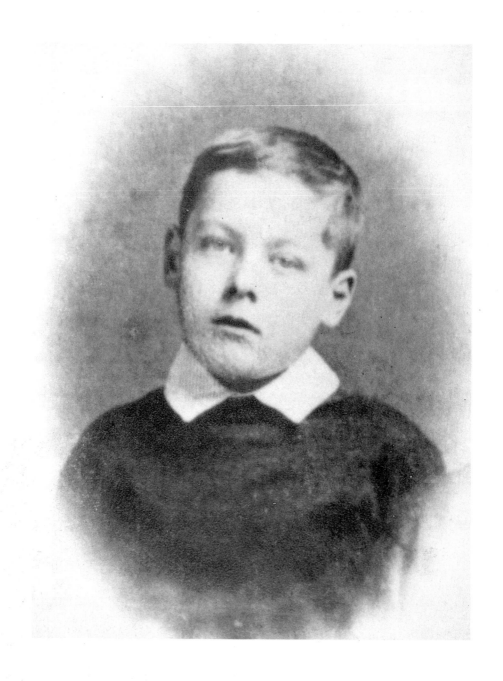

Robert Service aged eight, 1882

At the Hillhead Public School Drill Entertainment.

WM. CARTER, JUN., LITHO.

Hillhead Public School Drill Entertainment, May 1889, a *Quiz* Supplement, portraying drill instructor William Walker and headmaster Edward Ellice Macdonald (top and right)

Production of *Rob Roy* at the Grand Theatre, December 1892, a *Quiz* Supplement, with Georgina Robertson as Helen MacGregor (lower left) and Sergeant Hall as Bailie Nicol Jarvie (top)

Carter and Pratt, Litho and Printers, Glasgow.

"ROB ROY," BY THE 1ST L.R.V. DRAMATIC CLUB, AT THE GRAND THEATRE.

Canadian Bank of
Commerce, Dawson, Yukon
Territory, where Robert was
a teller, 1908–10

Robert's log cabin,
Dawson, where his second
volume of verse was
composed

Robert on the steps of his
cabin, 1910

Seated at his desk in the
cabin, 1911

Robert paddling his canoe *Coquette*, Fort Simpson, 1911

Robert, Dr Sandberg and the Douglas brothers in a voyageur scow, running the Big Cascade, Northern Canada, 4 June 1911. The elderly Indian ashore (foreground) was one of the two pilots

Robert in a cowboy hat at the Big Cascade, 1911, alongside ice left from winter overflowing

Robert Service in 1912

Mitchell's youngest reader of the period, who came every Saturday to browse through one or other of the bound volumes of *Punch* and copy the drawings therein. The Mitchell Library, then in its first location at Ingram Street in the centre of the city, was a couple of miles from Roxburgh Street, so Robert made a day of it, breaking off at noon to go to a nearby tea-room for a twopenny lunch of cakes and tea.

> What matter the poor fare! I was young and free, and my capacity for bright dreams was unlimited. Never was I more happy, and this because I felt so blissfully *alone*. When other boys of my age were playing games and idling away their leisure, I was living in an imaginative world of my own.[20]

It is significant that Robert makes little mention of his classmates, though he singled out one lad who was two years older than himself and who rejoiced in the nickname of Stinkey. Robert, by the way, admitted to being known as Beefy on account of his rosy, chubby cheeks. Stinkey presented a strange sight:

> He wore cotton-wool in his ears and a flannel bandage around his neck. He had a suit of green velveteen, with stockings pulled over long drawers. Spectacles handicapped him for sports, though he was wistful to hold his own in games. I figured I could lick him, but he had read a lot and mentally he was miles ahead of me. In class he was abstracted, treating the proceedings with weary disdain. I, too, was the object of his scorn, for he rarely spoke to me. Once he remarked:
>
> 'I see you have a sense of balance. You avoid the head of the class and also the ignominious bottom. To be average is to be comfortable. My father says that the boys who succeed are never the boys at the top of their class. I could beat those blighters but what's the use.' His father being a professor, I was inclined to believe there was something in what he said . . .
>
> He left school soon after, and I lost sight of him. Then some fifty years later I happened to read the obituaries in the London *Times* and there was a half column devoted to him. He had entered the Indian Civil Service and become high-muck-a-muck to a Maharajah. He had been knighted and lived a life of glory. It was hinted that he had burned the candle at both ends and had returned home with health broken . . .
>
> So my classmate became Sir Something Somebody and an honour

to the Empire; but if he killed himself in the process, I would rather be a live nonentity than a dead knight.[21]

The only person who fits this career description — indeed, one of the very few former pupils ever to attain a knighthood, was Sir John Rennie, who eventually became Governor of Mauritius. He was born in 1872 and, like Robert, was one of the inaugural pupils of Hillhead. His father, also called John Rennie, was not a professor, but private secretary and assistant at the physical laboratory of the University. In Robert's eyes, however, he clearly had professorial status and in 1890 he resigned his post in order to set himself up as a mechanical and electrical engineer with premises in the city's salubrious Bath Street, commuting each day from a large villa in the seaside resort of Helensburgh.[22]

Although a solitary child on his own admission, Robert did occasionally join other boys in their street adventures.

About this time I had what I will call the adventure of the Corpse in the Cooling Room. I would not mention it if it were not another illustration of that strange compulsion that made me do things against my will. Near us was a deserted building known as the Western Baths. Its promoters had gone into bankruptcy and for many years it had been left to silence and decay. Most of the windows were broken, while grass grew to the mouldy doors.

One day, with two chums, I went exploring around the basement, when under a stairway we discovered a window that opened to our pressure. We peered into the dark interior fearfully, and with a sense of sinister menace. I said: 'Come on, let's explore.' But to my surprise the others hung back. Shudderingly they tried to pierce that evil gloom. 'Come on, don't funk it. I'll go first,' I challenged; but I could not taunt them into following me.

However, the idea haunted me, and I felt I must brave that blackness or be a coward in my own eyes. So next day I stole away and slipped through the window. It was quite dark as I groped over rubbish and rubble. Then a glum light guided me, and stumbling up some stairs I came to the main floor. I was staring into the huge swimming tank, now cluttered with debris. The light that penetrated the glass roofing was evil and dubious. My slightest move made a startling echo, and I had a feeling that mocking eyes were on me. The very walls seemed to laugh derisively. I wanted to run away, but something kept urging me on.

Furtively I pushed open a door. Beyond was the room where the Turkish bathers reposed. Under a glass cupola that grudgingly yielded a pallid light were two lines of velvet couches. They were mouldy and gutted, and some rats scurried over them. Then I was conscious of a dreadful stench. I was shrinking back when suddenly I gasped with horror. Lying on a couch was the body of a man. His head was lower than his feet. I saw a black hole for a mouth and empty eyes. Through a mat of hair his face was the white of a shark's belly. His arms and legs sprawled wide, while one hand trailed on the rotted carpet. I had a feeling as if lice were creeping under my skin, and panting with fear I fled.

Oh, the joy of breathing clean air again! I decided to say nothing. No one had seen me go in, and I made sure no one would watch me leave. But the sight haunted me. I tried to make myself believe I had imagined it; I forced myself to think that the man was only a drunken derelict. But I could not sleep for the horror of it. I circled the building, fascinated as by an evil spell, while no power could have made me enter again.[23]

Shortly afterwards the Service family went away for their summer holiday by the sea, so this places the incident in June 1886. Throughout the weeks at the seaside, however, Robert's peace of mind was blighted by the memory, together with the fear that somehow he would be hunted down by the police as an accessory. He avoided reading the newspapers, but as the time came to return to Glasgow his spirits sank. Afterwards he steeled himself to return to the scene of the crime, and immediately a great burden was lifted from him when he perceived that the window had been boarded up.

There was a moment of panic a few days after the autumn term began, when two policemen visited the school and enquired 'Is there a boy called Service here?' While his classmates sighed with relief that the policemen were not on their trail, Robert rose uncertainly from his place, his legs turned to butter.

As I went out on the floor, I was preparing to make a full confession: 'I did not kill him . . . I swear I did not kill him . . .' when the policeman spoke:

'You did it. Admit you did it. You are the boy who *broke the lamp-post glass.*'

What a weight was lifted from me! I stoutly denied throwing the stone that broke the gas-light globe. In fact I had not seen it done. In fact I had been somewhere else. I protested my innocence, calling on my chum Silverman to testify that I had gone home peaceably on the afternoon in question. So the affair ended, and with it my last apprehension.

Curiously, the Western Baths is one of the few places specifically named in *Ploughman of the Moon*, although characteristically Robert was casual with details. This splendid edifice had been opened in Creswell Street on the eastern side of Byres Road in 1876. At first it prospered but then ran into difficulties; due to ancient mineworkings part of the building subsided and the floor of the pool cracked. The promoters were unable to raise the funds necessary for the repairs and the company went into liquidation in January 1884.[24] The building had been disused for two and a half years when this gruesome incident took place. Shortly before Robert made his hideous discovery, the company was reformed and the Baths eventually reopened in October 1886. While Robert was trying to erase the ghastly memory at the seaside the workmen brought in to refurbish the building found the corpse. Such a matter was a regular occurrence in Glasgow, and scarcely a day passed without the *Herald* chronicling the discovery of a bloated corpse in the river or the canal, or the putrescent remains of some tramp in some secluded corner. The discovery of 'the decomposed remains of a middle-aged man in a shabby black suit' in the Western Baths was briefly noted, with the comment that the cadaver had probably been there for several months. Identification was impossible and the case was closed before it was scarcely opened.[25]

At Hillhead, Robert's 'chief chum' was 'a Jew boy, brave and bright, but inclined to ironic humour', whom he disguised under the pseudonym of Silverman. From its inception Hillhead was a school which attracted the ablest boys and girls from the burgeoning Jewish community of the West End, the scions of families who had settled in Glasgow in the course of the century. The Hebrew Congregation had moved westwards from the centre of Glasgow to Garnethill in 1879, and its rabbi in the late 1880s was the Revd Isaac Levine. He had been born in Russian Poland in 1851 but about 1878 he had migrated to Glasgow with his wife Deborah and their first three sons, Abraham, Moses and Samuel. In Glasgow the Levines settled at 50 Great Western Road, Hillhead, where Rachel, Leah, Jacob, Ephraim, David, Lionel and Israel would follow in the 1880s and 1890s.[26]

Doubtless the Services and the Levines were not the only large families in Hillhead at the time, but Robert and Abraham Levine were of an age and were both eldest sons. What else they had in common seems to have been a

devil-may-care attitude towards authority. When Rabbi Levine was dissatis-
fied at his son's lack of progress he went to Edward Ellice Macdonald to
discuss the problem, saying that he gathered that his son's boon companion
was a boy called Service. The headmaster said that there were two boys of
that name in young Levine's class: 'One was the best boy in the school, the
other the worst.' The best boy was William Jack Nichol Service, son of the
eminent divine, the Revd Dr John Service, minister of Hyndland Church,
who had recently died. Willie Service would, in due course, follow in his
saintly father's footsteps and enter the ministry after graduating from
Glasgow University in 1894.[27] As far as can be ascertained, there was no
connection between the two Services, for Dr Service had been born at
Campsie, on the northern outskirts of the city, in 1833. Macdonald therefore
came to the conclusion that young Abraham was keeping bad company,
saying that Robert Service was a black sheep, lazy and incorrigible, inevitably
doomed to disaster. Robert greeted this news with mixed feelings.

> Silverman was a leg-puller and he may have exaggerated; but I knew I
> was in evil odour and the shadow of expulsion loomed ahead. What
> hurt was the prophecy that I was fated to failure. Well, I would fail
> colourfully. Better that than drab mediocrity. But the thought worried
> me not a little. It was the first suggestion that I was of the vagabond
> breed and destined to die in a ditch.[28]

Robert hated his last year at school. In 1887 David Bone entered the
Merchant Navy as a cadet and, although he does not say so, Robert must have
envied his erstwhile schoolmate. 'I wanted to go to sea. I dreamed of it night
and day. How I would swagger in brass buttons and grow tough and strong!'
His parents were deaf to his entreaties. He must remain at school for another
year. Robert resolved to drag his heels during that time. 'My rebellion began
gradually. It took the form of cheeky retorts that made boys laugh and the
teachers savage. I became the class wise-cracker.' Eventually his teachers simply
ignored his witty sallies, so he would sit aloof and brooding, often drawing cari-
catures of them. He positively dared the masters to punish him, but it was
unthinkable for a pupil in the eighth grade to be flogged. 'So I sat in insolent
isolation, paying no heed to the lesson. I turned up late, nonchalant and moody.
Things were rapidly coming to a head.'

From its inception, one of the undisputed institutions of Hillhead was
William Walker. Having served twenty-two years with the Northumberland
Fusiliers and retired with the rank of colour sergeant, he obtained the coveted
position of school janitor. In theory this was a lowly job, a cross between a

cleaner and a caretaker, but Walker was not slow in making his mark. Himself a strict disciplinarian, Macdonald gave his janitor a free hand to drill the boys and girls. The playground became a veritable parade ground and the annual drill displays at Hillhead each May soon came to be regarded as one of the sights of Glasgow. Walker, ramrod-straight and sporting a luxuriant moustache even by the standards of the day, cut a splendidly martial figure. Both boys and girls exercised with dumb-bells and Indian clubs, and were schooled in the mysteries of fencing and ring-drill; but it was the spectacle of youngsters marching with the precision of Prussian grenadiers that gladdened the headmaster's heart. The girls, in particular, took to this regimentation and there was intense competition to be chosen annually for The Sixteen, the élite female marching squad in their starched white frocks and red cowls. Following the outbreak of the Anglo-Boer War in 1899 a cadet corps was formed at Hillhead and small boys clamoured to wear the scarlet tunics and kilts of the Highland Light Infantry. Then William Walker, his old military rank restored, would strut around the school in uniform with three chevrons and the crossed flags of his rank proudly displayed.

Back in 1888, however, there was no cadet corps as such; but in practice a spirit of militarism that would have delighted Frederick the Great pervaded the school. It is small wonder that a maverick and a free spirit like Robert should have rebelled against this. Though he never gave Walker his name, Robert described the drillmaster as

an old soldier and fiery of nose and temper. He did not like me, but in virtue of my seniority I had command of one of the companies which we formed before marching into school. For we had a system of cadet training in which each class had its squad, the whole making up a battalion.

On this particular day I was in a devilish mood. I had charge of the last company, and as a rule the drillmaster told us 'Battalion, march off from the front,' but this time he shouted: 'Battalion, march off from the *rear.*'

He thought to catch me napping, hoping I would get balled up. In my confusion I said, 'Company, right-about turn.' They obeyed. Then suddenly I realised: Here I am, master of this company. I can make them do what I will. I regained my nerve. I would do something audacious. At first I thought I would order them into the street, so I gave the command: 'Quick march.' I could see they sensed some fun, they obeyed so readily. I gave them a left turn, flanking the battalion, then a right turn in front, and was wondering what to do next when I was aware of the Sergeant shouting at me. I turned to see him coming for me, his eyes blazing with fury. Now, I thought, he'll take over my company and disgrace me. How to save myself?

Right in front was a low building with the sign 'W.C.' in big letters. Then I had an inspiration. 'Left turn,' I yelled. They needed no second bidding. An order was an order. Joyfully they marched forward and ended up, laughing and tumbling, in the heart of the school latrine.

Then I turned to the Sergeant. 'Awfully sorry, sir. Lost my head. Piled my squad up in the privy. I am unworthy to command. I resign my position.'[29]

Sergeant Walker complained to the headmaster and a far from recalcitrant Robert was carpeted. Although Robert claimed that he was expelled from Hillhead, there is no note of this in the school records. The truth probably lies in Macdonald's laconic observation, 'You do not seem to be doing much good here.' He suggested that there might be some other sphere of action more worthy of Robert's abilities. 'Perhaps it might be better if you ceased coming.' Robert concluded that the head was sensibly sweet about it. 'It was really expulsion with kid gloves.'

So ended my school days. I was glad, for I was eager for the adventure of life. I have never gone back to my old school. Some day I may revisit it. I can see myself addressing the senior pupils and giving them a pep talk on success in life. I will tell them not to be lazy and disobedient, as I was, and point to myself as a horrible example of how I failed to be a bright business man and a respectable citizen. I hope they will take my homily to heart and follow in the sober path of their fathers.

In *Songs of a Sun-lover*, published in 1949, Robert gave poetic expression to this wish in the last stanza of 'Dunce':

Oh, I am old and worn and grey,
And maybe have not long to live;
Yet 'tis my hope at some Prize Day
At my old school the Head will give
A tome or two of mine to crown
Some pupil's well-deserved success —
Proving a scapegrace and a clown
May win at last to worthiness.

Regrettably, Robert never fulfilled this ambition. During the time when I was a pupil at Hillhead (1945–54) he was at the height of his fame, and after the publication of his two autobiographical books (in 1946 and 1948 respectively) the school basked in his reflected glory, but although he was a not infrequent visitor to Glasgow in those days, he never went near his old school.

CHAPTER 4

ADOLESCENCE, 1888-96

Said Father: 'Your son is a duffer,
A stupid and mischievous elf.'
Said Mother, who's rather a huffer:
'That's right — he takes after yourself.'

'My Future', in *Lyrics of a Lowbrow* (1951)

ROBERT WAS JUST TURNED FOURTEEN WHEN HE LEFT
school. By now Emily had had eight children and another (Janet Isabella) was
on the way. Some idea of the hand-to-mouth existence of the family at this
period is conveyed colourfully by Robert. Papa had a great opinion of his
business ability and studied the stock markets assiduously:

> He would often talk of Rio something or other, and when he was
> cheerful we knew it had gone up, but when he was glum we guessed
> it was down. In the end, like everything else he touched, something
> happened to wipe out his little stake. I see him now as a pathetic, frus-
> trated figure, forced to live on his wife's income because he was inca-
> pable of making one of his own.[1]

Having eventually come to terms with his failure as a businessman, Robert
Senior justified his existence by specialising in the intricate art of household

management. Raising a large family on a slender income was no easy feat. The canny Scot in him came to the fore; every day he trudged miles to purchase stale food in the cheapest markets of the slum districts: 'apples that were half-rotten, fish that smelt putrid, Irish butter tasting of turnips, eggs in which the yellow and white had wedded, and meat that was full of grubs'. His idea was that money saved was money earned, 'but we, as his poor family, were the ones who suffered from his penny-pinching'. As Robert Senior enjoyed his food, the family never went short, even if the quality was lacking. 'We had eggs for breakfast, a hot midday dinner, a high tea, and a supper at nine in the evening of coffee and fried fish.' Cooked food was highly seasoned, not only because that was how Robert Senior liked it, but condiments helped to disguise the foul taste.

Papa was a heavy smoker, but he made up for this self-indulgence by only smoking the cheapest clay pipes and mixing the tobacco himself, carefully preserving the clinkered dottle from the previous smoke to adulterate the next one. He took a pride in such matters as economy in clothing his large brood. On one occasion he obtained a job lot of green baize, the cloth used to cover billiard tables. From this he ran up suits for the four eldest boys. When the Service brothers turned up at school in their identical pea-green suits the class roared at the teacher's quip: 'The Service Circus meseems'. Robert Senior was also adept as a cobbler, mending the family's footwear with oddly assorted patches and reinforcing the soles and heels with enormous hobnails and steel plaques. 'It is as a cobbler I best remember him, beaming benevolently through his spectacles, his sleeves rolled up, grey stubble on his chin. In such a moment he looked benignant and contented.'

As the family increased in number, the Services could no longer afford the sixteen shillings a month for their domestic servants. They were given notice and thereafter Papa became official dish-washer. 'Thus by menial abnegation he tried to make up for his failure as a bread-earner, though he would have been the very last to admit failure. To the end he had to kid himself that he was a success, and in his own way he was.'

Not that Robert Senior could not keep up appearances when he felt it necessary. He only shaved twice a week. On the day he shaved he would dress up in his best suit, sprigged waistcoat and lavender spats. He sported the kind of hat later popularised by Winston Churchill 'that looked as if it was the result of a *liaison* between a bowler and a topper'. He was a pompous little man who affected an English accent (appropriate for Kelvinside, of course) and was an incorrigible name-dropper, referring to men in high office or public positions as 'My old friend . . .' The following day, however, when the stubble appeared on his chin, he donned a second-grade suit and looked like a small businessman. On the third he would dress like a tramp, with a red handkerchief under his bristly chin. In this scruffy character he enjoyed taking the younger children for walks, 'especially if it was Sunday and he could meet the well-dressed crowd coming from church. I admired his sense of dramatic fitness, but if I asked anyone to the house I was careful to do it on Papa's shaving day.'

Robert Senior was normally sober. 'He was one of the most abstemious men I have ever known. For three hundred and fifty-five days of the year he perched triumphantly on the water-waggon; then on the other ten he fell off with a mighty wallop.' The trouble was that these alcoholic binges came on with little warning, but as one became imminent the whole family suffered considerable stress, wondering exactly when the blow would fall. 'On the street, talking to a girl, we would keep a wary eye for Papa in the distance, taking up the sidewalk. Or if at home we had friends visiting, we were fearful of him barging in on us with bibulous geniality.' Robert Junior recalled that, on one occasion in 1884, 'we had a wealthy aunt staying with us when Papa developed a gloomy gaze and a mean manner'. The wealthy aunt could only have been Mary Jane from Southport, whose husband, Henry Pemberton, was a prosperous businessman. Jane's appearance alone must have served as a major reproach to the failed bank clerk, so it is hardly surprising that he turned to the bottle.

> . . . sure enough that evening he announced his intention of going out for a whiff of fresh air. I waited till he was well away, then followed at a distance. I was only ten at the time, but I felt the honour of the family was at stake. When he got to the first pub he disappeared inside, and after a little hesitation I followed. I was prepared to do my little: 'Father, dear father, come home with me now' stuff, and all braced for the part. He was standing up to the bar with a group of others, and before him was a tumbler of whisky. I went forward and took him by the arm. He turned round. At first his face showed amazement, then wrath.
>
> 'You young blackguard!' he shouted. 'What are you doing in this haunt of iniquity?' The group around him looked uncomfortable and crestfallen. So, taking *me* by the arm, he marched me out. 'What were you doing in that den of vice?' he demanded again with virtuous indignation.
>
> 'What were *you* doing?' I said.
>
> 'That's none of your affair. But anyway I was there on business. One of those men is a baker and I was arranging for a supply of

slightly stale bread at half-price. And over a glass of lemonade,' he added indignantly.

I felt guilt. Perhaps it had been lemonade and his motives innocent. So on the way home I let him lecture me on the evils of strong drink, and he made me promise that I would never enter a pub again. After all, I had to admit that he was a good example to me, for his bibulous spells only lasted two or three days, after which he became very sick. Then for a while he was abject in his misery; then almost angelic in his remorse. So much did he look the suffering martyr he made us feel as if *we* had driven him into the embrace of John Barleycorn. So he would remain a model of: 'Wouldn't touch a drop of the beastly stuff!' . . . till the next time.[2]

This candid, though not unaffectionate, pen-picture of the Micawberish paterfamilias was summed up neatly:

It will be seen from all this what an important part Papa played in our household. If he could not cut a swathe in the world of affairs he could at least be the big noise in his own home. By persistent pater-nity he bolstered up his self-respect, and if outsiders would not recog-nize him as a dominant personality he was determined his family would . . . A sentimental dreamer; kind to children and tender-hearted; a lover of freedom and good food — there have been worse men lauded to the skies, and I am grateful that here I am able to pay a small tribute to his memory.[3]

By contrast, Robert hardly mentioned his mother, and never provided even the sketchiest of descriptions.

Doubtless recollecting the splendid appearance of young David Bone in his smart naval uniform, Robert commented wistfully on those school chums who had gone into the Merchant Navy: 'They vanished for a while to reap-pear with brass buttons and brazen tales of far adventure'. Robert, however, was shrewd enough to realise that, underneath the bragging and swaggering, a life before the mast in the 1880s was no sinecure, though he thought that he would have stuck it out long enough 'to get a good sea-ground for a writer'. His parents put their foot down. Robert was destined for an office desk. In the end a compromise was effected when he obtained a job in a shipping office. The pay was meagre, a mere ten pounds a year, and as the company was only just starting up, the work was long, arduous and decidedly dodgy. A few years later James and Muirhead Bone were to collaborate on a delightful book entitled *Glasgow in 1901*, in which there appeared a profile of a shipping clerk, with his makeshift office on a Glasgow quayside:

> The clerk pops out and in his box all day long, just as do the pigeons in their dovecot over his head. Your proper head clerk is a kind of bonnet laird, who lives among his dogs and hens and turkeys, with maybe an old horse at the far end of the shed, and a sheep which — provided it is not demoralised by the lumpers into eating tobacco — is an ornament to any shipping business. The place is always like a farm, with piles of golden hay in the sides and grain on its floor. It is never free of cattle, and the head clerk holds long converse with dealers over the season's prospects and the North-country fairs. In his office a handful of new-laid eggs lie among his papers, and he will stop in the middle of his cash entries to run into the shed at the sound of an unprofitable hen clucking confidently at last. The under clerk is not like your office man, who has a guv'nor unsoothed by Arcadian joys, and no one but a boy to command . . . He acquires a curious, left-handed kind of knowledge from the broken men who now work the cargo, and the Highland mariners, which will not, perhaps, advance him towards a cashier's job, but makes him a good deal more interesting to his fellow-creatures. He learns many strange things, for the quayside is the harbour of wandering dogs and lost men . . .[4]

Robert's first employer definitely fell into the category of 'wandering dogs and lost men'. It did not take the boy long to realise that his boss was a shady customer indeed. 'He believed that credit was capital and that a man could measure his wealth by the amount he could borrow.' One of Robert's first tasks was to mail a batch of letters which invited widows and clergymen to invest in the business, with a guaranteed return of 100 per cent. Too late, it dawned on Robert that he had dropped the circulars into the mailbox without affixing the necessary stamps. Not surprisingly, this mail-shot produced a zero response.

> I can imagine gentle old ladies in their country homes and choleric Colonels in their clubs sniffing because they had to pay twopence postage; then snorting as they read the dazzling offer to allow them to share in an El Dorado. 'How can he make our fortunes if he cannot afford to stamp his letters?' I could hear them say.[5]

For want of a stamp a fortune was lost, or perhaps not. Robert speculated that his employer was a smart man who knew the shipping business intimately.

His scheme was to charter vessels on credit, but once he had control of them he would have run them to advantage. The failure of his prospectus to likely investors forced him to close down before long. Observing the rapid collapse of the business, Robert was conscience-stricken. 'Perhaps it was his small and irresponsible office boy who thwarted him from becoming the founder of a great shipping line.' Nemesis caught up with Robert when the boss received a letter one day from his fiancée, complaining that his last letter to her had arrived unstamped. In vain, Robert protested that he had stamped it but that the stamp must have fallen off. In future he was abjured to be more generous with his saliva.

Robert was paid monthly, in arrears. How he looked forward to receiving his first pay-packet which ought to have contained sixteen shillings and eightpence. In the meantime he had to trudge three miles along Dumbarton Road from his home in Roxburgh Street to the quay in Whiteinch, and three miles back again each evening, for he could not afford the penny tramfare. When he got home he was often too weary to eat supper, but consoled himself with the thought that, on the day of that first pay-packet, he would buy a hot lunch and chocolates. The day arrived, but there was no pay-packet. Another day passed without payment, and on the third Robert broached the subject with his boss who seemed surprised and not a little annoyed. 'All right; I'll pay you at the end of the week,' he promised casually. But the weekend came, and there was no sign of payment. Again Robert meekly suggested his need of money. He was scared, as if he were asking for something he had no right to. 'And he acted as if it were effrontery on my part. Huffily he promised to pay me at the end of the following week, but he made me feel so importunate I dared not ask again.'

The boss even began to grudge the money he disbursed for postage and took to checking the stamp book rigorously. This probably gave Robert an idea; he despatched two letters each day unstamped and pocketed the twopence which enabled him to purchase a mug of coffee and a bath bun at lunchtime. He selected letters addressed to big companies who were unlikely to complain and treated them in strict rotation. 'I do not suppose it did much harm,' he later wrote, but it was a form of petty theft that haunted his conscience for years after. 'Honesty is not natural; it is grafted on us. I was too youthful to understand its expedience.'

The business began to go downhill. Creditors haunted the office and the janitor called daily for the rent. Robert was instructed to tell callers that his boss was out, and he developed a theatrical technique for appearing to look into the inner office, only to be surprised to discover that the manager was absent (when, in fact, he was hiding beind his roll-top desk). 'You needn't be so damn realistic about it,' he would snap, but no doubt thought he had a very smart office boy. One day Robert had to keep a lookout for the janitor and while the coast was clear his boss did a lightning flit. A couple of draymen removed the roll-top desk which Robert spotted the following day in a nearby auction-room. 'I no longer worried about my salary, for I knew I was only a ranking creditor on the estate, if any.' Next day the boss did not turn up, and Robert never saw him again.

> I often wondered what became of him. He deserved fortune, for he had a bold, active mind. Perhaps he succeeded, and died with honour and dignity; but if so he must have been more discriminating in his choice of an office boy.[6]

Having worked for more than a month for no reward, Robert came up with an idea that gladdened his father's heart. One day he said, 'Papa, I'd like to go into a bank,' adding that at least he would be assured of his pay. 'Also, one gets all the holidays there are — and then some.'

Robert Senior was enthusiastic about his son's choice. On one of his shaving days he donned his Churchill bowler, sprigged waistcoat and lavender spats and took his eldest off to his old bank. 'There he introduced me to the clerks of his youth who had risen to position and power. My application was made, and soon after a certain branch wrote to say that they needed an apprentice, and would I present myself.'

Neither the bank, nor the branch in which he served his apprenticeship, are named in the autobiography:

> The office was only two miles from home and the way lay through a lovely park. Here would be a healthful walk for me; while the bank itself, situated in the vicinity of a slum, looked humanly interesting. Standing at a corner, it had all the allure of a licensed establishment; indeed, it was frequently taken for one by the drunken dockers of the neighbourhood.[7]

In fact the bank was the Stobcross branch of the Commercial Bank of Scotland. In the summer of 1888 when Robert embarked on his banking career he was only fourteen and a half. As a rule, the Commercial Bank did not engage apprentices under the age of fifteen, but Robert was a well-set-up lad who would easily pass for sixteen. John Hamilton, the bank agent, suggested that the boy accompany him to the head office in Edinburgh and get their dispensation. Robert had never been to the metropolis before and was considerably impressed by its venerable buildings in general and the Commercial Bank's headquarters in particular — 'a stately building in a staid old square . . . It had an air of fruity permanence that appealed to me.' He was duly wheeled before the personnel director and other august functionaries and apparently passed muster. It was a proud day for young Service, marred only by the fact that Hamilton dropped him like a hot potato as soon as they were back out on the street.

> He gave me a bun and his blessing and directed me to the station.
> Then he bustled off, looking very happy. I got the impression he had a
> girl friend in the city, and this was a diversion in an otherwise dull life.

As a brand-new apprentice Robert commenced with a salary of twenty pounds a year. This was paid without increment for five years, but there was no guarantee of any increase thereafter, and Robert was still drawing the salary he had started with, more than six years later, until he finished his apprenticeship. 'It paid for my clothes, my lunch and left me a fair amount of pocket-money. At first it was wonderful to gain so much, but latterly it hardly seemed adequate.' There was no mention of contributing to the hard-pressed family budget.

The Stobcross branch was located at 119 Dumbarton Road (now 995 Argyle Street). The beige sandstone building, at the corner of Argyle Street, Finnieston Street and Minerva Street, still stands and although it is now the premises of a retailer of wheelchairs and other aids for the handicapped, it is still a handsome building, with a noble, curved façade where the three streets intersect. As Robert inferred, it was situated in a rather mixed district. To the east and south lay the congested tenements of Finnieston and Anderston, but following the graceful sweep of Minerva Street was, and still is, St Vincent Crescent which had all the elegance of a Nash terrace and fronted on to a bowling green and park. A hundred yards away, on the northern side of Argyle Street, lies Kelvingrove Park, the 'lovely park' through which Robert walked to and from the bank each day. What is quite extraordinary, however, is that Robert fails to mention that, about the time he took up his appointment, the first of Glasgow's four great international exhibitions was inaugurated in that very park. On 8 May 1888 Their Royal Highnesses, the Prince and Princess of Wales (later King Edward VII and Queen Alexandra), drove through cheering crowds to unlock the doors of the Main Building. Daily Robert must have walked past the ornate triumphal arch which marked the Hillhead entrance to the Exhibition, but if it made any impression on him at all he failed to record it.

The shortest route from Roxburgh Street to Argyle Street would have been up Great George Street, a steep thoroughfare familiar from schooldays, thence by Southpark Avenue and the new University on Gilmorehill, then straight across the park to Kelvingrove Street. For the duration of the Exhibition, however, a slight detour round the enclosed grounds was necessary, but the palaces and pavilions of this, the greatest show of its kind since the Great Exhibition in London of 1862, must have been an exciting spectacle.

Robert's duties at the bank were not at all arduous:

> I always had a prejudice against hard work, or indeed any work. I would rather do little for poor pay than strain myself for a big salary. So here I was well suited. I would get down to the office at half past nine in the morning. There would be half an hour for lunch; then a walk to the chief office [in Buchanan Street] to collect the clearing house cheques. I would take an hour to this, walking, so that I might pocket the pennies allowed me for the car fare. At four by the clock I would lock the front door and go home. And there were the holidays. It seemed we were always having them, especially Bank Holidays which no one else had.[8]

Having narrowly escaped dismissal when the Bank Inspector made a snap examination of Robert's petty cash account and postage book — incredibly the Inspector assessed the stamped postcards at a penny each instead of a halfpenny, thus transforming a deficit of five shillings into a surplus of twopence — Robert vowed to himself to be scrupulously honest, at least in small things. As a politician once told him, 'Never be crooked unless you can be so in a big way'.

Robert had little to do with the branch manager, but the Accountant was his constant mentor and role model. He was Robert's immediate superior for seven years and seems to have tolerated the boy's idiosyncratic behaviour. 'It was obvious I had no vocation for banking, and the only reason I stuck to it was that it was an easier job than any other. Curse this business of making a living! I have always regarded it as a necessary evil.' In point of fact, the scanty records indicate that Robert was well thought of by his superiors and was a diligent, if unspectacular employee. Certainly his official duties by no means overtaxed him:

> And though my work was easy, I tried to make it still easier. I dawdled over my daily errands and dreamed over my ledger. I made rhymes as

I cast up columns of figures. It was so pleasant, with a big fire warming the spine, I crooked over my desk. Through the plate-glass window I could watch the cold grey street, where sailors and longshoremen met and wrangled. There were all sorts of Dickens-like characters meandering from pub to pub and an atmosphere of picturesque squalor that charmed me. I would gaze pensively from my high stool till a customer aroused me from my torpor.[9]

In the 1880s there was a public house on every street corner along Dumbarton Road. The Commercial Bank's Stobcross branch was probably the only street-corner establishment that did not conform to this pattern, so the confusion of drunken dockers was perfectly understandable. Watching the world go by was enormously stimulating; Robert's lifelong preoccupation with people and *types* was born here. Like Burns, he was often careless of, or indifferent to, places; it was the people in the landscape that mattered above all.

We know that Robert began rhyming at the tender age of six. It is to be assumed that the habit developed during his boyhood, although none of his juvenilia has survived. In the congenial atmosphere of the Stobcross bank branch, however, he succumbed to the temptation to rhyme:

> Then I took to writing verses during office hours, and this was the last straw as far as my Accountant was concerned. One day he grabbed a piece of paper I was scribbling on. It availed him little, however. I saw him gazing with stupefaction at the line spaced at intervals: 'But that was yesterday.' It was the refrain of a three-verse poem I was writing. I had the framework laid down, and all that remained was to fill in the body. Thus early was I adopting one of the tricks of the trade. My Accountant was mystified.
>
> 'What was yesterday?' he demanded with some indignation.
>
> 'That,' I answered vaguely.

The poem was, in fact, constructed on fairly mechanical lines. The first stanza was introductory, the second developed the theme and the the third climaxed it. There were four lines to each stanza and the fourth consisted of the punch-line 'But that was yesterday'. This tale of unrequited love ended with the couplet:

> Alas! my love is false to me,
> But *that* was yesterday.

Robert sent it off to a boys' magazine entitled *Ching Ching's Own*. Two weeks later it appeared, tucked away in the correspondence column with the editorial comment, 'You've got it bad, old fellow. But cheer up. You'll get over it.'[10]

At fifteen, Robert fell hopelessly in love for the first time. The object of his affections was 'a girl called Maisie McQuarrie, the perfection of prettiness'. Like virtually every other name in his autobiographies, this was false; but lest any lady of that name should materialise subsequently, Robert playfully concluded this chapter with

> I have a sudden doubt. Was her name not Daisy? It may have been. Funny how one can go off one's chump for a girl and later on hardly remember her name. Well, she was a lovely lass. I'll bet she made some man a perfect wife, but I have never regretted it was not I.[11]

Robert was overwhelmed by her 'saccharine pulchritude'. She was a picture of sweetness he hardly dared gaze at. 'To the last I never had one square look at her, but the mental image that haunted me day and night was one that in glamour exceeded reality.' From start to finish of this infatuation he never once spoke to her. If he encountered her in the street his legs wobbled and his bowels seemed to turn to water. Instead, he pretended elaborate indifference, hoping she would give him a passing glance, but she was probably quite oblivious of the effect she had on this shy, red-faced youth. He contented himself with haunting the street where she lived and gazing up at the window he fondly imagined was hers.

'The McQuarries were a snooty family,' wrote Robert. The only clue to their identity was that they lived in Sunnybrae Crescent (elsewhere referred to as Sunnybrae Gardens and, in reality, Athole Gardens). The only family which vaguely fits the meagre description given by Robert was that of Alexander Grant, a manufacturer residing at 7 Athole Gardens, whose daughter Marian was three years Robert's junior.[12] Robert's description of Mr McQuarrie as a high official in the railway does not, in fact, match any of the denizens of Athole Gardens. The Grants were adherents of Kelvinside Church, on the corner of Byres Road and Great Western Road, and this was the church to which Robert Senior packed off his brood every Sunday. Robert had been an indifferent church-goer until Maisie/Marian cast her spell on him. She and her parents occupied the pew immediately behind the Service family so that, although he could not *see* her, he fancied that he was inhaling her perfume.

During the course of the infatuation Robert was a zealous attender at Kelvinside Church. Even on the wettest day he would trudge to the morning service. By squinting round he might get the occasional glimpse of her, though he dared not do this often.

> Did she notice me, I wondered? Did she ask herself who was the poetic youth with the air of romantic melancholy? He must be some one unusual, perhaps a genius. I was sorry my face was so plump and red and sucked my cheeks in to make my profile more interesting. I only hoped I was making an impression.

This one-sided affair lasted for seven months, but ended in farce. The girl's father was bony of face, with a choleric eye. He always dressed smartly, with a fine frock-coat and a shiny top-hat.

> It so happened that one day I arrived very late for church and hurried to my place. The congregation was singing the first hymn when I pushed into my seat. I was conscious of Maisie looking at me in an amused way, so flustered was I. I was aware of Mr McQuarrie directly behind me, singing lustily in a voice like a corn-crake. Then as I sat down to make the usual perfunctory prayer, I was further aware of a dreadful cracking sound. It dominated the singing; it curdled my blood! it paralyzed me with horror . . . I was sitting squarely on Mr McQuarrie's gleaming silk topper.
>
> Will I ever forget the sickening sensation as it buckled under me, and my too tardy reflex as I rose with a startled 'Oh!' I was aware of the petrified stare of its owner. He suspended his singing, looking aghast as he realized what had happened. I turned to face him. He held out his hand for the hat. I took it up, but before I gave it to him, I instinctively put my hand inside and straightened it out. I remember the big cracks and the drunken disreputable look of it. It was squashed almost flat. With a most unchristian look on his face he snatched at it. And it was then, I am afraid, I added insult to injury, for I said the thing that came into my head. As I tried to push it back into shape I stammered: 'Awfully sorry, sir. Pity it wasn't your opera hat; then it wouldn't have mattered, would it?'

At that, for the first and only time, the girl smiled. Robert would always treasure the memory of that smile, but the game was up, the spell was broken. As he watched McQuarrie trying to look dignified under his battered tile on the way home, Robert realised that he could never have been his father-in-law. Then the funny side of it struck him and he laughed. 'I was free from the thrall of love, and how happy I was! Maisie could go to the devil now. I no longer cared for her.'

Yet he must have nurtured a lingering affection for her. Years later, when he heard that she had enrolled at the old teacher-training college in Dundas Vale, he was inspired to compose a ballade:

> You've pupil teacher turned, they say,
> And at the knowledge I declare
> I wish I were a child to-day,
> That pupil I might claim your care;
> Ah, then how gladly would I fare;
> Each day to your sweet presence free,
> Each day to hear with eyes astare
> The lesson that you taught to me.

And so on, three verses and the *envoi*. Robert regarded it as a perfect specimen of the ballade form, so he sent it to her, but anonymously. He was surprised to find his ballade, some years later, in the poet's corner of the Glasgow *Weekly Herald*. It was printed as he wrote it, but it bore other initials than his. 'Not Maisie's either. I wondered who had stolen it. It amused me, but at that time I had switched from poetry to another of my interests and I was too careless to investigate . . .'[13]

This young lady inspired a fair amount of verse, if Robert is to be believed. It was invariably the poetry of renunciation and despair. One piece entitled 'Love's Lament' consisted of the usual three stanzas and Robert was particularly pleased with a couplet in the second verse:

> Love's exultant roundelay
> Issues in a wail of pain.

'In fact, I was so tickled with it, that being Scotch, I saved it up and used it on three later occasions under somewhat similar but less reticent circumstances.'[14] Robert now embarked wholeheartedly on his first poetic phase, which apparently occupied about twelve months. Other girls might fleetingly attract his attention but he was gauche and had a tendency to bore them. Of one girl he later wrote: 'I talked of books instead of her looks. I gave her Keats when she wanted cuddling.'

In his sixteenth year he was obsessed by poetry. He always carried a volume of poems and would devour it whenever he had an odd moment, even when seated on the toilet. He had a 'tiny Tennyson and a brownie

Browning' and was especially fond of the latter, which he called his bob's worth of Browning. It will be noted that Robert not only had a penchant for rhyme — even in casual conversation he often spoke in couplets — but he was hopelessly addicted to alliteration, as the titles of his prose and poetic works would later testify. Commuting between home and the bank he often had his nose in one of these volumes and was so engrossed that he frequently risked being run down by a horse tram or a bone-shaker bicycle. Both Tennyson and Browning were still alive at the time, and Robert speculated what might have been their reaction on learning that a young boy had been knocked down while reading 'Ulysses' or 'A Toccata of Galuppi'.

But although he never lost his appreciation of these poetic giants, Robert was drawn 'for real enjoyment' to the late-Victorian minor poets such as Owen Meredith and Coventry Patmore. 'Even more I liked verse-makers. Thackeray and Tom Hood were my favourites, and I took them as models.' He preferred verse 'with lots of rhyming'. He was always in love with rhyme.

> If two lines could be made to clink it seemed to me to go a long way to justify them. Perhaps it was because I had such facility in that direction. I could take a paragraph from the paper and turn it into doggerel, while at home I often spoke in stanzas. Rhyming has my ruin been. With less deftness I might have produced real poetry.[15]

Even in this prose passage he unconsciously falls into the rhymer's habit of inversion. The first of his more mature pieces was called 'The Song of the Social Failure'. It had three stanzas and a refrain which ran:

> The Might Have Been, the Might Have Been,
> The haunting, taunting Might Have Been;
> We all can hear in our hearts, I ween,
> The grim reproach of the Might Have Been.

This was published in due course, though Robert omitted to say which magazine or paper it appeared in. 'I wonder if the Editor who printed my morbid and disillusioned poem had any suspicion that his contributor was a beardless boy?' His next effort was a comic one entitled 'It Must Be Done'. The idea came one wintry morning as Robert poised over his icy bath. It began:

> He stands upon the water brink
> With pale and anguished brow,

And shudders as he murmurs low:
'It must be done — and now.'

There were the usual three verses and the closing couplet packed the surprise:

It's over now . . . he's only had
His morning bath — no more.

Robert was inordinately fond of italics in his punch-lines. At this juncture he never attempted anything grander. 'I was wise enough to know that three verses were the limit of a reader's tolerance.' But he had not yet learned that he must not let rhyme beat him. This poem was despatched to a periodical called *Scottish Nights*. Two weeks later, on purchasing a copy, he was pleasantly surprised to find his verse on the front page. He was even more gratified when he received a letter containing a postal order for two shillings and sixpence. 'That was a great day, though little did I dream that my wonderful half-crown was the portent of future fortune.' The Accountant cashed his order with enthusiasm, while even John Hamilton was tickled by his junior clerk's success. 'They saw me from a new angle, and I blushed and decided it must be an accident. One didn't make money like that.'[16]

Robert soon learned that, while magazines were quite happy to print his verse they very seldom paid for it. A month later he had a serious and rather high-minded poem, entitled 'Shun Not the Strife', published in the *People's Friend*:

Shun not the savage brawl of Life,
O you who would divorce your soul
From self and win love's highest goal!
Shun not but mingle with the strife.

'Probably on account of the nobility of its sentiments the Editor did not insult me by offering me filthy lucre for it. So I learned early in the game that verse may pay, but poetry is its own reward.' This was an important distinction. Much later in life, when he was habitually patronised by 'real poets', Robert would often comfort himself with the thought that he might only be a versifier, but he had money in the bank while they had not. Indeed, he would make a virtue of necessity and was quick to correct anyone misguided enough to call him a poet. He was a versifier, a rhymester, and defiantly proud of his particular calling.

At the beginning of the 1890s he went back to writing light verse and had several pieces published in a local paper. They brought favourable comment but no cash. 'However, it was a bright little rag and I was pleased to see my stuff in it.' The periodical was *Quiz*, a humorous weekly published in Glasgow. These pieces were sometimes identified by their authors' initials but more often they were published anonymously. The editor, who never refused a contribution, had no idea who Robert was, and he was too timid to visit him.

About this time Robert became fascinated by the structure and form of poetry. The series of pocket books with the generic title of the Canterbury Poets was then in progress and Robert read the volumes on French patterns and sonnets.

> Their very difficulty was a challenge to me. I accomplished several ballades and a sequence of sonnets. I had a peculiar way of working. I would choose easy rhymes, write them in a string and pick out the likeliest. With these I would make the rhyming ends of my sonnet or ballade. Once having set up this framework I would write in lines to suit my rhymes. A carpenter job you will say. Maybe, but it worked. I did not know anything about the mechanics of verse. Even today I do not know what is an iambic or a trochee. To me scansion was a matter of ear, and if one followed good models one could not go wrong. I aped Keats for sonnets and Austin Dobson for ballades, and turned out fair imitations of each. It was good practice and great fun, but the secret of my success was my joy in jingles.[17]

By the time he was sixteen Robert had contributed over a score of poems to weekly periodicals. He boasted that he never had a single rejection, because he had the good sense not to send them to a paper unless they had a 75 per cent chance of acceptance. 'I gauged this by the poems they had already accepted; in fact I often modelled my own on these. I never read a poem I admired but what (*sic*) I tried to emulate it.'

One day he ran into Jimmy Bone, bubbling over as usual. He was writing a series of poems for *Quiz*. Robert interjected that he had written poems for this periodical too.

'But they pay me,' said Jimmy with dignity.

Robert was crushed by this retort; but some months later he met him again and said, 'I read your things in *Quiz*. I enjoyed them very much. Why have you stopped contributing?'

'They did not pay me,' was the answer.

It is impossible to say which of the anonymous pieces in *Quiz* came from Robert's own pen, but one poem of three stanzas entitled 'Her Part and Mine!', which appeared in the issue of 21 March 1890 has his hallmark:

Thrice in a little drawing room
　　We met: she used me free; —
I never felt like loving her
　　When *she* — loved me!

We were alone: 'twas still and clear;
　　'Neath May moon's witchery;
I never thought of kissing her
　　When *she* — kissed me!

Months passed. I came to need her love,
　　Oh, with what fervency!
I never dreamt of leaving her
　　When *she* — left me!

Another chance encounter with Jimmy Bone triggered off an interest that, for a time, became almost an obsession. 'He was as dynamic as ever. He seemed to gobble life voraciously.' Jimmy introduced Robert to the music-hall scene. Hearing a girl singing 'After the Ball', Robert wrote a parody entitled 'Under the Mould':

After the fight is over,
After the strife is done,
After the bells are pealing
After the triumph won;
What is life's sum of glory
When all the tale is told?—
A shroud and a feast for the blindworm
UNDER THE MOULD.

'The profound pessimism of callow youth! At sixteen how I revelled in the macabre. It was as if I were ending my days instead of beginning them.'

The only other acquaintance of his Glasgow period whom Robert identified — although, characteristically, he never actually named him — was

a sandy-haired youth who smoked cigarettes and dressed dapperly. He had a lazy, humorous regard and a nonchalant manner. Because he was some years older than I and knew some reporters, I held him in awe. Then one day a paper-covered publication appeared on the bookstalls. The title was *Wee MacGreegor*. Almost overnight it catapulted its author to fame. He became a professional writer and never looked back. Though none of his books had the success of his first, many of them had more merit. A real writer, humorous and original — though in his youth he high-hatted me, I salute his shade.[18]

The writer was John Joy Bell, three years Robert's senior. He, too, lived in Hillhead (at 8 Bank Street), which is probably where their paths crossed; but Bell was out of a higher social class altogether, his father being one of Glasgow's tobacco magnates. J.J., as he was always known, was by this time halfway through the Arts course at the University. More importantly, he edited the undergraduate weekly magazine *G.U.M.* which was a nursery for many who later achieved literary fame. As if these editorial duties were not arduous enough, Bell began contributing short stories and features to the Glasgow newspapers. Robert was right about *Wee MacGreegor*. The book was an overnight sensation and became a classic, frequently reprinted to the present day, with John Hassall's famous drawing of the eponymous hero. There were sequels, but none of them captured the imagination like the original book. Robert's memory, however, was faulty on this occasion for Bell's first book *New Noah's Ark* was not published till 1898 — two years after Robert emigrated to Canada, while *Wee MacGreegor* was not published till 1902.

Before his death in 1934 Bell also published two volumes of memoirs entitled *I Remember* and *Do You Remember?*, which evoked the spirit of Glasgow and the splendours of Hillhead in the closing years of the nineteenth century. Intriguingly, although he never mentioned Robert at all, he too mentioned their mutual friend, the Jewish boy who became an analytical chemist. Bell did not resort to the subterfuge of giving him an alias like Silverman. Writing of his first visit to London at the turn of the century, he said, 'I had an old college friend who, a few years earlier, had left Glasgow for London as an analytical chemist to a manufacturing firm. To him I was to owe the gayer experiences of the visit . . .'[19] In the 1891 Census Abraham Levine was described as a 'student of science'. After graduating from Glasgow University he went to Jesus College, Cambridge, before settling in London.[20]

By contrast Robert regarded himself as a failure:

When I look back I am impressed by the number of lads I knew who have won distinction. And among those bright boys I cut a poor figure. I was regarded as a nonentity, so that in moods of gloom I felt I was destined to fail. But when I smarted under a snub I got out my copy-book in which were pasted my accepted poems. Reading them reassured me; yet for fear of ridicule I showed them to few. And looking over them years later I was surprised by their competence. Technically I could find little fault with them. I shirked no rhyme. My measure was exact. Most of my pieces were on the three-verse pattern — attack, build-up and pay-off, I called it. That my formula was a good one was proved by acceptance. The proof of a poem is in the printing.

That may be due, perhaps, to the judgment I showed in the selection of papers. Although I only wrote to please myself (and no one can do otherwise) in the end I tried to please my editors, who in turn tried to please the public. Instinctively I knew what they preferred, and perhaps I unconsciously catered to them. But I was so young, and to be published gave me such a thrill. After all, what I wrote was only newspaper verse, neat but negligible. I was conscientious in my craftsmanship, and the careless rapture of my lyrics was the result of patient toil.[21]

Regrettably, Robert's early passion for poetry proved to be little more than a passing fancy. It had a final flicker when he discovered Bret Harte and Eugene Field and added them to his models. Oddly enough, he seems not to have been aware of the fact that Bret Harte had been American Consul in Glasgow for five years (1880–85). Many of his rollicking yarns of the Californian pioneers were, in fact, written in his rooms at the Grand Hotel, Charing Cross, although, as the 'Consulate of St Kentigern', there is an uncannily accurate description of his own office in *The Heir of the McHulishes*. Interestingly, Bret Harte had a reputation, when in Glasgow, of being of a very retiring disposition, shunning public appearances. At the *Glasgow Herald* centenary banquet in 1882 he was scheduled to propose the toast to the Press, but at the last moment he excused himself saying that 'after spending a week or two studying the US Constitution in order to find out whether he might attend such a gathering, and considering the importance of the toast, he had prepared a speech which would take at least five hours to deliver'. This threat fully excused him, and a substitute was hastily found.[22]

In the 1890s Robert developed a feeling of satiety which ended in revolt. 'I began to dislike poetical words and to prefer blunt Saxon speech.' Then he was repelled by the preciousness and pretentiousness of poetry, particularly its subject matter which tended to dwell on the beauties of nature.

Why should poetry concern itself with beauty and not with ugliness, which is just as fascinating? Why should it deal with virtue when vice is more interesting? Why did poets write about flowers and love and the stars? Why not about eating and drinking, and lusts and common people? I was a rebel. Poets, I complained, cared more for the way of saying things than for the thing said. I was tired of ideals and abstractions, flowery language, words musically arranged and coloured like a garden — no, I did not react to that any more. Poetry farewell!

But I stuck to verse. Though I turned from nectar I still liked beer. I could rhyme with the best and make verse with facility. But I practised it less and less, and the time came when I confined my efforts to limericks, of which the least said the better.

So ended my poetical period. It was a happy one and no doubt served me well. Though for years I did not write another line, that early training was not wasted. For when I began again to make verse it came as easy to me as slipping off a log.[23]

In *Ploughman of the Moon* Robert devoted chapters to the activities that fleetingly caught his attention. In 'Artificial Athlete' he tells how, for a season, he took up rugby with a savage enthusiasm. Coached by 'MacSporran', and wearing boots with lead-weighted toe-caps, he earned a deadly reputation as a full-back. MacSporran was well over six foot. 'His face, like mine, was ruddy, and when we walked together Silverman said we looked like a lobster and a shrimp.' Who this coach really was, Robert did not say. We learn, however, that he was a Highlander, or at least of Highland extraction, and that he worked in a lawyer's office. Later he became 'a flowery orator and ended up in Parliament as a silent member for a Gaelic constituency'. He had been a good all-round athlete in his youth but had strained his heart tossing the caber, so he was content to coach others in his spare time. This description, scant though it is, identifies Robert's coach as Thomas Hedderwick, the second son of Robert Hedderwick, a minor poet as well as founder and editor of the Glasgow *Weekly Citizen*, a Liberal newspaper. Thomas was an Arts graduate of Glasgow University before going into law. He unsuccessfully contested South Lanarkshire at the 1892 General Election but eventually became MP for the Northern Burghs (1896–1900). As well as sports, he was an avid book collector. Latterly he lived in London, where he had a fatal heart attack in February 1918.[24]

Having improved Robert's kicking abilities, Tom Hedderwick subsequently trained him to tackle low. 'Take a running dive at your opponent's shins', he would say; and Robert practised and practised turning himself into a human projectile until he was black and blue all over. In September 1891 he went off to a farm for his annual holiday and practised tackling with a sack of bran in the hay-loft. This single-mindedness paid off when Robert got a trial with a team and turned in a star performance, with three spectacular tackles and some impressive footwork.

Hedderwick was pleased with his protégé. 'I have created a full-back,' he said. 'And now I am going to be your press-agent.' He sent an account of the match to the sporting editions of the newspapers, in which Robert's name figured flamboyantly. 'My position was assured; I finished the season in a simmer of satisfaction.' But in the last match of the season Robert blotted his copy-book. Why couldn't a back score? Anyone else could make a touch-down and get the glory of it. He was thus ruminating when he saw the ball coming towards him and he collared it. Instead of kicking, he began to run:

> I think the field was too astonished to do anything about it. They imagined I had gone mad. So as they gaped and hesitated I ran for all I was worth. I dodged a half-back, pushed over a quarter, ran round the full-back, and touched the ball down behind the posts. The crowd cheered and laughed, but my captain was furious. He accused me of showing off and threatened to suspend me. This ended my football career, for by the next season I was on another tack. By then, not only did I forswear the game, but for the rest of my life nothing could induce me to watch a match.[25]

When the rugger season ended, Robert turned to cricket and his friend drilled him in that sport also. Hedderwick had a scientific approach to games. He believed that if, instead of being an all-round player, one could concentrate on a specific aspect, success might be achieved. Putting this theory to the test he decided that Robert's talents might lie in short-catching. 'Concentrate. Stand as close to the batsman as possible. Watch every ball as it comes in and act as though you expect it to be batted to you. What's better still, *will* the batsman to play into your hands.'

Having got a trial with the second XI of the prestigious West of Scotland Club, whose grounds were located in Partick, Robert played in his chosen position.

> I hovered close to the wicket. I bent forward, tense, eager, holding my hands in readiness for the ball that I was sure was going to nestle there. But most of all I willed the batsman to put it there. Perhaps there was something in my suggestion, for he frequently did. And as sure as it came near me I snapped it up. In my first match I made

three catches, one of them so close to the ground that I got a cheer from the crowd. After that my position was assured, and I rarely failed to bring off at least two catches in every match. I simply willed the batsman to play into my hands and the weaker ones did. Oh, I did not become a cricketer. My batting average was two not-out, as I went in last man. But I did become a mid-wicketer; thus proving MacSporran's theory that specialization will win where all-round ability will get a man nowhere.[26]

Considering that Robert was 'not made for sport' and actually hated competitive games, one can only marvel at his single-mindedness. Like his other enthusiasms, his passion for cricket did not survive the season, but all this strenuous exercise did him good. 'It kept me much in the open air, made me objective and healthy in mind and body. Altogether it was a rather radiant year . . .'

The sporting life toughened Robert and built up his confidence. 'No longer was I a shy, sensitive youth, sending secret verse to the local rags. I now thought myself a man about town, able to swagger into a pub and down a pint of beer with the best. And it was by way of the bar-room and the music-hall that I continued my education.'[27]

One evening, in the gallery of one of the variety palaces, Robert was hailed by 'Tommy Twitchell', his old rugger captain who was apparently hoping to become a music-hall artiste. He was an excellent song-and-dance man, good at impersonating Dan Leno and Little Tich, but he succumbed to parental pressure and entered the family drapery business instead. Robert deplored his lack of daring to take the plunge. 'Last time I saw him he was wielding a yard-stick and on the fairway to successful mediocrity. But O the glorious adventure he missed!'[28]

Another of the frustrated souls whom Robert recalled was a near neighbour whom he ran into at the Royalty Theatre during a performance of the operetta *Marjorie* in April 1891. He happened to be occupying the next seat and Robert thought he recognised him. During the interval Robert asked him, 'Don't you live in Ferndale Terrace?' The young man replied, 'Yes. You live in Roselea. I've seen you passing our house.'

As already mentioned, these street names were wholly fictitious. The boy invited Robert home and entertained him by playing and singing some of the songs popularised by Albert Chevalier.

That was the beginning of a brief but bright friendship. His name was Horace Pewgrass and he lived with his mother. But he had the theatre in his blood, and I never knew a boy so keen to get on the boards.

Unlike Tommy, he would have chucked the best job to go on the stage. It was the love of his life. It was his tragedy too, for he had the heart of a romantic lead and the body of a buffoon. At the piano he was a good entertainer of the Grossmith type; but he looked pathetic with his heavy head awry on his twisted neck. He was like a grotesque gnome, and his voice was a penetrating croak.[29]

Horace Pewgrass was, in fact, William Pettigrew, who lived with his widowed mother at 5 Roxburgh Street.[30] It is interesting to note that, although Robert conferred the customary fictional name on his friend, the fictional and real surnames were not entirely dissimilar. Pettigrew was an ardent devotee of the theatre and for a time he and Robert went to see all the great actors when they came to Glasgow. This was the era of Henry Irving and Ellen Terry, of Wyndham and Willard. After the performance, Robert and his friend would adjourn to a pub frequented by actors and look with adulation at the professionals. 'How proud was I to buy a drink for a slim youth who played a footman in a current comedy. The fact that he subsequently rose to fame justifies my hero-worship.' Robert admired the old English comedies staged by Edward Compton (father of Compton Mackenzie), but the star he really worshipped was the redoubtable Shakespearian actor, Osmond Tearle. 'I saw him time after time, and tried to echo his mournful cadence. In doing so I lowered the pitch of my own voice till I was speaking in chesty tones instead of throaty ones.'

Then suddenly Robert became stage-struck. He got out *Hamlet* and *Macbeth* and declaimed them as he had done with Pat Dougan at Kilwinning so many years previously. 'I ignored the sense of the lines; the sound was what I was after. I intoned the blank verse sonorously. Poetry seemed now to be only a medium to exploit my voice. And in front of my bedroom mirror I grimaced, spouted and postured.' He even expended some of his earnings on elocution lessons at the Athenaeum, but abandoned them after a few weeks because they were too elementary. Some time later, however, he happened to be in that august building when the end-of-term examination was in progress. On the spur of the moment Robert entered the room and recited Browning's 'Pied Piper'. He got as far as an imitation of the rage of the burgomaster when the examiners stopped him. Thinking that he had made a fool of himself, Robert bowed out and put the matter from his mind. A few days later the exam results were published and he was astonished to find his name at the top of the list.

This encouraged him to embark on 'a fell career as an elocutionist'. He learned several of the dramatic poems then so popular:

I did nothing but dramatic stuff and I loved to let myself go. I became in demand for church-halls and beer-halls, and soon I was launched as an entertainer. I can see now how learning by heart and reciting dramatic pieces had an effect on my future verse. I must confess that I often write with an eye to the reciter.[31]

At the same time, Robert was hanging round stage-doors. Occasionally he got a job as an extra, but the professional supers resented him and he had to propitiate them with beer and cigarettes. These walk-on parts earned a shilling a night. Robert carried a banner in a revival of *Marmion* and played second watchman in *Macbeth*. His first real engagement, however, came in a big production of *Rob Roy*. Then, for the only time in his life, he saw his name on a theatrical play-bill. It was last in the cast, and in the smallest of type.

In the late eighteenth century, John Hume's drama *Douglas*, had stirred the patriotic feelings of the Scots. This was the play at the end of whose première a member of the audience had leaped to his feet and shouted 'Whaur's yer Wullie Shakespeare noo!' Robert Burns, regretting that Scotland was relatively poorly served, had ambitions to emulate Hume and got as far as sketching out a play, to be entitled *Rob McQuechan's Elshon* about King Robert Bruce, but he never developed it. In 1817 Walter Scott published anonymously his novel *Rob Roy* and a year later a dramatic version made its début in Glasgow, followed by performances in Perth, Dundee and Edinburgh. Thereafter, and especially after the copyright lapsed, this play was incredibly popular. As late as the 1890s there might be up to four different productions of this perennial favourite in the Glasgow theatres alone. The story of the Highland freebooter changed none too subtly with the passage of time, till he was elevated to a kind of latter-day Wallace or Bruce, fighting for the liberty of Scotland against the hated English. The drama was packed with action, giving immense scope for every ham-actor of the period. The script was familiar to the audience and there was often considerable repartee and audience participation. It was, in effect, a patriotic pantomime on the grand scale.

The play was usually staged by professionals, but sometimes there would be amateur productions, with a hard core of pros to give it polish. Such a one was the three-night production mounted by the officers and other ranks of the First Lanark Rifle Volunteers Amateur Dramatic Society at the Grand Theatre at the beginning of December 1892. This followed a rival production by the Third Lanark Rifle Volunteers at the Royal Princess Theatre earlier that year. The first battalion, however, scored heavily by enlisting the talents of Georgina Robertson as their leading lady. Although *Rob Roy* was sometimes staged at the Grand by Ernest Stevens, with his own wife in the role of Helen MacGregor, the actress who had otherwise a virtual monopoly of this role was the redoubtable Miss Robertson, whose name crops up frequently in both professional and amateur productions of this play, at the Grand and many other theatres. She was tall and Junoesque, and would not have been out of place playing Brunhilde in Wagnerian opera. Eighteen-year-old Robert Service was cast as her son, Young Rob.

Robert's role was minute, yet essential to the dramatic effect. He had to rush on, panting and panicky, to announce the capture of Rob Roy:

> My mother, Helen MacGregor, grabbed me and cried: 'Where's yuh fathah?'
>
> 'A prisoner of the Sassenach,' I said brokenly. In an impulse of wrath, she threw me on my back. I twisted round, ducked my head and quivered my shoulders with a simulation of grief. Helen then indulged in a fierce tirade, ending up: 'They have not yet subdued Rob Roy.' As she finished, with a flourish of her claymore, she saw me prostrate at her feet. Then she grabbed me up again and clutched me to her capacious bosom; after which she proceeded to shed tears down my neck. And strange though it may seem, this scene was most effective; for in those days 'ham' acting was taken seriously. So I felt that, though I had no illusion as to its banality, I must not let my mother down. Maybe we might be worthy of a curtain call . . .[32]

This went well enough at rehearsals. On the opening night, however, Robert donned a magnificent Highland costume, complete with red wig and Balmoral bonnet. Then Sergeant William Hall, playing Bailie Nicol Jarvie, suggested that what Robert needed was a slug of Scotch to brace his first-night nerves. They adjourned to the bar for a 'wee hauf'. The spirits were having their effect when one of the other actors burst in saying that Miss Robertson was frantic. 'The old girl's up in the air,' he warned. It then transpired that Georgina was a rabid teetotaller. When told that Robert was in the bar, she shrieked, 'My Robert drinking! Oh, the young rascal! Fetch him to me at once. I'll give him such a spanking.'

'She wull too,' said Hall. 'She'll lift yer kilt and skelp ye.' Then he twisted Robert's sporran round till it protected his rear. 'There! That'll tak' aff the brunt o' it.'

They had another drink, and Robert was downing the last of the whisky when the call-boy came running, 'You're on.' Robert made a dash for the stage:

I arrived just in time for my entry, but as I emerged from the wings I heard an anguished howl from the stage manager: 'For God's sake stop him! He's got his kilt on backwards.'

With a shock I realized that my sporran was dangling behind instead of in front; but it was too late. There, in the middle of the stage, I heard a twitter from the front rows, then a rumble of laughter as the house realized my plight. Helen was gazing at me with horror. Then she threw me to the ground with vicious force. As I lay I struggled to adjust my kilt, but in my efforts I felt that something had slipped and the whole thing was coming down. As she yanked me up again I felt my kilt dropping to my ankles, but with a swift movement she happed me round in her voluminous plaid. Then, as she sobbed over me: 'My son, my precious boy!' she hissed: 'You little devil! I'll flay you for this . . .' But as the curtain fell to mingled applause and laughter, I ducked under her arm and fled the scene.[33]

Thus ended Robert's one and only appearance on the professional stage. 'I was mortified, and my love of the theatre died right there.' He immediately corrected himself:

No. I must not say that. It has never died. Today the lure of the footlights is as strong as ever. In any case, the world has been a stage for me, and I have played the parts my imagination conceived. Rarely have I confronted reality. Now at seventy it seems as if I had never lived at all — just dreamed and played at living . . .

Every day, on his way to and from work, Robert passed close to the immense neo-Gothic pile on Gilmorehill. The University had begun moving out of its medieval site in the High Street in 1864 and the main buildings, designed by Sir George Gilbert Scott, were erected in the 1880s. Scott died in 1878, shortly after completing the drawings, so the work devolved on his son, Jon Oldrid Scott who was solely responsible for the hundred-foot-high central tower completing the structure. This was erected in 1887–91 and is to Glasgow what the Eiffel Tower is to Paris or Tower Bridge is to London. Watching the daily progress of the great tower, 'its serene beauty high soaring from the hill', Robert imagined himself in cap and gown as a student. But he was acutely aware of his educational shortcomings, having left school at fourteen without the necessary matriculation certificate. His proficiency in English language and literature enabled him to enrol as a part-time student for the sum of two guineas. For an hour each day he attended lectures held in the late afternoon, after the normal banking hours. There were about two hundred students in the steeply tiered class-room: 'poor boobs, to be pitied'. The majority of his fellow students were destined for the schoolroom or the manse. They lacked his sophistication, his ability to drink bitter beer and chat up barmaids. It was with high hopes that he began the course in the autumn of 1892, and he did well at first, coming fourth in the examinations shortly before Christmas. In his self-deprecatory style Robert attributed his success to learning the lecturer's notes off by heart.

Disillusionment with academia set in dramatically during the spring term. The pressure to conform to academic views of literature began to rankle. Students were definitely not encouraged to think for themselves. He submitted an essay on the character of Ophelia in *Hamlet*. Robert considered her 'a bit of a slut' and that it was her wantonness which caused Hamlet's distracted condition. Robert was inordinately pleased with himself, and was confident that the essay would earn at least 90 per cent of the marks. His disappointment at getting only 23 per cent was compounded by the lecturer's comment that the essay was a 'perverse and obscene bit of work, unworthy of a student of this class'. He challenged the teacher to step outside and settle the matter in the time-honoured fashion. The lecturer declined the challenge to fisticuffs and threatened to summon the bedellus and have Robert forcibly ejected. Before such summary action, Robert flounced out of the room, and vowed never to return. Yet he never lost some lingering affection for the University and made provision in his will for the establishment of an essay prize which was instituted by his widow in 1961.[34]

One day Robert bumped into 'Tevendale', who had been the star pupil in the class. He was sitting in a pub, half-cut, with a small blonde draped across him. When Robert confessed that he had dropped out of class, Tevendale agreed wholeheartedly that the University was hidebound by tradition. 'This is the real life — wine, women, song. Give me the man that dares to live.' He asked Robert if he knew French literature — Baudelaire, Huysmans, Mallarmé. 'There's a people who know how to live, because they know how to reconcile the flesh and the spirit.'

Tevendale went on to reminisce about 'a drinking tour' which he had undertaken through France the previous summer:

On the shores of the Mediterranean I rested awhile. There, where the sea is eternally blue and the sun shines the year long, the people are gay and laugh and sing and love ... Well, I would like to go back there and be as one of them. I would live in a little red cottage, wear a *béret* and wine-coloured overalls and rope-soled sandals. I would be like a peasant with a boat and a net and a bit of land. I would grow purple

cabbage and tomatoes and onions and garlic and red peppers. I would
live with a dark, passionate Dago girl and eat mountains of spaghetti;
and I would write a book on the success of failure.[35]

This monologue may have sown the seeds of desire that drew Robert to the
Riviera a quarter of a century later, though, bearing in mind when and where
he recalled this passage of his autobiography (Hollywood, 1944), there seems
to be a hint of longing to return to a part of the world and the idyllic lifestyle
which he had enjoyed in the 1930s.

The next phase Robert called his political period, but there was a
tongue-in-cheek character to the chapter entitled 'Proletarian Prig' which
described his brief flirtation with socialism. He chanced upon a pamphlet
entitled *Merrie England* by Robert Blatchford, editor of the *Clarion*. This was
a tempestuous period; the newly enfranchised working men were about to
flex their political muscles. Hitherto the working classes had looked to the
Liberals for improvement in their lot, but at the General Election of 1892 the
Ayrshire miner James Keir Hardie was elected on the Independent Labour
ticket, as MP for South West Ham. He had founded the Scottish Labour
Party in 1888 and five years later took a leading part in the formation of the
Independent Labour Party. Robert was swept up in the enthusiasm for
socialism in the run-up to the General Election. He was persuaded to
address the crowds of the idle and curious who congregated on street
corners.

I saw myself a fiery orator, inflaming the passions of the mob, carrying
a red banner as I stormed a barricade. I cursed the capitalists. I was
one of the have-nots, hating the haves. In short, I was an egregious
young ass.[36]

He confessed that his street-corner oratory failed to make a single
convert. Even the hopelessly poor were much more interested in football. As
for his own class, the subject bored them and they arrogantly brushed aside
his arguments. But what finally put Robert off was meeting fellow workers
for the cause. Socialism would be charming, he thought, if one could elimi-
nate the socialist. 'I have always found that my own ideas antagonize me
when they are held by others,' he wrote, 'so I now found fellow-socialists
antipathetic to me.' Their manner grated, they had one-track minds. Often
they were narrow, ignorant and bigoted. They spouted the same old clap-trap.
They allowed their leaders to think for them. Robert began to doubt their
intelligence, then their sincerity.

I got so sick of hearing the stock platitudes — the exploitation of labour, the profit motive in industry, a classless society. Because I was well dressed I was looked on with suspicion. I should have worn a cloth cap and a flannel shirt. Obviously I was not of the proletariat. As to its dictature, it dawned on me that I did not want any kind of dictature. I wanted to be free.

One can understand an essentially kindly and generous spirit as Robert Service being drawn to the ideals of socialism, especially in this formative period; but such a free spirit could never have been regimented in politics, any more than it was in any other sphere. Half a century later he admitted that he found it pleasant to be a 'carpet-slipper socialist', living in comfort and security on the royalties from his writings.

> With my reasoning mind I accept the logic of socialism, but my selfish human nature keeps me from doing anything to further it. By nature I am indolent, dreamy and peace-loving. I have never cast a vote. I have avoided public life. I live abroad to escape responsibilities. In short, I am a very bad citizen indeed.[37]

And not long after these words were written in 1944, Robert and his family moved to Monaco, the haven of the super-rich where income tax and death duty were unknown.

Robert continued to read omnivorously. As he approached the end of his teens he was reading Stevenson, Kipling, Thoreau and Borrow. He was fascinated by the travel writings as much as the adventure yarns of Stevenson, then Scotland's most famous writer although by that time resident in Samoa. So too Kipling aroused once more a desire to visit the outposts of Empire. But Thoreau's *Walden* proffered a 'simplicity of expression', with 'a clean new world of tonic air and diamond clarity'. Thoreau 'fostered the recluse' and perhaps also the latent farmer in Robert. George Borrow's *Lavengro* introduced him to 'a great and original writer . . . a fine, handsome man, a fighter and lover of horses, a friend of gypsies, a rover and a student'. Borrow revealed to Robert 'the gift of vagrancy'. Above all, it was Borrow who unsettled the young bank clerk as he viewed a further forty years ahead of him chained to a desk or imprisoned in a teller's cage. He it was who 'kindled the wanderlust'.

The lure of vagabondage was strong. Robert was essentially a loner and this was a characteristic which became more marked in his twenties and thirties. Under the influence of Levine, now training as an analytical chemist, Robert dabbled in radicalism and materialism and became a confirmed agnostic. On the brink of manhood, however, he went through his bohemian phase, when he associated with a group of young men whose common bond was their ambition to become writers. The leader of this coterie, as usual, was given a pseudonym — Mugson.

> He was a bantam with a head like Caesar's. He spiked his moustache to pin-points, and kept his hair cropped to the roots. He rarely had his pipe out of his mouth, which was a cemetery of decayed teeth. His cheeks were a bright pink, his chin gun-metal blue. His voice was a squeaky drawl that made his least remark sound humorous. But he was witty in himself and made us laugh without effort. He was one of the few men who can be unfailingly funny. He had a comic spirit and a gibing tongue.[38]

It is interesting to note that one of Robert's many nicknames for his daughter Iris was Muggsum, which may have been a subconscious harking back to his own youth. From tantalising references to Mugson's literary efforts, however, I have been able to identify him as John Ferguson of Garriochmill Road, North Kelvinside. He contributed light verse and humorous sketches to the *Glasgow Weekly Herald* and other periodicals, often using the non-de-plume of Painter Jock. His circle of friends was 'a gay gang' — the term used here in its original sense, not the modern idiom. These rather idealistic young men were preoccupied with sport, the theatre and their aspiring business careers, and literature seldom entered into conversation. It was an asexual atmosphere. They never talked smut and the only expletives that peppered their conversation infrequently were 'Damn' and 'Hell'. 'As to the other Anglo-Saxon terms, we did not foul our mouths with them,' adds Robert primly.

> I think one reason we were so decent was that we all had sisters, and insisted on a proper respect for the girls we knew. We may have known them but we never went with them. We were a band of ceno-bites. To have been seen 'girling' would have disgraced us and proclaimed us 'sissies'. We cultivated a manly disdain for women, and though some of us hinted at secret adventures, I am sure we were all virginal. I think our contempt for the soft sex was a form of shyness. In my case it was. For years I scarcely spoke to a girl. I was afraid of them, and if by chance I met one I was self-conscious and tongue-tied.[39]

Ferguson's literary début was made with a humorous account of a visit to Loch Lomond, which was actually made by Robert, when he had been almost eaten alive by midges. Robert did not consider this a suitable subject for an article, but his friend tackled it gleefully and made a very entertaining story out of it, for which he was paid ten shillings. Thus encouraged, he turned out stories and articles distinguished by humour and biting wit. By this means he was able to augment his wages as a whisky salesman, but he really hit the big time with a serial, published in a weekly paper.

> It was called: *Tom, Dick and Harry*, and we were all in it. It was the forerunner of a school that was called the New Humour. Jerome, Barry Pain and Jacobs were its leading exponents, and the *Idler* and *To-day* its chief vehicles. If Mugson had lived he would have rivalled any of them. But in his twenties he had a stroke and became paralyzed. Even then he tried to carry on, still sending stories and sketches to the local papers; but his brain flagged, refusals became frequent, and it was evident he was doomed.[40]

Another fellow, whom Service does not even grace with the usual pseudonym, had already had a book published. It was a five-act tragedy inspired by Ford and Massinger. This young man also wrote a sequence of sixty love sonnets, 'though I don't believe he had ever been familiar with a girl'. Robert recalled the opening line of one of these poems: 'I am a lazzarone in the lands of love' and thought it very beautiful. 'I often wondered what became of him. Probably went to London and sank in the struggle.' Admittedly, this description is very scanty, but the only writer who fits it was George Eyre-Todd whose novel *Anne of Argyle, or Cavalier and Covenant* was published in 1895. Eyre-Todd became a prolific writer in prose and verse at the turn of the century. He was a member of the Glasgow Ballad Club (founded in 1875) and three of his pieces were published in the Club's anthology *Ballads and Poems* (1898). George Eyre-Todd seems to have spent his entire career in Glasgow, where he died in 1937.[41]

About 1894 Robert took Tevendale's advice and began studying French literature. He was attracted to the realism of Zola, whose writings were then banned from the public libraries. He read Flaubert, de Maupassant and the Goncourts. 'I harked back to Balzac and Hugo', and during an entire winter read nothing but French books. George Moore was his guide. His *Confessions of a Young Man* was a literary landmark. 'He made me long to live in a Paris garret and emulate the heroes of Murger, which at a later date I did.'

But it was a book of another character altogether that had the greatest influence on Robert, now entering his twenties.

It was *A Western Avernus* by Morley Roberts. It first kindled the spirit of vagabondage in me. I determined I would go to America and become a hobo.

By now Robert had settled into a rut, a pleasant enough existence bounded by the bank and the library and his circle of friends. The latter was by now a group of about ten. One played the banjo, another one sang, a third was a boxer, while a fourth painted quite nicely. 'We organized debates and got up sketches. We had sing-songs and entertainments.' But their most triumphant expression was their magazine.

We all contributed. It was typed and neatly bound and had a great success. I was represented by two triolets and a villanelle in which I aped Austin Dobson and Arthur Symonds. We all looked forward to the next number, when suddenly everything crashed and our whole community split and dissolved.[42]

It seems that Ferguson's rich Uncle Archie had recently married a lady evangelist who lost no time in proselytising her nephew and his friends. First Levine, then Ferguson himself, were converted to the salvationist doctrines, their born-again convictions reinforced by exciting new jobs secured for them by Uncle Archie. Levine was supposed to be going off to Western Australia to become an assayer in the Coolgardie goldfields, while Ferguson was to be given employment by a firm of tobacco importers. Before they departed, however, they persuaded Robert to join them at Uncle Archie's country retreat for a prayer meeting. Against his better nature, Robert went along but refused to join the others at their conventicle upstairs. In the lounge he concentrated on reading *Alley Sloper's Half Holiday*, the most inane comic paper of its kind at the time, and playing with Aunt Tibbie's dog. By and by he fell asleep, and when Aunt Tibbie came down to claim his soul he was snoring like a pig. As Ferguson told him afterwards: 'Then she knew the jig was up and called off the meeting. She thinks you're a hard case — too fat to feel spiritual grace.'

It is not clear whether it was Ferguson's new-found zealotry (which was short-lived) or Robert's habitual flitting from place to place which broke up the coterie; perhaps it was a bit of both. At any rate, when he was twenty-one, Robert resolved to lose weight. He was over-fond of chocolates and though he still walked two or three miles daily going to and from work, he had taken no really strenuous exercise since giving up cricket and rugby. He was sharply confronted with his flabbiness on beholding his brother Peter who had gone off to work on a farm in Fife. A year later he returned, no longer the puny stripling but a rugged stalwart, towering over his eldest brother as if to say 'You little fat bank clerk, I could take you over my knee and spank you'. Peter roused Robert's inferiority complex. 'He seemed to be someone I might have been; he was so ruddy, strong and full of energy.'

This episode triggered off what Robert liked to call his bucolic phase. Inspired by Thoreau, he would become a farmer, but first he would have to toughen himself up. Now he enrolled at the University gymnasium and took up weight-lifting and a punishing routine of callisthenics. At the same time he joined the Western Baths in a determined effort to whittle off the fat. The reformed, renovated and refurbished Baths of the 1890s would have been a far cry from the derelict building where Robert had stumbled upon his first corpse a few years earlier; nevertheless, one cannot help wondering whether the memory of that ghastly encounter did not sometimes flash into his mind. Perhaps he confined his activities to the swimming-pool and shunned the Turkish baths or at least the luxurious couches of the Cooling Room.

His ambition to break away from the rut of banking was thwarted by lack of cash. He simply could not afford to make the break. But it was an ambition which he articulated frequently. It provoked consternation and dismay from his parents. To leave the bank was unthinkable; he was courting disaster. Robert explained his motives to family and friends, saying to some that he had a sense of vocation for the farming life, to others that it was for the good of his health. Without exception, they tried to talk him out of it.

Ironically, the only person who was inclined to agree with him was the Accountant at the Stobcross branch.

> Born on a farm, he had left it too young to be sickened by its endless toil, Standing before the fire with his coat-tails pulled frontally so that his behind got the comfort of its warmth, he spoke only of the pleasant side of farming.
>
> As he spoke of cattle and crops, the breath of the moors seemed to sweep into the dusty bank, exhilarating me and confirming me in my sense of destiny. I think he encouraged me because he was so discontented with his own career. I hated figures and the problems of high finance inspired my repulsion. Banking for me would be a blind alley; but, as I see it now, with my unstable temperament, all of my life would have been a blind alley. I was as destined to failure as the sparks fly upwards.[43]

Every Sunday Robert walked far into the countryside and revelled in the sights, sounds and smells of farming. 'I had a perpetual spring-morning feel-

ing in my brain. As I thought of the destiny in store for me I sang with joy.'
Then he realised that his dream was impossible without some capital. He
consulted his farmworker brother about the problem. Peter suggested emigration as a way out of the dilemma, proposing Canada as the ideal. Robert went
to the Canadian Emigration Office and got all kinds of pamphlets. It seemed
the solution. He went to the library and read everything he could lay his
hands on. He made himself an authority on the Dominion. 'I translated
myself into prairie life. Already I was a sturdy settler, raising cattle and grain,
or riding a bronco and roping steers.'

The notion of being a cowboy appealed immensely. In preparation for
this role Robert purchased a big hunting knife and an air-pistol and practised
the fast draw. All of his former interests and enthusiasms were jettisoned in
favour of pistol shooting, the target being a match-box on top of his bed-post.
The lack of cash, even the six pounds for the steerage ticket, continued to
thwart his plans. At first Ferguson tried to talk him out of it, pointing out
shrewdly that someone whose sole experience of riding had been a seaside
donkey would find a bronco a totally different steed. But when Robert was
adamant he generously offered to fund the trip with the ten pounds he had
earned from his magazine serial. Robert declined the offer, being too proud
(and canny) to borrow money.

The opportunity came in 1895 when he completed his apprenticeship.
As a fully qualified clerk, he could now command an annual salary of
seventy pounds, a huge jump after years on twenty pounds per annum.
Promotion also meant a transfer to what Robert termed the St Mungo
branch, but in fact the Commercial Bank's branch at 152 St Vincent Street.
Before Robert left Stobcross, he was handed a testimonial by the
Accountant which extolled his willingness, industry and intelligence —
'everything I was not'. Robert pocketed the testimonial and treasured it for
years. 'It was the only certificate anyone ever gave me, and it was to play a
decisive part in my destiny.'

Over the ensuing months Robert scrimped and saved, though his
expenses at this city branch were greater as he had to dress better and take his
lunch at a restaurant. His work, never of the most diligent, was now
performed in a perfunctory manner, earning him numerous rebukes from his
new Accountant. 'But I was prudent in my imprudence. I wanted to wait
until I was twenty-one before giving notice. Spring would best give me a
happy start to a life of hazard.'[44]

In this, Robert's memory played him false, though it explains the widespread notion that he went to Canada in 1895.[45] In fact, his resignation from
the Commercial Bank took effect on 31 March 1896. Robert was just turned

twenty-two at the time, fitter than he had ever been before. The day he gave in his notice was a memorable one. He was ushered into the Manager's office at his own request and resigned verbally.

The Manager of the St Vincent Street branch was Andrew Mackinnon, a forty-seven-year-old widower with three young children and a thirty-year-old widow as housekeeper, whom he would subsequently marry. Robert described him as 'a dignified man with a pendulous stomach', wearing 'gold-rimmed eye-glasses, astride a red and bulbous nose'. Initial surprise at Robert's announcement that he intended to go cattle-ranching in Canada soon gave way to the laconic observation that Robert must know his own business best. Mackinnon said, 'I suppose you realize that the bank offers you a safe and permanent position. You may even rise to be a manager like myself.' The prospect did not appeal to Robert as he eyed the dent made by the desk on his boss's ponderous stomach. 'I also suppose you know that if you serve another forty years you may retire on a pension.'

Robert thought of his fellow clerks, their pallor and grey hair. They were waiting for that pension. When they got it they would be ready to die. 'I quite appreciate that,' said Robert. 'But I want a free life. I've always been interested in horses and cattle.' Mackinnon stared absently out of the window:

> I, too, stared. His look was wistful, even dreamy. At that moment I saw him transfigured . . . *He was a rugged Highland Scot, clad in the tartan, high up on a misty mountain, with a pair of shaggy dogs and a herd of huge-horned cattle.* That was what he should have been. He had missed his destiny and he knew it. So after a little he turned to me: 'Well, you know best. I only wish I had your years. Then, by Goad, my lad, *I'd go along with ye.*'[46]

More than half a century later Robert paid one of his flying visits to Glasgow and was interviewed by the editor of *The Griffin*, house journal of the Commercial Bank of Scotland. In the course of the interview Robert was asked what advice he would give to aspiring young bankers. His answer was characteristic: 'Don't try to write poetry and tote columns of figures at the same time — and give every customer the same glad smile you would give a glamorous blonde.'[47]

CHAPTER 5

PACIFIC COAST VAGABOND

Living in camps with men-folk, a lonely and loveless life;
Never knew kiss of sweetheart, never caress of wife.

'The Song of the Wage-Slave' in *Songs of a Sourdough* (1907)

ROBERT'S RESIGNATION FROM THE BANK TOOK EFFECT AT
the end of March 1896. This left him little more than a fortnight to make his
preparations to emigrate. Fortunately, Donaldson Brothers of St Vincent
Street offered direct sailings from Glasgow to Montreal and, in fact, the first
ship of the season was due to leave the Clyde on 15 April. Robert, of course,
does not name the ship which bore him with such high hopes to the New
World, but he described it as a tramp steamer. Many of the passengers were
returning to Canada 'for the spring work after spending the winter in the old
country', and Robert also mentioned 'the drovers who had come over with
shipments of cattle. They were wild fellows, who drank and swore and
scoffed at the idea of settling down.'[1]

The ship was, in fact, the SS *Concordia* which, with a tonnage of 1,617,
was hardly the most luxurious or comfortable medium for crossing the
Atlantic. Conditions aboard were extremely cramped, humans being
secondary to the ship's main cargo. On this voyage the passengers were
accompanied by 1,531 sheep, 339 cattle and 16 horses, exported from
Scotland to swell the agriculture of the young dominion.[2]

It was a fine spring morning when Robert went down to Berth 75 at Queen's Dock. He was pleasantly surprised, and not a little touched, to discover that his pals were there to give him a rousing send-off. They presented him with a silver flask and, to his embarrassed shame, sang 'For he's a jolly good fellow'.

> I was wishing they would dry up when Papa appeared. The old man came running down the wharf, carrying a small package which he handed to me. Outwardly he was smiling a twisted smile, but I could see he was crying bitterly — inside. Well, I have always disliked displays of emotion, so I hurried on board the boat. As it edged out, I could see his very blue eyes in his very red face staring wistfully after me. Maybe I was doing what he would have loved to have done; for besides being a dreamer I think he would have enjoyed adventure.[3]

But Robert Senior, now aged sixty, was burdened with the responsibilities of raising his large brood. By 1896 the family was complete, and though Janet Isabella was now at school, Albert, the last of the ten children, was still a toddler. Perhaps Emily was preoccupied at home with the little boy; otherwise it seems strange that she did not come down to the quay to take her farewell of her eldest son. With candour Robert added:

> I cannot reproach [my father] for his failings, for they were my own — laziness, day-dreaming, a hatred of authority and a quick temper. And even more than he, I had the equipment of a first-class failure, Yes, I hated to work for others, and freedom meant more to me than all else. I, too, was of the race of men who don't fit in.

After the ship weighed anchor and slid down the Clyde, Robert opened the slim packet to examine his father's parting gift. It was a bible. 'I am sorry to say I never read it. Yet I kept it sentimentally for many years; and, in wild camps of thieves and vagabonds, that was the one possession no one ever tried to steal.' Robert Senior also pressed on him his ivory-handled razor, the very one that Robert had guiltily used to sharpen his pencils. He shaved with it for years across half the world, until it was stolen in the bunkhouse of a Californian labour camp. Robert wondered what its ultimate fate was. 'Maybe it cut the throat of a nigger.'

He never saw his father again. There was a certain callousness in Robert's subsequent treatment of his father. 'He wrote to me many times, and in a final letter begged me to pay him a last visit.' The old man pleaded, 'Even if you cannot come, just write and say you will.' About 1904 the Service family followed Robert to Canada, settling for a time in Toronto. In 1905 they went west to take up a farm at Vegreville, fifty-six miles east of Edmonton, whither Peter Service, the farmer of the family had gone ahead a few months previously to secure the homestead where the family lived for many years. When his father died six years later, following a stroke, Robert felt only a sense of relief. 'His letters had become increasingly pathetic, and he was quite infirm. His passing would make things easier for my mother, who was much younger and who had borne a hard burden.' A burden, it should be added, not made any lighter by her eldest son's indifference.

Fortunately for Robert, the voyage across the Atlantic was blessed with constant sunshine and calm seas. 'The sea was a shimmering, gold-spangled plain through which we ploughed. It welcomed us, laughing and leaping in little waves. The sky was without a cloud. Never before had I seen a cloudless sky.' Robert, who had grown up on the banks of the Clyde, had taken the obligatory trips 'doon the watter' on the many pleasure steamers that thronged that busy river and its magnificent estuary; but setting foot aboard the *Concordia* was a novel experience and, despite poor food and hard, cramped berths, he enjoyed the ocean voyage. 'The air was so tonic; the sea rippled in rosy waves; everyone seemed so full of hope and happiness . . .'

It is doubtful whether, in the spring of 1896, Robert had any firm ideas of what he wanted to do, or where he wished to go. He had a second cousin, Andrew Gray Service, already well set up on a farm at Alberni on Vancouver Island, British Columbia,[4] and it was to that part of Canada that Robert gravitated, although there is no record of him having visited his relative, far less worked with him. 'A vagabond life, I thought, may be more constructive than a sedentary one. I would give myself three years of roaming, then settle down.' Even in the apparent aimlessness of the ensuing years, there was a sense of purpose. At the back of his mind Robert hankered to be a writer. Stevenson was his model; a pocket edition of *An Amateur Emigrant* was eagerly read and later constantly compared with his own experiences. Stevenson had travelled by emigrant ship and transcontinental railroad to California in 1879.

Foolishly Robert had mis-labelled his luggage, and his Gladstone bag containing his clothing and toilet articles had been stowed away in the hold, so that he had nothing but what he stood up in. Alliteratively he described his predicament: 'Every day my collar became grimier and my chin shaggier. I shunned observation. Shabby, unshorn, I shrank into my shell.' There were some bonnie lasses aboard but he became invisible to them. 'I took comfort in the thought that I was actually roughing it from the start, and wondered how the philosophy of Stevenson would have stood the strain.'

As the voyage neared its end, expectation mounted to excitement. Robert gives only a lightning sketch of his first impressions: 'There was fog . . . icebergs . . . the bleak shores of Newfoundland. Quebec . . . toylike houses . . . villages with church spires . . . a man driving a buggy.' He uses ellipses here to convey the fleeting moment rather than imply words omitted. Though he could ill afford it, he grandly chipped in half a crown for the steward, when others were content with a penny or twopence. His wealth on landing at Montreal amounted to one pound sterling, which then translated into five dollars. After purchasing a few provisions at the railway wharf he had exactly a dollar and ninety-five cents left to his name. Few people could have set out on such a great adventure so ill-prepared. He looked down on a band of Armenian peasants who were also on the 'emigrant wagon' — until a fellow passenger pointed out that each of them had at least a hundred dollars tucked in his belt.

Robert was up bright and early on the first morning of the cross-country train-ride for a much-needed shave and change of clothing. In the toilet he changed into the rig appropriate to the occasion. This was a Buffalo Bill costume which had been discarded by Hengler's Cirque in Wellington Street and which Papa had thoughtfully purchased at an auction. Clad in chaps, high-heeled boots and a Mexican sombrero, Robert amused his fellow passengers with demonstrations of his skill in drawing his airgun from its holster and drawing a bead on some imaginary target.

He was entranced and intoxicated with the unfolding landscape. To be sure, he saw little from the train but fire-scorched woods and the occasional surprise of a lake. 'It was a blue eye staring up from the forest-grey, but it gave me a thrill. How happy I could be on its shores with a rod, a gun and a canoe!' There was an exuberance tinged with innocence about Robert's initial impressions of Canada — not, it may be added, a rosy-hued view shared by the other emigrants.

> To see the ordinary with eyes of marvel may be a gift; or it may be there is no ordinary and wonder is the true vision. In any case it keeps one spiritually intact; and it must be a rare quality, for none of my fellow-travellers had it. Most of them grumbled at the casual progress of our train, which dawdled to such an extent that I was tempted to jump off and run alongside.[5]

The leisurely journey across the vast high plains took several days, but even the very monotony of the prairie at first delighted Robert. He saw cattle eating from straw-stacks and men ploughing with oxen. Here, he felt, was his future home. 'I will settle on a section like this and dwell in one of these doll-like houses that look doubly diminutive in the vast emptiness.' They called at small villages whose names enchanted him. One was called Moose Jaw and then consisted of a muddy street lined with shacks. Here Robert spent the last of his money on hard-tack, sardines and jam that would barely keep him going till he reached his destination at Vancouver.

In one of the saloons lining the muddy street he saw some of the younger lads from the ship, drinking and laughing. Among them was a boy of Robert's age, from Renton, Dunbartonshire, whose consuming passion was playing football. They were hilariously happy when suddenly came a warning whistle from the train. Robert leaped aboard as it moved off. Looking back, he saw the party from the pub running to catch it. There were three of them and the first two managed to clamber on board, but the third stumbled and slid under the train. The Negro porter grimaced: 'He's killed for sure. Ain't dat no luck? Jes' when folks is goin' in for lunch! Dey ain't goin' to have no appetite.' Robert was drawn up short by the swiftness with which tragedy had struck.

> The train stopped. Some distance away I saw a small crowd gathered round a figure on the ground. I ran back. On my way I passed a red boot and a sock and the protruding splinter of a shin bone; but I did not pick them up. Lying in the midst of the group was the footballer. His face was chalky white and he was moaning: 'Mither! I want ma mither.' Then a man came along holding a boot and a jagged section of bone and flesh. 'Every wheel went over him,' he said; 'every bloody wheel.'[6]

Disillusionment set in at Winnipeg. One of Robert's fellow-travellers was a hatter, hell-bent on changing his way of life. His wife was to meet him at the station and then they would take the stage-coach out to their prairie homestead. 'Tomorrow I'll be raising vegetables in my own garden. I'll be chopping the firewood and bringing water from the well. Won't I be the happy man!' It was the moment he had dreamed of. No more felts for him. No more grubby city streets. He was realising the dream of a lifetime. But on the platform he was greeted by his wife and married daughter who informed him flatly that they had no intention of returning to the homestead. They had had their fill of the farming life. 'It's dreadful on the prairie,' said the younger woman. 'It's all right for European peasants, but for a civilised woman it's appalling. I'll never rejoin my husband there. I want him to sell up the farm and come back to town.' The older woman took up the refrain: 'You're not going out there, John. You're just going to stay here with us two. We like

Winnipeg, but the prairie — oh, it's simply terrible. You can get a job here. We've already got one promised for you. They want good hatters . . .' Robert left them arguing, but by the way they led off poor John he doubted whether he stood a chance against them. 'I expect he spent the rest of his life cleaning and blocking hats.'

This had a rather depressing effect on Robert, but he reflected that it did not matter. He had a ticket for British Columbia and could keep going till he reached the Pacific coast. Perhaps the prairie was fit only for Armenians, Swedes and Slovaks.

> Besides, the prairie was so devastatingly flat. I was afraid it might bore me. It did not seem a fit frame for a dashing young man who wore Napoleonic boots and a Spanish hat and who looked like the ring-master in a circus.[7]

Yet he had to admit ruefully that his cowboy outfit caused little excitement. There were so many outlandish costumes around him — Hungarian, Italian and Romanian — that his seemed quite commonplace. By the time he reached Alberta the endless prospect of the prairie was beginning to overwhelm him. But the more he travelled, the more he wanted to keep going. By now the shortage of cash was beginning to worry him. He sold his Gladstone bag for ten dollars, purchasing for three dollars a canvas holdall that suited his purpose better. On the train, he disposed of his Harris tweed suit for six dollars; at Winnipeg he sold his gun for a 'ten spot'; at Calgary he let his camera go for fifteen. His westward trail was studded with items from his outfit as he realised them for cash.

> I felt some compunction when I thought of how poor Papa had combed auction rooms for these articles and presented them to me with such pride. Yet he got so much joy in doing it that the thought consoled me. My outfit served me well, though not in the way it was intended.

The sight of the Rockies, however, 'justified my joust at jeopardy'. He marvelled at the great jagged peaks, the glaciers and the tremendous rivers roaring through vast canyons. It was so gorgeous that he grudged every minute that he could not devour the scenery with his eyes, and got up at dawn so that he should miss nothing. 'But I was alone. None of my companions shared my ecstasies.'

Then they left the Rockies behind. 'I awoke one morning to find we were speeding through a land of forest to the sounding sea. My Nemesis of toil was nearing. I began to be afraid.'

By June 1896 this rolling stone had come to a temporary halt. At Vancouver Robert had taken the ferry to Victoria, then moved north to the Cowichan Valley, inspired by Morley Roberts whose *Western Avernus* was now his bible. Roberts, in turn, had been inspired by Bret Harte, another of Service's heroes, and his book abounded with racy descriptions of the Far West, with chapters on Manitoba and the Rockies, the Kicking Horse Pass, the railroad camps, Kamloops, the Fraser Canyon, New Westminster and finally Vancouver Island and Victoria. This was the route that young Robert now took. Although he lived in and around Cowichan for two short periods only (in 1896–97 and 1898–1903), the inhabitants are proud of the connection. In the Robert Service Memorial Park there stands today an impressive monument, marred only by the errors in his dates (1875–1959) on the bronze plaque.

In a chapter entitled 'Mud Pupil' Robert says that his first employment was with 'the MacTartans, a Shetland family who some ten years before had rounded Cape Horn to found a new home'. Like almost every other name in this book, it is fictitious, and even less likely than most. Lockhart[8] identified the MacTartans as the Colvins at MacPherson's Landing, the only Shetlanders in the Cowichan Valley at this period. Mrs Colvin earned her place in the history of the Valley for having taught the Fair Isle knitting pattern to the Siwash Indians who produce fine sweaters in this distinctive style for sale to the tourists to this day. Her son Magnus, at least, was a friend of Robert, and was one of the few people with whom he corresponded throughout his long life. Indeed, the correspondence, with Robert's widow Germaine, continued till 1960.[9] But it has now been ascertained that Shetland was, itself, a red herring. The family were, indeed, islanders, but they hailed from the Inner Hebrides.

James M. Mutter, formerly a magistrate in Islay, and a major in the Argyll and Bute Artillery Volunteers, was a man of substance, being a junior partner in the family firm of W. and J. Mutter which owned the Bowmore Distillery as well as bonded warehouses in Glasgow. In 1889 James and Isabella Mutter, with their six children, left Islay and settled at Ashgrove Terrace in Partickhill.[10] James Junior, later known as Jock to distinguish him from his father, was a few months younger than Robert and it is not impossible that they were known to each other at that time. Early in 1891, however, Major Mutter emigrated to British Columbia, his family joining him there a few months later. Their farm was at Somenos in the Cowichan Valley. By 1896 the elder Mutter boys, 'Jock' (James, then aged twenty-one) and 'Bung' (Alexander, aged eighteen) were 'six-foot stalwarts with a genial tolerance and a gift for ragging their very green mud pupil'. Pitted against them, Robert soon discovered that his 'gymnasium muscles' were sadly wanting. 'I was ashamed of the way I played out so quickly when it came to packing hay in a hot mow, but my humiliation spurred me to grim effort and gradually my muscles took on the tough fibre of the labourer.'

He soon found that there were some jobs he preferred to others. Not surprisingly, he liked work that left his mind free, that was not too hard, and that made no demands on either skill or resource. He hated handling horses, and he disliked competitive work in which he had to keep up with the other fellow. 'I liked to toil alone, and I did not mind how monotonous the job was as long as it was mechanical.'

His first task was picking up stones from a field. It was about an acre in extent and Robert thought he would have it cleared in a day or two. He set to with a will and bagged the stones which he carried to the side of the field. But the more he picked the more there seemed to be. 'They were laughing at me, I thought — multiplying before my eyes. I grew discouraged. What price the fat little bank-clerk who thought he was going to be a dashing cowboy!'

His next job, weeding a field of turnips, was even less to his taste. As he toiled over this back-breaking task he turned introspective:

> I had to crawl up the rows, tearing away the weeds, and eliminating most of the baby turnips. A cruel business. Surely weeds had a right to live. It was only because they were unwanted they were called weeds. The unwanted people of this world were weeds and should be destroyed. Poor weeds! Maybe I was one myself . . . And the young turnips so ruthlessly sacrificed that their fortunate brothers should thrive and grow strong. Sad superfluous turnip plants! They made me think of the underdogs of the world.[11]

The work might be monotonous and back-breaking but it allowed Robert to muse and dream and let his mind wander and his imagination soar. And if he was largely indifferent to the labour of the field-hand he was always conscious of the beauty of his surroundings.

> To cheer me I looked at the blue purity of the sky, the mountains that rose to meet it, the unexplored bush that came right down to the clearing . . . Here was a dream world worthy of a dreamer. I was quite alone. The silence was one of murmurous sound, of the droning of innumerable insects. The heat radiated like wavering sheets of cellophane. I hated the grovelling toil. I despised myself for doing it; but — well, if it was the price I had to pay for all this beauty, then I was glad to pay it. So with a sense of fulfilment I turned again to my turnip rows.

In high summer the haymaking got under way. Robert enjoyed this much better. On the other hand, he never became a proficient milker. He was given the poorest cows on which to practise, but they, one and all, refused to yield their milk. 'Still, it was restful with my head butted into the cow's flank and my right leg between her two hind ones, so that she could not kick me over.' The wife of a Japanese farm-hand came to the rescue and helped him with the milking. She had a tiny baby strapped to her back as she squatted under the cow. The treatment of this tiny morsel of humanity appalled Robert:

> It was just like a doll, but it was shamefully neglected. All day it lay in their wretched shack and never cried. It did not even know how. Flies crawled over its face, even walking into its wide black eyes, but it did not blink. It seemed to have lost all sensitiveness to discomfort and pain. It was inevitable that in the cold and damp of the winter it should perish. It did, and was buried, I was told, in a soap-box behind the cow barn.

Summer in Vancouver Island, in the scrub land close to virgin forest, produced not only flies but mosquitoes which would 'settle on an arm, dig down and swell with blood'. Robert and the Mutter boys indulged in a grim sport, squashing these mosquitoes just as they were full to capacity. 'Sometimes one waited a second too long and I saw it take off, gorged to the gills. Then profanity was in order. Otherwise a broad red smudge testified to one's timing. The game was to see who could show the biggest blood-splotch.' Apart from the mosquitoes, there were the sandflies which irritated but did not bite so hard. Worst of all was the black fly. 'It had a way of getting under one's collar. Its bite was poisonous and the swelling often lasted for days.' In one of his first letters home Robert enclosed a fine specimen of a mosquito which had bitten him.

Infinitely more irritating than the insects were many of the people. Even today, Vancouver Island and its capital, Victoria, are probably the most British parts of Canada in atmosphere, but a century ago this feeling must have been infinitely more accentuated. The bulk of the settlers were first-generation English, Scots and Welsh. They may have thought of themselves occasionally as British Columbians, with the emphasis on the first word, but certainly not as Canadians. Although the Dominion of Canada had been created three decades earlier, British Columbia had not joined until 1871, and then only reluctantly. When the Dominion government failed to keep its promise and construct a transcontinental railway, British Columbia threatened to secede. The completion of this vital communications link in 1886 led to the foundation of the seaport of Vancouver on the mainland. Although it soon overtook Victoria in size and commercial importance, Vancouver City was a world away from Vancouver Island in the 1890s.

Robert soon discovered that he was living in a settlement glorified by the Old School Tie. 'I do not suppose that in all the Empire there was a community so dominated by the public school mentality.' On one occasion he remarked to an Englishman that 'the trouble with us was that we thought we were the finest people in the world'. In amazement the Englishman replied, 'Well, we jolly well are, aren't we?' The expatriate community divided into two main groups. Most of the older men were retired military or naval officers who prided themselves on their 'little bit of old England, by Gad!'. They dressed like squires and expected hired hands like Robert to touch their forelock to them. Then there were the Younger Sons, remittance men sent out by their families who were glad to be rid of them. They kept ponies and played polo. They dressed in yellow leggings, knee breeches and Norfolk jackets.

> Many of these young bloods came to the house in the evening and the conversation consisted entirely of horses and dogs, guns and fishing. One would have thought that art and literature did not exist. Indeed, to have mentioned such subjects would have tabbed one a bit of a bounder. As I sat tongue-tied in their company, no doubt they regarded me with suspicion. How often I wished I could steal away and read a book, any kind of book.[12]

He still had his cowboy complex, although this was severely dented when Jock gave him his first ride on horseback. Robert mounted the bare back of a bronco, which set off at a mad gallop when Jock slapped its rump. 'For about a mile I slithered around, finally locking my arms about its neck. Fortunately I managed to hang on.' Then one day Bung took him for a ride to visit some neighbours for afternoon tea. Clad in his circus boots and white flannel trousers, Robert mounted the horse, but on arriving at the tea-party he discovered, to his horror, that he was firmly glued to the saddle.

> At the tea-party was a fat girl who made a poem on my plight. Afterwards she became famous as a writer. Most people know her name so I will not give it; but if she reads this she may remember that her virgin muse was first inspired by the gory seat of my pants. After

that, I felt less cowboy-minded. It was nice to have experience, but I
felt I was going to pay bitterly for mine.

According to the unpublished reminiscences of John Frederick Corfield
(1884–1975), now preserved in the British Columbia Archives in Victoria,
BC, the young woman whom Robert describes so unflatteringly was Jean
Mutter, the eldest of the Mutter children and a year older than Robert
himself. Jean did indeed become a writer later in life, best remembered nowadays for her evocative poems of the turn of the century entitled *Mud Pup: a
Sequence in Light Verse.*[13]
Robert indicates that, although he was no more than a farm-labourer, he
was treated as one of the family and on the same footing socially as the other
settlers; yet he felt an outsider and, indeed, was more intent on being an
observer than a participant. But, he added ruefully, 'Can it be wondered that
my inferiority complex flourished in their midst and that I felt a shabby
vulgarian? They regarded me with such patronizing sufferance I felt it was a
privilege to endure them.'
A valuable lesson learned at this time was that money, as such, had no
bearing on class. This was a community where cash was so scarce that 'a silver
dollar was almost something to put in a glass case'. Business was done by
barter, the farmers trading their grain, fruit and dairy products for flour, tea,
sugar and tobacco. Everyone was poor, but there was no want. There might
be little cash around, but no one needed it, so its importance was diminished.
Robert looked wryly at the posturing and pretensions of 'the Snob crowd'
drawn from the impoverished county families. While sons and husbands
toiled like field-hands the womenfolk, dolled up in old-fashioned finery,
drove in rickety buggies with superannuated farm horses, to leave cards on
their friends. 'They lived in a mid-Victorian atmosphere of tea, tattle and
tennis.' Sunday church was the social high-point of the week. 'It was
Anglican, of course, as the native Canadian usually went to Chapel.'
Robert himself, though later professing a curious brand of ecumenism
mingled with agnosticism, became an adherent of the Anglican church at this
time. Indeed, for all his avowed distaste of the people he lived among, he is
fondly remembered in Cowichan to this day. His rich tenor voice became a
useful addition to the choir of St Peter's Anglican Church.[14] Beatrice Day, one
of the early settlers at Cowichan who attained her centenary, fondly recalled
how Robert sang alongside her. Mary Marriner remembered Robert taking
part in an operetta got up by the Amateur Dramatic Society, but she chiefly
noted him as a champion hand-shaker — a startling comment, at variance
with Robert's self-portrait as a loner. And the Share family, regarded as the

leading socialites of the Valley, were proud of the fact that Robert was a frequent guest at their house parties, though this may have been a view mellowed by retrospect. One must suppose that Robert's own impressions reflect fairly accurately his feelings at the time.

Robert made a clear-cut distinction between this Anglo-Scottish community and the native Canadians (not the Siwash Indians, of course, but the whites who had been born there and were the true pioneers). His innate egalitarianism was offended.

> I do not know what the future has to offer us in the way of a classless society, but when I think of the deep cleavage that divided our community I feel as if I had lived in a past century. The English emigrants regarded the Canadian pioneers with disdain and called them mossbacks. On the other hand, the Canadian frontiersmen who had carved homes from the wilderness spoke of 'damn fool Englishmen' and felt for them contempt and dislike.

In the end, however, the challenge of wresting a living from the soil was the great leveller. The Englishman and the Canadian were united in a determination to work hard. The patrician and the roughneck did not differ in that respect. The standard of merit was a man's fitness to do hard physical work. 'If you could sweat all down your back you were a worthy member of society. If you could not, you were a loafer and beyond the pale.'

This was a lesson which Robert learned early. At first it was his dogged pride that made him keep his end up, but gradually it came to him that if a job was worth doing it was worth doing well, that even the most menial task could be dignified with a sense of achievement.

> For instance, I was told to clean out a pigsty. The manure was packed so tight it was like cement. I could have dawdled all day at the job. I might have dreamed the hours away, for one can dream even in a pigsty. But I plied my four-pronged fork with a will and had the job finished by noon. It was some satisfaction that when I sat down to lunch the stink of me was so strong the female members of the family had to leave the table.

At the end of the summer of 1896 Robert took stock of the situation. He had been initiated into farmwork and had passed with flying colours. He was leaner, fitter and more bronzed than when he arrived in Canada a few months earlier. Some jobs were more congenial than others, but he discovered that, when faced with a choice, he preferred dirty work to strenuous effort. He worked harder than ever in his life; or rather, he was working hard for the first time in his life. This led him to thinking that he hated hard labour. With mounting horror, he realised that he had made a hideous mistake:

> For from now on, nothing but hard work lay before me. I had sold myself to serfdom. I had freedom only to starve, I had relinquished my heritage of easy living for the grimmest life I could have chosen. True, farm work was not so gruelling as other forms of labour, but there was no end to it. I had plunged myself into a morass from which I saw no way out.

After six months with the Mutters Robert tired of the rather claustro-phobic atmosphere of Somenos and moved up-country to a more remote farm. Here he lived with an old 'mossback' whom he calls Hank, actually a Welshman named Harry Evans.[15] Robert found this a much more congenial experience. He described his new home as a 'frame shack' cowering in the shade of the pines. Ramshackle, rain-sodden and innocent of paint, 'it made a disreputable blot in the clearing'. Knee-high grass grew up to its walls and a rickety scaffolding caged it in.

> Thirty years before, young Hank had rigged up that scaffolding, intending to add another storey to his home. He had answered an ad in which an attractive widow wanted a loving mate. She was to come out and join him and they would be married in the new house. But something slipped and the lady backed out. Young Hank had not the heart to take down the scaffolding, so there it remained, a witness of frustrated hopes and dreams . . .[16]

Now old Hank, 'rather a lovable man, gentle, patient and slovenly', was lonely. He wanted someone to keep him company during the winter, so Robert took on the job. The shack was the most remote house in the Valley, a three-mile tramp through the woods, and beyond it was a land that had never been crossed by human foot. The nearest neighbours, a half-hour hike through the bush, were a misshapen dwarf and his mother.

> At first sight he affected me painfully. Later I got used to him and came rather to like him . . . I would help him to get his sheep into the fold, or do other chores around the house. For he had little arms like

flippers and tiny twisted legs that allowed him to squat on the ground with imperceptible effort. He could neither run on his stubby feet nor do much with his pudgy hands. But he had the torso of a normal man and a head twice as big.

He did not appreciate the solicitude of his mother; in fact, I sometimes thought he hated her for having brought him into the world. He snarled at her and looked with rancour at his stalwart brothers. He said to me once: 'Why couldn't she have made such a good job of *me*? Or why didn't she smother me in my cradle?'

He was the cruellest man I have ever known. He seemed to get real pleasure from the infliction of pain on animals, and his chief victim was his old grey mare. She was skin and bone, but he drove her mercilessly. On her back she had a big open sore that was full of maggots. To the lash of his whip he had attached a wire nail and with this he used to flick the mare on the raw place. It made her jump and pull like mad.[17]

One day in midwinter, Robert heard the jingle of sleigh-bells and encountered the dwarf who ordered him to join him on the sleigh. He had 'a peremptory way that brooked no denial'. The dwarf produced a bottle of whisky and ordered Robert to uncork it, for he could not do this for himself. He tilted 'the raw liquor to his lips' and drank long and deep, polishing off half the contents at one go. He made Robert re-cork the bottle and hide it in the straw, but in a few minutes he fell senseless. Robert took the reins and drove him home. The mare, sensing a gentler hand on the reins, became unruly and almost upset the sleigh on a sharp bend. At the little homestead Robert hefted the dwarf and dumped him on his bed. His mother railed bitterly against the 'God-damned saloon keepers' of Cowichan who had let her son have the whisky, although they had been ordered by the police not to do so. 'Anything to make a dirty dollar,' she wailed. 'Oh, he's broken my heart long ago.' Robert surrendered the bottle and the old lady poured the rest on to the ground. The following day the dwarf turned up at the shack, demanding his bottle. When Robert told him what had happened he got a tirade of violent abuse for his trouble. Then he turned his murderous invective against his mother. Robert was frightened, and for several days hovered near their cottage, but as long as he saw a lamp lit he knew all was well. Nevertheless, he had a feeling of foreboding.

It was Hank who told him of the outcome. He had been chatting to the old woman when they saw the mare trotting up the trail with no one in the wagon. Hank drove back down the trail, and at the sharp bend he found the dwarf in the ditch with the marks of the wagon-wheels halfway down the bank. He had apparently fallen asleep in the driving seat. The curious thing was that his skull was indented with a blow from a shod hoof. Hank reckoned the mare had taken her revenge. Robert's graphic description of the dwarf occupies almost three pages of his book. Before and afterwards, he was always drawn to, and fascinated by, grotesquerie, either in appearance or in character. Ugly people were infinitely more interesting than beautiful ones; vice, in its many forms, was preferable to virtue. Consciously or unconsciously, Robert was adding to the rich store of memories and impressions which would later serve him so well, both as a versifier and as a novelist.

For a time he luxuriated in the lonely wilderness. Giant Douglas pine engulfed the clearing where Hank had his humble abode. Enough had been felled to give it a breathing space, and to ensure that none was near enough to crash on to the shack during a storm. The fallen trees lay criss-cross where they had been felled and made a barrier around the shack. Hank kept about twenty head of cattle which roamed the mountain all summer and came home in winter. Robert was now living on the nearest thing he was ever to get to a cattle ranch, a cowboy without a horse. 'Hank had a lazy man's idea of farming, the less labour the better. It was also mine.'

The shack consisted of a living-room and a bedroom, though Hank himself slept in a cubby-hole under the roof, mounting to the loft by a ladder which he drew up after him at night. He was believed to have a hoard of money up there and to be afraid of robbers. After Robert arrived, politeness forbade Hank drawing up his ladder, although Robert was never privileged to enter the den.

> I believe the reason he discouraged visits was that it was very filthy. Every morning he descended carrying a 'jerry' which he told me had once belonged to the Premier of the Province. He was very proud of it, and it was precious, as he suffered from prostatitis.

Robert had the bedroom to sleep in, but it had no bed. Indeed, it was totally bereft of furniture. 'I couched on the floor, lying on a buffalo-robe and wrapped in a mackinaw blanket.' From the moment he went there, for all of seven years, Robert claimed that he never slept between sheets.

Fired by his newly discovered hatred of hard work, Robert 'energetically cultivated laziness'. He lit the morning fire, swept out the living-room, baked the bread and helped Hank feed the cattle. Occasionally there were logs to be sawn for firewood. Otherwise, Robert had a life of leisure. 'Oh, the joy of liberty after six months of slavery!' Freedom was the finest thing in the world.

Later he would come to regard health as more important, but in his early twenties liberty was what he prized above all else.

> I was as careless as a breeze. I gave the future no thought. When the evil day came I would meet it; in the meantime let me live lyrically. But I would control my destiny. I would never allow myself to be shaped by circumstances.

At this period Thoreau was his mentor, *Walden* his bible. The words quoted above were written almost half a century later, from the position of fame and fortune, so it is difficult to calculate how much sense of destiny Robert had in 1896–97. But it is evident that, like his other role-model, Morley Roberts, he was storing up experiences, indeed actually creating them, with an eye to publication at some future date.

> Perhaps I might become a writer. The thought was always at the back of my mind. I might commit all kinds of folly, but my pen would save me in the end. It may have been that instinctive confidence that made me so jaunty in assurance and challengeful of fate. All this, I thought, was but a preparation. Some day I would get my chance and I would take it.

Robert did not realise how he had been mentally starved during the previous six months until he found in the shack a pile of old *Harper's Magazines*. Greedily he devoured every page, savouring each printed word. Nothing bored him; much enraptured him. 'Every page had the pulse of life in it, and many passages had the preciousness of words engraved on brass.' Most luminous of all were some articles about Southern California. They waxed lyrical about the citrus groves, the vineyards and the apple orchards. These articles were like a beckoning light, giving Robert a new incentive, a fresh inspiration. 'My plans might be excitingly uncertain, but I was on the trail of adventure.' Untrammelled by material possessions or emotional ties, Robert was a free spirit and he revelled in the prospect of warmer climes. 'I would pick oranges and grapefruit, olives, figs, walnuts in that wonderful sunshine.'

The images conjured up by the magazines were augmented by the old man's yarns. Hank had spent many years in California. Apropos of nothing in particular, Robert added that he had four brothers who looked like apostles. 'Hank was the black sheep. He had been a bit of a Casanova and still nosed round certain bitches of the settlement.' This *non sequitur* positively leaps off the printed page. During this period — indeed, for the ensuing sixteen years — there is no mention of any emotional entanglement. Robert posed as a backwoods philosopher. He would live like Thoreau, in a log cabin on the edge of a lake somewhere in the virgin forest. 'I would fish, hunt, raise a few potatoes, and maybe keep a few sheep.' But if the thought of getting himself a wife ever crossed his mind at this time, he never committed the thought to paper.

Elsewhere, however, he hints that 'though I loved my loneliness' he had reactions when he craved society. He began visiting the neighbouring homesteads, 'simple, hearty people' whose innate reserve he eventually broke down. These were 'small farmers for the most part' who had built their log barns and 'carved their stump-garnished fields from the virgin forest'. On the other hand, Robert the roughneck antagonised his former friends by his 'democratic brashness'. He wore a black shirt, white tie and black stetson, looking more like a *mafioso* than a backwoodsman. 'I dropped my English accent and tried to adopt the vernacular.' By 'English' Robert presumably meant the accent he had emigrated with, for it would have been the tones of Ayrshire and Glasgow rather than of Preston. Many years later, newspaper reporters would describe his voice as a soft burr, its Scottishness mixed with a transatlantic drawl. Robert had not lost his earlier socialist ideals, but when he voiced them these sentiments fell on deaf ears. 'The community was individualistic to the backbone, and I realized that any preachments (*sic*) for the betterment of the underdog comes ill from one who is himself an underdog.'

Regarded by the men in knee breeches as something of a pariah, Robert did not win ready acceptance among the mossbacks either. It was only by his entertainment value that he was finally accepted. Hank had a battered banjo and Robert soon succeeded in learning the principal keys and was able to strum a few chords while he sang the popular ballads of the day. He had some innate musical ability and a good ear for a tune. Ever since he could remember, he had made music on some instrument or other. In early childhood this had been a 'penny wheep'; from the tin whistle he had graduated to the flute and then the piccolo. In his late teens he had taken up the concertina, discovering harmony as well as melody. Piano lessons at the age of nine had ended abruptly when the spinster music teacher had actually kissed him.

Now, as his reputation with the banjo spread, Robert found himself being invited to parties and social evenings. He strummed his banjo and improvised ditties. He sang the old familiar songs, and got the appreciative audience to join in the chorus. Some of his happiest memories of this period are of community sing-songs in log cabins on the fringe of the forest. 'Often I would set out over a six-mile trail in the pitchy dark.'

But the best times of all were in the shack late at night after Hank had retired to his loft. Robert would sit in the firelight, seeing pictures in the flame.

It was then I had an itch to write something, and a sense of frustration overwhelmed me. I could not express all the emotion I felt. I would sit brooding till the fire died down, then creep, still musing, to my blanket. I had a feeling of secret excitement. I did not know where I was going, nor what would become of me, but I had faith that my good angel would save me in the end.

With the return of spring Robert felt the wanderlust. Lack of cash prevented him from heading south immediately, but he went to work with renewed vigour, spending the spring and summer of 1897 on a dairy farm on the outskirts of Duncan as a 'cow-juice jerker' — not a cowboy in the accepted sense, but at least a cowman, a 'manipulator of manure', at the largest ranch in the Valley. The four-hundred-acre Eureka Farm, midway between Duncan and Cowichan Bay, belonged to George Treffry Corfield who had migrated from Cornwall and eventually farmed most of the land around Cowichan.[18] Many years later Norman Corfield, the baby of the family, recalled the day the 'little red-faced Scotsman' turned up at their place 'with a pack on his back.' Unlike his time with the Mutters, Robert was not, on this occasion, treated as one of the family.

Instead, he dossed in the bunkhouse with a dozen or so other cowhands, a situation reminiscent of his boyhood in Roxburgh Street. In the evenings the men threw themselves on their bunks and smoked and chatted. A few wrote letters but no one read. In spite of being physically tired Robert had difficulty adjusting to the sounds and smells of the dormitory and slept badly for several nights. On the fourth evening, desperately seeking some escape from this sordid environment, he took out a volume of Rossetti's sonnets from his dunnage bag and began reading — a strange activity that soon excited the curiosity of his companions. When a bed-bug ran across the page, a neighbour promptly squashed it — right on top of one of the most beautiful sonnets. For many years Robert was reminded of this incident every time he saw the rusty stain on the page. Discovering that his bunk (and his alone) was heavily infested, he dumped it in the river, slept that night in the hay-barn, and fashioned a new bed out of some lumber the following day.

The Eureka interlude was chiefly memorable for Robert's detailed sketches of his workmates. There were the two Englishmen, the one an ex-stockbroker's clerk and soldier of fortune, wounded in the Graeco-Turkish War of 1886, who was to die in action during the Boer War, the other with psychopathic tendencies, believed to have been an officer in the Royal Navy but dismissed from the service. They were alcoholics and 'after the usual row with the boss, both of these men vanished in an odour of whisky'.

Then there was the Irish couple, tall and gangly Mike from Ulster who was 'cranky of temper', and pint-sized Patsy from County Cork, over seventy, the best worker on the ranch, but possessed of an evil tongue and a master of poisonous insinuation. On one occasion Robert was on the receiving end of a vitriolic outburst. When he finished, Robert said quietly, 'Look here, Patsy, I'm not going to waste words on you. I'm too sorry for you.' Then he went on to air his modicum of medical knowledge, diagnosing that the Irishman had 'sarcoma of the duodenum' and that he had only two years to live, at which point he would die in great agony. Instead, he suggested that Patsy should go and pray to his God to save him from the hell-fires that threatened him. Poor ignorant, pious, superstitious Patsy became a changed man, even attending twice-weekly Mass at the Catholic church three miles away. 'But the point is,' concludes Robert, 'that he did die in two years' time. And it was a stomach ulcer that finished him. I only hope worry over my words did not bring it on.'

There were three Canadians, and Robert explored their characters thoroughly. Ted, 'a grand worker but very cantankerous', saved his money with the single-mindedness of a miser. Some years later, he came into the bank where Robert was then working and subsequently the latter checked Ted's account, only to discover that he had several thousand dollars tucked away. The second Ontarian was a youth who, though lacking formal education, was a brilliant debater. Again, Robert bumped into him years later on a Pullman, 'looking like a million dollars' in real estate. The third, Ralph, hailed from Quebec and was for ever dreaming up business schemes. At Robert's suggestion, he bought an Edison phonograph, then an expensive novelty. He would tour the country giving gramophone recitals in church-halls and schoolrooms. Robert even drafted a handbill for this backwoods impresario before he went off on tour. When Robert himself was famous, he had a letter from Ralph saying he was manager of an express company in St Louis and very pleased with himself.

Robert dwelled on these ranch hands at some length because he believed that the most ordinary people could be interesting; though sometimes, while he was studying them, he wondered what they were making of him.

I can still see myself in that squalid bunkhouse, under the low, shingle roof, writing painfully but with a sort of ecstasy. The table was ramshackle, the lamp smoky, my seat a nail keg. From the gloom about me came snores in various keys. I alone was awake. As I paused to inhale the stink of sweat and filth, I mused: 'Life is queer. Is this I, this tired youth in dung-caked overalls? What am I doing in this sordid place with these clodhoppers who think I am a crank? No one of them has a trace of culture in his head. Yet are they any the worse? Nay, they are better; for they are paid twenty dollars a month, while I get fifteen. True, I can read Heine and Verlaine in the original, but I cannot plough a straight furrow. They have never heard of Marcus Aurelius, but they can milk two cows to my one.'

Something was wrong with me. Or was it only that I had taken a false turning? A man who could soar to the sky had no right to sink to the mire. Was it too late to save myself?[19]

There was the hilarious tale of how big red-haired Fergus the charge-hand lost his lady-love. He was caked from head to foot in cow manure one day when she rode by, 'a picture worthy of Rotten Row', with some young dandy of a remittance man in tow. She giggled immoderately at the spectacle, wrinkled up her elegant nose, and went her charming way. At this point in the narrative Robert interjected, 'I had a little romance of my own, which might have ended unfortunately'. At one point a gang of Siwash Indians were hired for an extra job of weeding and Robert was given the task of supervising them. He was attracted to a half-breed named Minnie; her father was a respectable member of the Church who, having sired half a dozen children by a 'klootch', abandoned his Indian family and married a white woman. 'None of his white daughters had the glamour of that half-caste girl. There was something tragic about her, a lost loveliness that added to her charm.' Robert's incipient ardour was abruptly dampened, however, when he was attacked by Minnie's beau, Johnny Fat, who hurled a pitchfork at him, narrowly missing his crotch. Lest his readers might suspect him of interest in the 'many good-looking half-breed girls in the nearby reservation', Robert added hastily:

> there was nothing Don Juanish about us farm hands. When a man works sixteen hours a day, it takes all the lasciviousness out of his system. The toiler is virtuous because he has no energy left for vice. It is only during an idle spell his thoughts turn to sex.

With autumn the active work of the ranch came to an end and, one by one, the men were paid off. Robert was one of the handful kept on at the end of the season, but incessant rain and then the bitter cold at the onset of an early winter rekindled his yearning for the sunshine of California. In November, faced with the prospect of blowing a month's wages on heavy underwear, gumboots and a mackintosh slicker, he gave notice to quit. The boss paid out a hundred dollars and promised him work if he liked to return in the spring.

> Well, it had been a good experience. I was pleased to see how I had risen to the occasion. I could earn my bread by the sweat of my brow. I had proved my manhood. I was not a little proud, and ready for the next phase in adventurous living.

A month later he was in Seattle, seriously worried. In four weeks his precious capital had dwindled to fifty dollars. He had calculated that he could live on twenty-five a month, but here he was spending twice as much. Meals cost a quarter and a room another two bits; a dollar a day should have covered him at the most. But there had been travelling expenses (he had presumably sailed from Victoria direct to the Washington seaport, though he omits this detail), and little luxuries like oranges and chocolates (an addiction acquired in Glasgow). In this, his first American city, he fell in with a homosexual variety artiste. In his naive way Robert thought him 'such a nice little fellow, grey-haired, fine-featured', yet there was something in his hot clutch that gave him the creeps. The Great Zanzini took him back to his cheap lodgings and gave him a recital, playing Mendelssohn's *Spring Song* on the Chinese fiddle, Handel's *Largo* on the concertina, and *Otchi Tchornia* on the balalaika. He promised Robert a fine career as his stooge, but there was something in those hot eyes that repelled the younger man.

Robert agreed to think it over, however, and was still considering the proposition when he chanced upon a large poster in a shipping office window, advertising the SS *Mariposa* leaving for San Francisco that day. The one-way fare was only a dollar. It was a special price, aimed at winning passengers away from rival companies, but Robert seized the opportunity. The accommodation was scarcely worth the buck: extra bunks had been hastily thrown up in the steerage quarters, in three tiers, four to a row, separated only by a very narrow passage. A hundred hobos were Robert's travelling companions, yet he felt a sense of destiny again and 'it was with some elation I realized that I had partly achieved one of my ambitions'. Instead of waiting for adventure, he would go to meet it. 'I would seek experience so that I might write about it; and the more colourful it was, the more arresting would be my copy.'

The voyage south was appalling. Robert was very sea-sick and had to share a bunk with a large Swede who kept rolling on top of him.

> We were packed like sardines, and the air was so thick you felt you could slice it like Camembert. The man below had already thrown up

his supper, and the one above was beginning to do likewise. It seemed every one of these hundred passengers was busy voiding his stomach. The Swede alongside joined in the general chorus of eructation. As he heaved himself over me I was afraid he was going to lose his self-control; but fortunately he made the passage-way, and there he puked prodigiously.

Then I, too, had my moment. It was all the more violent as my stomach was empty. Several spasms left me limp and gasping; and, with around me a mob of retching men, I probed the depths of misery. So utterly exhausted was I that when the vomit of the man above me spattered on my face I had not the energy to turn my head away.[20]

Although he slept fitfully his slumbers were disturbed by the 'crawling crowds of cockroaches . . . dancing a quadrille on the underside of the mattress'. In the early dawn Robert staggered from his bunk and slithered along the companionway to the pure air of the deck. Suddenly he noticed a gentle warmth in the wind, and a balmy quality in the breath of the sea. All next day he recuperated and even managed to force down a few mouthfuls of tough steak and the kind of rotten potatoes usually fed to pigs. The second night aboard was spent on deck, lulled by a soft wind and cradled by a gentle sea.

Robert spent a month in San Francisco, exploring the city minutely. He sat on a bench in the Golden Gate Park admiring the memorial to Robert Louis Stevenson which had been unveiled only a few weeks previously. During the hour he sat there, only three people paused to read the inscription. 'The monument seemed sadly out of place in this hurly-burly city, but to me it was the centre of everything. All San Francisco was a setting for that little bronze galleon on its granite shaft.'

Of all the cities in the world, this was the one that most kindled Robert's imagination. Bret Harte, the Argonauts and the Forty-nine gold rush had romanticised it for him. It had no rich literary tradition, but even as Robert dreamed in the sunshine of the Plaza one was in the making. Gelett Burgess, Wallace Irwin, Frank Norris, George Sterling, Ambrose Bierce, Joaquin Miller, W.L. Stoddard and Jack London were then struggling young writers there. The last-named was to be drawn to the Far North just after Robert got to San Francisco, and was to do in prose what Robert achieved in verse a few years later.

At first Robert stayed in a hotel at the base of Telegraph Hill, but he could ill afford the half-dollar a day and soon moved across to the Latin

Quarter where he obtained a large room with a French family. The main article of furniture in his room was a huge four-poster bed which Robert considered to be well worth the two dollars a week charged. He slept badly for several nights before it dawned on him that the four-poster was alive with bed-bugs. The rest of the week he slept on the floor. 'It was of no use complaining. The people of the house spoke no English.' One wonders why the man who could read Verlaine in the original was unable to communicate with his hosts.

During the four weeks he spent in San Francisco Robert got to know the city intimately. The Barbary Coast thrilled him but it was Chinatown that intrigued him most. Many years later he could vividly conjure up the opium dens and the brothels where white drug-addicts catered to the sexual needs of Chinamen. Although he hung around their doorways, observing the comings and goings, he was too poor — and too timid — to enter. 'Theatres, restaurants, joss-houses — to me wonderful in their novelty.' Robert lived in a state of exhilaration and excitement. 'I was terribly happy and, though alone, I had no fear of the future. I might be down in the gutter, but I had faith in my star.' The descriptive passages in the chapter entitled 'Barbary Coaster' are as evocative as anything written about this rumbustious seaport at the end of the nineteenth century. Both here, and many times later in both autobiographical volumes, one has the feeling that Robert's true *métier* was that of the travel writer, a genre in which he dabbled only briefly some seventeen years later. Significantly, it was the colourful characters encountered along the way which made those passages so lively.

After some hair-raising escapades (he purchased a knuckle-duster for self-protection) Robert would return to the Stevenson Memorial to muse. 'In these moments I felt the spirit of the Master, and the urge to write possessed me.' Everywhere was colour and romance. Adventure lurked around the corner. 'Around me was a roaring city, exultant in its ribald brutality.' A chance meeting with a freelance journalist in a bookshop — they discussed contemporary French literature — triggered off more longing and an intense feeling of frustration. 'How I envied him! To write, to write, even if I starved . . .' San Francisco, so vibrant with vitality, inspired Robert as no other city did. 'I felt serene for, in its lowest dens of depravity, I could read Omar Khayyam, and dream of beauty.'

Then one day he awoke, stared at his last ten-dollar bill, and said, 'Young fellow, where are you going to?' He had his first feeling of fear. He had seen so much 'of the misery of a great city, its derelicts, its down-and-outs, that their degradation filled me with disgust'. Soon he would be one of them, and the prospect appalled him. He began studying the Wanted Labour advertisements in the paper, but was depressed to find that the Work Wanted ads were equally vehement. In the offices of Murray and Ready, where he had gone in response to an advert for labourers in the Los Angeles area at two dollars a day, Robert had a chance encounter with a man who was looking for 'a handyman, half coachman, half gardener, for two old ladies' at twenty-five dollars a month. He was actually offered the job. 'Here was one of those cross-roads of destiny.' If he had accepted, he might have settled down in California, perhaps ending up with a small farm and a big family, poor but honest. But on the spur of the moment he turned it down 'for one that proved to be a bit of hell'.

At nine o'clock the following morning he and a bunch of other desperate men boarded the Southern Pacific bound for Los Angeles four hundred miles to the south. Pay was two dollars a day, from which seventy-five cents was to be deducted for board and lodging. The cost of the train ride was also to be taken out of the first wages earned. At Sacramento ten of their number disappeared, either because they had come to their senses, or because their homes were in that locality. At Los Angeles they were met by the contractor who had hired them. They were now closely guarded to ensure that no one escaped at the station, and entrained on a local bound for the countryside. So far, no one knew where they were going, or what sort of work they were expected to do for their meagre pittance. It was dark when the train stopped at Azuza. The fifty who had left San Francisco had now dwindled to thirty. They were marched to a small hotel, eyed by hostile inhabitants who shouted 'Bloody strike-breakers!' at them. After a sleepless night in a tiny attic, Robert joined his comrades for an early breakfast. Two stage-coaches swiftly bore them off to the San Gabriel Canyon where a construction camp was in course of erection. Robert became part of a gang driving a tunnel half a mile long through the wall of the canyon to bring the water of the San Gabriel River to the valley. For ten hours a day they toiled in the dark, damp tunnel. Robert had never been in the bowels of the earth before and hated it. He had to wear leather gloves that cost a dollar a pair and lasted only a few days. On the first day he had worked with his bare hands, so that by night-time they were torn and bleeding.

Although he subsequently transferred to work in the gravel pit, Robert quit his job on Christmas Eve. On claiming his wages he was given a cheque for twenty dollars which could only be cashed at the contractor's office in Oakland. Needing cash desperately, Robert was compelled to sell it for half its value. On the trail down the canyon he had found a packet of blueprints for the tunnel project and tried to trade it to Schrader, the project manager at Azuza. Schrader promised to cash the cheque, but having got his hands on the precious plans which were holding up the work, he welshed on the deal. 'He turned his back on me with contempt. I was just another bum to be treated like a dog.' In the end the stage-coach driver offered ten dollars, knowing full well that he would be able to get the full amount himself. This episode left Robert with the realisation of how helpless he was, and how callous were those around him. 'I was a bit of flotsam to be spat on, scorned.' Bitterly he considered how to keep on going 'forward to whatever destiny' awaited him.

The ensuing forty pages of *Ploughman of the Moon* chart Robert's erratic progress on the Pacific Coast. On Christmas Day, after a night in a flea-infested chicken-coop, he took the train to Los Angeles where he subsisted with other bums in an evangelical mission, getting by on a dollar a day for the rent of a tiny room at the mission and fifteen cents for food. For ten cents one could get a five-course meal at Smith's Restaurant on Spring Street, while a huge plate of baked beans and a coffee cost only five cents.[21] In Los Angeles he found the public library where he could sit and read all day. San Francisco had made him want to write stories, but this city 'made me want to make poetry'. But he was more attracted to verse than poetry, the sort of newspaper verse that 'simple folk clip out and paste in scrap-books'. He sent some specimens to the local papers and they were promptly published. In one, entitled 'The Hobo's Lullaby', the line 'My belly's got a bulge with Christmas Cheer' was typical of Robert's penchant for the coarse and the concrete. 'Thus early I discovered that I would rather win the approval of a barman than the praise of a professor . . .'[22]

There were sketches of the other inmates of the mission, the Socialist, the Hypochondriac, the Corn Doctor, the Quartz Miner, the Section Foreman and the Book Agent, all good practice for the budding writer. As dishwasher at the Pacific Gospel Saloon, Robert could scrounge as much bread as he wanted, so he did not actually starve, though his diet was undeniably deficient. When a man caught Robert scraping with his teeth a banana skin which he had just thrown away on the sidewalk, and offered him a dime, he proudly refused the coin. He had not sunk quite that low! It was thus, literally on the bread-line, that Robert passed his twenty-fourth birthday and saw little ahead but poverty punctuated by occasional bouts of gruelling labour. He had a three-day stint as a sandwich-board man which earned him a dollar.

Then the orange-picking season started. Robert was hired by a Mexican contractor not as a picker but as a washer, the lowest job of all. Many years later he identified the orange grove, 'at the foot of Broadway and Hill Street, about a mile from the present Union station'.[23] On average he made fifty-five cents a day and after two weeks managed to save three dollars. Then he moved to another grove and was promoted to picker, averaging seventy-five cents a day, a real boost to his income. Half a century later and living in a comfortable bungalow in Hollywood, Robert remembered his time in the orange groves as one of the brief halcyon periods as a drifter.

Having saved eleven dollars before this job came to an abrupt end, Robert then advertised in a local paper for a job requiring some education:

> Stone-broke in a strange city. Young man. University non-graduate, desires employment of any kind. Understands Latin and Greek. Speaks French, German and Chinook. Knowledge of book-keeping and shorthand; also of Art and Literature. Accept any job, but secretarial work preferred.[24]

There was only one response which brought him the offer of a position in San Diego as 'a sort of tutor' to three girls who needed cultural conversation. The Villa Lilla was in a remote suburb, 'a low, mission-like building with a red-tiled roof'. Madame Ambrose, 'a broad-bosomed lady', turned out to be a madame indeed, for the Villa Lilla was a high-class whorehouse. Robert substituted for the black handyman who had landed in jail, and for thirty dollars a month, all found, he had a wide variety of odd jobs, mostly congenial. As for the three 'daughters' of the house, Laura was the highbrow of the family and read books, Lotta was musical and Rose painted in watercolours. Laura lent him Nietzsche's *Thus Spake Zarathustra* — 'the finest of soporifics'. Lotta was more amiable and talkative. Robert tuned her Spanish guitar and tried to teach her how to play it. At this time he discovered that he could compose music as well as write the lyrics. 'In after years I published about thirty of these efforts, all of which were highly unsuccessful.'[25]

This idyllic situation came to an end with the imminent return of Big Pete, 'a razor toting coon' who would raise Cain if he found Robert sleeping in his cabin. The following Sunday morning Madame Ambrose paid him for the full month, while Lotta presented her guitar in its brown leather case as a parting gift, appropriate equipment for the wandering minstrel. 'In that Mission setting, they might have been a Mother Superior and three Sisters. God bless them . . .' Robert concluded irreverently as he left the villa.

With five gold half-eagles sewn into his shirt and a guitar on his back, Robert headed for the open road south and the 'collection of hovels called Tia Juana', if for no other reason than that he wished to send home a card with a Mexican postmark.

> It would be so nice if Papa, in answer to inquiries, would be able to reply: 'Oh, he's travelling in Mexico. Taking a little holiday from his arduous duties as a horticulturist.'[26]

He tramped on, trudging through the desert by day, camping near haciendas at night, accepting the hospitality of poor farmers and singing for his supper by strumming his guitar. In this 'rambling, gypsy fashion' he got as far as Ensenada, some seventy miles down the Mexican coast, 'a bronzed, lean-jawed roughneck', very different from the pink-faced, pudgy little bank clerk of not so long before. By now the novelty of Mexico had worn off. 'I had glutted my appetite for loneliness, and the monotony of the mesa was beginning to weary me. I was sick of cactus and yucca tree, of *frijoles* and *cassava*.' When he returned to the American border he was agreeably surprised to find that his ten-day jaunt to Mexico had cost him exactly a dollar. He found that he could easily tramp thirty miles a day but, concerned for the state of his boots, he preferred to walk barefoot whenever he came to a good highway. Because the nights were so cold, he rested up during the heat of the day and tramped after dark. Along the way he fell in with several genuine hobos, and these provided him with further material for perceptive pen-portraits. One day he splurged a quarter on a can of corned beef. Oh, the extravagance of it! In the 'village town' of Santa Ana Robert ventured into a Japanese restaurant and had a breaded cutlet. 'It cost me ten cents, but I enjoyed it hugely.'

Approaching Los Angeles again he 'felt suddenly forlorn'. There was no place for him in this opulent land. 'Where was I driving to?' The previous night he had had a strange confrontation, in a rude shack which he had put together with old railway sleepers, with a hobo whom he suspected as the serial killer then believed to be roaming the district. Robert had crawled out of the hut and taken refuge in a hollow full of dried leaves. Then fate intervened. On the road into the city he encountered a schoolboy whose name was Jimmy Service. On the strength of a shared surname, Robert was invited home to meet another Scottish family. Yet Robert was suddenly reluctant, ashamed of his appearance. It was another of those 'cross-roads of destiny, in which my choice would make the greatest difference to my future. Here might be a chance to make good.' Contemplating that here, at last, might be the opportunity he had been waiting for, he was on the point of accepting the invitation as they turned off the road at a big house.

> Then something seemed to twist me right round, and, bidding him good-bye, I went off in the opposite direction. Once more I mused: What is directing my steps? . . . Well, a force stronger than myself seemed to be drawing me on to another destiny, and, even though it looked a gloomy one, I must fulfil it.[27]

That night he camped on the outskirts of Los Angeles. In the early morning he entered the city 'like a whipped dog'. He had not the heart to return to his old lodgings, 'to face the old gang with failure written on my face'. Instead, he headed for the Salvation Army hostel where, for ten cents a night, he had a small cubicle, clean but windowless. Lunch of beans and dinner of hash cost five cents a meal, and for a further five cents he could get some bread and oranges. Thus, on a quarter a day, Robert joined the army of the Great Unwanted, 'incapable of hard work and unable to get soft jobs'. Life with the hobos at the hostel was an education in itself. Robert learned how to 'batter the burg': where one could scrounge a free meal or pick up a dime. The grizzled, weather-beaten tramps with their gunny sacks, however, were 'outcasts, accepting their fate, awaiting their time to die like dogs in ditches'. Robert had rugged health, but not the hands for heavy labour, or even for dishwashing. What he longed for was a white-collar job. The mere wish was a small step up, but he had little confidence in his ability. He avoided decisions by musing fatalistically

> What will be must be. The future as well as the past is a fixation. To-day was conditioned by yesterday, and to-morrow will be conditioned by to-day. Life is a pattern, woven to the last thread. What I do is the only thing I can do.

Robert was down at heel but not yet down-and-out. He considered writing home for funds, but promptly rejected this. He was too proud: 'Better to perish than to admit defeat.' In the meantime, he took another labouring job. This time he got 'work with pick and shovel in the face of clay and rock' as an army of navvies burrowed into the hillside above the city to make a tunnel for the tramway. During his first morning on the job there was a cave-in and two men were borne away on stretchers. The air was bad, the light evil, and when at noon he emerged into the blessed sunshine 'I did not return to the gloom. I made the city a present of my labour.' This brief experience inspired a poem entitled 'The Wage Slave' which Robert says he never submitted to any newspaper, although many years later he saw it in print, in an anthology compiled by Upton Sinclair.[28]

Next, he became a dishwasher in a big hotel, but soon discovered that there was a world of difference between washing a few plates and mugs at the Pacific Gospel Saloon and dealing with the mountain of dishes in a busy restaurant. Robert, lagging well behind the other washers, was fired at midnight on the first day and paid off with a dollar. As this was the sum he had handed over as a placement fee to the employment bureau his labour, yet again, had gone for nothing.

Even as an unskilled labourer, Robert was a failure. Sitting on a park bench the following day, resigned to his uselessness, he chanced upon a head-line in the paper read by the man next to him. A TON OF GOLD COMES OUT OF THE FROZEN NORTH. 'It did not interest me a bit. *The Klondike.* Bah! Let others seek their fortune in that icy land. Give me the sunshine and the South.' The man walked away, leaving his paper on the bench, and Robert read on about the gold rush which was being hailed as a worthy successor to the fabled Forty-nine. 'Maybe it will have its dramatic aspects. No doubt another Bret Harte will arise and sing of it in colourful verse,' he read, unmoved. What concern was that to him, a hapless hobo on a park bench? But the words 'arise and sing' kept ringing in his ears. 'I could do both. The troubadour spirit in me was not dead.' Here was Robert's destiny at last — by singing of the gold rush, to make the richest strike of all — but not yet.

Thus inspired, he spent almost two years wandering through the American South-West, roaming over the states of Utah, Texas, Arizona, Nevada and Colorado. During this happy, carefree period, the wandering minstrel played and sang for a meal here, a bunk there, earning the odd buck by casual labour: weeding a lemon grove for five dollars, a job that lasted a week, was about his main source of employment. Though he never sank to the moral depths of the typical hobo, Robert was a self-confessed vagabond. Time and again this word appears in both his prose and his poetry. He cheer-fully exchanged the bondage (of a settled existence) for vagabondage. Among his cherished souvenirs was a worn dime.

> I think I must have tendered it a hundred times with a hollow smile, saying: 'Excuse me, ma'am, but I'm so hungry I'm willing to give my last ten cents for a bit of dry bread and a glass of water. I'm not a bum, ma'am. Please let me pay.'
>
> They never did, and in most cases I had more than dry bread. In fact I often had a real feed.[29]

Robert salved his conscience by offering to perform chores to express his gratitude, but this was usually refused. Then, if they felt like it, he would give them some music. The cowboy songs were the most popular, but the sentimental ballads of Stephen Foster were also a sure hit. After half a dozen numbers Robert felt that he had earned his meal. 'In this way, without begging, I was able to provide myself with nourishment at little expense.' With his packet of tea and occasional tin of salmon in his back-pack, he was never a vagrant in the accepted sense. The canny Scot in him carefully budgeted at five dollars a month, 'and I seldom exceeded this'. Most of this sum went on small luxury items: 'food played a big part in my vagabond days'.

Robert wandered for many months, his zigzag progress taking him all over the West. 'Much of my wayfaring was monotonous and is now vague in my memory,' he wrote later. This kind of aimless drifting might have gone on indefinitely, but for an accident while traversing the four-thousand-foot Tehachapi Pass in south-eastern California. On this occasion he had abandoned the highway and was walking along the railroad track when he came to a long trestle, one of those flimsy wooden bridges supporting the single track. He was halfway across it when a train caught up with him. He tried to make it to the end of the bridge before the locomotive ran him down but realised to his horror that he was not going to make it. Every twenty ties or so there was a beam that jutted over the abyss. He was about to crawl out and wrap himself around one of these when he remembered the burden on his back. In a panic he detached it and let it fall to the bottom of the ravine, and had just time to crawl out on to the projecting timber before the train thundered past, barely inches from his head. Afterwards he regained firm ground and descended into the ravine. He found his pack, wet from the sluggish stream but none the worse for the drop; but nearby lay his precious guitar, smashed to pieces.

> I almost cried as I looked at the faithful old thing. Well, I left it there, and with something gone out of me I took up the trail. But I was about through. After that I had no more zest for wandering, so by devious ways I returned to Los Angeles. There in the square were the same old crocks and misfits. Would I become like them? As I surveyed myself, I thought bitterly: Heir of all the ages, in the foremost files of time.[30]

Once more, a newspaper on a park bench seemed to point the way. An advertisement for the US Marines caught his eye. The war with Spain was then at its height, and the country was ablaze with patriotic fervour, spurred on by the exploits of Colonel Teddy Roosevelt and his Rough Riders.[31] Robert considered this prospect for a moment. 'It might help me rehabilitate myself, and there was a recruiting station a few blocks away.' But something seemed to hold him back. Then he turned a page and his eyes fell on a paragraph about British Columbia. 'Suddenly I decided I would return there, and that very night I took the boat for the North.'

This time he got as far as Portland, Oregon. Out of money again, he signed on at a sawmill where he managed to hold down a job for three whole days, but shifting lumber was the worst sort of back-breaking labour, so he took his cheque, paid off his hotel bill, and pressed on towards Canada once more. His objective was the Corfield ranch in the Cowichan Valley where he had proven his ability to work with cattle. Within three weeks of leaving Los Angeles he was back at work with the Corfields, his first job as swineherd:

> Pigs are often preferable to some people. I can see poetry in a pigsty, and, in those days of inhibitions and complexes, a hog wallowing in the mire is a sight to restore sanity. I mention my occupation because it is another instance of my capacity for misdirected energy.

This led him to thinking, once again, that Nature had intended him to be a dud. 'She gave me tiny talents which could only mean frustration. They diverted me from the true objective of my being.' He could draw, play and act a little, but in each his achievement mocked his aspiration. He also regretted that there were 'years and years when literature did not exist for me, and I gave myself up to vain pursuits.'

In the late autumn he was promoted as cattleman in charge of a herd of fifty cows and twenty calves. Robert was happy in this position. 'I loved working with beasts, but not with men.' There were even many poetic sides to the job, if one had but the time to appreciate them, but it was really one rush from dawn to dark.

There were only four men in the bunkhouse, for now most of the hired hands were Japanese who had their own quarters. The calibre of the hired help had also noticeably improved. One of the bunkies was a heavily tattooed ex-sailor who read philosophy and had fierce arguments with Robert over the relative merits of Schopenhauer and Nietzsche. 'It must have seemed droll to see two mucky men on a dung-heap discussing metaphysics.'

The onset of winter doubled Robert's responsibilities, as a band of young cattle came in from the hills. One morning in December 1898, while Robert was taking the big Holstein bull to pasture, he was knocked to the ground by the brute and only saved from disembowelment when the Philosopher leapt the fence and distracted the maddened animal momentarily, giving Robert just time to crawl to safety. Two of his ribs were cracked.

This brought to an abrupt end Robert's career as a cattleman. The ground floor of the bunkhouse accommodated a general store run by 'a waggish youth' named Bill. About the time of Robert's encounter with the Holstein, Bill chucked his job to go off as a mule-skinner and Robert was installed as storekeeper in his place.

> I have had great moments in my life — when it seemed the gates of heaven opened wide and I stepped through them from the depths of hell. This was one of them.[32]

Luck had come to his rescue; at last he was 'once again a white-collar man'. On Monday he had hustled sixteen hours a day. On Thursday he was watching others hustle and getting the same pay for it. It seemed too good to be true. He moved out of the bunkhouse and dined with the Corfields.

> Here I sat with the family, in a blue serge suit, eating in the dining-room, while through the intervening door of the kitchen I could see the farm-hands in their grimy overalls gobbling down their food. For a long time, I am sorry to say, I got pleasure from this dolorous contrast. It is true that through the misery of others we appreciate our own well-being.[33]

Rising at eight-thirty (instead of five-thirty), Robert breakfasted in the family dining-room. 'Taking my napkin out of its silver ring, I daintily toyed with eggs and bacon.' At nine he opened the store (which was also the Cowichan post office) and attended to duties which must have been familiar from his time at Kilwinning. At nine-thirty he hitched the pony to the wagon, collecting the cans of cream on the stands along the way and delivering the mailbags to the railway station. He unloaded the cans at the creamery, reloaded with empty cans, and started back around eleven, calling at the station for the incoming mailbags. At noon he was back at the store, sorting the mail and distributing it before lunch. Thus two hours a day were spent jogging behind a pony, 'smoking, meditating, and enjoying pleasant scenery'. Afternoons were spent in the store. 'Occasional customers came in, but I would serve them without enthusiasm.' Most of them were Siwashes from the reservation, to whom Robert, in an inspired moment, sold a long-hidden consignment of chamber pots which Bill had been too coy to display. Now promoted as Etruscan vases, Robert flogged them off as all-purpose utensils for marriage presents, parlour ornaments, coffee urns and punch bowls for festive occasions.

> My stock vanished overnight, and the boss considered ordering a fresh consignment. But alas! it was my only success as a shopman. Even to-day it humiliates me to think that my one brilliant achievement in the commercial field should have been as an advocate of porcelain propriety.

Robert had no illusions about his abilities as a 'counter-jumper'. He hated himself for selling shoddy goods to the Indians at inflated prices, but he carried on this job of 'petty huckstering' for four years because he who had been on the verge of vagrancy was now warm, well-fed and dry. He was looked on by the Corfields as one of the family. 'Consideration by people of my own class was not wasted on me, and gratitude for that kindness made me prolong my stay from year to year.' He had been handled harshly by the world and taking up the struggle frightened him. 'So I continued to follow lethargically the lovely line of least resistance.' His duties, on the whole, were very light, although they included tutoring the Corfield boys, looking after the tennis court (the first in Canada) and slaughtering cattle in the neighbourhood, the butchering being usually done on the spot. Cowichan Valley journalist and historian Jack Fleetwood has preserved memories of Robert, 'habitually sitting in the shade of a particular maple in the club policies reading his dictionary'.[34] His name appears in the centre of a tablecloth which the ladies of the tennis club embroidered in 1901, showing the signatures of the members.

Fifty years later, Robert still had a sharp mental image of his quarters at Cowichan:

> The store stood on the bank of the river. To the right on entering was the post office. Around one side and back was a counter. Behind the counter the dry goods began, then the shoes, then the shirts and underwear. The back of the store was devoted to groceries, and underwear. Outside of the counter were nail kegs and boxes of hardtack. There was a space for hardware, another for flour, and a table on which was piled cheap clothing.
>
> The stove was of the barrel variety and sat in a bed of cinders. Above it hung a large oil lamp. Near it was a wooden stair mounting to an attic through a trap-door. Part of the attic had been partitioned off to form a small room. It held a bed, a table, two chairs. There was also a basin, a jug, a mirror. The bed had two grey cotton blankets, but no sheets. The pillow slip was changed weekly.[35]

Robert had a very pleasant, congenial existence. He attended parties, where he was much in demand for his dramatic recitations of Newbold and Kipling. He rejoined the choir at St Peter's and threw himself enthusiastically into the round of amateur theatricals, taking roles in *The Area Belle*, *Ici On Parle Français* and *Box and Cox*. He became a proficient horseman, a crack shot and a keen salmon-fisher. An energetic swimmer since boyhood, he enjoyed nothing better than a dip in the Koksilah River in high summer, when the weather was warm enough. Then he would accompany the Corfield boys. Fred, the eldest, was closest to Robert in age and was probably responsible for the apocryphal tale that the Scot 'got his first inspiration to write poems while working on the monotonous grind of separating cream'.[36] Norman, when in his eighties, could still recite one of them, inspired by a swim in the local river. The lines were, in fact, a free rendering of the 'cold bath' verses which Robert had got into print in Glasgow a few years earlier and which he also submitted to the *Duncan Enterprise*.

Most of all, Robert valued the local library where he read novels incessantly. 'But though Nature at times filled me with the old ecstasy, I was never moved to express my feelings in writing. During those years I made no music and composed no verse.'

This is oddly at variance with the facts, as set out in the Corfield reminiscences and elsewhere. Although he was to ignore it in his autobiography, Robert composed a sentimental ballad of four verses during the Boer War and sent it to Charles Harrison Gibbons who published it in one of the local newspapers, the *Victoria Colonist*. Entitled 'The Christmas Card', it described with pathos the feelings of a young soldier, fighting for Queen and Empire, far from home and loved ones.[37] Contrary to the popular belief that Robert had no interest in the Yukon before he went there, he sent a poem from Cowichan in 1902 to the editor of the *Whitehorse Star*.[38] To the same period clearly belongs the longer poem 'Fighting Mac' which sticks out, like a sore thumb, among the Yukon ballads in Robert's first published volume, for this 'life tragedy' was evidently composed in March 1903, when news broke of the suicide of General Sir Hector Macdonald in Paris, on his way home from Ceylon to face a court martial for gross indecency with his native bearer.

On reflection, Robert felt that the four years at Cowichan was a period of stagnation. 'My days were rubber-stamp days, each year a stencil repeated from season to season.' Although he was aware that he was wasting his life and often resolved to break away, he was 'too cowardly and indolent' to do so. As usual, external factors eventually forced his hand. Competition from other traders, not as fastidious as Robert about cheating the Indians or selling them contraband liquor, stole away most of his customers. One day an old mossback, observing Robert meticulously measuring out a yard of knicker elastic for a Siwash woman, told him bluntly, 'You'll never make a trader. Why don't you try something more in your line?' Being so honest, why did he not try school-teaching?

The idea had immediate appeal. 'From a blanket-stiff I had climbed to white-collarism: now I was going to mount to a profession.' In fact Robert was already augmenting his income by tutoring the Corfields' seven sons. What they remembered most, many years later, was Robert's consummate abilities as a raconteur and spellbinding spinner of yarns. Some of the tales he told the impressionable youngsters, in the barn converted into a schoolroom, were pretty 'wild and woolly'.

A careless accident with the pony and wagon, resulting in cans of Jersey cream flooding the highway, clinched matters. Having to fork out two dollars fifty cents for spilled cream decided Robert that he had had enough of Siwash trading. He decided to go to McGill University. While redoubling his efforts in the store and post office to save sufficient to pay his way through college, he abjured novels and began studying seriously for the matriculation exam. This proved to be tougher than expected for he had lost the knack of study.

In May 1903, when he had saved two hundred dollars, he handed his resignation to George Corfield and moved from his attic to the shack of a friend where he could cram for his exam in total solitude. This was no solution, for the shack was infested with cat fleas which distracted the reluctant student. Inclined to be a dreamer at the best of times, Robert often found his attention straying from his text-books. 'Often I wanted to throw the hated things out of the window and write mad sonnets to the moon.' All he managed was a three-verse lyric which 'came as easy as eating pie'. The poem entitled 'Apart and Together' was later sent off to *Munsey's Magazine*. In due course it appeared in print, in the December issue, and Robert received a cheque for five dollars. 'Five dollars for half an hour's work! Five dollars for filling only a page of Munsey's!'

After two months in the flea-infested shack Robert obtained temporary work with a road gang. 'Take it easy and make the job last,' advised the road boss. 'Remember you're employed by the Government.' By day Robert worked on the roads, 'grading, mending culverts, chopping brush'. Summer passed cutting a trail through woodlands. At night Robert studied by the light of a candle in his tent. Then the job came to an end and he was paid off. In the autumn he went down to Victoria, his two hundred dollars intact. He took a room in a boarding-house for thirty dollars a month, but as his little savings dwindled he moved out, to a small room in a private house at fifteen dollars a month. In due course he took the examination. 'It lasted three days and I suffered from the strain.' Robert scored 100 per cent in arithmetic, which was routine, but the 90 per cent score in English literature was exceptional. He scraped through in geometry and Latin, scored well in Canadian history, but flunked in algebra which he hated. This poor showing in maths was to be expected, but Robert was shocked to learn that his French paper had earned him a single derisory mark. The examiner, however, was a French Canadian, and anything less than perfect in translation was savagely marked down. Once more Robert felt frustrated rage and an insane desire to inflict physical violence on a pompous professor.

He was advised to do the re-sit in algebra and French, and to this end enrolled at a college in Victoria where his fellow students were fresh out of high-school and about half his age. Robert felt stupid and out of place. They were well dressed while his clothes were worn and shabby. He bought a new outfit to raise his morale and half his hard-won savings vanished at a stroke. The cost of text-books eroded the other half and by the time he began full-time classes he was down to a bare sixty dollars, enough to last two months. 'What would happen after that I did not dare to think. I could only carry on, hoping something would turn up to save me . . .'

To make matters worse, Robert fell behind in his class work. He could not compete against younger, more nimble brains. One morning he played truant and went for a long walk in the park. Conscience-stricken, he passed a sleepless night, resolved to work harder than before, but 'next morning I found a grim exultation in the thought that never again would I sit in my classes. My university career was over.'

He had now only enough money to keep himself for a week or two. 'To what shabby fate was I drifting? I tasted the dregs of defeat and felt cast into the outer darkness.' He applied for jobs and was easily rebuffed. Instead of drowning his despair in alcohol he exercised fiercely, going for long, punishing hikes, often at night and preferably by moonlight. 'Then a certain peace and serenity would come to me, and I would imagine all the jobs I could have enjoyed doing.' These ranged from ragtime pianist in a honky-tonk to rose gardener and rural postman. Bitterly, Robert faced the fact that he was trifling with his life, 'a minion of the Moon, whose silver emptiness mocked me'. What a mess he had made of things, and now he was at the end of his tether.

CHAPTER 6

BANK CLERK IN BRITISH COLUMBIA AND THE YUKON

This is the Law of the Yukon, that only the Strong shall thrive;
That surely the Weak shall perish, and only the Fit survive.

'The Law of the Yukon' in *Songs of a Sourdough* (1907)

WHEN A PERT STENOGRAPHER TURNED HIM DOWN FOR AN office job — 'Sorry, but we only wanted an office boy' — Robert admitted to himself that he was sunk. He thanked her with as much dignity as he could muster to hide his chagrin. Back on the corner of a busy street in Vancouver City, he bent to examine his watch, then remembered that he had pawned it and was living off the proceeds. No one would have suspected the dire straits he was in, for he was smartly dressed in his new serge suit and overcoat. But it was his darkest hour. 'Where now was that guardian angel who had always interposed to save me in my extremities?'

Then fate, as usual, intervened. He was accosted by a biscuit salesman whom he had known in his storekeeping days. When asked what he was doing in 'the big burg', Robert replied despondently that he was looking for a job. The salesman briskly asked him what was his special line. Robert admitted to having trained as a bank clerk. 'Well, what's the matter with the bank you're looking at? Ain't it good enough for you?' Robert was characteristically diffident; the bank was like a veritable palace. He doubted whether he would be good enough and was frightened that he would be thrown out. But his friend urged him to give it a try. 'Again I looked at the bank, and no sinner ever gazed more longingly through the gates of Paradise.'

Taking from his pocket that old testimonial from the Commercial Bank of Scotland which he had miraculously preserved through all his wanderings, Robert entered the building with considerable trepidation. Approaching a stern-faced young man at the Accountant's window, Robert proffered the dog-eared document, saying huskily that he was looking for a job. The young man did not stare contemptuously at him, nor turn him away as so many had done. Instead, he said rather kindly, 'You'd better see the Inspector. You'll find him in his room upstairs.' Upstairs another stern-faced youth received him. Robert presented his certificate and repeated his faltering plea. He left Robert quaking in his shoes and went into a private room. Presently he returned. 'The Inspector will see you,' he said kindly. The Inspector, 'a gruff, grey man', asked him why he had come to Canada and how old he was. Robert said he was twenty-seven, 'understating my age by two years', which he judged to be prudent. By now almost thirty, Robert realised that he was no longer in the first flush of youth. This was the first, but by no means the last, time that he would lie about his age.

The Inspector replied that the bank did not usually hire men as old as that, but was inclined to give him a chance on the strength of the glowing testimonial. However, Robert would require three sponsors. Thinking rapidly, he came up with three names and addresses. The Inspector asked him to return a week later, by which time the bank would have received answers to its enquiries. On his return to his lodgings Robert wrote to his three referees begging them to put in a good word for him. The ensuing seven days were the longest in his life. 'I walked a good deal. I ate as little as possible. I kept spruce and neat. But though I smiled cheerfully, anxiety rowelled me.'

Then he went back to see the Inspector, immediately aware of a change in his manner. 'This frosty man had thawed toward me.' The references had been satisfactory and the bank would give him a probationary appointment for six months at fifty dollars a month. 'Report on Monday at our Island Office,' he snapped, then, returning the testimonial, he dismissed Robert abruptly. That, at least, is the story Robert narrates in *Ploughman of the Moon*. The truth, however, may be more prosaic. In a very self-revealing article, published a few years earlier, he merely states that a friend introduced him to a bank inspector.

In no time at all I was safe and secure behind the very sort of counter I'd quit so gallantly in Scotland. Imagine the disillusionment of my old manager in Glasgow had he known. He wanted me to be a cowboy too![1]

When he took the ferry back to Victoria Robert was down to his last half-dollar. On the boat, however, he fell into conversation with a draper from Dundee who offered him a ten-dollar bill to tide him over. Robert politely refused the man's generosity but gladly accepted his offer to vouch for him with the landlady of his boarding-house, so that he did not have to stump up the customary rent in advance. After a cheering breakfast of ham and eggs he presented himself at the Victoria branch of the Canadian Bank of Commerce at eight o'clock on the morning of Monday, 10 October 1903. The very bank in which Robert resumed his chosen career still stands, at the corner of Fort and Government Streets, although the name has slightly changed.[2]

As the most junior of the senior clerks, Robert was required to sleep on the premises, with a nicely furnished apartment above the strong-room at the rear of the building. A trap-door in his bedroom floor opened on to the two-tiered bank vault; Robert was expected to sleep with a revolver at his side, ready to take pot shots at anyone prowling below, though he confesses that he was such a sound sleeper that it would have required a detonation of nitro-glycerine to waken him. The interior of the bank was modernised in the 1950s and the vault and trap-door are no longer in existence.[3]

Robert could hardly believe his good fortune when he beheld the sitting-room, bedroom and bathroom which were now his. That night, for the first time in years, he slept in a proper bed with real linen sheets. After paying off his boarding-house landlady Robert was left with thirty dollars from his first pay-cheque. Quixotically, his first act was to hire a piano which he installed in his sitting-room; his second was to buy a ready-made dinner-jacket. In Scotland bank clerks were of no account, but in British Columbia they were the backbone of society. During the next six months Robert attended numerous parties and dances. 'I used to devote myself to girls who were wallflowers . . . I would sail to their rescue. I don't think I ever danced with a popular girl. I was too sensitive to the pathos of the wallflower and the cruelty of youth.' He went to the theatre in evening dress and played golf appropriately attired. 'I found it paid to be well groomed, so I spent most of my spare money on clothes.' Robert was now mixing with two quite different classes of people. There were his friends at the bank and there were his old pals at the boarding-house. 'I preferred the latter. They might be common, but they were more fun.'

At work Robert was conscientious, *too* conscientious, for he often worked late into the evenings, and was mildly rebuked by the Accountant: 'I don't like to see men in the office after hours. Speed up your work and get out in good time.' Robert had been used to a more leisurely pace in Glasgow; here, every-thing was done in a rush. 'It was more important to be quick than to be neat, most important to be accurate.' Robert was neat and fairly correct, but he realised that he would never be a fast worker. 'I was too incurably a dreamer to concentrate on figures.'

Robert cultivated the sloping handwriting required of Canadian bank clerks: 'In those days penmanship seemed to me more important than literary composition.' In March 1904 his appointment became permanent and he was given a ten-dollar raise. It was one of the proudest days of his career. Then one day the Accountant told Robert that he was being transferred to an inland town on the mainland.

> I went with regret. I had never gotten over my first exultation at work-
> ing in that office. I regretted my apartment, my piano, my friends.
> Every day of my life there I had congratulated myself on my good luck.
> Well, perhaps, my new post would be equally enjoyable.

On 9 July 1904 Robert reported to the bank's branch in Kamloops, then a small country town of fewer than two thousand people, at the junction of the north and south branches of the Thompson River in the southern central region of the province. It was in the heart of the cattle country. Doubtless Robert remembered the chapter in *A Western Avernus* devoted to this little town, with its 'long straight street of wooden houses, some of them quite hand-some structures' on a high bank above the river. Robert found Kamloops even more agreeable than Victoria. It had a bracing climate (the bank allegedly sent its tubercular staff there to recuperate) but the rolling countryside was ideal for horse-riding. Robert's first act was to buy a pony and take up polo. This was pure swank. 'I hated the game and never could hit the ball with certainty.' He even had himself photographed in his polo costume and sent a copy to his father. 'Playing that most aristocratic of games was even more impressive than touring Mexico. I could hear the old man telling the world his son was a prominent official in a big Canadian bank.' This infers that Robert Senior was still living in Scotland at the time. The family disappears from the Glasgow directories in 1899 and virtually nothing is known of their subsequent move-ments. John Alexander, at least, is known to have come to Alberta in 1904[4] and Peter's son Kelvin has confirmed that the family as a whole settled in the area either late in 1904 (after Robert's transfer to Kamloops) or early in 1905. He states that his father Peter had gone ahead of the others and had obtained the arm at Vegreville east of Edmonton where Robert and Emily Service, with heir entire family (apart from Robert Junior), made their home.

Even in a small country town like Kamloops there were the same social distinctions. Robert's set comprised the government officials, the professional men and the country ranchers.

> We in the bank kept aloof from the tradespeople. At public dances it was curious to see on one side of the hall the shopkeeping crowd, and on the other the so-called *élite*. I never dared to dance with girls who worked in stores, though I wanted to, because they were the prettiest. But to have done so would have queered me with my own set.[5]

In Kamloops Robert did not have a piano, but he bought a banjo, tuned it like a guitar and strummed away happily. During this period he scarcely ever read a book and literature ceased to exist as far as he was concered. 'My sense of poetry, so strong in my poverty and my desert wanderings, now seemed to have deserted me.' His whole ambition was to get on in the bank, and he was prepared 'to give it my lifelong loyalty'. Other men had similar ambitions, but were also blessed with the bureaucratic mind that went with them. 'I never would have. All I asked was a small country branch, with little responsibility.'

From time to time he read exciting stories of the Klondike, but he claims to have paid them little heed. It was all so remote and inaccessible. 'None of the romance of the gold rush had been exploited.' Yet little did he dream that, while other men were seeking their Eldorados, they were also making one for him. The Bank of Commerce had been quick to open a Yukon branch, at Whitehorse in 1898, shortly after the spectacular strike that triggered off the gold rush. Stories of the adventures and hardships endured by the staff sent to man this lonely branch, half shack, half tent, where miners brought their pokes of gold dust panned from the creeks, were commonplace.

> It was the romance spot in the bank's history; but of all the officials sent up there, a little junior, humped over a big ledger, was about the only one to win a sizeable stake.

The 'little junior' was, of course Robert himself.[6] A posting to the Yukon was apparently regarded as something of a prize. Clerks seconded to the Whitehorse branch were given an outfit allowance of two hundred dollars in order to purchase the obligatory coonskin coat. They also got a special food allowance of fifty dollars a month because supplies were short and prices astronomical: tins of corned beef cost $5, eggs were $12 a dozen, beer and whisky $5 and $10 a bottle respectively. Apart from their grub, the bank staff had good quarters with all living expenses paid. According to Robert, the move to the Yukon took him by surprise:

> I will never forget the morning the Manager beckoned me into his room. 'You are being transferred to White Horse,' he said. 'You must prepare to go at once. You are very fortunate.'
>
> In a daze I went into the outer office. The others were staring at me. 'It's the Yukon,' I said. Envy was in their eyes. As for me, I had to take a firm grip on myself, and it was some time before the significance of the change of life began to sink in. Yet I was sorry to leave that branch. Life there had been delightful.[7]

So far there was no hint of romance in Robert's life, but he had now turned thirty and in his first year in the bank's employment he enjoyed a lifestyle and a social standing which must surely have set him thinking of finding a wife and settling down. Neither Klinck (1976) nor Lockhart (1991) mention any romantic attachment, following Robert who was himself, of course, totally silent on the matter. Yet from various sources have come isolated pieces of a jigsaw that point to an affair at Kamloops. When Robert published his first slim but best-selling volume of poems little more than two years later (March 1907) he dedicated it cryptically 'to C.M.' although he never mentioned the fact, far less explained the dedication. Fred Corfield, eldest of George's sons, was Robert's closest friend from the Cowichan period and was the source of the story that Robert had actually asked for a transfer to Whitehorse, after an unhappy love affair. 'His bosses gladly accepted, as the average span of service at that branch was only a couple of months, the incumbents leaving to go gold prospecting, dying of fever or getting shot.'[8] Corfield recalled that the girl's name was Catherine. Robert's daughter also remembered a curious letter sent to her mother after the poet's death. The writer was herself the daughter of a lady to whom Robert had written a series of passionate love letters. Would Mrs Service, she wondered, like to have them? Mrs Service declined, and it was surmised that the owner of the precious bundle deposited them with a library in British Columbia.[9] While there is a school of thought which maintains that Robert would never have dedicated his first book to the girl who turned him down, others speculate that it was rather touching, besides being a clever way to put two fingers up at the girl who might have been married to a celebrated author; and I am bound to say that I agree.

At any rate Robert sold his pony, gave away his banjo, and said goodbye to his friends. Back in Vancouver he got his clothing allowance, bought a coonskin coat at Johnston & Kerfoot on Cordova Street for a hundred dollars, and cannily pocketed the rest. On a cold, crisp morning at the beginning of November he boarded the Canadian Pacific steamer *Princess Beatrice* bound for Skagway. 'I had an idea that a new and wonderful chapter in my life was about to begin.'

The sail northwards up the Inner Passage is one of the most spectacular voyages in the world. It may be likened to a cruise along the fiords of Norway from Bergen to Kirkenes, but that pales into insignificance by comparison. The mountains are more majestic, the ice-blue glaciers infinitely more spectacular, the pine-forests more breathtaking. By day there is the spectacle of killer whales cavorting round the ship; by night there is that grandest of all natural wonders, the aurora borealis, transforming the sky into a gigantic flickering screen. Small wonder that Robert was entranced by it all. Introspective as usual, he wondered at himself most of all, enjoying so much wonder without it costing him a cent.

> It was the first time I had ever made a voyage at the expense of someone else; and, believe me, it tripled the enjoyment. And to think that I was being paid for having a marvellous time! Not only my pleasure was being given me free, but I was being handed two dollars a day for accepting it. To my Scotch mind it didn't make sense.[10]

On the five-day voyage north Robert got to thinking. How gorgeous it would be to live all his life at the expense of others! And so easy too. All he had to do was to acquire a certain amount of capital, and he could live off the interest. Five thousand dollars at 5 per cent would yield an income of twenty dollars a month. He reckoned that he could get by on that, and perhaps augment this from his pen from time to time. This was the kernel of what he fondly called 'my Escape Idea'. Underneath lay the notion which he called the Author Complex. 'Perhaps I could dodge my destiny by being a pot-bellied banker, and even publish a little book.' Published at his own expense, of course: 'I might become one of those amateur authors who are such a nuisance. It would salve my vanity.' Thus he mused, alliteratively as usual, 'in the moonlight of mountain magnificence, inspired by sublime scenery to sordid schemes of self-enrichment.'

Characteristically, the breathtaking vistas along the ninety- mile Lynn Canal, the spectacular seaway which terminates in the dazzling beaches of Skagway and Dyea, were not mentioned. No doubt Robert appreciated the sheer mountains that rise from the brilliant turquoise water, their lofty peaks mantled in gleaming snow reflected in the glassy sea. The port of Skagway, until shortly before a sprawling tent city but by 1904 a small town of wooden shacks and unpaved streets, was wreathed in rain when Robert disembarked. 'The Portal of Romance' was how the Alaska tourist brochures of the period described it, but the reality was extremely disappointing and Robert wasted no time dallying there. He boarded the train whose narrow-gauge railway line climbed steeply from sea-level to almost three thousand feet. This was a major triumph of engineering, mute testament to man's ability to conquer natural obstacles when the goal was worth it. By the time it was completed, offering a track of 111 miles between Skagway and Whitehorse, the reason for its construction had all but disappeared. From the comfort of the little railway carriage Robert, the detached observer, could look down on the notorious Trail of Ninety-Eight far below, the narrow, winding trail worn by the tramping feet of thousands of pioneers. 'It looked tough enough, though.' The carriage windows were opaque with ice. 'I could not see much of the scenery, but what I did glimpse was dreary and depressing.' Stunted pines pricked through the deep snow and cruel crags reared over black abysmal lakes. 'A tough country indeed. I was glad I had not been one of those grim stalwarts of the Great Stampede.' There was no mention of the vertiginous drop, visible from the carriage, into the aptly named Dead Horse Gulch where three thousand pack animals perished in the summer of 1897.

The railroad rose to the summit of the White Pass. Six years earlier, following the first torrent of gold-hungry humanity, the Canadian government, fearful of America's plans to push its frontier all the way up to Whitehorse, had hurriedly despatched a company of the Royal North West Mounted Police. At the top of the pass they had erected their tents and constantly manned a Gatling machine-gun aimed at the endless line of toiling goldseekers. The invasion crisis passed off by the end of 1898 but ever afterwards the Mounties had rigorously controlled the border. Robert was singularly unimpressed by his first Mountie, for the latter pounced on a pair of felt boots which Robert had purchased in Skagway and demanded two dollars import duty. 'As I paid I could have kicked myself with them. Two dollars shot to Hades! A nice beginning to my campaign of economic independence.'

The rest of the journey passed without mention. Robert seems to have been oblivious to the breathtaking beauty of Tormentation Valley which in later years would make the Yukon and White Pass Railway one of the world's greatest, if least accessible, tourist attractions. The line tortuously writhed across the British Columbia panhandle. At Bennett it skirted the eastern side of the lake of the same name, ringed by spectacular mile-high mountain peaks reflected in the mirror stillness, then crossed a narrow arm of the lake into the Yukon Territory. Just north of the territorial boundary was a railway station that took its name from the peregrinations of the local quadrupeds, though in later years Caribou Crossing was abbreviated to Carcross. Today its railway station, long disused, has been transformed into the Robert Service Museum. Thus from the moment of entering the Yukon one is confronted with the affection, amounting almost to reverence, with which Robert's memory is kept alive.

In Whitehorse Robert stepped out on to the wooden platform at the terminus. His immediate impression was the sea of heavy coonskin coats. 'But for the rosy faces of the men inside them, it might have been a coon carnival.'

Then one of the strange fur-coated figures addressed him, telling him to put on his coat. Robert seems to have been unaware that it was thirty below. 'You don't feel [the cold] because you're a cheechako. Your blood's like soup. When you've been here a year you'll get cold-conscious.' With this advice the latest cheechako (tenderfoot) was greeted by his bank manager with whom he was to lodge. The manager had the unique distinction of being the world's only sea captain to turn banker.

> Of an eminent clerical family, but of an adventurous mind, he had defied family tradition by taking to the ocean. He might have been a parson: he preferred to be a tar. Then, after roving the Seven Seas, he decided that he and Neptune had just about enough. He would give the land a chance. So he did, but soon realized that working on a farm was a mug's game. There were easier ways of winning one's meal ticket, and banking might be a good bet.
>
> There are two types of managers, the bureaucratic and the popular. Our skipper was of the latter. He was perhaps the most popular man in town. He was a virtuoso in slang, and his conversation was rich with it. He was a good mixer, oozed geniality, and had great gifts of chaff and humour. His wife was little more than a girl, with a *chic* that was Parisian. Unusually pretty and dainty of figure, in the setting of that rough mining camp, she stood out like a jewel in a junk heap. Yet she looked after us with a maternal solicitude that won our gratitude. She called us her 'boys' and we called her 'Missis'. Few real families of four were more united and happy.[11]

Mr and Mrs Leonard De Gex were a childless couple, but they were like a mother and father to Robert and the bank teller. Harold Tylor was a brilliant boy, as surely destined to success as Robert was to failure:

> He might have been a millionaire if he had not preferred to nurse the millions of others. As it was, he did pretty well for himself. He was a mass of energy that nothing seemed to exhaust. He had an insatiable appetite for life and a great gift for popularity. He excelled in games, was a hunter, a fisherman, and as keen a swimmer as myself. In all gatherings he was a human dynamo. He neither drank nor smoked and claimed he had never tasted tea or coffee in his life. In fact he was so viceless that he was almost vicious.

A drinking man, as Robert then was, could not compete. Every time he bought a whisky and soda, he felt that Tylor was that much ahead financially.

Robert accused him playfully of exploiting his continence. 'There is nothing so immoral as morality.' But Harold was saving hard in order to marry a girl back home, to whom he wrote copious letters every day. Robert had an understandably jaundiced view of matrimony at this particular time and saw Tylor's goal as a surrender of liberty. But his friend's exemplary conduct proved to be a model for Robert's own ambitions to win economic freedom. Henceforward he would match him as a miser. He immediately gave up drinking (which had been the occupational hazard of so many of his predecessors) and put fifty dollars from his monthly pay-cheque into a savings account. With undisguised joy he watched his nest-egg grow. 'I stinted myself the smallest pleasures. I scrimped, I scraped. Thrift grows on one. The more I saved the more I wanted to save.'

Tylor, like De Gex, was immensely likeable and popular with everyone. Robert envied them their easy amiability, ruefully recording in his autobiography that he himself had never been popular 'in all my existence'. Many of the newspaper memoirs published either at the time of his death (1958) or his birth centenary (1974) referred to the little Scotsman as stand-offish, and Robert himself confessed that he shrank from popularity — 'maybe I disliked it'.

> Due to my solitary spirit I always wanted to take a back seat. I was as morose as a malamute. But my reticence was partly due to shyness, partly to indifference. I had no disdain for those around me: on the contrary I admired them because they could do so many things I could not. So I enjoyed the popularity of my colleague and trotted meekly at his heels. After all, he was a man of action, I a feckless dreamer.

The De Gexes, Tylor and Robert were a happy quartet and the last-named could not recall a sour note to mar their harmony. Meals were occasions of sheer merriment, the Skipper punctuating the conversation with racy remarks which would provoke the reaction from his wife, 'Hubs, if you don't stop your nonsense I'll leave the table.' But she would laugh at his drolleries, delivered with never the crack of a smile.

In one sense at least Robert was fortunate in arriving in Whitehorse when he did. The winters were so harsh that gold-prospecting came to an abrupt halt. Placer gold, the only kind found in the Klondike, cannot be mined without water, nor can it be extracted from the earth until the permafrost above the pay-streak has been thawed all the way to the bedrock. At the onset of winter the rivers and lakes froze, deep snow blanketed everything, and the miners fled south, to Seattle and San Francisco where they so often drank, whored and gambled away their fortunes. In the spring the population of

Skagway, Haines and Dyea would momentarily explode as thousands of eager miners, prospectors and newcomers would wait impatiently for the Chilkoot and White Passes to open again when the frenetic rush could resume. For five months of the year, however, the Yukon was in a virtual state of suspended animation. This gave Robert a leisurely introduction to his new branch and ample time to reflect and dream, or, donning a pair of snowshoes and his coonskin coat, to go for long hikes into the surrounding wilderness.

Spring in the Far North is negligible but summer, accompanied by almost total daylight and a brilliant sunshine that rapidly warms up the land, arrives suddenly 'with midnight melody of birds and myriads of mosquitoes'. Robert records the thrill he got when he saw the snow suddenly vanish and the brown earth bob up: 'to watch the ice crack, break and go in rearing slabs; to behold the eager green springing to the caress of the lingering sun'. It is a magic change that happens almost overnight, giving one a sense of unreality. The spectacle of the stunted trees in their fresh spring foliage, the bright greens contrasting sharply with the thick carpet of crimson fireweed, is a breathtaking sight. Not that Robert seems to have noticed; he was, as always, more interested in the human element:

> Then from Outside came the inflowing tide of workers resuming their jobs, and residents returning to their homes. All had enthusiastic tales of their travels, but declared they were glad to be back. The shipwrights returned, the pilots and crews of the boats reappeared: the scene suddenly became a bustling one as every train brought new crowds going into the Interior. Then navigation opened, and the season was in full swing.

Whitehorse lies at the southern tip of Lake Laberge which Robert was later to make world famous, albeit in a misspelled form. The northern end of the lake empties into a tributary of the mighty Yukon River which rises only fifteen miles from Skagway but then flows two thousand miles through Alaska to empty into the Bering Sea. This provided a reasonably convenient means of getting from Whitehorse to Dawson, three hundred miles to the north-west, where the bulk of the mining was then taking place. Although Robert had missed the great days of the gold rush, when Dawson's population had swollen to almost forty thousand, and the lake had been covered with an incredible flotilla — 7,124 boats of every description from kayaks to scows, from rafts to stern-wheelers, had spearheaded the great stampede in May 1898 — excitement and eager expectancy still pervaded the atmosphere. The original gold fever had barely lasted two years, from midsummer 1897 when the news of George Carmack's fabulous strike at Bonanza Creek had first reached the outside world, to July 1899 when word of even greater gold at Nome in Alaska had emptied Dawson overnight. The earliest prospectors had panned gold out of the creeks, but in April 1898 gold was discovered in the hills and benches as well as the riverbeds. This required the sinking of shafts and the construction of flumes and sluices; gradually the pattern of goldmining changed, the individual prospectors giving way to syndicates operating sophisticated machinery. This, in turn, produced a greatly reduced but more settled level of activity. The great age of lucky strikes and claim-jumping was over long before Robert reached the Yukon, but there were plenty of old-timers and ever-optimistic prospectors around, with yarns of spectacular nuggets and rumours of lodes as yet unlocated to fire the imagination of the quiet bank clerk.

During the five summer months the bank in the gateway to the north was kept extremely busy:

> The stream of travel was in full spate, while the local mines were working night and day. In fact, there was little darkness, and we were able to play tennis at midnight. We also paid a daily visit to the swimming hole, a pool formed by the back-up of the river. On Sundays we never failed to attend church, because the Skipper was a strict sectarian and insisted we decorate the family pew.

De Gex was head deacon and used to pass the plate, saying 'Come on, you old stiff, loosen up,' or some similar remark. It was of him that Robert thought when in one of his ballads he wrote the lines:

> Me that's a pillar of the church an' takes the rake-off there,
> An' says 'God damn you, dig for the Lord', if the boys don't
> ante fair.

After a time De Gex said to Robert, 'You have a pious mug. I think you'd make a good deacon.' So he became one and passed the plate in his turn, urging the tightwads to come through. Robert enjoyed the dramatic moment when he held up the collection before the parson for his blessing.

> He himself was a literary man, and when he was not writing sermons he was composing best-sellers. He published a score of novels, many of which were popular. So far as I knew he was the only one in that community who had a taste for letters.[12]

Minutes of the Whitehorse Episcopal Church, written in Robert's neat angular script, are preserved in the church archives to this day.

The incumbent at this period was the redoubtable Isaac Stringer, subsequently Bishop of the Arctic. His writings are no longer read, but he is still remembered on account of a strange adventure in the winter of 1910 when he was stranded in a snowstorm on the notorious Edmonton Trail, on a journey between Fort McPherson and Dawson. Having used up his meagre rations, Bishop Stringer boiled his sealskin and walrus boots for seven hours then baked them on hot stones before consuming them. Later he confessed that the leather was 'tough and stringy, but palatable and satisfying'. After several weeks in the wilderness he was discovered, barely alive, having lost fifty pounds in weight. Bishop Stringer's experience was the source of the well-known scene in the film *Gold Rush* in which Charlie Chaplin ate his boots.

Robert recounts how the two handsomest men in the Yukon, friends of his, met tragic deaths. One was the superintendent engineer of the river flotilla who was badly injured in an accident and sent Outside for an abdominal operation. This was a fairly simple routine matter, but afterwards it was discovered that a pair of scissors was embedded in his intestines. He had to be cut open again but succumbed to the shock. 'The poor chap died, a victim of someone's carelessness.'[13]

The other unnamed unfortunate was 'the nephew of an earl and related to half the English nobility'. This six-foot Adonis might have been a film-star or a naval officer, but when Robert knew him he was a deckhand on a Yukon stern-wheeler. If it had been a windjammer on the high seas Robert could have understood, for there was romance and danger there; but on the placid river there could not have been a more secure billet. Yet even the Yukon had its perils. One peaceful evening the steamer was nosing its way upstream, pushing a scow laden with hundreds of small tin barrels. A young cabin boy, spotting a duck flying towards the boat, rushed for his shotgun. In his haste, he tripped, the gun went off, and sent a blast into those tin barrels . . . of gunpowder. There was no explosion, just a sheet of flame that engulfed both scow and steamer.

> The flame-swept decks below were strewn with charred bodies, among them my friend. He died a few hours later. He asked to see me, and his last words were: 'God curse the man who invented gunpowder.'

What an incomprehensible world it seemed! 'An insignificant shrimp' like Robert was permitted to survive while so many fine fellows were stamped out. More and more, Robert came to the firm conviction that he had a guardian angel. Although he would later profess agnosticism and had a distaste for religion, he believed in churches, which gave him a sense of social stability.

Occasionally he regretted his lack of faith. Certainly few professed, church-going Christians could have agonised so often or so long about their beliefs in the way Robert did.

The summer passed quickly. Then the crowds which had flowed in with the spring began to flow out again. 'It was a human tide whose final ebbing was one wild welter of escape.' The last boats were crammed to the gunwhales. Then the rivers and lakes froze overnight, navigation was closed and the season ended. Now, so far as Robert was concerned, the real life of the Yukon could begin. There was a very real feeling of 'us and them', between the transient majority who came only for the earth's bounty, and the resident minority, the sourdoughs, who had a sense of belonging to the hard, unyielding High North. The latter were 'happy helpful people'. The Wild brought out virtues in people which were not readily apparent in the cities — brotherhood, sympathy, high honesty. 'As if to combat the harshness of Nature, human nature makes an effort to be at its best.'

With his innate antipathy for hard and sustained work, especially if it were monotonous and repetitive, Robert welcomed the wintertime when the bank's business fell by three-quarters.

> I joyed to think that for the coming six months I could loaf and dream. For now I realized my dreaming was creative, that from my reveries came thoughts and fancies I might one day put on paper. It was an incubation of all worth while in my life.[14]

Robert the loner became notorious as a solitary walker, going off by himself as soon as work was done, into the Great White Silence. 'My lonely walks were my real life; the sheer joy of them thrilled me. I exulted in my love of Nature and rarely have I been happier.' At four o' clock he would close his ledger, his cocker spaniel would rush to the closet and fetch his arctics, and then they would set off together through the strangely deserted, snow-bound streets. Other dogs would join them and sometimes Robert had as many as five leaping and barking joyously around him. He would climb the bench above the town and strike through the woods.

> There were trails everywhere, and slender pines on which chipmunks barked shrewishly. Sometimes I would shake a tree till I dislodged the little creature. The dogs would wait, full of excitement, and make a dash for it as it fell; but they would never catch it, for which I was devoutly thankful . . . Oh, those tramps in that world of crystalline purity, when I shared the joy of my canine companions! And my return after three hours of march, so keen set for supper, with glowing cheeks and sparkling eyes! Never was life more wonderful.

On Sundays, after morning service, he would spend the entire day on snowshoes, exploring the frozen wastes beyond the river. It was then that he realised the poetry of his surroundings: 'I just felt it with that inarticulate sense people feel in the presence of serene beauty.' In the evenings, however, Robert was dragged into the constant round of parties and dances; scarcely a night passed without some social distraction. Whitehorse boasted a fine ice-rink where Robert and his friends met their girls and waltzed on the ice to the music of the orchestra. There was the exhilaration and excitement of tobogganing on the snow-clad hillsides. There were whist-drives which Robert hated, giving rise to the mistaken assumption that he had an aversion to cards. In fact, he was particularly fond of solitaire, a game which he enjoyed right through into old age, but it was probably the social aspects of card-playing which he detested, not the cards themselves. But there were also dances, which he loved. In the club, there was a handball court as well as a large hall for indoor baseball, played with a soft ball that bounced off the walls. 'I do not believe as small a community ever packed so much pleasure into its leisure.'

Whitehorse, by 1905, had a population of less than a thousand souls. It was a straggling little town, half hidden in greenery, sprawling along the river-bank. Its front street was a strange medley of log cabins, false-fronted stores and timber-framed government offices. Nearby was a boneyard of derelict lake steamers, made redundant by the collapse of the gold rush. Indians and droves of huskies roamed the river-banks. Like Duncan and Kamloops, however, Whitehorse was a town with two clearly divided communities. The rip-roaring days of the original gold rush were long gone and Whitehorse was well on the way to becoming the staid little town that it is today. Nevertheless, there was a sharp division between the town itself and the Settlement where the miners lived. By 1900 many of the earliest residents had brought their wives and families and they undoubtedly contributed largely to the civilising influence of Whitehorse. In the mining camps, however, it was a different matter. There, drunken brawls that led to knifings and shootings were still all too frequent. The rough life there was something that Robert observed from a safe distance; given his social position in Whitehorse, there is no way that he would ever have ventured into the Settlement, far less have participated in saloon life.

The social events which Robert attended were conducted with the great-est decorum and at least a modicum of sobriety. In his three years in Whitehorse Robert says that he never tasted a drop of alcohol. It was too expen-sive, and drinking socially entailed buying a round of drinks for one's compan-ions. Such conviviality did not fit in with Robert's savings scheme.

The permanent residents were regularly drilled and instructed in fire prevention. In a town which was entirely built of wood, a well-organised fire brigade was essential. In 1899 Dawson had been razed to the ground in a conflagration that reduced the boom town to ashes in a matter of hours. Whenever the fire siren sounded, everyone turned out promptly, whether it was the middle of the night or not. Around three o'clock one morning in the spring of 1906 the citizens of Whitehorse were roused by the nightmarish wail of the siren. Fire had broken out in the White Pass Hotel. The volunteer firemen manned the apparatus and swiftly ran out the hoses, but no water came. Then it was discovered that the pump-house door was locked. The crowd became unruly when it was realised that the engineer was not at his post. Things were beginning to look ugly when a flustered little man scurried up, fearful of a lynching if he did not unlock the engine-room. The hotel was only a hundred yards from the pump-house; soon all would be well. But the engineer lost his head and failed to get the pump started. Every second counted, as the smoke grew thicker, blacker, deeper.

At last the engine coughed into life and the hoses began to swell with water as the pressure built up. The fire seemed to be under control as the hoses played on it. Then, to everyone's horror, the jet of water died to a trickle and then stopped. As if to mock their efforts, the fire suddenly crackled into life again. The engineer was dragged screaming from the pump-house when it was discovered that he had failed to maintain the water level in the storage tanks. Despair overwhelmed the crowd; they cried, cursed or prayed, but to no avail. A huge column of flame shot into the grey dawn sky and the hotel was doomed. Efforts had to be made to prevent the fire from spreading. A chain of buckets was swiftly organised to save the grocery store on the opposite side of the street where the proprietor was vainly trying to keep the roof dampened. Clouds of steam rose from the roof and suddenly a tongue of flame licked it hungrily. Scorched horribly, the old man on the roof rolled down and fell into the street. A second later, the store was well ablaze.

As the conflagration spread with horrific speed, staff of the White Pass Railway vainly tried to salvage stores and records from the station. Then the station caught fire, then the freight shed. Soon the flames had engulfed the town centre, as frightened shopkeepers tried to evacuate their precious stocks. Robert himself tried to help the daughter of one storekeeper, as she humped sacks of potatoes. Then he spotted cans of petrol in the rear and, like a man possessed with demonic strength, he hoisted them out of the building to the relative safety of the street before they exploded.

The bank was located in a fairly isolated spot, but it soon became apparent that it, too, was threatened. De Gex called on his staff to help him douse

Germaine Bougeoin aged 24, 1911

Robert and Germaine on their wedding day, June 1913

Robert, Germaine and their best man, Frank C. Dodd (right) in the Luxembourg Gardens, Paris, June 1913

Robert and Germaine in the 'Rabbit Hutch', their Paris apartment, October 1913

Dream Haven, Lancieux,
Brittany, 1913

Shrimp netting at Lancieux,
1913, with Germaine (far
left), Robert (second from
right) and Archie Ker
Bruce (far right)

Germaine (left) and Carola
Armington in the sea at
Lancieux, 1914

On the beach below
Dream Haven

Robert in the uniform of the American Ambulance Corps, Lancre,
June 1915. The message on the back of this postcard to Germaine
reads: 'Was awfully glad to get your letter today. Have just got in
from the trenches and living again in the Chateau. Bon baisers,
Robert.'

Robert in the uniform of the Canadian Army Intelligence, 1918

Iris and Germaine, Dinard, 1922

Robert with his wife and daughter, Lancieux, 1922

the walls with the water from the four enormous rain-barrels outside, but even as they swished water up the sides the walls began to smoke ominously. Only the courage and agility of the old sea-dog prevented disaster. Leonard clambered on to the balcony with extraordinary skill and kept a constant deluge playing on the steaming walls. Even when the building opposite suddenly burst into flames, the bank miraculously survived. Even dainty little Mrs De Gex showed her mettle by lugging enormous buckets of water.

At daybreak the citizens surveyed the ghastly scene. Only the customs house, court house, post office and bank had survived the holocaust. A thriving and happy community had been reduced in a matter of hours to a charred and smoking eyesore.

Over the ensuing four months Whitehorse was rebuilt. An army of carpenters arrived, but even before the cinders had cooled down many merchants had erected tents and makeshift huts and were trying to do business as usual. Robert reckoned that they must have done pretty well out of the insurance, for the new stores were finer than the old and their stock richer. With the return of the miners in early summer the town was beginning to look better than ever. That was the most frantic period of Robert's entire career, and there was precious little time for tennis that summer. At the end of the 1906 season Harold Tylor was transferred to Dawson and Robert was promoted to teller in his place. Before Harold left, he and Robert compared their bank balances, and the latter was pleased to note that his savings had now passed the four-figure mark. Tylor was much better off, of course, and now well on the way to achieving his goal of matrimony. Shrewdly, Robert realised that it was only in the Yukon that he could have managed to save a thousand dollars so quickly. 'On the Outside it would have taken me five years.'

Robert's place on the ledger was taken by 'a champion tennis player, a handsome fellow, with a quick Irish wit and a fine singing voice', just the sort of fellow who would be an asset to the community. 'His gift of popularity made up for my lack.' They shared a taste for entertainment and between them they organised theatricals. Robert produced *The Area Belle*, the female parts being taken by members of the Mounted Police — which must have been a hilarious sight as they were all, to a man, fiercely moustached.

'My only claim to social consideration at this time was as an entertainer, and a pretty punk one at that. I could sing a song and vamp an accompaniment, but mainly I was a prize specimen of that ingenuous ass, the amateur reciter.' Robert's repertoire consisted of the perennial favourites of the period: 'Casey at the Bat', 'Gunga Din' and 'The Face on the Bar-room Floor'. They were effective enough, but the moment came when they were staled by repetition. When he was asked to participate in a church social, Robert wondered what to do. It was then that Stroller White, the editor of the *Whitehorse Star*, provided a solution. From time to time Robert had sent him samples of light verse which he had promptly published. Now he suggested that Robert should recite something of his own composition. 'Give us something about our own bit of earth. We sure would appreciate it. There's a rich paystreak waiting for someone to work. Why don't you go in and stake it?' Robert agreed to think this over.

> I went for a long walk, and did think, considerably. The idea intrigued me, but I hadn't the foggiest notion how I was going to proceed. All I knew was that I wanted to write a dramatic ballad suitable for recitation. I questioned very much if I would be able, for I started from nothing. I doubt if ever another successful ballad has been produced out of such unbelievable blankness. I said to myself: 'First, you have to have a theme. What about revenge? . . . Then you have to have a story to embody your theme. What about the old triangle, the faithless wife, the betrayed husband? Sure-fire stuff . . . Give it a setting in a Yukon saloon and make the two guys shoot it out . . . No, that would be too banal. Give a new twist to it. What about introducing music? Tell the story by musical suggestion. That would be different, maybe interesting.'[15]

Robert applied his usual 'synthetic approach to the job', but nothing tangible formed in his mind. It was a Saturday night, and from the various bars he heard sounds of revelry. The line suddenly popped into his mind: 'A bunch of the boys were whooping it up' and it stuck there. When he returned to the bank house everyone was asleep. Robert was on fire to get started so he crept downstairs to the darkened office and worked in his teller's cage. Then disaster struck, and the budding poet was almost cut down before his career was launched.

> I had not reckoned with the ledger-keeper in the guard-room. He awoke from a dream in which he had been playing single-handed against two tennis champions, and licking them. Suddenly he heard a noise near the safe. Burglars! Looking through the trap-door he saw a furtive shadow. He gripped his revolver, and closing his eyes, he pointed it at the skulking shade . . . Fortunately he was a poor shot or the *Shooting of Dan McGrew* might never have been written. No doubt some people will say: 'Unfortunately,' and I sympathize with them. Anyhow, with the sensation of a bullet whizzing past my head, and a detonation ringing in my ears, the ballad was achieved.

The ballad simply tumbled out of him, so that even he was amazed at his facility. 'It was as if someone was whispering in my ear.' As he composed stanza after stanza, the story seemed to evolve itself. By the time he crawled to bed at five in the morning, the ballad was in the bag. At the time, Robert was only concerned to make a dramatic monologue but, 'owing to the cuss-words', he was unable to recite it at the church concert after all. He tossed the manuscript into a drawer and promptly forgot all about it. What had come to him so easily, he reckoned could not have any literary value. Memories of his pompous lecturer at Glasgow University assailed him and he speculated as to what sarcastic, withering comment he might have made about Dangerous Dan and the Lady that's known as Lou. Robert consoled himself: 'Better the college of crude reality and the culture of the common lot.'

He wrote nothing more for a month, and the second ballad was the result of an accident. He gatecrashed a party one evening and found himself 'staring gloomily at a fat fellow across the table'. He was an important mining man from Dawson and he scarcely acknowledged his introduction to the little bank clerk. He puffed away at his fat cigar, then leaned forward and said suddenly, 'I'll tell you a story Jack London never got.' Then he regaled the company with a yarn about a man who had cremated his pal. The story had a surprise punch-line that occasioned much laughter. Robert, however, did not join in; 'I had a feeling that here was a decisive moment of destiny'. Then he added smugly: 'The fat man who ignored me went his way to bankruptcy, but he had pointed me the road to fortune.' Thirty years later, of course, Mike Mahoney would claim that *he* was the inspiration of Robert's second great ballad; shortly before, he had made an epic trek of four hundred miles through the wilderness, carrying the frozen corpse of Judge Hume and fighting off a pack of hungry wolves most of the way.

Feverish with impatience to get started, Robert excused himself from the party. Instead of going straight home, he took the woodland trail, his mind seething with excitement and a strange ecstasy.

> As I started in: *There are strange things done in the midnight sun*, verse after verse developed with scarce a check. As I clinched my rhymes I tucked the finished stanza away in my head and tackled the next. For six hours I tramped those silver glades, and when I rolled happily into bed, my ballad was cinched. Next day, with scarcely any effort of memory, I put it on paper. Word and rhyme came easily to heel. My moonlight improvisation was secure, and though I did not know it 'McGee' was to be the keystone of my success.[16]

Actual composition seems to have been not quite so spontaneous, for the Yukon Archives preserve a number of Robert's manuscripts and it is obvious how much work went into his most famous poems. It is revealing to note the extent to which Robert polished and refined the ballads before they evolved in their final form. Just how different this could be is demonstrated by the earliest version of 'The Cremation of Sam McGee', which begins:

> There are strange things done after half past one
> By the men who search for gold,
> The arctic histories have their eerie mysteries
> That would make your feet go cold.
> The Aurora Borealis has seen where Montreal is,
> But the queerest it ever did spot
> Was the night on the periphery of Lake McKiflery
> I cremated Sam McKlot.

Klinck[17] deduced from the narrative in *Ploughman of the Moon* that Robert wrote 'Dan McGrew' in the autumn of 1906, which would have placed it a few months before Christmas that year when Robert took the momentous decision to publish. Indeed, this is suggested by the tale of the gun-toting ledger-keeper which places composition after Harold Tylor left for Dawson. Robert, however, then contradicts himself, the narrative in his autobiography declaring composition of the early ballads over a much longer period. One is left with the inescapable conclusion that the story of the attempted shooting of Robert Service is apocryphal. It first appeared in *Ploughman of the Moon* and was frequently repeated in newspaper and magazine articles in later years, but it may be significant that the ledger-clerk was never identified, far less came forward to confirm the story.

'Dan McGrew' and 'Sam McGee' were obviously written in autumn, but the ensuing passage implies that composition actually took place at the onset of winter 1904, soon after Robert's arrival in the territory, with a month between them. According to this account, Robert carelessly put his second ballad with the first and went about his humdrum duties; but on the long tramps through the woods he now carried a volume of Kipling 'and would rant poetic stanzas to chipmunks and porcupines'. He then goes on to say that 'one early spring' he stood on the heights of Miles Canyon, with a magnificent panorama around him. Suddenly the line *I have gazed on naked grandeur where there's nothing else to gaze on* came into his head and this led, in turn, to the poem which he entitled 'The Call of the Wild' inspired by the stupendous scenery above the Whitehorse Rapids. 'Early spring' in this context can only have been in 1905. In the two months that followed (which would bring us to the beginning of the sub-arctic summer) Robert wrote something almost every day, and always during those lonely walks through the woods. 'I looked forward to them because I knew the Voice would whisper in my ear, and that I would just as surely express my feelings.'

If we are to accept his own word for it, 1905 was Robert's *annus mirabilis*. He was deliriously happy. 'Sometimes I thought I would burst with sheer delight.' Words and rhymes came to him without any effort. 'I bubbled verse like an artesian well.' In this summer period he wrote 'The Spell of the Yukon', 'The Law of the Yukon' and many others, 'a solitary pedestrian pounding out his rhymes from the intense gusto of living.'

As he finished each poem he filed it away with the others and forgot it. It never occurred to him that his work might have any value. 'It was just a diversion, maybe a foolish one. The impulse to express my rapture in a world of beauty and grandeur was stronger than myself, and I did it with no thought of publication.'

Significantly, 'nature was not enough'. Robert returned to his original theme by concentrating on human nature and its foibles and weaknesses. He wrote of the life of the mining camp, of the rough miners and the dance-hall girls. At this time, the Revd John Pringle of the Presbyterian faith was waging a campaign to close the dance-halls and stamp out the prostitution that thrived therein. His one-man campaign had a political dimension that reverberated all the way to Prime Minister Laurier in Ottawa.[18] It became a hotly debated matter for most of 1906–7 and the citizens of Whitehorse and Dawson were fiercely divided over Pringle's tirades against the calumny and corruption of the public officials who turned a blind eye to the immorality and lawlessness of the territory. Robert, with his fascination for vice, deliberately set out to chronicle the 'Red Light atmosphere', but Pringle's vituperations may have led him to keep quiet about his racy ballads. Every day his pile of manuscripts was growing higher and higher but he dumped his shirts on top and forgot them. 'Then, as suddenly as it had begun, the flow of inspiration ceased. My bits of verse lay where I left them, neglected and forgotten *for more than a year*' (my italics).

Then, one day in the late autumn or early winter of 1906, Robert chanced upon his manuscripts again. He regarded the pile bitterly; how much time he had wasted in idle scribbling! Then, as he read them over, a thought crossed his mind. He gave the bundle to Mrs De Gex to glance at. 'Some of it's not so dusty' was her verdict. Why did Robert not make a little book out of it, and give it to his friends for Christmas? It would make a nice souvenir of the Yukon. Of course, he would have to leave out such rough things as the McGrew and the McGee poems, and a lot of things like 'The Harpy' and 'My Madonna' which offended her sense of delicacy. Robert agreed with her, but in the end he decided to send the whole lot for publication. The fortuitous advent of a hundred-dollar Christmas bonus clinched the matter. Rather than add this unexpected windfall to his growing nest-egg, Robert decided in a weak moment of vanity to blow the lot on the little book.

> I would squander it in egregious authorship. I would herd my flock into a snug fold. I visioned a tiny volume of verse which I would present to pals, who would receive it with that embarrassment with which one accepts books from amateur authors. I would get a hundred copies printed, and maybe during my lifetime I could bestow them, with apologetic wistfulness, on my kindly acquaintances.

Before staking his hundred dollars on such a rash venture, however, Robert approached a local businessman, a fellow Scot, suggesting that he might share the risk. For fifty dollars Robert was prepared to part with a half interest. When the businessman discovered that it was a volume of poetry he exclaimed, 'D'ye take me for daft? Who buys poetry in this blasted burg? Not a damned soul.' He pointed to a shelf full of similar volumes at the back of his shop which he had never managed to shift in years. 'Now if it were stories like that Rex Beach writes, well, I might consider it. But poetry, laddie, oh, no . . .'

> He was so rude I went away like a whipped dog. Yet years after, when he realized his fifty dollars would have brought him in about fifty thousand, I think it broke his heart. I know it would have broken mine if I had been obliged to give him half the dough that book brought me in royalties.[19]

In the years since 'Dan McGrew' and 'Sam McGee' first saw the light of day, there was endless speculation about their origins. Sam McGee was a real person, whose name Robert lifted from the bank ledger, but there was never a Dan McGrew. Nevertheless, some of the lesser characters in that ballad were real enough. There really was a Malamute Saloon, and the Ragtime Kid was Hartley Claude Myrick, born in England in 1885. The Kid's mother became a piano teacher in Chicago, and from her he acquired a thorough training at an early age. When he was thirteen he accompanied his father to the Klondike and later played piano in all the honky-tonks and dives from Dawson to Skagway, hence his nickname. He was working in Whitehorse in 1906–7 and knew Robert well in that period. Thanks to the poet, the epithet Ragtime Kid stuck to him all his life, though he left the High North in 1916 and moved to Seattle where he died in July 1950.[20]

Even stranger was the true story of the Lady known as Lou. In real life she was the cabaret singer Lulu Johnson who was well known as a performer at various dance-halls and saloons in Alaska and the Yukon territories at the turn of the century. She was drowned when the Canadian Pacific steamer *Princess Sophia* sank in the Lynn Canal on 25 October 1918 with the loss of all hands.[21]

CHAPTER 7

FIRST BOOKS

I have no doubt at all the Devil grins,
  As seas of ink I spatter.
Ye gods, forgive my 'literary' sins —
  The other kind don't matter.

Dedication in *Songs of a Sourdough* (1907)

ALTHOUGH THE *Whitehorse Star* COULD HAVE PRINTED THE
book, Robert sent his poems Outside.

> So I arranged my pieces, retyped them and sent them, care of Papa, to a
> firm of publishers who did amateur work. I remember so well the
> morning I posted that envelope. 'Good riddance to bad rubbish,' I
> thought, as I dropped it in the letter box, and instantly regretted my act.
> I did not register the envelope, I felt so careless and indifferent, and told
> myself: 'Silly ass! Why didn't you burn the stuff?'[1]

The Services were living in Alberta at the time, not Toronto as Klinck
surmised from the simple fact that that was where the publisher was.[2] In his
autobiography Robert was maddeningly laconic about the actual manner in
which his first book was produced, neither naming the publisher nor explaining
how it came to be printed. The fact that the manuscript was sent 'care of Papa'

implies that Robert did not know who to send it to, and trusted his father to find a printer for him. No doubt Robert Senior scanned the advertisements in the newspapers and selected the Methodist Book and Publishing House in Toronto because it offered a service in vanity publishing as a sideline to the main business of producing religious works. The firm was headed by William Briggs and was, at the time, the largest book publisher in Canada. Briggs often brought out books of poetry for their authors, invariably at their expense, for such little volumes were not considered commercially viable from a publisher's standpoint. Doubtless some of the books by 'padded poets' that Robert saw on the shelves of the store in Whitehorse bore the Briggs imprint — if Robert had taken the trouble to enquire.

At any rate, the manuscript was sent to Briggs in December 1906. The following month Edward Caswell, the firm's literary editor, went down to the wholesale department and handed a set of galley proofs to twenty-three-year-old Robert Bond saying, 'We're bringing out a book of poetry for a man who lives in the Yukon. You're going to the west coast — you may be able to sell some to the trade out there. It's the author's publication and we're printing it for him. Try to sell some for him, if you can.'[3]

Bond's sample trunks had already gone to the station, as he was leaving that very evening for his annual trip west. At the last moment he shoved the proof sheets into his pocket and thought no more about them. Certainly a new book of Canadian poetry was nothing to be excited about. As he was sitting in the dining-car that night, however, he suddenly remembered the proofs and, having nothing better to do, he began reading them. When he got to 'The Cremation of Sam McGee' he became so enthralled that he forgot his meal, and on reaching the punch-line he burst out laughing. The man seated opposite, a commercial traveller, was intrigued. 'You must have something good there, brother. Let's have it.'

'It's poetry,' said Bond. The traveller's face fell, but he asked, 'What made you laugh? Bond replied, 'It's unusual, and it's Canadian, and it might even sell.'

'Well, try it on me,' suggested the traveller. 'What's it all about?'

So Bond read it to him. The traveller giggled, then burst out laughing so heartily that he coughed till he choked and had to leave the dining-car. As Bond passed the smoking-room from the diner he heard him telling his friends about it. Bond came back later on for a smoke and at once was asked to read 'Sam McGee' to the crowd. As he recited the poem the crowd grew, until there was standing room only. When he finished, bedlam broke loose, everyone talking at once. Some of the men even quoted lines that had stuck in their minds. Then the inevitable happened. Someone came in late, wondering what all the commotion was about, and Bond was compelled to read the poem again. He gave several more renderings of 'Sam McGee' before the night was over.

He had it off by heart before he reached Fort William, his first stop. This would be the true test; would he be able to sell a book of Canadian verse in profitable quantities? As soon as Bond mentioned a new book of Canadian poetry, Mackenzie the bookseller cut him short, 'We'll skip that' and went on to discuss more saleable fare, such as W.H. Drummond's *Habitant* poems. Bond saw that he was not going to get far. To read an entire poem, with the kick in the last line, was going to take too much time in the bookseller's sample room where Mackenzie had allocated no more than an hour to all the wares Bond had to show. Bond waited till he saw Mackenzie in the store later in the day and then raised the subject again. This time Mackenzie said, 'Is this the poetry you were reading on the train to some travellers? They told me about it.' Bond nodded, and started to recite the poem, but they were interrupted by customers. Bond never finished the recitation, but Mackenzie said that he would take five copies. This was a promising start for, in a place like Fort William, the usual order for Canadian poetry was one or two copies, but more often than not none at all.

Shrewdly Bond realised that it would be impossible to sell the book cold. The secret lay in word of mouth, so wherever he went he lost no opportunity to recite the poems. By this method he managed to place a few copies with almost every bookstore across the country. At Portage la Prairie the bookseller was an Englishman named Bagshaw who riled Bond by saying that Billy Bell (the doyen of Canadian book salesmen) would *really* sell the book. However, he let Bond recite McGee and became enthusiastic, placing an order for seven copies. 'I remember the number well because it was so unusual.'

At the hotel in Indian Head, Saskatchewan, Bond ran into a group of travelling entertainers. The elocutionist of the group overheard him reciting 'Sam McGee' in the lounge and asked if she could borrow the proof sheets to learn the poem so that she could recite it that night in the village hall. The idea was appealing, but Bond was worried that this might infringe the copyright and reluctantly demurred. Nevertheless, it got the book talked about. The book was entitled *Songs of a Sourdough* but it was not till he reached Linton Brothers' bookshop in Calgary that Bond learned that a sourdough was a gold prospector who had spent at least one year in the Yukon, the name being derived from the use of fermenting yeast to make bread in the mining camps. Jim Linton had been an old-timer out west and was so captivated by the book that he promptly ordered twenty-five — Bond's largest order up to that time.

Now Bond began pushing the book harder than ever. At Lethbridge, Alberta, he got the druggist (who was also a bookseller) to listen while he read

'The Shooting of Dan McGrew' as well as 'Sam McGee'. He was so impressed that he asked to borrow the galley proofs, to read them at lunchtime to the men at the club. That afternoon, when he returned the proofs, the druggist placed an order for thirty-six copies. As a result, there were probably more copies of the original author's edition in that town than anywhere else in Canada. Many years later Bond advertised in the *Lethbridge Herald*, offering to purchase one of these copies, but without success.

Bond was in Revelstoke, a railway town in British Columbia, when he received his first sample copy of the book itself, early in March. His first impression was most unfavourable. 'It was a poor-looking, thin book, bound in green cloth, marked Author's Edition.' But more important than its appearance was the price. It was listed at seventy-five cents retail. Bond wrote back to William Briggs immediately saying that he had been selling it at a dollar. Furthermore, if the accounts department were to check the figures, they would see that the first edition of five hundred was almost sold out. Bond offered the opinion that it was the first book of Canadian poetry the firm had published that had good commercial possibilities, and urged Briggs to take over publication on a royalty basis.

It was on Bond's recommendation therefore that Briggs wrote to Robert, returning his hundred-dollar cheque. Robert's immediate reaction on seeing his cheque inside the envelope was to deduce that the Methodist Book and Publishing House did not wish to print his poems as they were too coarse. He was preoccupied with bank business when the mail arrived, and had no time to read the long letter that accompanied the cheque, but his feelings were of 'relief tinctured with chagrin'. He had been about to make a fool of himself. 'Well, I would burn the darned stuff. So much the better.'

Later that day, however, he took up the letter:

What was this? With a growing sense of stupefaction, I read. With a sense of unbelief, I re-read. The words danced before my eyes. But it was a dance of joy. And at the same moment my whole being seemed lit up with rapture. For the letter told quite a story. It seemed that when they sent the manuscript to their composing-room, the foreman noticed how quickly the typesetting had been completed. 'The fastest job ever done in the office,' he said. He smelled a rat, as it were. Taking the galley proofs to the office, he had shown them around. One of the travellers had scanned them carelessly, then become suddenly enthusiastic. He was an amateur reciter, and it was the McGee ballad that attracted him. He said: 'Here, let me see . . . This looks like the real thing.' He had declaimed it to the staff with great effect. Then he cried: 'Say, just lemme have those proofs. Maybe I can *sell* this stuff.'

He did. He went around the trade reciting McGee, and booking orders so fast it made his head swim. He dropped everything else to push the book . . . This was the story the publishers told me at some length in their letter. They told it with jubilation in the telling. Then they added that they had sold seventeen hundred copies from the galley proofs alone, and only in their city. Would I allow them to be my publishers, and they would pay me a ten per cent royalty on a dollar book?[4]

Robert was probably quoting from memory, coloured no doubt by the way the legend had grown over the years. In fact no copies were sold in Toronto till May 1907, and it was Bond, just back from his western trip, who was given the job of taking samples round the bookshops. Reaction to *Songs of a Sourdough* was understandably muted in the metropolis. One bookseller looked over the book and said, 'You know, old man, this isn't our kind of book, but I'll take two copies'. Before Christmas, however, he was asking for quotations on lots of a hundred.

Briggs bought the book on a royalty basis and thus Robert did not have to pay for the printing of the first edition. And it stayed at a dollar retail, so that the author got ten cents instead of the seven and a half which Briggs had originally envisaged. After the author's modest edition, two other impressions, each of a thousand copies, were produced before the first copy actually went on sale late in March, but before the year was out it ran to fifteen impressions, each one larger than its predecessor.

Meanwhile, Bond was still on his sales trip. When he had got as far as Vancouver Island, he decided to take the steamer from Victoria to Seattle, the jumping-off point for Alaska and the Yukon. In Seattle he sounded out a bookseller, but the latter did not like the idea of importing books from Canada and was not sure about customs duty. He told Bond that he would think about it. After leaving a copy of the book with him, Bond went off; but later he remembered that selling a book in the United States before it was copyrighted might affect the chances of getting a copyright later, so he retrieved the book quickly, much to the bookseller's annoyance and disappointment. When the book was published later that year in the United States, by Barse & Hopkins in New York and E. Stern & Company in Philadelphia, it appeared under the title of *The Spell of the Yukon and Other Verses*. It was also published, under its original title, by T. Fisher Unwin in London.

Robert's reaction to the offer of royalties was immediate. 'I telegraphed acceptance so quick I did not give them a chance to change their minds.' Robert himself recorded his feelings on receipt of his first royalty cheque, and Bond recalled the letter which the author had sent to Briggs. Robert suggested that there might be some mistake, and ventured to ask how long the royalties might continue. Never in his wildest dreams could he have realised that he would still be earning royalties on that little book more than half a century later. Estimates of sales of *Songs of a Sourdough* vary widely. Fisher Unwin produced the twenty-third impression in 1910 and the thirty-sixth in 1917, but new editions continued, under the imprints of Ryerson of Toronto, Dodd Mead of New York and Ernest Benn of London, for many years thereafter. Dodd Mead claimed that three million copies had been sold by 1940; Robert himself, in a letter to Bond written early in 1958, more modestly put the total at 'far more than a million'. This accords with the figure of a hundred thousand dollars quoted in his autobiography (1945), although he was earlier quoted in various newspaper interviews as saying that 'Dan McGrew' and 'Sam McGee' had earned him half a million dollars.

In the first parcel post when rail communications reopened in the spring of 1907, Robert received the package containing the two dozen copies he had ordered for himself.

I gave them away apologetically, and they were received with embarrassment. People in that town hardly ever read verse, and now I was putting them in a spot. They would be forced to scan my book, to pay me the compliments politeness demanded. That was taking a mean advantage of friendship. I almost felt like begging their pardon for bothering them with my egregious effort.

Yet strange to say, even the least literary of my friends seemed to find something extenuating in it, while a few were quite enthusiastic. People whom I had never suspected of poetic leanings impulsively shook my hand. A lawyer we called the Judge, who up to now had never noticed me, said with feeling: 'My boy, I've read your book. It's out of sight. I mean it — out of sight.' Coming from an old whisky soak I appreciated the compliment.

Robert's own feelings, when he 'caressed this bratling of my muse, were, I suppose, like the rapture of a mother over her first-born'. He gazed with awe and emotion at the 'slim, drab, insignificant volume'. Immediately he was struck with the thought that, by this act, he had achieved immortality. 'I would rot in my shroud, but it would remain a testimony to my brief breath of being.' Shortly afterwards, copies went on sale in the shops in Whitehorse. Even the canny Scot who had declined a half share in the venture had taken twenty copies, on the understanding that Robert would take them off his hands if he got stuck with them. When he sold out he had the cheek to approach Robert and scrounge a dozen of his author's copies at the trade price.

But within three days he was back again to say he was sold out and had telegraphed to the publisher for fifty by the first mail.

Songs of a Sourdough, in its title, was true to Robert's penchant for alliteration, a habit he never lost. It was well named for it consisted mainly of lyrics by an experienced resident of a mining community, rather than ballads about the miners themselves. A sourdough was officially defined as someone who had spent an entire year in the Yukon; unofficially, you qualified for the epithet if you had shot a bear and slept with a squaw, though some wag claimed that most sourdoughs would have preferred to shoot the squaw and sleep with the bear.

Despite Robert's claims in his autobiography that *Songs of a Sourdough* were written at Whitehorse in several months, it is obvious that composition was spread over a much longer period. At least two pieces had already appeared in print, 'The Song of the Wage-Slave' in a Los Angeles newspaper in 1898 and 'The Old Log Cabin' which had appeared in the *Whitehorse Star* of 10 May 1902. Interestingly, for someone who professed to have no interest in the Yukon at that time, Robert had sent the poem to Stroller White from Cowichan.[5] Others, such as 'The March of the Dead', must have been written while the Boer War of 1899–1902 was in progress, whereas 'The Younger Son' and 'Tramps' reflected the imperial sentiment of British Columbia at the turn of the century. Throughout the book there was a considerable scattering of pieces that clearly demonstrate the influence of Poe, Verlaine and other poets whom Robert had read years earlier.

Robert did not arrange his verses in chronological order. Instead he began the volume with 'The Spell of the Yukon', followed by 'The Heart of the Sourdough'. Such poems as 'The Law of the Yukon', 'The Call of the Wild' and 'The Lure of Little Voices' followed. 'Dan McGrew' and 'Sam McGee' occupied the place of honour, in the middle of the book, but there were few other dramatic monologues. Even in 'The Parson's Son' and 'The Rhyme of the Remittance Man', balladry served the purposes of song rather than of narrative. To appreciate them fully one must read them aloud; mere silent reading off the page does not bring to life the rich cadences and the lyrical quality of these pieces.

The first major review of the book appeared in *Saturday Night* in June 1907. The reviewer used the words 'Canadian Kipling'; the term caught on, others used it, and Robert was saddled with the epithet for the rest of his life. He himself once admitted that he 'bowed the knee' to Kipling, but in truth Kipling was only one of many of the influences on Robert. Indeed, he was eclectic in the sources of his literary models, though, strangely, the one influence conspicuous by his absence was Burns.

In Whitehorse reaction to the book was mixed:

Many thought me a presumptuous young pup, trying to exploit the town to my profit. To some I was a freak, to others a fourflusher. A few liked it and complimented me mildly, half afraid to show too much appreciation. No one saw in it a record-breaking success.

Robert's main antagonism came from the church. The first to express disapproval was one of his fellow deacons who called at the bank one morning to complain that his wife had been reading the book. She and the other ladies of the sewing-circle thought that it was a pity that Robert had only written about the bad women of the town, and said nothing about the good ones. Robert responded mildly that we took the good ones for granted, adding that vice had more colour than virtue. 'I write to please the public, and, though I have nothing against virtue, I've frequently remarked that a lot of people look on it as rather a bore.' The deacon was speechless. Robert half-expected him to demand his resignation from the church, but he 'clung to my collection plate like a drowning sailor to a life-buoy. It seemed my sole hold on respectability.' Certainly those who knew him were astounded at the raw earthiness and the Rabelaisian humour of those pieces which, nowadays, are regarded as his best work and classics of their genre. Who could ever imagine that the quiet-spoken, rather diffident little bank clerk, always so prim and proper in his high, starched collars, would be capable of such verse? The citizens of Whitehorse, or the poetry-reading ones at least, preferred the high moral tone of 'Comfort' whose punch-line was the banal 'You've got God, and God is love.'

Public opinion changed, however, with the opening of the season, when citizens returned from the south with the news that the book was a best-seller. It was in all the bookshops and people were talking about it. Robert was reputed to be making hundreds of dollars out of it and he observed cynically that, to most people, money was the standard of success. 'If a book sold well, why, it must be good. If a man made money, well, he must be smart.' In high summer, when the tourists arrived, respect for Robert increased. Every tourist had a copy of the book and quoted it with enthusiasm. 'They crowded to the bank, pushing it through my wicket with requests for autographs. The other members of the staff sicked them on to me, deriving a sardonic glee from my embarrassment.'

To his dismay, Robert discovered that he was regarded as one of the tourist attractions, perhaps the main one. Blushingly he tried to evade his admirers and fled to the woodlands whenever he could. But in his teller's cage at the bank there was no escape from rubbernecking literati. Thankfully, the tourist season was a short one and soon Whitehorse settled down for yet another long winter. He had been looking forward to the tranquillity of the sparkling zero weather, but one day De Gex announced that Robert was due three months' leave, his first break from Whitehorse in three years. He was compelled to take a long holiday *with* pay. Robert bade goodbye to Whitehorse with real regret. In the autumn of 1907 he retraced his steps to Skagway and thence by steamer to Vancouver. The city was wreathed in fog and rain the day he landed, and it remained depressingly fog-bound throughout his long vacation. Robert lived in a boarding-house 'with twenty boarders and one bath'. His depression was compounded by the unpleasant discovery that his book was little known. The tourists had told him that he was a celebrity Outside, but in truth he was 'a small frog in a big puddle'. Disconsolately, Robert wandered round the park in the cheerless drizzle and revisited the scenes of his former hardships. In the raw, damp weather he caught a string of colds from which, in the Yukon, he had been immune.

Robert was due for re-assignment and he dreaded the prospect. He desperately wanted to get back to the Far North. He wished to write more about it, to interpret it. 'I felt I had another book in me, and would be desperate if I did not get a chance to do it.' At length, his holiday came to an end and he had to report to the Inspector, the same 'gruff character' who had interviewed him more than four years earlier. He made no reference to Robert's literary effort. This was no surprise as Robert had soon found that officials of the bank resented his 'trespass into the Land of Letters'; but he had the feeling that the Inspector *had* read the book and wanted to give him a chance to write another. There was a twinkle in his eye as he said, 'Well, you'll be sorry to hear you're going back to the North. I have decided to send you to Dawson as teller.'

Robert was to report there on 8 April 1908. Once more he boarded the steamer for Skagway, then took the train to Whitehorse. He was buoyed up with 'serene happiness and faith in the future'. He was keen to get to Dawson. 'I wanted to write the story of the Yukon from the inside, and the essential story of the Yukon was that of the Klondike.' No one had done it, in verse or prose. Perhaps he would be the one to work out that vein of rich ore. Nursing the conceit that he might become the Bret Harte of the Northland, he journeyed on. In summer the trip from Whitehorse could be accomplished in comfort, by steamer along 460 miles of the Yukon River. In late March, when Robert left Whitehorse, the river was still frozen over and the snow lay thick on the ground.

> From Whitehorse to Dawson was six days by open sleigh. It was then I realized the vastness of the land and its unconquerable reservation. The temperature was about thirty below zero. With bells jingling, we swept through a fairyland of crystalline loveliness, each pine bough freighted with lace and gems, and a stillness that made silence seem like sound. Day after day, serene and sunny solitude, as we hunched in our coon coats, half doped by the monotony of bitter brightness.
>
> Our breath froze on our fur collars; our lashes and eyebrows were

hoar; our cheeks pinky bright, as we took shallow breaths of the Arctic air. Every now and then the driver would have to break icicles out of the nostrils of his horses. Sometimes the sleigh would upset, and often we would have to get out and push through waist-high snowdrifts. Twice a day we stopped at roadhouses to change horses. There we would find a meal prepared and be obliged to eat. As we had no exercise, we suffered from surfeited stomachs and had to take laxatives. Meals and beds cost two dollars each. When we woke up in the morning we would say: 'Six o'clock, six dollars.'[6]

The overland trip from Whitehorse to Dawson, the longest continuous stage-coach journey in the world, lay almost four hundred miles through a frozen wilderness. The coach, mounted on runners, jolted, slipped and slid up and down steep and icy hillsides, over frozen rivers and lakes, stopping every fifteen or twenty miles at roadhouses where the team of six horses was changed. Robert was fortunate that his trip was accomplished in six days; ten days or a fortnight was more usual, especially in the depths of winter when the snow lay deep on the ground. The roadhouses were crude cabins where passengers of both sexes bedded down for the night in a single dormitory. The toilet facilities were even more primitive, and many a lady traveller never recovered from the trauma of seeing a row of bare buttocks protruding below the skimpy hem of the hessian curtain that fronted the line of communal latrines.

Dawson City, named after George M. Dawson, Director of the Canadian Geological Survey, had sprung dramatically out of the frozen wilderness following the discovery of gold at Bonanza Creek on 17 August 1896. Within two years, at the height of the gold rush, Dawson had a population of almost forty thousand, making it the largest Canadian city west of Winnipeg. When gold was discovered at Nome in Alaska in August 1899, Dawson emptied rapidly. By 1901 the population had dropped to 9,142; seven years later it stood at 4,000. Though a shadow of its former self, it was still a much larger town than Whitehorse. In 1898 it had become the capital of the Yukon Territory and in Edwardian times the palatial governor's mansion was only one of the many splendid structures to be seen. The city was ravaged by fire in 1898 and again in 1899; each time it arose phoenix-like, more splendid than before.

George Washington Carmack who, with two Indians, Skookum Jim and Tagish Charlie, made the first strike, is believed to have extracted forty million dollars' worth of gold in 1898 alone. In one short stretch along the creek there were more than thirty claims worth over a million apiece. Even the smallest claim, the fabulous Dick Lowe Fraction barely eighty feet across at its greatest width, had yielded over half a million dollars for the drunken muleskinner that staked it. Colossal fortunes were made, and lost, in the Klondike. In the wake of the miners and prospectors came the businessmen, the conmen, the swindlers and the hucksters. Hundreds of prostitutes plied their trade along Paradise Alley; broad-rumped girls imported from Belgium were the most popular. Champagne cost sixty dollars a bottle, and in the season of 1898 alone some 120,000 gallons of it were consumed. Those who struck it rich seemed to have an 'easy come, easy go' attitude to their spectacular, new-found wealth. Nigger Jim Daugherty had a $2,500 husky team to draw his luxury sleigh with its built-in bar. Coatless Curly Munro spent $4,320 on dog food for his six puppies. Clarence Berry laid out $400 a ton for hay to feed the only Jersey cow in town, so that he could have fresh milk daily. Others put their gold into building sumptuous dance-halls and theatres. In an orgy of building after the 1899 fire Dawson became a city of plate-glass windows and carpeted floors, of Turkish baths and linen napery, of silver and crystal, grand pianos, electricity.[7] But the city had passed its peak. Then news of the discovery of gold on the beaches of Nome reached Dawson and in a single week that August over eight thousand people left the town, never to return.

In its heyday Dawson was essentially a rumbustious American city, where the Fourth of July was just as important a public holiday as Dominion Day three days earlier, resulting in a four-day binge of prodigiously riotous proportions. By 1908, with almost nine-tenths of its former population gone, Dawson was more conventionally Canadian in character. Goldmining was still its main industry and the branch of the Canadian Bank of Commerce, much larger and more opulent than its Whitehorse counterpart, was largely concerned with the purchase of gold dust and nuggets at sixteen dollars the ounce troy.

Instead of rooming with the manager and his wife, as he had done in Whitehorse, Robert now found himself, with a dozen young bachelors, in the bank mess, a low building which had originally been the bank. At the height of the gold rush the yellow dust was handled rather carelessly and it was rumoured that there was enough of it under the floorboards to make a fortune. When the bank moved to its present location after the First World War, Lyman Munger extracted several hundred dollars' worth of gold dust from the soil under the old floor.

The Overland Stage, otherwise known as the Whitehorse Sleigh, ran fortnightly in winter bringing in the mail. In spring it ran weekly and carried passengers as well. Robert, in fact, was on board the second passenger run of 1908, and in due course the list of passengers was published in the *Dawson Daily News*. Had he been on the first run, at the beginning of March, he would have encountered the customs official H.D. Stammers *and wife*. Stammers, an Australian, had been shacked up with Montreal Marie who had previously plied her trade in Paradise Alley. It was Marie who had raised the money to let Stammers go Outside for a long overdue holiday, leaving her and their two children for three months. When he was Outside, however, he acquired a pretty young wife, which set all the tongues wagging. Marie took her two little girls and returned to her cabin in Lousetown (the largest red-light district north of the Forty-ninth Parallel) and once more hung out her sign. Mrs Stammers died in childbirth that autumn while Stammers himself was shot in a hold-up. What became of Montreal Marie is not known, but she was immortalised in several of Robert's later ballads.

Robert arrived in Dawson at night, to be met by a lugubrious youth, resembling a young Abe Lincoln, who turned out to be the bank's gold-buyer. On the way to the mess, Robert's one-man reception committee warned him that his reputation for bawdiness and booze had gone ahead of him, but that the mess would not tolerate profanity. 'We have meetings and sing hymns every evening,' he said primly. 'No doubt you will join us in prayer.' Robert assented, willing to be agreeable. On arriving at the mess, however, he found a dozen fellows in a long, low room, some standing at the bar, others playing cards, one playing the piano. As Robert entered he was greeted with cries of 'Here comes the bloody Bard'. Then there was a shout, 'Hail to the lousy Bard'. 'The Bard of Bawdyville,' announced the pianist, 'come to poison our innocent minds with his vicious verse.' Robert took the ragging with a good grace and downed the glass of whisky thrust into his hand — his first drink in more than three years. The police barracks was next door and the Mounties added to the generally convivial atmosphere. When the mail was delivered later the same evening by old Alec Ross, the bank's messenger, bringing Robert's first annual royalty cheque, he celebrated the thousand dollars by ordering three bottles of whisky for the mess; but soon he reverted to his customary abstemiousness and applied himself to saving as much money as possible. His goal of five thousand dollars now seemed much nearer. Incidentally, Alec Ross, though occupying a humble position in the bank, left over $100,000 to his relatives on his death.

Robert had just got off to sleep on his first night when he was unceremoniously dragged out of bed and carried down to the mess-hall where the party had been enlivened by the presence of two of the dance-hall girls who had expressed a wish to meet the poet. The unusually literate whores were Dogface Kitty and Spanish Jeanette, a young lady who, when she said that she hailed from Castile, provoked the riposte from one client, 'Castile? Hell! You sure don't get to the castile [soap] often enough!' Robert, clad only in pyjamas, was introduced to the girls, plied with whisky again and induced to sing some of his songs at the piano. 'It was in the wee small hours when I was able to sneak off to bed, yet still the boys were whooping it up.'

The Accountant in this branch was a bookish young man who presided over dinner in the mess with his nose buried in a novel and never uttered a word. He and Robert became firm friends because they shared an interest in poetry and literature. He had an extensive library and Robert had the run of it. He introduced Robert to A.E. Houseman, lending him *A Shropshire Lad.*

On his first working day Robert was interviewed by the Manager, a man of about his own age who addressed him crisply by his surname and gave him his orders. Robert sirred him in return, but inwardly he was seething.

> I have always resented stuffed-shirtism. Why should a man who drinks with you at a bar assume an attitude of dignity behind his roll-top desk? Dignity is the camouflage of charlatans. What man is dignified with his pants down, or in the act of perpetuating his species? Dignified men are hypocrites and frauds. No man who has the honesty to see himself as he really is can be anything but humble. Only fools take themselves seriously . . .[8]

Suddenly it dawned on Robert that this new-found streak of rebelliousness was brought about by the cheque nestling in his pocket. Another cheque or two like that and he would soon be able to chuck banking for ever. The interview was soon terminated, but later in the day the Manager came to him, bearing the cheque which Robert had paid into his account. 'All this money,' he said. 'What does it represent?'

'Verse,' replied Robert. 'Just verse.'

The Manager looked bewildered. 'It's a strange world,' he sighed and scratched his head.

Thereafter Robert redoubled his efforts to save money. He cultivated thrift to the point of frugality and gloated over his growing bank balance. It was not the love of money that made him save so eagerly; it was the hope of freedom which it represented. 'If I achieved a reputation of a tight-wad, it was put down to my Scotch nationality.' His one indulgence was a weekly cigar, lit on his way to church. By the time he reached the door, however, it was only half smoked so he would stick it in the snow and retrieve it after the service. 'The others chaffed me about this, but at the time it seemed to me a natural thing to do.'

After his book was published in the United States Robert began receiving monthly royalty cheques from New York and Philadelphia. He could count on cheques for twenty-five dollars, but suddenly they jumped to fifty, then a hundred, then a hundred and fifty. There they levelled out. In 1908 he earned more than four thousand dollars from his royalties, compared with his bank salary of nine hundred. Increasingly Robert questioned his continuing role at the bank. As a teller, he felt unsuccessful and far from happy. He who hated responsibility was accountable for huge sums of money every day. He agonised over the currency in his care and his fear of making a mistake made him overcautious, so that he was slow in paying out. At the close of business each day his nervousness in balancing the cash amounted to fear. 'I seldom got a first-shot balance and generally had to hunt for a shortage.' This meant a feverish and anxious hunt for the error, leaving poor Robert with a headache that lasted till dinner-time. 'In my painstaking way I was a poor man to be on the cash.'

Robert also realised his shortcomings in dealing with customers. A teller's greatest asset was affability. Customers liked to be greeted with a joke or a humorous sally but Robert never had the gift of facile chat. 'In my strict attention to business I was grim and monosyllabic.' Captain T.V. Fleming of the North West Mounted Police would later recall that he never saw Robert 'without a stiff collar about six inches high'.[9] Laura Berton was living in Dawson at the time and got to know the dapper little bank teller fairly well. She left a graphic first impression of him:

> He slid into town one day without any great fanfare, and was soon to be seen weighing out gold dust in the teller's cage of the Canadian Bank of Commerce on Front Street. By this time his first and most famous book, *Songs of a Sourdough*, was on everybody's lips and the whole camp was reciting *The Shooting of Dan McGrew*, *The Cremation of Sam McGee* and *The Spell of the Yukon* — wild ballads with a Kiplingesque lilt written about totally imaginary events in the Klondike of '98 by a man who had never been there, and yet withal strangely authentic and true to the land.
>
> Miss Hamtorf and I having missed Service in Whitehorse, immediately made a hurried excuse to turn up at the bank for a glimpse of the man whose poems we had already committed to memory. We had thought of him as a rip-roaring roisterer, but instead we found a shy and nondescript man in his mid thirties, with a fresh complexion, clear blue eyes and a boyish figure that made him look younger. He had a soft, well-modulated voice and spoke with a slight drawl. 'An English inflection, an American drawl and Scottish overtones.'
>
> Service was never much of a talker, but he was a good listener and he got the inspiration for many of his poems listening to old-timers ramble on in Whitehorse. We now saw him strolling curiously about in the spring sunshine, peering at the boarded-up gaming-houses and the shuttered dance-halls, which had given place to schools, churches, fraternal houses and even a Carnegie library. He was a good mixer among men and spent a lot of time with sourdoughs, but we could never get him to any of our parties.[10]

As time passed Robert settled to the routine of the bank and the boisterousness of the mess, but his heart was in neither. A growing dislike for the job made him determined to be done with it for good. If only he could be sure that his present income from writing would continue. Then he realised that he had to follow up his success with a second volume. There was no opportunity to write during the summer and by the time he had balanced the books he was too exhausted for poetic inspiration. Nevertheless, he began assembling material, gathering notes, against the time when he would have the vitality to use it. Though much bigger than Whitehorse, Dawson, by 1908, was well on the way to becoming a ghost town. Fewer than a third of the buildings were now occupied, and much of the former city had a dilapidated and deserted look. Soon after his arrival the only dance-hall to survive from the rip-roaring days shut down, thanks to the efforts of the Revd John Pringle. Dawson, in fact, was now in the grip of a religious mania. Not only the churches, but the lodges, were doing good business. Robert joined two of these secret societies, becoming a Wow-Wow and an Arctic Brother, though he never went very far with either. 'Brotherhood was not much in my line.' He suspected that many members joined out of self-interest, though he was not backward in exploiting membership himself. Among the Arctic Brotherhood were men who had come in over the Trail of Ninety-Eight. 'I wormed their stories out of them and tucked away many a colourful yarn.' He was like a reporter ferreting out details of a story that would be a scoop. 'My only wonder was that no other writer had grabbed the rich stuff waiting to be won,' he wrote, apparently oblivious of *The Call of the Wild* which Jack London, a *real* Klondiker, had published five years earlier.

Round midnight Robert would wander the streets of the abandoned city, the summer sun still bright enough to read by:

> I tried to summon up the ghosts of the argonauts. The log cabins, in their desolation, were pathetic reminders of a populous past. I loved the midnight melancholy of the haunted streets, with the misguided birds singing, and the neglected flowers springing. As I pensively roamed these empty ways, a solitary and dreamful mourner, ghosts were all about me, whispering and pleading in the mystic twilight. Thus I absorbed an atmosphere that eluded all others; thus I garnered material for another book. Oh, my Dawson of those days was a rich soil from which I reaped a plentiful harvest.[11]

Laura Berton, then Miss Laura Thompson, had come from Ontario to Dawson a year earlier than Robert. Four years his junior, she earned more than twice his salary as superintendent of the kindergarten department of the local school. She and her teaching colleague Miss Hamtorf shared a cabin on the outskirts of town. Eventually Laura was to fall in love with Frank Berton, a mining engineer who gave French lessons in his spare time, but in 1908 she was still fancy-free and got to know Robert very well. In her memoirs *I Married the Klondike*, published in 1955, Robert supplied a foreword which ended:

> In the evening of life it is a ray of sunshine to have achieved success in a strange field, and I hope the author will reap a rich harvest. It is nigh on half a century since I escorted her to a Dawson dance . . .
>> Dear lady, I will not forget,
>> Though fifty years ago,
>> Your maiden tresses black as jet
>> — Now white as snow.

Laura Berton has left the best eye-witness account of Robert in the Dawson period. She recounted how, one morning in late September 1908, a condemned murderer was led out of the police barracks and mounted the scaffold. Robert had wangled permission to attend the execution. 'He was a man who felt he had to undergo every type of experience, and it was this persistent search for local colour that gave his poems their authenticity.' Robert remained at the scene until the black flag fluttered up the mast, and then, pale and visibly unnerved, he staggered back to the mess-house where he spoke not a word but poured himself a tumbler of straight whisky and gulped it down.

> This was unusual, for all of the time he was in Dawson he neither smoked nor drank. He was a man who liked best of all to go for long, lonely walks in the hills or along the river bank, where, I think, he did most of his composing. We would see him occasionally on the A.C. Trail, swinging along athletically, looking a bit vacant-eyed. He was always cordial and pleasant, but he had no close friends, as far as I know, and nobody knew him well.

Although the memory of that hanging remained vivid till the end of his days, making Robert a fervent abolitionist, more than thirty years would pass before he could bring himself to write a poem derived from this terrible experience. The incident provided the material for 'The Ballad of Hank the Finn' which appeared in *Bar-room Ballads*, published in 1940.

With the onset of winter 1908 Robert got down to serious writing, producing his second book in four months, working from midnight till three in the morning. Any other hours were impossible because of the rumpus about him. Robert's colleagues whooped it up every evening, but he would retire to bed at nine and sleep till twelve, then make a pot of strong, black tea and begin to write. When he went back to bed, however, he would be so imaginatively excited that he could not sleep, and would rise for breakfast feeling hung-over. In writing this book he found that he had to *think* more than he usually did. He preferred to sit down and hope for the inspiration which had sustained his first efforts. But this time he really had to get down and dig. 'Instead of my usual joyous exuberance, I blasted out my rhymes with grim determination. When I finished the last line my relief was enormous.'

It was with considerable misgivings that Robert despatched the manuscript to Briggs. 'By all precedents this volume should have been a failure. It was forced. It was a product of the midnight oil. It was that luckless effort, a second book, written to follow up the success of the first.' He was only too well aware that it lacked the sheer inspiration of the first volume. Unlike the random, hotch-potch nature of *Songs of a Sourdough*, this volume, entitled *Ballads of a Cheechako*, was deliberately planned and constructed. There was nothing miscellaneous about it; all of it was 'steeped in the spirit of the Klondike, written on the spot and reeking with reality'. A perusal of this volume confirms Robert's own terse opinion that 'there was little lyric verse and most of the descriptive ballads were over-long'. But he was satisfied with it: 'technically it was an improvement on my first work'.

He was dismayed to receive a letter from Briggs telling him that they were loath to publish it. Briggs complained about the 'coarseness of his language' and his 'lack of morality'. Anger succeeded amazement and Robert immediately telegraphed Briggs, telling him to hand over the manuscript to a rival firm. Briggs cabled back: 'Reconsidering decision. Await letter.' This made Robert madder than ever. He wired back: 'Reconsideration superfluous. Have advised other firm to take over.' Then he received a telegram from the other firm: 'Will be glad to publish anything you write.' When the mail arrived, there were two letters, one from Briggs and one from the rival publisher. Briggs, despite his moralising and fears for the reputation of the Methodist Book and Publishing House, was reluctant to lose such a lucrative deal. With the threat of Robert taking his book elsewhere, he begged him to make some minor changes and omit a ballad dealing with the Tenderloin, or red-light district of Dawson.

Robert revelled in pitting one publisher against another. Cynically he wrote back to Briggs saying that he had no reputation to consider, and that morality had nothing to do with literature. However, he wanted all his work to appear under the one imprint, so he agreed to remove the offending ballad, though it would cost them five per cent more in royalties. Briggs agreed to these terms and, shortly after *Ballads of a Cheechako* appeared, Robert received a cheque for three thousand dollars. The book was published, more or less simultaneously, by Barse and Hopkins in New York and Stern in Philadelphia.

Laura Berton recalled in her memoirs that, on one of his visits to her cabin, Robert discussed some of the new poems he was preparing for *Ballads of a Cheechako*.

In his soft voice, well modulated but always strangely vibrant and emotional when he talked of the Yukon, he read me parts of 'The Ballad of Blasphemous Bill'. I cannot say I was greatly impressed, for it seemed to me a near duplicate of the Sam McGee story, and I said so.

'I mean it's the same style — one man's body stuffed in a fiery furnace — the other's a frozen corpse sewn up and jammed in a coffin,' I told him.

'Exactly,' said Service. 'That's what I tried for. That's the stuff the public wants. That's what they pay for. And I mean to give it to them.'

The hint of things to come, expressed in the first volume, was fully realised in the second. Though slightly larger, at eighty-eight pages, it contained only twenty-one pieces, beginning with an address 'To the Man of the High North' and ending with a lengthy 'Envoi'. Successive pieces extolled the men of the High North and some of the colourful characters Robert had met or at least heard about. There were the ballads of Pious Pete, Blasphemous Bill, One-eyed Mike and Hard-luck Henry. In the Dawson monologues readers were introduced to Ole Olsen the sailor Swede, Gum-Boot Ben, the Dago Kid, Claw-fingered Kitty, the man from Eldorado and Muckluck Meg. The black sheep of an aristocratic family who joined the Mounties, the telegraph operator, the prospector and the wood-cutter were apostrophised in turn. In 'The Prospector', which dealt comprehensively with the army of gold-seekers in the days of the great gold rush, we find the germ of the idea which Robert was soon to cultivate in his first novel, *The Trail of Ninety-Eight*.

Although he had now achieved his target of five thousand dollars in the bank, Robert did not resign. 'Ten thousand would put me in a spot where I could thumb my nose at the world.' The royalties were now coming in from England as well as Canada and the United States and Robert likened his bank account to a pool constantly fed by small streams.

He wrote nothing else for almost two years. 'I loathed the thought of writing and wondered if the desire to express myself in authorship would ever return.' Thereafter, or until the publication of *Ploughman of the Moon* in 1945 at any rate, the pattern of four months hard work, followed by twenty-four of idleness, was usually adhered to. Resigned to continuing as teller for a while longer, Robert earned his salary. As Dawson continued to decline in population and importance, Robert's bank duties became less onerous. He resumed his habit of long hikes into the wilderness, and tramped along the fabled Klondike or, if it was a fine moonlit night, he would climb to the summit of the Midnight Dome. In Dawson, even in decline, there was no shortage of entertainment and diversion. There was ice-skating and bobsleighing, snowshoe parties and sleigh-rides.

Indoors, there was an embarrassment of choice. There were two dances each week and frequent balls at the sumptuous Arctic Brotherhood Hall, not to mention card parties and dinners where everyone dressed to the nines and their feet froze in silk socks and patent leather shoes. Robert did his best to enter into the social whirl, doing everything 'but curl, drink whisky and play poker'. He looked on curling as an old man's game, 'while hooch and cards meant spending money, and I was determined to save mine'. His own memoirs deal very cursorily with the social scene in Dawson, but other writers have left vivid pictures of the incredible style which continued in this unreal northern city till the outbreak of the First World War. Laura Berton and Martha Black have both left graphic accounts of the lavish banquets, the *bals poudrés*, the fancy-dress balls and grand dances where the ladies sported their five-hundred-dollar gowns from Madame Albert and etiquette was as rigidly observed as in London or Paris. Regarding one of these occasions, Laura Berton wrote of Robert:

> He was an absent-minded man, his thoughts always far away from the business of the moment. He danced with me once during one of his rare social appearances in the A. B. Hall. It was the custom at Dawson balls to divide the dance numbers by a long promenade around the hall. When the music stopped for this interlude, Service, deep in meditation, forgot to remove his arm from my waist. We meandered, thus entwined, around the entire floor, and in those days a man's arm around a lady's waist meant a great deal more than it does now. The whole assembly noticed it and grinned and whispered until Service came out of his brown study.

Intriguingly, Laura also mentioned that Robert kept company with a pretty, young stenographer who worked for the Government, although the girl was not named.

> I remember how he would watch the Government buildings from his vantage point on the hillside, and race down to meet her when she emerged. They did not marry. The report we had was that her family did not approve of Service. His wild verses upset them and, because of his themes, they were convinced that he drank.

Then it was summertime again and business became frenetic once more. Robert's only relaxation was to go up the Klondike on fishing trips. It was then that the idea came to him. Why not write a novel about the gold rush? The most colourful episode in northern history was just asking to be put into fiction. The more he thought about it, the more he became obsessed by it.

> My book must be an authentic record of the Great Stampede and of the gold delirium. It must be tragic and moral in its implications, a vivid scene painted on a big canvas. The characters must be types, the treatment a blend of realism and romance . . .

These thoughts whirled in his mind as he whipped two-pound grayling from the pools of the Klondike, not far from the scene of Carmack's discovery. With two successful books to his credit, Robert now felt supremely confident of his abilities. 'When it came to roping up a bunch of words and licking them into shape I felt I could hold my own with most.' He cast himself in the role of a Zola who would chronicle the epic of Ninety-Eight. He looked forward to the winter months when he would get down to writing his novel. When the time came, however, he found to his disgust that the words eluded him and his imagination was dull. Then he realised that he needed seclusion to brood in. Contact with the boisterous mess threw him off his stride. Laura Berton has left an interesting impression of Robert at this period:

> . . . we could never get him to any of our parties. 'I'm not a party man,' he would say. 'Ask me sometime when you're by yourselves.' He seldom attended the various receptions or dinner-parties or Government House affairs which went on unceasingly, and soon people got out of the habit of inviting him. Sometimes when distinguished visitors arrived in town, he would have to be hunted up at the last moment, for they always insisted on seeing him, and the poet, if pressed, dutifully put in an appearance. I remember how Earl Grey, the Governor-General of Canada, on a visit to Dawson, electrified the town by asking why Service hadn't been included among the guests at a reception. We had all forgotten how important the poet was.

It was in August 1909 that Earl Grey, accompanied by his daughter Lady Sybil, the Hon. Miss Middleton and Lord Lascelles, the Governor-General's ADC (and later husband of the Princess Royal), arrived in the capital of the Yukon Territory. Early on the first morning Earl Grey asked Alex Henderson, the Territorial Commissioner, 'Does Robert Service live far from here?'

'No. Only next door.'

'I would like to meet him. Send for him to breakfast with us.'

This summons was regarded as virtually regal recognition, and the whole of Dawson was agog. Until then the Yukoners had not paid much attention to the shy young bank clerk. Later on, Lascelles was quite concerned that Robert had not sent a formal acceptance to his invitation to dinner, and took up the matter with Clement Burns, the Commissioner's Secretary. Within the hour, Burns had Alec Ross speeding over with the required RSVP. Robert more than made up for his gaffe by presenting Lady Sybil and Miss Middleton with auto-graphed copies of *Songs of a Sourdough.*[12]

Alex Henderson had become a devoted fan of Robert's poetry before coming to the Yukon as governor. On his appointment a civic banquet was held in his honour, and his first question was 'Where is Robert Service?' But the poet had not been invited. This anecdote is related by Martha Black in her memoirs, and sounds suspiciously like the story narrated by Laura Berton in her book. It may be that the overlooked invitation happened on one or other occasion, if not both. According to Martha Black, Robert was hastily summoned and Henderson asked him to recite some of his verses. 'Oh, I couldn't do that without the book,' said Robert nervously. Many thought that this was just an excuse to cover up his shyness, but other Yukoners said that Robert actually forgot his poems as soon as they were committed to paper.

Clement Burns was also secretary of the Dawson Amateur Athletic Society, and he managed to persuade Robert to attend the annual banquet as his guest. Robert accepted the invitation but only on condition that he would not be asked to recite. As the night wore on, however, Robert mellowed and, lean-ing towards the secretary, said, 'Burnsie, I've written an unpublished and uncensored poem or so, which I might recite . . .' Burns lost no time in getting the word to the chairman, and cheers lasting several minutes greeted the announcement. Robert thereupon recited 'Touch-the-Button Nell', probably that 'ballad of the Tenderloin' which Briggs had insisted be omitted from *Ballads of a Cheechako:*

> They gave a dance in Lousetown, and the Tenderloin was there,
> The girls were fresh and frolicsome, and nearly all were fair.
> They flaunted on their backs the spoil of half-a-dozen towns;
> And some they blazed in gems of price, and some wore Paris
>   gowns.
> The voting was divided as to who might be the belle;
> But all opined, the winsomest was Touch-the-Button Nell.

This long ballad was eventually to see the light of day in good black print, in *Bar-room Ballads* published in 1940, but thirty years earlier it is recorded that three of Dawson's leading clergymen hurriedly left the room as Robert warmed to his theme! Martha Black could only recall one occasion when Robert appeared in public before the whole of Dawson. This was a charity performance organised by Mrs Sinclair, wife of the Presbyterian minister, 'a most cultured woman who, before her marriage, had been an artist on *Punch*'.

Robert might have continued in his familiar routine, just as he had stayed at the Corfield store for four years, had not fate, yet again, intervened. One morning he was summoned to the Manager's office and informed that he was being promoted to Relieving Manager at Whitehorse, with immediate effect. He was to leave on the first available stage-coach. Initial elation swiftly gave way to dismay as the responsibilities of the promotion sank in. Moreover, with his novel germinating, the last thing he wanted was to leave Dawson. On the spur of the moment Robert tendered his resignation, saying that he wished to pursue his literary career. When the Manager asked him how much he was earning, Robert replied 'Oh, about five thousand a year from my books and a thousand from the bank. Six in all.' This was more than the Manager was earning, and his manner changed like magic. He was friendly and affable as he agreed with Robert's decision. 'Grasp your opportunities. The trouble is we bankers don't get any.' Instead of congratulating him on his promotion he congratulated him on his judgment in refusing it.

Characteristically, Robert was overwhelmed with the enormity of what he had done, almost as soon as he had done it. As he penned his formal letter of resignation, his innate timidity rose to the surface. 'Perhaps my impulse had been foolish.' But the very next mail contained his bank book showing that the balance now ran to five figures. He had achieved his stake for life. The interest on this sum would yield forty dollars a month on which he felt he could live quite comfortably. Besides, there was no sign of those royalty cheques petering out.

Robert's resignation took effect on 15 November 1909. On leaving the bank mess he rented a log cabin on Eighth Avenue high on the hillside. Behind it was the mountain; below, the valley of the Yukon and the town. The view was inspiring, the isolation all that he could have wished. The cabin had a porch on which he slung a hammock. Indoors, there was a sitting-room and a bedroom, both furnished austerely. He brightened the place by hanging photos on the walls, painting the sitting-room pale blue, and buying flannelette sheets for his well-sprung double bed. 'Everything was snug and shipshape in what was to be my home for two years.'

Away from the rigid routine of the bank, Robert soon slipped into a bohemian existence. 'I kept fantastic hours. Sometimes it would be two o' clock in the afternoon when I had breakfast.' Once he went earlier, but Front Street was abustle with lunchtime animation. It gave him an uneasy feeling to see those people working while he was doing nothing. He took comfort from the ten thousand dollars' worth of bank stock, at five per cent, which he had purchased, recalling the pleasure with which he had written out his first five-figure cheque. Again, luck was on Robert's side, for the bank prospered and paid handsome dividends as its stock doubled in value. Before he realised it, he found the time slipping past in congenial idleness.

> All this time I could not settle down to work, for I was enjoying the casual and irresponsible life that best suited my temperament. I would take supper about ten in the evening and smoke and talk till midnight. It was the bohemian life in the shadow of the Pole. Going home to my bright cabin I would read to the early hours, then sleep till eleven. I would exercise, bathe and descend to town for a leisurely breakfast, returning about three for a siesta. At five I would make tea and strum a guitar, after which I would go for a tramp on the mountain. I did a lot of physical culture, took many cold baths and practised self-massage till the muscles rippled under my skin. It was this passion for physical fitness that made the debauchery of the town repugnant to me.

With a kitten rescued on the frozen trail, and a huge Siberian bearhound called Mike — 'I think, the biggest in the Yukon' — for company, Robert got down to the serious business of the novel, but claims in *Ploughman of the Moon* that he frittered away several months without finding a satisfactory beginning. In the end, it was the offer of an initial royalty of fifteen per cent from Dodd Mead of New York that got him started. However, these statements are at variance with the chronology which demonstrates that he must have been hard at work from the moment he resigned from the bank. He began labouring long and hard on the project, combing through back numbers of the *Dawson News* in the Carnegie library and soaking up the yarns of the old-timers. The book totally absorbed him, 'a slave to the task until it was completed'.

Many of the characters are two-dimensional and the plotting rather contrived, but it is in the lyrically descriptive passages that *The Trail of Ninety-Eight* comes to life. It was narrated in the first person by the hero, Athol Meldrum, a young Scotsman, scion of a landed family in the West Highlands. Describing the writing of this book, Robert likened it to the scenes in a film being unreeled before his eyes. He had to inject an element of romance into it, so he created a heroine Berna (the name came from a brand of condensed milk) but this cardboard cut-out never quite comes to life and Robert's romantic interludes are perfunctory to say the least, in his impatience to get on with the main narrative dealing with the epic struggle of the early gold-seekers. The book was studded with heroes and villains drawn from real life, and as robust as they come. The heroes are often flawed, which makes them more interesting, while the tough guys were seldom completely bad.

In the principal character of Athol Meldrum, however, we can perceive strains of autobiographical writing. 'To avoid any charge of false psychology I exploited certain phases of my own character in the person of my hero. I made him a romantic dreamer, unable to come to grips with reality and at odds with his environment.' In the early part of the novel, Athol's aimless drifting along the Pacific coast of Canada and the United States was clearly derived from Robert's own experiences. The descriptions of the Yukon and its people, rivalling in prose the language of the *Sourdough* and *Cheechako* verses, show Robert writing at his best, but the melodramatic effect has an oddly dated character, owing much to late-Victorian moralising literature (Briggs urged Robert to make Berna 'an inspiration to virtue') and to the silent movies of the Edwardian era. Indeed, *The Trail of Ninety-Eight* was eventually made into a film, directed by Clarence Brown. Ralph Forbes played the part of Larry (Athol in the novel), while Dolores Del Rio played Berna. It was premièred at the Astor Theatre in New York on 20 March 1928, before an audience which a reviewer described as 'critical and appreciative'.[13] He also found the film to be 'highly exciting, not without its melodramatic moments and its flashes of symbolism'. Greater realism was imparted by the judicious use of actual footage from the gold rush of 1898 itself.

The first draft of the novel was written in pencil in school note-books. According to Robert it was written 'over five months, averaging a thousand words a day. There were days I did three thousand words and days I only bit my nails.' As the novel progressed, however, Robert attacked it with demonic intensity. In one final burst he knocked off twelve thousand words, scattering the sheets on the floor in his frenzy and suffering from an aching wrist and stiff fingers as a consequence. The second draft allegedly took three months, during which Robert discarded over thirty thousand words and went over each phrase, testing it and seeking to improve it. If, as he states, he expended eight months on writing his first novel, he must have started work on it as soon as he left the bank, for it was completed in April 1910. This makes a nonsense of his professed dilatoriness, and the confession that he frittered away an entire winter before he hit upon an opening page.

The final version was neatly typed out. Although Robert disliked typing he got a kick out of watching his work evolve in print. The man who had been so casual about his first book that he never bothered to register the package now went to extraordinary lengths over his first novel. Instead of sending it by post he resolved to deliver it in person, at Dodd Mead's offices in New York. By stage-coach, railway and steamer Robert returned to Vancouver.

There is no mention of his brief stay in the city before he took a Pullman heading east, but a brief account of the occasion was given by a fellow Scot, Robert Bruce Lockhart, then a young rubber planter on his way home from

Malaya to recover from malaria and enter the foreign service. Then twenty-nine to Service's thirty-six, he was to achieve fame a few years later as British high commissioner in Moscow at the height of the Bolshevik Revolution, being for a time imprisoned in the Kremlin as a suspected counter-revolutionary. Many years later Sir Robert recalled:

> When we arrived in Vancouver, I was introduced to Robert Service, and for the first time in months blood came back to my cheeks. I was a shy youth and could still blush, and Service, then at the height of his fame, was the first British author I had met. He gave me autographed copies of his *Songs of a Sourdough* and his *Ballads of a Cheechako*. Today, with the rest of my books, they are doubtless gracing the shelves of a Bolshevik library, unless, which is highly probable, they have been burnt by the Moscow hangman as imperialistic effluvia, and, therefore, noxious to Moscow nostrils.[14]

By the end of April 1910 Robert was in Toronto.[15] William Briggs was still his publisher in Canada but responsibility for editorial work on the manuscript was to rest with Frank C. Dodd, senior partner in Dodd Mead of New York. Early in May Robert boarded a train for the United States. He had lived in the Far North for six years and had grown unused to the ways of the outside world. On this train he foolishly left his wallet on his seat and not surprisingly it disappeared, with all his money except some loose change in his pocket. He used some of it to telegraph for fifty dollars to be sent to him in Chicago, and then had to get by on a dollar and sixty-five cents until he reached that city. Ironically, for a man who was now relatively wealthy, with twenty thousand dollars in the bank, the trip had echoes of his vagabond days, and secretly Robert rather relished the situation. On sixty-five cents he lived for four days. 'I bought a sack of apples and a bag of doughnuts, and that is all I ate during this trip.' He dared not spend the dollar, 'for the Negro autocrat of the car would expect it for a tip', even though he was the man Robert suspected of stealing his wallet. Towards the end of the trip he became quite light-headed with hunger, 'but I cinched my belt tighter and told myself I must take it'. This was absurd, for by now he was quite well known and several of his fellow passengers tried to lend him money, but he haughtily brushed them aside. At Chicago he could not afford a taxi and did not appreciate the size of the city. When he reached the First National Bank there was some difficulty over identification but eventually he got his money and took a taxi back to the station, only to see his train departing. In the station, waiting for the next train to New York, he whiled away the time by revising his manuscript, irritated by smuts settling on his white collar. 'In Dawson one could wear a collar a week; here one would have to change it twice a day.'

On the banks of the Yukon River above Five Fingers, Robert had encountered an artist known as the Miner Painter who took a liking to him and promised that, if ever he found himself in New York, he could put up at his studio in the National Arts Club. When he arrived in New York, Robert was rather unnerved by the grandness of his surroundings and disillusioned by the seediness of Madison Square and Broadway which totally failed to live up to his expectations. Seeing the derelicts and dossers harrowed him 'to the soul'. As for the upper classes of New York, Robert found them superior and patronising. More and more he realised that he was kin to the man in the crowd. He preferred Child's to Delmonico's and the Bowery to Fifth Avenue. At Dodd Mead he ran into problems with his novel because it was pronounced *bawdy*. He was exhorted to go away and purge and purify his heroine who was, to Robert's way of thinking, 'purely imaginary and unimaginably pure' as it was. He was also ordered to write a new ending. Meekly he did as he was told, but even so, the novel was later banned in Boston (which probably boosted sales in Lowell and Fall River).

At the National Arts Club Robert rubbed shoulders with editors like McClure and Bob Davis, novelists like Hamlin Garland and George Barr McCutcheon and fellow poets such as Madison Cawein and Will Carleton; but, as a rule, he steered clear of his fellow writers. 'I had a feeling they high-hatted me and were often contemptuous.' One day, Robert was correcting proofs at the club when a shot rang out, and he was an eye-witness to the death of the novelist Graham Phillips who had been shot by a madman. What Robert's reaction was to this dramatic incident is not recorded, as he merely states the fact in a few words, without comment. Probably he was too stunned at the time, and later, when he came to recall the incident, the memory of it was only a blur.

In New York Robert roamed the ethnic districts, the Jewish section, Harlem, Chinatown and Hell's Kitchen. 'All that was sordid delighted me, while the skyscrapers and palatial hotels left me cold.' Even as he haunted Greenwich Village 'the vagabond in me came out and once more I wanted to be free'. As soon as he had concluded his business with Dodd Mead he set off for the South. On impulse he decided to *walk* to New Orleans. Not surprisingly, people thought he was crazy, or that he was a fugitive from justice. The weather deteriorated and it rained, sleeted or snowed along the way. Far too often Robert was stranded in some one-horse town, kicking his heels in some dreary rooming-house. Three months in New York had made him lazy and over-weight. He was in poor shape for the rough road, and was assailed by colds and a persistent cough. After three weeks he had only got as far as a small town in

Pennsylvania. When the station porter tried to move him on as a suspect vagrant Robert finally snapped. He asked the booking clerk for a ticket to Philadelphia, then changed his mind and booked all the way through to New Orleans. All the while, the porter was watching him nastily, so he showed him the ticket — first class, Pullman, observation car, all the frills. 'Is it forbidden for passengers to wait for trains in this station? Are you dumb or are you just a son-of-a-bitch? You dare to insult passengers! If you were not such a poor swine I would report you to the station-master.'

Perhaps the porter was right, mused Robert. 'He may have been over-zealous or he may have been a born bully. I did look a little like a hobo at that moment . . .' At first Robert regretted giving way. 'I felt a miserable worm, spineless spawn of the Effete East,' but an hour later he was luxuriating in a Pullman drawing-room. With high hopes of finding colour and romance he approached New Orleans, but it was picturesque only in spots and the colour was sometimes drab. He was disgusted by the colour bar, and embarrassed when he accidentally took a seat in a streetcar at the rear, where black people had to sit. The French quarter was run down and the Negro district squalid. But he was also touched with the sincerity and warmth of Southern hospitality.

At length he bade goodbye to New Orleans and took the ship to Cuba. He was looking for something 'violently different' and in Havana he found it. Cuba, grossly misgoverned for generations, had thrown off the Spanish yoke barely eleven years previously, and the American troops who guaranteed some semblance of law and order had departed only a few months earlier. It was hopelessly corrupt, morally depraved, insanitary and dirty, but here was the riot of colour that Robert craved. In the plazas he found a 'torrid zone of Latin pulchritude'. On a park bench he encountered an old salt, a survivor of the US battleship *Maine*, whose destruction in Havana Harbour in 1898 had triggered off the Spanish-American War. Here was effervescence, colour, emotion. 'To the devil with Anglo-Saxon efficiency. Give me this open-air café with its tumult, its mercurial gaiety, the stars above the palms. Give me this street seething with ardent movement, this high-pitched, hectic living.'

Too many *pina frias* and three-hour siestas, however, played havoc with his waistline, so he decided to take to the open road and walk to Santiago; but after a few days in the heat and total humidity, combined with disgusting accommodation, he was forced to return to Havana. Tired of the 'relentless sun-blaze' and by now bored with the South, he longed for 'the snow and tonic air of the North'. Then one day, seated on the Prado and leafing through an American magazine, he chanced upon an article entitled *I Had a Good Mother*. 'Suddenly I thought: I, too, had a perfectly good mother. She was living in Alberta and I had not seen her in thirteen years.' Robert Senior had died a couple of years previously, though he had lived long enough to witness his son's first spectacular success. Robert had even sent Papa one of his author's copies, dutifully auto-graphed, though he doubted whether the old man had ever looked at it.

Now he decided to 'do the prodigal son in reverse'. He would return to the family homestead, pay off the mortgage and make the acquaintance of brothers and sisters he hardly remembered and scarcely knew. So, yielding to sentimental emotion, he packed his Gladstone bag, bade farewell to Havana and started out for the virile North. Back in North America, he found that his novel had been published. Both Canadian and American editions included four illus-trations by Maynard Dixon. Later editions were illustrated instead with photographs, stills taken from the 1928 film.

It was late autumn when he finally reached the Service homestead at Vegreville. Winter had already set in and there was deep snow, sunshine and a temperature well below zero on that vast plain as he set off in a hired sleigh to visit his family.

> Through the deep snow a toe-path led to the frame farm-house. As I knocked at the frosted door it was cautiously opened to reveal the face of a very pretty girl. This must be one of my sisters, I thought; but which I could not guess, so I said: 'I represent the Encyclopaedia Britannica. Perhaps I could interest you in that monumental enterprise.'
>
> At that the door was opened wide enough to reveal a cosy but primi-tive kitchen. A little, elderly woman was washing dishes at the sink, and a tall, comely girl was thawing out a newly born calf by the stove. Then the little woman came forward drying her hands.
>
> 'Why, if it isn't our Willie.' We Scotch are economical of our emotions. We exchanged the same conventional kiss we had indulged in when I left, nearly fifteen years before. My sisters were introduced and I pecked at their cheeks.
>
> 'What about a cup of tea, Ma?' I said. 'I could do with a spot.'

Robert was soon 'hefting the dogie up on its wabbly legs' and rubbing it down. It seemed like old times, reminding him of his days as a cattleman at Cowichan. He soon got to know his family again. Emily Service proved to be a spare little woman of intense activity, who 'loved the farm life and never regret-ted the shabby gentility of a city suburb'. Robert remembered her as rather sickly and tired; now she was 'almost pathetic in her eagerness to be brisk and bright'. She laughed a great deal and Robert felt pleased to see her so happy. 'But they all were. That was one of the happiest homes, three boys, three girls, full of health and high spirits, and the old lady smiling cheerfully in the back-ground. I can honestly say I have never seen a sweeter home than that humble steading nestling on the vast loneliness of the prairie.'[16] At that time the three youngest sons, Stanley, Peter and Albert, were living with their mother, along with their sisters Agnes, Jane and Janet. Agnes would subsequently marry David Todd and settle at Manville a few miles east of Vegreville, but Stanley would go off to medical college and a busy Toronto hospital, while Peter would migrate to Vancouver where, for many years, he ran a second-hand bookshop appropriately named The Sourdough. Albert, the baby of the family and his mother's favourite, was to die in the trenches of the First World War as a lieutenant in the Canadian Infantry.

Robert spent the winter of 1910–11 in what he termed his 'prairie idyll'. He mucked in, doing chores about the farm, and went for long walks into the undulating countryside. On one memorable occasion he helped defend the homestead when a prairie fire threatened to engulf it. But with the coming of spring and the melting of the snows something of the vagabond stirred in his blood. 'I would escape from domesticity and let the sun and wind work their will with me. So I took staff and satchel and started out. I had no idea where I was going, but the North drew me like a magnet.' For ten days he tramped around Alberta, covering some two hundred miles and stopping at night in Norwegian, Romanian, Slav or French settlements, whose diversity added to the interest of the journey. Robert was 'a born tramp' and he got a tremendous kick out of these twenty-mile hikes each day in the invigorating countryside. He rejoiced in his superb health which awoke in him a longing for the High North and the Midnight Sun.

In Dawson he had met a young man who had come to the Klondike the patriotic, hard, all-Canadian way, overland on the notorious Edmonton Trail, taking two years to accomplish the two-thousand-mile journey. Now Robert intended to 'pack and track like the pioneers'. Some forty pages of *Ploughman of the Moon* (343–82) are devoted to this epic journey. It is one of the best and most exciting stories he ever wrote, far surpassing anything in his novels. It is not only a personal account of a part of the Canadian North West which even today is little known, but it is also a modest, yet dramatic, revelation of the intrepid spirit, dogged endurance and sheer courage of the banker-poet. At the age of thirty-seven, Robert was at the peak of physical perfection. All the flabbiness of Havana had been burned off by hard work on the farm. The stamina built up over the past fifteen years and the hardiness of the northern explorer stood him in good stead; without them he would never have survived the rugged hardships and dangers he encountered on this terrible overland route. Had he never made this journey, his reputation as the Bard of the Yukon would have been secure enough; but he *did* make this incredible journey and out of his experiences along the way he would distil the poetry which appeared in his third volume of verse entitled appropriately *Rhymes of a Rolling Stone*. Although it was compiled after his return to Dawson it is not strictly a Yukon book, for the subject matter deals with the Canadian Arctic. Hitherto Robert had admired the Klondikers who lived below the Arctic Circle, but after his epic journey he could boast that the man who had travelled north of that imaginary line 'strutted it over the man from the subarctic'.

Perhaps Robert's motive in undertaking such a hazardous venture was to prove himself. He was acutely aware that although he had chronicled the Yukon in verse and prose, he was something of a fraud. He had not actually been on the Trail of Ninety-Eight and the gold rush that inspired him had been all but over by the time he got there. He made for Edmonton, the Alberta provincial capital and jumping-off point for the Athabasca River, a two-day journey by stage-coach although even then there were automobiles that covered the hundred-mile trip in four hours. At Athabasca Landing Robert met 'Peace River' Jim Cornwall, who was to make a fortune developing the area. Jim offered Robert a section at three hundred dollars which, in time, he promised would be worth ten times as much. If he had said a hundred times as much he would have been more accurate. For the first, but by no means the last, time Robert declined to speculate in land, thus denying himself the chance to become a multi-millionaire — 'such a fate I would not wish on anyone'.

Robert discovered that the Hudson's Bay Company barges had departed two days previously to replenish their trading posts after the winter, so he borrowed a canoe and, with a Swedish doctor named Sandberg and an Indian guide, set off after them on 25 May. Two brothers, a mining engineer and a retired naval officer named George and Lionel Douglas, raced them in another canoe. Dr Sandberg and Robert 'dug in like niggers' but it was three days before they caught up with the barges. Along the way they passed through an oil region, with a strong odour in the air and scum on the water. At nightfall on the second day they came upon a flaming jet of natural gas rising twenty feet into the air.

On the afternoon of the third day they caught up with the Company flotilla. A dozen barges were strung along the bank and supper was in preparation. They were allotted to one of the barges and the canoes were hauled aboard. There were about a dozen passengers in all distributed among the barges. At night they bivouacked on the river-bank, rigging up one-man pup tents and mosquito nets. Although Robert's account of the trip is extremely vague regarding dates, George Douglas took a number of photographs (which he developed and printed *en route*) and his captions on the back of them have helped to pinpoint the earlier part of the journey. On the fourth evening, 29 May, the travellers camped on the river-bank near Grand Rapids.

As usual, Robert found his fellow travellers exceedingly entertaining. On the barge he read and dozed in the sunshine. 'It was pleasant but boring.' He looked forward to mealtimes and began to put on weight again. There was nothing to mar the pleasant monotony, except when it rained and they had to shelter under tarpaulins. Then they came to a series of rapids, and George Douglas suggested a canoe race. 'It was a needless bit of bravado, but I felt I must take part.' The thrills and spills of white-water canoeing were well described, but when one of the barges ran aground, its steersman diverted by Robert's antics, he and Douglas were forbidden to do 'these silly stunts'.

The arrival of the barges at Fort MacMurray on 2 June had a carnival atmosphere. 'The little settlement was hectic, and the whisky-starved population was making up for lost time. The scene was like a fiesta, for it was the end of months of cold and deprivation.' From a canoe and then a scow, Robert progressed to a river steamer on the next stage of his journey. This was the stern-wheeler *Grahame* which Robert and his companions boarded two days later. He had a stateroom, 'misty with mosquitoes', donned moccasins and slacks, and prepared for a spell of 'delicious laziness'. Any time his Calvinist conscience pricked him on account of such idleness he took comfort from the fact that, for every dollar he spent, he was earning two from his royalties. Although the Indian agent at the Fort, a former parson, told him that the journey he was contemplating was foolhardy in the extreme, Robert brushed his gloomy prognostications airily aside.

It took a week to switch cargoes from the barges to the steamer and start on the trip down the Athabasca River on 9 June. Robert's last view of the barges was of the Athabasca Brigade — long lines, each of a hundred men, hauling on the ropes to tow the ungainly scows back upstream, 'a Volga boatman scene'. The steamer took two days to pass down the Athabasca River. They were at Chipewyan by 11 June where the ship crossed Lake Athabasca and entered the mouth of the Peace River. A hundred miles upstream, at Smith's Landing, a series of rapids made the river impossible to navigate, so the freight had to be carried twenty miles to Fort Smith on the Slave River. There, on 27 June, Robert embarked on another steamer which took him on, through the western arm of the Great Slave Lake and up the Mackenzie River, to Fort Simpson. On this stretch of the journey Robert purchased a birch-bark canoe, which he christened *Coquette*.

I bought it at Great Slave Lake from an old Indian who was considered the best canoe-maker of his tribe. He judged it a masterpiece and truly, it was like a flame upon the water. A gaudy patchwork of purple, scarlet, primrose and silver, it danced on the ripple as lightly as a leaf. The old man sighed as he parted with it. He had gone far to select the bark. He had sewn it with wood fibre and lashed it with willow wands. It had taken him a year to fashion, and now he looked at it with the sadness of an artist who sees his finest work being sold. With reluctance, he took the twenty-five dollars I offered him.

On the mighty Mackenzie River Robert enjoyed every minute of the voyage by steamer, but did not go into details, other than to note 'We visited a score of forts and met many Factors who hailed from the Hebrides'. These Hudson's Bay posts were a mine for the story-teller, but the grim men who manned them had no sense of the romance of destiny. Robert hoped to write a book about the trip and made copious notes, which were eventually distilled into the account in his autobiography; but it is to be regretted that he never realised his ambition of expanding his notes into a full-blown travel book. What we are given in *Ploughman of the Moon* is but a taste of what might have been.

At one post an Indian came in to report that a cabin belonging to two trappers had been deserted for a month or more. The men had not been seen, but an evil odour was coming from it. Robert went along with the Mounties to investigate. The stench of decaying human flesh was overpowering. The door was bolted on the inside but the troopers broke it down, releasing a vast black cloud of bluebottles. Only when the flies dispersed did the Mounties venture inside. Although the corpses were badly decomposed and crawling with maggots and lice it was obvious that the trappers had quarrelled to the death. Both skulls were smashed by bullets fired at close range and nearby lay a rifle, with one discharged shell in the breech and another lying on the floor. On a table Robert found a small notebook which one of the men had kept as a diary. This chronicled the rapid deterioration of relations between the diarist and his partner, both of whom appear to have gone mad. The last entry in the book was a suicide note, written in an almost indecipherable hand after the writer had shot his sleeping comrade. Robert would later aver that life along the Mackenzie was much harsher than in the Yukon and the strains placed on the people who lived there well-nigh intolerable. Many of the men he met on his journey were to die violent deaths.

The steamer journey terminated at Fort Macpherson, where the Peel River joined the Mackenzie. By now Robert was well north of the Arctic Circle in a strange land of tundra. The Factor here was John North who appealed to Robert's vanity by saying that he had read his books. He sold Robert sacks of flour and sides of bacon as well as dispensing the sound advice to go back the way he had come, 'like a good little boy'. The officer in charge of the police post was equally pessimistic and reminded him of the Lost Patrol, a four-man party of Mounties which had set off for the Yukon and had disappeared without trace. Undaunted, Robert pressed on, pitching his tent near an Eskimo encampment where he swapped his safety razor for a fish-hook of walrus ivory. He hoped to cross the hundred miles of the Great Divide, carrying his little canoe before heading down the Bell and the Porcupine to the Yukon River where he would paddle upstream to Dawson. He fondly imagined that, along the way, he would encounter Indians who would assist with the portages to the headwaters. In this he was grievously disappointed, despite generous offers of payment.

Fortunately, one day he saw a scow coming up the river with two men and a woman aboard. The men he called Captain McTosh and Jake Skilly had named their scow the *Ophelia* and the woman was allegedly McTosh's wife. They were mavericks who would have nothing to do with the Hudson's Bay Company posts or their steamship. Robert fell in with them, and they journeyed together for many days. Jake and Robert paddled the canoe, while the McToshes and two Indians crewed the *Ophelia*. Paddling up the Peel River was 'serenely monotonous'. At the mouth of the Rat River they made camp. Later the canoe was loaded on to the scow and Robert became a galley slave, working harder than at any other time of his life. *Ophelia*, fully laden, weighed half a ton, and poling her upstream against the mean white waters was both hard and dangerous work. Gradually the water became shallower, until they reached a point where there was nothing for it but to haul the scow up to the Divide and over to the other side. Now everyone donned rope harness and prepared to tug the boat over many miles of trackless waste. Often over the ensuing days Robert would ask himself 'What am I doing here?'

Twelve hours a day on the tow-line, often knee-high in water, brought an unexpected bonus. Hitherto Robert's feet had been plagued by corns, but now they miraculously vanished and never reappeared. Sometimes the travellers came to a valley where the river forked into a dozen channels; then the problem was to decide on the likeliest channel. Sometimes they made the wrong choice and ran out of water altogether; then the scow had to be unloaded, mounted on runners, and hauled over dry land. Some days they travelled barely half a mile, a heart-breaking job of hoisting the scow inch by inch over that rocky bed. They were lucky with the weather, which remained sunny so that the water was tepid. As they climbed higher and higher, the mountains seemed to close in around them and the river narrowed to a single channel. Suddenly the water, which had been muddy till now, became crystal clear. Just as this was raising their spirits, however, the two Indians decided to quit. Grimly Robert suspected that these so-called guides had lost their way and had decided to leave the others before the awful truth emerged. Again, the river forked and they had to choose which channel to follow. Theoretically the correct channel would lead them to a small lake at the head of the Divide. To miss the lake would be disaster. They chose the channel that seemed to have the greatest bulk of water. As the days passed, however, fears that they had chosen the wrong channel assailed them.

On one occasion, after a particularly discouraging day, they collapsed at a sandspit for a brew-up. Robert went on ahead and found a tree on which Buffalo Jones had carved his name. The sight of the name of this well-known Klondiker put fresh heart in him.

> Indeed, so elated was I by my discovery that for the next week my exertions were herculean. No one hefted *Ophelia* more enthusiastically than I, and as I helped to heave her upstream I almost liked her. For I had a vision of myself in my Dawson cabin, swinging in my hammock, with the river gleaming blue and the birds singing. Oh, how I would rest and read and sleep! No more wandering for little Willie.

There was new life in them, but the worst was yet to come. The stream narrowed to a brook, then a ditch overgrown with willows. Suddenly they realised that they were on the height of land forming the Divide. 'We were no longer climbing. We were pushing on the level. We were pulling over a small prairie . . .' And then, there in the near distance was a small lake, 'shining like a jewel under the cold blue sky'. Appearances were deceptive, for the approach to the lake was swampy and it took ten hours of wading and pulling, up to their waists in mud, before they reached the clear waters of the lake. Here they rested for two days and recovered their strength. At the Bell River they parted company, Robert going ahead in *Coquette*. This was an extremely foolhardy course of action, for even a minor accident could have spelled total disaster and death. Fortunately the river was placid, its banks well stocked with game, and Robert drifted downstream for two hundred miles, fishing and hunting as he went. The weather broke when he reached the Porcupine. Here he ran into the crew of the *Ophelia* again. By now Jake Skilly had fallen out with his companions, so Robert unwisely agreed to take him on down to Dawson. Skilly was a chain-smoker who rolled his own cigarettes, but when he ran out of paper he began to fear life without nicotine. Robert was not in the least reassured by Jake's harrowing tales of the men in the wilds who went insane or quarrelled over trivial matters, ending in sudden death for one or both of the antagonists. He began to be alarmed when Jake, suffering withdrawal symptoms, behaved irrationally. It was with immense relief that he encountered a sternwheeler and, hoisting *Coquette* on board, booked his passage to Dawson. Skilly would later return to the Arctic to trap, but eventually he shot himself. The celebrated ballad 'When the Ice-Worms Nest Again' was allegedly composed aboard the Porcupine sternwheeler, for Robert taught it to the crew who sang it for years thereafter. In fact, it was based on a song which he inserted into his novel, in print some two years earlier.

In Dawson, Robert quickly settled down to his quiet Bohemian lifestyle. As winter returned he donned his snowshoes and revelled in long hikes along his beloved woodland trails. Over the winter months he worked on his third book of verse. He pinned rolls of blank wallpaper to the cabin walls and wrote out his poems with a stick of charcoal in large block lettering. Then he would stand back and study the lines, adjusting and changing words and phrases until he achieved the desired effect. Years later, tourists visiting the lonely cabin would bear away portions of the verse-covered wallpaper as mementoes.

One day he set off to visit some friends who lived almost fifty miles from Dawson. He made the outward journey without incident and spent the night there, but on the following day he lost his bearings and became hopelessly lost as night closed in. Fatigued by the long trudge through the forests and suffering exposure as the temperature plunged to forty below, Robert was afraid to go on lest he fell into a snowdrift from which he would never escape. In the end he selected a tall pine and began walking slowly round it, hoping to get his bearings. He was at the end of his endurance and thought his number was up, when suddenly the moon broke through and there, not a hundred yards away, was a cabin. He staggered towards it, opened the unlocked door, and found the stove ready to be lit. Somehow he managed to eat a little food before collapsing on the bed. In the morning the owner returned, made sure that Robert was properly fed, and persuaded him to spend a second night keeping him company. That night, however, as they split a bottle of whisky between them, Robert's host became wilder and wilder and began brandishing his shotgun in a menacing manner. It was then that he revealed that he was none other than Cannibal Joe, who had earned his grisly epithet from the rumour that he had killed and eaten his partner when the two of them had run out of food while prospecting in the Barren Lands. In a terrifyingly tense atmosphere Joe gave his version of the story, how his partner had died and with his dying gasp had told Joe to save himself by using his corpse. It would not have been the first time that trappers and prospectors, caught in similar situations, had resorted to cannibalism, and it would not be the last either. But Joe was adamant. 'I never et Bob. I never et a single slice of him. No, that's not what I want to tell you. . . What did I do? Listen — God curse me! I never et Bob, but *I fed him to the dogs and I et the bloody dogs*.' With that, he collapsed on the floor in a drunken stupor. When Robert woke in the morning his host was frying eggs and bacon. He showed no trace of a hangover, and with his white beard and snowy hair, he was mild, almost gentle, reminding Robert of Walt Whitman. As they parted company he remarked casually, 'Say, friend, if ye had a bad dream last night ye jest want to ferget it. Y'understand?'

Robert finished his book in the late spring of 1912, adding to his gallery of characters such immortals as Eddie Malone of Fond-du-lac, Athabaska Dick from Lac Labiche, Barb-Wire Bill, Happy Jack, Flap-jack Billy (given the cow-juice cure), Tom Thorne, Chewed-ear Jenkins, Guinneyver McGee, the Squaw Man and Little Laughing Eyes. The ballads were more thoughtful, more senti-mental than in the preceding volume, the men of the Arctic dreaming nostalgi-cally of home and loved ones. There was a liveliness, a sense of urgency even, about many of the verses, composed so soon after his epic journey through the Arctic.

This was also a more ambitious volume than its predecessors, for it ran to a hundred and twenty pages and contained fifty-one pieces.

Having completed the volume, however, he relaxed and enjoyed a last summer in the High North, leaving Dawson with real regret on the last steamer of the season. South of Vancouver he spent a couple of months, camp-ing in a tent in the foothills of the Olympic Mountains where he revised and polished his poems before taking the manuscript to William Briggs. He was in Toronto by late September 1912,[17] and probably went on to New York soon afterwards, for Dodd Mead brought out their edition of *Rhymes of a Rolling Stone* before the end of the year.

Laura Berton summed up Robert's literary achievement of this period succinctly:

And yet of the hundreds of writers who came through the North and produced whole libraries of books about it, many of them pioneers who watched history being made before their eyes, only this quiet, colourless bank clerk succeeded in capturing the strange mixture of magic and tragedy, hope and heartbreak, of which the gold camps of the Yukon are compounded. It is a tribute to him that his books sell nowhere as well as they do in Dawson itself.[18]

Robert would probably have been amused — and not a little flattered — to learn how often some of these writers claimed to have known him, in places and at times which cannot possibly be true. Pierre Berton, son of Laura, in a trenchant note on sources appended to his own masterpiece,[19] enumerates some of the authors who made false claims. The Hon. James Wickersham, a distin-guished American judge writing in *Old Yukon*, said that in the summer of 1900 in Skagway 'in one of the banks a gentlemanly clerk named Bob Service was introduced smilingly, as a writer of poetry'. In *Far North Country*, Thames Williamson wrote, 'Service was in the Klondike during the fevered days of the gold rush' and Glenn Chesney Quiett falls into the same error in *Pay Dirt*. And Stanley Scearce in *Northern Lights to Fields of Gold* says that he met Robert Service in Dawson in 1898 (ten years before the poet actually arrived there).

CHAPTER 8

BALKAN INTERLUDE

I've tinkered at my bits of rhymes
In weary, woeful, waiting times.

Foreword to *Rhymes of a Red Cross Man* (1916)

HAVING DELIVERED TO HIS PUBLISHERS THE MANUSCRIPT OF *Rhymes of a Rolling Stone*, to his publishers, Robert planned to go to the South Seas for the winter. 'I dreamed of palms, starry-eyed sirens, strumming ukuleles on coral strands.' Instead, he was approached by the editor of the *Toronto Star* who wished to 'send this bold boy to the blood bath of the Balkans'. He appears to have been in New York when he got the letter proposing to make him a war correspondent; 'with curses in my heart I cabled acceptance'. Then, with a copy of his *Rhymes* fresh off the press in his valise, 'superb as to health, but uncouth through long living near to Nature, I departed for sophisticated Europe'. On this note, Robert concluded *Ploughman of the Moon*. Considering that this was one of the major turning points of his life, Robert made surprisingly little of this decision, although the impression is conveyed that he was reluctant to go. 'With curses in my heart I cabled acceptance' does not infer eagerness on Robert's part, but this may be nothing more than his usual tendency to dramatise his actions. The solution may be more prosaic, however. Robert was at a loose end, and while it was comforting to think of the royalties coming in from his verse, his deeply engrained Calvinist upbringing pricked his conscience. He was probably relieved to get the commission, while the prospects of new worlds to explore and new challenges to conquer would have appealed to him.

The second autobiographical volume, entitled *Harper of Heaven,* took up the story in 'sinister Stamboul' a month or two later. As in the first volume, this book of 450-odd pages was rich in impressions drawn from a colourful life but maddeningly deficient in names, dates and details of places visited. He crossed the Atlantic on a German luxury liner, 'so different from the roach-ridden old tramp in which I had crossed fifteen years before'. Though the ship was not named, it has now been ascertained that Robert, in fact, travelled on the 16,000-ton *Deutschland* of the Hamburg-American Line which had been launched in 1900, and in addition to her regular transatlantic crossings offered cruises to the Mediterranean. Although he says dismissively 'I never liked Germans', Robert struck up an acquaintance with at least one other passenger, Ludwig Beuttenmueller from Baden-Baden, to whom he subsequently sent his personal postcard with Christmas wishes. The card, incidentally, showed a scout-hatted Robert seated in *Coquette* during his epic Arctic journey the previous year.[1]

Robert's description of the voyage was impressionistic, studded with lightning sketches of fellow passengers and members of the crew. What comes over clearly, however, is that the Teutonic arrogance of the ship's officers and most of the passengers was subjective, feeding Robert's innate inferiority complex. Of a publisher, 'a little grey man who looked like a pocket edition of General Grant', Robert wrote, 'Although I have four best-sellers to my credit he takes no more notice of me than if I was an earwig. No one does on this bloody boat. I'm just a lousy little nobody.' The voyage terminated at Naples and Robert then travelled by rail to Brindisi and took a ship to Athens, thence across the Aegean by moonlight. 'So by seas of cornflower blue I came to ten-tiered Istamboul (*sic*) with its domes and minarets gleaming in the sunrise . . .'

Bulgaria, Serbia, Greece and Montenegro had mobilised their forces on 30 September 1912 for a concerted attack on the crumbling Ottoman Empire, the misgovernment of Macedonia being the immediate pretext for the war. The Turks fielded about 240,000 men but the Allies had 310,000 and these were better armed, trained and led. War was declared on 17 October and severe fighting ensued almost immediately. In Thrace, the Bulgars besieged Edirne (Adrianople) and defeated the Turks in a series of bloody battles. The Ottoman forces retreated in confusion to the Chatalja Lines on the outskirts of Istanbul itself, but the victors were too exhausted to pursue them. The Bulgarian onslaught on Chatalja took place on 17 November but was repulsed with heavy losses. It was apparently on that very day that Robert landed in Istanbul, for 'over all boomed ceaselessly the guns of Tchatalje'. The Bulgarian high command, sobered by this salutary experience, refrained from trying again. The fighting in Thrace now came to a standstill for a fortnight and then, on 3 December, a truce was signed between Turkey and the Allies.

Clad in khaki tunic and breeches, Robert looked the part but he was unable to get to the Lines where gunfire rumbled all day and night across the city. While he listened to the gunfire Robert was content to sit on the terrace of the city's finest café, playing a part: 'a fez cocked over one eye, a gilt-tipped cigarette between my lips and a gorgeous concoction called a *Susanna* at my elbow — marvellously happy and delightfully lit up'.

In order to get closer to the action, he enrolled in the Red Crescent and pinned the emblem to his sleeve. 'As I saw myself in the mirror I felt quite impressed, a semi-soldier, capable of deeds of near-danger'. But he was repelled by the misery and wretched condition of the wounded soldiers whose cots cluttered the floor of the Aghia Sofia Mosque, converted into a temporary hospital. Troops passed continually, Turks in new uniforms, goose-stepping to the orders of German-trained officers, mountain Kurds, 'small wiry men with donkeys carrying light guns and wearing no special uniform', and everywhere streams of refugees. During the lull in the fighting, Robert's boss, Doctor Dilly, sent him to the cholera camp at San Stefano with a ton of rice. Robert was disgusted that the Turks should levy import duty on the rice before he was allowed to take it into the camp, even though he was bringing it to feed their own troops. There was a melodramatic encounter with two suspected German agents, 'Levantines capable of cutting a throat for a dollar'.

While his fellow correspondents, the morose Australian Grimstone and the bandy-legged Scot McHaggie planned to get to Edirne where the siege was expected to culminate in a major battle any moment, Robert loaded his sacks of rice at a wharf on the Golden Horn. It was midday before his launch reached San Stefano. In peacetime it had been a summer resort for wealthy Turks; now the Greek school had been made into a hospital. Robert's description of the appalling scene which met his eyes is one of the most gruesome to be found in either autobiographical volume. Robert was immediately set to work carrying corpses out of the building. It was too much for him and hastily he made his escape. 'The stink of death was in my nostrils, so I sought the beach and there in the Sea of Marmora I swam till I felt fairly clean again.' Yet horror fascinated him, and he returned to the camp where thousands of tents had been set up: 'in each half a dozen men lay on the bare ground, writhing and retching'. Every now and then one would get feebly to his feet and stagger to the door of his tent. Alongside was a shallow ditch, and on the edge of this he would cower weakly, convulsed by violent spasms of diarrhoea, and scarcely unable to unbutton his breeches. Robert's lasting memory of San Stefano was the acrid stench and 'a long line of men, crouched on the edge of the ditch, their lean buttocks gleaming pallidly in the pale sunshine'.

That night, he slept on the floor of a villa rented by the Red Crescent. The bedrooms were occupied by Austrian nurses but 'not even the homeliest of them would invite [me] to share her couch', he complained. Instead of returning to the cholera camp, he went for a swim the following morning, thinking of Leander and wondering where exactly was the Hellespont. On the beach, however, Robert was peremptorily dismissed when the colonel in charge discovered that he was 'one of those newspaper pests'. Thus ended Robert's first encounter with the horrors of war. During the evening he left San Stefano on a paddle-steamer crowded with Anatolian conscripts whose officers beat them with the flats of their swords to pack them in more tightly. Back in Istanbul he packed away his uniform and resumed civilian clothes. He was all set to join Grimstone and McHaggie on their foray to Adrianople. Instead, he had a visit from two plain-clothes men who examined his documents and ordered him to appear at the Commissariat of Police at three o' clock the following day. Robert did not wait for the anticipated interrogation. As soon as the policemen had departed he went to a travel agency near his hotel and booked his passage to Constanza by the first vessel leaving the following day. He was so worried that he could not sleep that night, his life-long horror of authority asserting itself. At eleven the following morning he boarded a Romanian steamer and when he should have been at the Commissariat he was actually vomiting over the rail into the unsympathetic Black Sea.

The next six months were spent aimlessly wandering through eastern and central Europe, a parallel to his vagabond days on the Pacific coast although now he had the money to travel in some comfort. On the Orient Express he ran into an English aristocrat whom he called Sir Pelham Pelham, Bart. In a footnote — the only one in either volume of autobiography — he explained:

> The repetition of his name, he told me, he owed to a great-aunt who, when asked what he should be called, said, 'Why, Pelham, of course. Where could you find a nobler name?' I asked him why he did not hyphenate it and stick another Pelham in front, but he gave me his 'We are not amused' look.[2]

Needless to say, there never was a baronet of this name, nor has any with identical Christian and surnames been traced. The question then arises, was he a figment of Robert's fertile imagination? The answer is, very probably. Sir Pelham Pelham bobs up years later, when Robert was taking the cure at Royat in the Auvergne, and the elderly *roué* was having an affair with Claribel, Countess of Camlachie (actually a slum district in Glasgow). The subsequent chapters in which this fictional baronet occurred added nothing to the autobiography.

There was an unreal quality about Robert's wanderings, as a sort of Childe Harold of the Far North. In Bucharest, his first stop after leaving Turkey, he stayed at the opulent Palace Hotel. His enchantment with the Romanian capital, the Paris of the Balkans, was almost intoxicating.

> Bucharest thrilled me. I wrote bright articles of army officers in Merry Widow uniforms, of gargantuan coachmen driving their teams like the wind, of gay incongruities where East meets West and crude peasants gazing at the debonair boulevards.

Robert claims that he received a cheque for three hundred dollars in respect of four articles he wrote at this time, but the editor of the *Toronto Star* must have spiked them, for nothing from this period under his byline ever appeared. Later in life Robert was to say that he had played many roles. Role-playing was what the Balkan interlude and its aftermath were all about. The chapter entitled 'Innocent Abroad' is one of Robert's raciest, packed with yarns about predatory women, whom he warded off by purchasing a photograph of a lady and pretending that she was his wife. When one of the predators, an East European princess, saw the photograph she laughed derisively. 'Your precious wife! Do you know who that is? I should, for before I was divorced I was her bosom friend . . . Fool! Imposter! That picture on the floor is the portrait of Her Royal Highness the *Queen of Romania*.' With those words she gave him a stinging slap and flounced out of the room. There is an obvious discrepancy in this story, for the Queen at this time was Elizabeth, a seventy-year-old better known to posterity as Carmen Sylva, the name she used in writing books of poetry and Romanian folklore with the help of her lady-in-waiting, Mite Kremnitz. Perhaps Princess Marie, daughter of the sailor Duke of Edinburgh and grand-daughter of Queen Victoria, was meant instead. She was the wife of Crown-Prince Ferdinand who ascended the Romanian throne in 1914.

Early in December Robert took the train to Budapest, travelling third class by mistake. Thus he found himself sharing a compartment with three generations of a peasant family but was disgusted by the lavatorial exploits of the youngest who defecated on his lap. He spent a month in Budapest; he did not name the hotel where he stayed but it was so nondescript that on his first night on the town he forgot its name. It was 'a smallish hotel, one of a score in the neighbourhood' and all he could remember about it was that the receptionist was a fat man with a wen on his nose. Not surprisingly, it took him half the night to relocate his lodgings. The most remarkable feature of his stay in the Hungarian capital was that he did not speak to a soul throughout the entire month.

And how I enjoyed my silence! I glutted my hunger for obscurity. I realised how self-obliteration was a passion with me. Content to observe the life about me I dreamfully absorbed my impressions.

He grew fond of his 'shabby room, one corner of which was the yellow-tiled wall of the huge stove'. He enjoyed hunting out cheap restaurants in back streets, where he ate 'the rich greasy food of the people!'. Again he realised that there was something common, even vulgar, in his nature that made him prefer the poor to the rich and the slums to the sleek boulevards.

In January 1913 even Budapest was beginning to pall, so he decided to press on to Vienna. Here, a cab-driver 'who thought all Americans were millionaires' took him to Sacher's Hotel where he bumped into the amorous baronet again. This time Sir Pelham's quarry was a Castilian countess. The description of the baronet, polishing his monocle and preening his moustache as he set about his latest conquest, has a stereotypical, two-dimensional quality, half-real, half-artificial. Robert himself admitted that Sir Pelham was 'a cardboard Casanova'. These episodes set the tone of much of Robert's later writing, particularly the fiction. In *Ploughman of the Moon* Robert was to reveal as little of himself as possible; and having got away with that, he took this a step farther in *Harper of Heaven*. Carl Klinck, who made a detailed analysis of Robert's prose as well as his verse, concluded that 'cardboard characterization' solved many of his technical problems:

> 'Cardboard' became one of his ways of masking himself as he wrote two-dimensional stories in which a third dimension of subjective involvement on the part of the author was veiled. He practised the art of letting his characters in song and story tell their own tales — in the first-person point-of-view — but he generally planted clues which pointed away from himself.[3]

When the baronet departed, Robert moved from Sacher's to a cheaper hotel behind St Stephen's Cathedral and resumed his 'grubby poking amid mean streets, getting the local colour' that appealed most to him. He pretended to himself that he was a poor scribbler making his living precariously. 'It's fun pretending one is poor when one isn't — and it saves a lot of money.' As he scratched his flea-bites in his shabby room and bathed in the wash-basin, it tickled him to think that while he lived on a dollar a day he was earning ten times that amount from his book royalties. 'So I took long walks, returning cheerfully tired and brimming over with health.' Later in life, when asked which city he had most loved in Europe before the First World War, he would reply Vienna. 'But that was after I had tired of Paris,' he added. 'For fifteen years Paris was to be my only love, and it was now to this golden goal I turned my eyes.'

CHAPTER 9

THE LATIN QUARTER

Here is my Garret up five flights of stairs;
Here's where I deal in dreams and ply my fancies,
Here is the wonder-shop of all my wares,
My sounding sonnets and my red romances.

'My Garret' in *Ballads of a Bohemian* (1921)

IN MARCH 1913 ROBERT COMPLETED HIS LEISURELY TRIP
from the Balkans and arrived in Paris. It was a bright sunny morning when he
stepped out of the Gare de l'Est and hailed a horse-cab and asked to be taken to
Notre Dame. As they ambled along, Robert felt that his dreams were coming
true:

> My reading of Paris had been ravenous; from every corner remem-
> bered names leapt at me. I was living again in the pages of Hugo,
> Daudet, Zola. In that adorable spring morning each twist and turn gave
> me a new thrill. I felt as if I were coming home and my heart sang.
> Here, I thought, is where I fit in. I will remain at least a couple of
> months . . . I remained for fifteen years.[1]

He had studied a model of Notre Dame in New York's Metropolitan
Museum, but the real thing was more beautiful than he could have imagined.

After a blissful spell of contemplation he started out on 'the grandest walk in the world'. He strolled along the banks of the Seine, past the print-sellers and the book-bins, as far as the Institut, then crossed the Pont des Arts to the Louvre. From there he tramped up the Tuileries to the Place de la Concorde and mounted the Champs Elysées to the Arc de Triomphe. 'On that brilliant day everything was at its best and I had no words to fashion my delight.' From one seductive street to another he marched on till he came to the Madeleine and thence to the Opéra. After a leisurely lunch on the terrace of the Café de la Paix, he resumed his enthusiastic exploration. The Eiffel Tower, the Invalides, the great Boulevard St Michel and the Luxembourg — he visited them all through that memorable afternoon. Though he was footsore by evening he climbed to the Sacré Coeur and Montmartre, his joy sustained to the last. 'To be young, free, primed with romance and with a full purse — what could be nearer Paradise than Paris in the spring?'

On his arrival he had booked in at a hotel near the railway station. This cost him seven francs a night, then the equivalent of six shillings sterling (or thirty pence in modern currency). Cannily, however, he soon moved to a four-franc attic in an ancient hotel at 17 Quai Voltaire. From here he could look down at the Seine: 'the shining river, the trim quays, the gay green of the poplars and the book-bins beneath all gave me an exquisite pleasure'. The hotel is still there, and the scenery has not changed with the passage of time, although the Quai Voltaire has moved up-market, with a profusion of expensive boutiques and fine art shops. From his mansard window, set high above the street, Robert had a stunning view of the spires of the Sainte Chapelle and the towers of Notre Dame, while downstream were the Tuileries and the bridges culminating in the Pont Alexandre. 'That panorama never failed to enchant me, so that from dawn to dark I could sit there entranced.'

Characteristically, he was so absorbed by the city that it was some time before he established any human contacts. The Paris correspondent of a New York newspaper interviewed him at his hotel and then invited him to breakfast at Ciro's. Although he does not name the man, Robert described him as an Englishman 'with a rich voice' and a knowledge of every capital in Europe.

> He had a personality I lacked and he made me look a poor dub, even
> though I *had* written best sellers. I visioned success for him and I was
> not wrong. In the World War he became Colonel, wrote a book, made
> a handsome marriage and clinched his career with a knighthood.[2]

The 'Englishman' was, in fact, George Jefferys Adam, nine years Robert's junior. Despite his rich English accent, he was actually born and raised in

Edinburgh, a descendant of the famous family of architects. From 1901 till 1912 he was head of Reuter's press agency in Paris and simultaneously European correspondent for both the New York *Herald* and *Sun*. Shortly after Robert met him, George Adam moved to *The Times*, becoming their chief correspondent the following year. He did, indeed, have a brilliant war, attaining the rank of colonel, but his knighthood was French, not British, for he became a Chevalier of the Legion d'Honneur. He married an heiress named Pearl Humphrey and, in fact, wrote several books including a history of France (1921) and a biography of Clémenceau which was published shortly before he died on 22 March 1930.

Robert's best friends were a Canadian couple. 'Sweethearts in the same prairie village, linked by a love of art', they had studied in city schools and finally gravitated to Paris. Robert envied their tales of the places they had visited all over Europe, returning with their sketch-books to their studio in Montparnasse to put their impressions on to canvas.

> Theirs was an ideal marriage for not only were they devoted in their
> ordinary lives, but their art was a spiritual passion binding them. So in
> their painting and etching they shared each other's pains and triumphs.
> In their perfect partnership they inspired me, and for years I enjoyed
> their gentle friendship, until like so many they passed on . . .

The Canadians were Frank Armington, who had been born at Fordwich, Ontario, in 1876, and his wife Caroline Helena Wilkinson, born at Brampton, Ontario, in 1875.[3] Neither of these towns could be described as 'a prairie village' but this could have been yet another of those pieces of disinformation with which Robert covered his tracks and those of his friends. The couple actually met and married while both were studying art in Toronto and then, from 1901 till 1905, they had taught and painted in Winnipeg. Afterwards they had moved to Paris where they continued to paint. The outbreak of the Second World War decided them to return to North America, and Caroline died in New York in 1939, Frank surviving her by two years. Through the Armingtons Robert met many other painters until gradually his life took on an artistic trend. Now he conceived himself in the role of a *rapin*. As a schoolboy, he had been pretty handy with a pencil and sketchpad; now he bought a sketch-book and enrolled for lessons in the studio of Colarossi in the rue de la Grande Chaumière. For a franc, he was admitted to the life class and, with trepidation, watched the girl model undress. 'As it was the first time I had seen a naked female I fear my conscientious nudes were affected by my modesty.' In keeping with the part he was now creating, he dressed in a broad-brimmed hat with a butterfly tie and velveteen jacket. 'I dramatised myself in my new role, for, like an actor, I was never happy unless I was playing a part. Most people play only one character in their lives; I have enacted a dozen, and always with my whole heart.'

As usual, Robert's memory of chronology was faulty. 'This *Vie de Bohème* phase must have lasted a year,' he writes, but in fact it lasted no more than a few months. It probably seemed much longer because he certainly packed a lot of interest and excitement into it. He learned 'to loaf on the terrace of the Dôme Café, waggle a smudgy thumb as I talked of modelling, making surreptitious sketches of my fellow wine-bibbers and pile up my own stack of saucers'. Although he had reverted to drinking in this period, he stuck to small *bocks*. He also visited the picture galleries; the Luxembourg was most to his taste, the Louvre lulling him 'into somnolence'. On the other hand, he found that 'excessive modernism' irritated him.

> I got to know many of the long-haired freaks who spent their time between the Dôme and the Rotonde, crossing from the one to the other their only exercise. Poles and Swedes were peculiar enough but the Muscovites were the maddest of all. There were middle-west Americans, too, who absorbed the colour of the Quarter to the point of eccentricity.

On the other hand, there were American artists who worked with passion, 'grudging every moment they could not be at their easels'. Robert would often accompany them on their daily excursions into the surrounding countryside, 'sketching amateurishly while they plied the professional brush', yet he had a feeling that they were exploiting beauty while he was worshipping it. Artists, on the whole, were a pretty dull crowd, caring nothing for music nor literature. When not at their easels all they wanted to do was play snooker or go to a cinema. 'But what a blithe brotherhood! Their technical absorption saved them from that introspection that is the curse of the author.'

While the identity of friends was carefully concealed in his autobiography, Robert had no compunction about naming names when it came to more casual acquaintances. Thus the man who invited him to tea one Sunday, 'a designer of book plates, balanced between literature and art', was not named, although the two other men at the tea-party were.

> In his studio were two men — the first small and thin, with a pear-shaped head, a Swinburnian brow, dark eloquent eyes and crinkly black hair. The other was short, but sturdy, with a round face, sharp eyes peering through glasses, and a virile manner. I was introduced to them: 'James Stephens, the Irish poet, and Gellett Burgess, the American humorist.'

Robert was thrilled to meet two men whose work he had 'long admired' (in fact, Stephens had only achieved literary fame a few months earlier, with the publication of *Crock of Gold*, a collection of fairytales distinguished by its exquisite prose). Burgess is now long-forgotten, but in the early years of the century he achieved modest fame with a satirical volume entitled *Bromides*. Burgess, the funny man, had a sly dig at Robert, asking him why he was not whooping it up in the Yukon. Robert answered with as much dignity as he could muster that he was an art student, experimenting in the life of the Quarter. Soon the conversation turned to poetry. Burgess and Stephens recited some of their poems and Robert was asked to recite one of his. 'This I did with diffidence' — he does not add which one he declaimed. When he had finished, Stephens (whose first slim volume of poetry entitled *Insurrections* had appeared in 1909) loftily commented, 'Very good *newspaper* verse'. Robert was so humble in this rarefied atmosphere that he was quite flattered at this pronouncement. Actually Robert and Stephens, eight years his junior, eventually became quite close friends; later on, the Irish poet was Robert's landlord for a time, before he returned to Dublin to further the Nationalist cause. James, 'pale and frail, a man of delicate health', made a considerable impression on Robert who devoted two pages of *Harper of Heaven* to describing him in the minutest detail.[4] Stephens cut a very strange figure, standing only four foot six inches in his high-heeled elevator shoes. His large eyes and full throat (due to goitre) prevented people from thinking of him as a dwarf, although they often saw him as a leprechaun and sometimes a changeling.

'These literary lights of my salad days looked, I fear, with justifiable disdain on the brash boy from the Yukon,' comments Robert, though he was several years older than either of them and now in his fortieth year, with three volumes of verse and a best-selling novel under his belt. They, on the other hand, had published relatively little and earned even less. Here again, one suspects that subjectivity and an overwhelming sense of inferiority coloured Robert's judgment. On the other hand, lest Robert ever get delusions about his literary worth, he was 'severely put in his place' from time to time. On one occasion an unnamed friend asked him to dinner to meet the celebrated Edmund Gosse. Robert even went so far as to purchase an evening-dress suit for the occasion. 'Gosse was handsome, distinguished, a famous talker' who enthralled his audience with his stories of Browning, Rossetti and Swinburne. For Robert, who had devoured their poetry with manic intensity, this must have been heady stuff indeed. Robert had brought along a copy of *Rhymes of a Rolling Stone* which he duly presented to the great man. 'Rather a pretty binding,' remarked Gosse grudgingly but he never had the grace to open the volume, and ignored its author during the entire evening. Robert, needled by the eminent poet's supercilious attitude, observed to Edmund as the party was breaking up, 'We have at least one thing in common — our names are French.' As *gosse* is French slang for 'kid', the remark was received with withering silence.

Confrontations of this sort, with acknowledged poets, left Robert in no doubt as to his standing — or lack of it — in that rather precious fraternity:

> In those days I took contumely meekly. I regarded myself as a cross between Kipling and G.R. Sims. I was inclined to agree with the dispraise of the mandarins of letters. If people did not buy my books they might purchase others more worthy. I was sorry I was an obstructionist in the fair path of poesy but I did not see what I could do about it. Alas, I write as I feel! I fear I can never do otherwise.

George Robert Sims (1847–1922) was Tom Hood's successor as editor of *Fun* and enjoyed a huge popularity in late-Victorian times for his melodramas and his volumes of light verse. Gosse (1849–1928), on the other hand, was, at the time Robert met him, combining a lucrative career as a poet, biographer and literary critic with his day job as Librarian of the House of Lords and he was actually in Paris in 1913 to receive the *palmes* of the Académie Française, arguably the crowning glory of his brilliant career, although he eventually received a knighthood as well.

Robert also struck up a friendship with James Hopper, a writer of short stories. Like Robert, he was on the short side, reticent and self-effacing. They would sit together silently, each wrapped in his own thoughts, on the terrace of a café. 'No doubt he was hypnotised by the passing throng, or maybe dreaming one of his distinguished stories.' Another friend of this period was the novelist Jeffrey Farnol, who had the same English publisher as Robert. When he offered *The Broad Highway* to Fisher Unwin he was told that it was too lengthy. Savagely he tore out a chunk from the middle, saying, 'That will make it short enough.' Even then, it was overlong, but the publisher accepted it and it was an immediate success. 'In Paris society he wore a huge pair of knee-high boots, but despite them he was gay and ebullient as if he had on dancing pumps.'

One day at Brentano's Robert espied a very distinguished-looking figure, whom the salesman identified for him as Richard Harding Davis. 'My old hero! I watched him with admiring respect,' but apparently did not screw up the courage to approach him. Davis, ten years older than Robert, was then the doyen of American war correspondents, having followed a successful career as a travel-writer with best-sellers about the Graeco-Turkish War of 1897 and the Spanish-American War of 1898. 'He was well groomed and handsome, but he did not look a hale man. As I saw myself the picture of health I did not wish to be in his shoes. I was wise, for shortly after I read of his death.' Davis, in fact, lived long enough to cover the opening campaigns of the First World War, from which he produced a minor classic, *Somewhere in France* (1915). He died near Mount Kisco, New York, in April 1916, some three years after the brief encounter at Brentano's.

During this bohemian period Robert rubbed shoulders with a number of international journalists. He attended a dinner in Larue's in honour of Neil Munro, 'the only Scots author with more than a local reputation', and present on that august occasion were 'Adam of *The Times*, Jerrold and Grey of *The Telegraph*, MacAlpine of the *Daily Mail*, Hill of the *Montreal Star* and Donahoe the Australian journalist'. Laurence Jerrold, a year older than Robert, was actually the reporter for the *Daily Chronicle* on the Western Front in 1914–15 but died barely a month before the Armistice. Previously, Robert had been introduced to Munro at the Napolitain, a favourite watering-hole of the expatriate literati:

> Neil was a slim, fair man, not outwardly striking, yet giving an impression of being fey. He asked me about my work and I assured him I was doing nothing with great enthusiasm. He shook his head sadly: 'I'd give a lot to be independent and write only books. But there's the grey grind of a newspaper office, and by the time I get home my imagination just won't work. Yet my heart's in the Highlands, in the good old days when clansmen clashed and claymores flashed. I was born a hundred years too late.' 'Damned if I feel that way,' I told him. 'I'd rather be here drinking a bonny dram with you than stinking in the coffin of the great Sir Walter. But I get your point, and here's to Romance.'

What Neil Munro made of this brash compatriot is not recorded. Born in Inveraray, Argyll, in 1864, he had come to Glasgow in his youth and spent the rest of his life on Clydeside. 'His heart and genius were in the writing of romances; and yet his instinct and his talent were for journalism,' wrote George Blake in a preface to Munro's autobiography, *The Brave Days*, published shortly after his death in 1930. When Robert met him, Munro was the chief reporter on the Glasgow *Evening News* and took over as editor in 1919. Robert had, he confessed, never read any of Munro's novels, such as *John Splendid*, *The Daft Days* and *Gillian the Dreamer* which had made him a household name in Scotland at least. They were what Robert dismissed as 'tushery'; he was always too much a lover of the present to be interested in the past. Today, Munro is best remembered for his humorous Para Handy stories about the crew of a West Highland puffer.

Another celebrity whom Robert met at this time was Vicente Blasco Ibáñez, the Spanish novelist then in self-imposed exile in Paris. They were introduced by their publisher, T. Fisher Unwin, who asked Robert to act as interpreter in the delicate negotiations which would lead to the appearance of an English translation of his great masterpiece *Blood and Sand* later that year. A few years later it was to be eclipsed by his epic *The Four Horsemen of the Apocalypse* on which his posthumous reputation now rests. The Spaniard, some six and a half years older than Robert, 'was as romantic as Neil [Munro] was prosaic. He was brimming over with a vitality that would not let him rest a moment. A big, handsome, dynamic man . . .' Years later, Robert ran into him again as he was walking across the courtyard of the Louvre.

> Gone was his exuberant zest. He was flabby and stooped with dull eyes and a pasty face. He told me he was having trouble with the Spanish Government who had denounced him as a traitor, while even the French authorities regarded him invidiously. Rich, world-famous but broken-hearted, soon after he passed on. I believe his last regret was that he could not die fighting for his country.

In Paris, Blasco Ibáñez became the centre of a group of Spanish politicians with anti-monarchical views. Although a republican, he also held curiously conservative views on the role of women and was rabidly anti-feminist in outlook. He died there in 1928, during Robert's last full year in Paris.

Robert also enjoyed sitting on park benches in the Jardin du Luxembourg, watching the world go by. One day, he was joined by another idler, 'a young man with a long beard and an ironic smile'. They struck up a conversation and over the months the friendship ripened. He was living in a room that gave on to a back court where, 'with the cats and the ashcans, he cultivated his sense of derision'. His eyes never lost their satiric gleam, even when he became rich and famous. 'I knew him when he had scarce a *sou*,' wrote Robert. 'I never admired his pictures and often wondered if through them he was not mocking the world as he did in the olden days in the leafy garden of the Luxembourg.' The sardonic artist was Kees van Dongen.

Significantly, the man with whom Robert was most intimate in his Bohemian period, and his closest friend for many years thereafter, was disguised by the pseudonym of Peter McQuattie.

> I was sitting lonely on the terrace of the Dôme when an oldish man approached me. He made me think of a Skye terrier, for he had a shaggy moustache and friendly blue eyes under a thatch of eyebrow. He addressed me with a Scotch accent that immediately appealed to me.

His real name was Archibald Ker Bruce[5] and he introduced himself as 'a journalist of sorts and I would like to write an article on you for the *Morning Post'*. Though usually known to family and friends as Archie, he was invariably referred to by Robert as AK. He had been a schoolmaster 'in a wee Scotch toon' before going to France in the early 1890s as tutor to a millionaire's son. For some time he had lived in Tours where he made the friendship of Hugh Walpole, then a young student on the brink of his literary career. He had eventually gravitated to Paris where he later scraped a living writing a weekly column for an English Sunday paper at three guineas a time. An apparently confirmed bachelor without a care in the world, he acquired a sense of responsibility during the war when he was appointed manager of Reuter's Paris office, and subsequently married 'a Scotch lassie, a child sweetheart' whose widowed mother was very wealthy. In the 1920s Archie Bruce and his wife Elizabeth bought a palatial villa at Vence on the Riviera where he had 'a Rolls and a chauffeur, and about a dozen domestics'.[6]

Archie's great ambition was to write a novel about Paris. It was to be called *Youth and a City* and was to recapture his first rapture on arriving, but it never progressed beyond the title. As he settled down to life in the Quarter, however, Robert told his friend that he would take over this ambition. Bruce was less than enthusiastic, giving Robert his 'schoolmaster look' and reminding him that he had not been in Paris long enough. Robert riposted that Archie had been there too long. 'You know it over well. You'll never write your book.' Robert had hoped to goad his friend into getting down to serious work on the project, but he hesitated to make a start. In the end Robert went off 'and wrote and wrote'. Six months later he produced the manuscript. 'Here's your book. Only *I* wrote it. I did it in six months, but I kept my nose to the grindstone. It's the only way.'

In 1914 Robert's second novel, *The Pretender*, was published by Dodd Mead. It was subtitled *A Story of the Latin Quarter* and was concerned with literary circles in New York, London and Paris. The first edition had a quatrain on the fly-leaf, omitted in later editions but characteristically Service in flavour:

Of Books and Scribes there is no end:
This Plague — and who can doubt it?
Dismays me so, I've sadly penned
Another book about it.

Also in the first edition was a note on the title page: 'In deference to the opinion of the publisher the Author has consented to certain alterations being made in his work.' One can only speculate as to what these changes were.

The sequence of events, the love affairs and adventures of James Madden, the hero, were quite fictitious of course, but the book is not without considerable interest in shedding light on Robert's impressions of the literary scene in these cities, brought to life by 'personification, dramatisation, exaggeration, satire, sardonic mockery, absurdity and sentiment'.[7] Contemporary critics, however, did not think much of it. Typical of the reviews that greeted the publication of this novel was that which appeared in *The Times* on 3 May 1915: 'Mr Service's poetry led us to expect better than this uninteresting succession of sentimental and sensational episodes held together by the mere semblance of a plot'.

The title of the book was well chosen for the hero was a pretender in more ways than one, both as an aspiring writer and as one who refuses to separate reality from fantasy. None of the characters in this book is quite what he or she appears at first sight; the entire work is riddled with ambiguities and dualities. The hero is James H. Madden, 'a man of affairs' one moment, and J. Horace Madden 'dilettante and dreamer' the next. To complicate matters further, Madden adopts the pseudonym of Harold Dane when he takes up writing.

The descriptive passages are rather mixed. Those dealing with New York reflect Robert's own feelings of boorishness and lack of sophistication when he first went there from the Yukon. The London passage, by contrast, is rather perfunctory. Until the summer of 1913 he had, in fact, never been there, and his acquaintance with that city was, as will be revealed, understandably brief and sketchy, confined largely to visits to the Reading Room of the British Museum and book-browsing in Bloomsbury. But it is in the Parisian chapters that the novel really comes to life. There are many layers to this densely woven romance. An entire chapter is devoted to a novel called *Tom, Dick and Harry*, identical to that serial written by Robert's Glasgow friend Ferguson, which Madden, now using the pseudonym of Silenus Starset, eventually gets published by McWaddy and Wedge in their Frivolous Fiction Library. Klinck expends many pages of his biography searching for hidden meanings in the text of *The Pretender*, even speculating as to the identity of 'McWaddy and Wedge'. On page 161 of the novel, for example, there is a list of sixteen articles written by Madden, submitted to twelve different magazines in Britain. Klinck carefully examined this list but failed to tie any of the supposed articles to any real magazines.

One wonders whether the articles, stories and novels attributed to Madden in 1913 were ever written, and whether there is in them any information whatever about Service's literary efforts in 1913. Are these titles fictional masks for writing still buried in files of old magazines, or perhaps puzzling clues to experiments forever lost?[8]

In fact, Robert's experiences in this period produced the material for six articles which appeared, under the generic heading of 'Zig-zags of a Vagabond', in the *Toronto Star* between 16 December 1913 and 10 January 1914. Each of these weekly articles was illustrated by photographs and bore the respective titles of 'Paris, A City of Alienating Seduction', 'The Lure of the Latin Quarter', 'Montmartre, the Monstrosity', 'Afoot in Fontainebleau', 'Baedekering in Brittany' and 'The Fisher-Folk of Finistère'. Into these articles Robert put all his enthusiasm and zest for living:

> From every facet I flashed joy as I wrote of my beloved city. It was easy to write those articles for I was so supremely happy. Again and again I thanked the Gods for their gift of ecstasy. Little things that others took for granted — my morning croissant and coffee on the terrace of a tavern, my reflective pipe, my lonely walk along the Seine, evenings under the trees in the purple twilight — all of these were to me sources of divine content. I was amazed at my former idleness and rattled on my typewriter with exuberant ease. Again I discovered the rich satisfaction of creative effort. How I radiated joy! It did not seem right to be so lyric with gladness. I was so happy it almost hurt.

Now he resumed work, throwing off the bohemian image. 'I had no time to waste in café loafing. I despised the fourflushers and failures who crowded the Dôme' and urged his friend Bruce to disassociate himself from 'a bunch of boozing wasters', but to no avail. Always a prodigious walker, Robert indulged his passion more violently than ever. 'No man had ever stauncher legs and they carried me all over Paris till I came to know it like my pocket.' The better he knew it, the better he loved it. 'I do not believe there was another writer of English who knew the City as well as I,' he claimed with pardonable exaggeration.

The *Toronto Star* was well pleased with the material he was sending them and demanded more. Robert broadened his horizons by wandering 'dithyrambic with delight' in the woodlands of Barbizon, although he had a narrow escape when he encountered a lion which had escaped from the set of a film which Pathé were making at Melun. Fortunately his Yukon training stood him in good stead, and he shinned up the nearest tree with agility.

Having exhausted the possibilities of Paris and its environs on foot, Robert purchased a bicycle and began exploring farther and farther afield. 'The first day I did fifty miles with enthusiasm, the second, ten with a sore fanny.' Thereafter he averaged twenty miles, depending on the distance between pubs. In this manner he explored Normandy and then went on to Brittany. 'From the sky-blue sardine nets of Douarnanez to the grim cairns of Carnac; from the quaint *coiffes* of Concarneau to the brilliant brocades of Landerneau' he loved every bit of it. Then one day he stumbled across a pretty village on 'a sea coast famed for its charm' whose beauty took his breath away. He spent several idyllically happy days there, clad only in trunks, catching lobsters, conger eels and jumbo shrimps in the rock pools. 'As I stalked the sands with spear and shrimping net I was like a primitive savage.' He would swim and sun-bathe, his mind a ferment of poetic images which he longed to set down on paper.

According to Robert's own account in *Harper of Heaven* he was attracted to a little red-roofed house that stood on a rock jutting into the sea, set far apart from others. It seemed to be begging him to buy it. Some enquiries at the hotel revealed that the house had once been a coastguard station but now belonged to the local mayor who wanted twenty-five thousand francs for it. When Robert asked if the owner might reduce the price, the hotelier replied, 'Not if you begged him with your *derrière* sticking out of your pants.' This gave Robert an idea and he went to see the vendor wearing stained trousers, a ragged shirt, a broken straw hat and disreputable sandals. Even the local inhabitants seemed more respectable. 'I want to buy your house,' he said, 'and I offer you seventeen thousand francs.' The mayor was dismissive, but Robert proposed a strange deal. He said that all he actually had was seven thousand francs. He would have to beg, borrow or steal the other ten, and was not sure that he would be able to raise the balance. He offered to pay seven thousand down and try to pay the remainder by noon the following Saturday. If he could not complete the deal, he would forfeit the seven thousand francs. With that he pulled seven large *milles* from his ragged shirt and spread them out before the mayor. Urged on by his wife, the mayor took the notes and made out a contract. Robert had three days to come up with the rest.

That night he took the train to Paris, withdrew ten thousand francs from the bank, and the following day was back in Brittany. With the local lawyer he set out for the *mairie* at eleven o'clock that fateful Saturday, arriving only minutes before the deadline. 'I'll never forget the look of disgust on his face as he saw me. For now I was togged up in flannels made by a Paris tailor.' Swallowing his chagrin, the mayor signed the papers, the payment was made, and the house was Robert's. It was fully furnished, right down to a car in the garage; when the mayor asked if Robert wished to check the inventory, he declined. 'I do not want to see the interior of the house. I fell in love with the outside and I want the inside to be a pleasure in store.' Pausing only to name the house Dream Haven he returned to Paris:

> I wanted to keep it a dream, something insubstantial and only half conceived. I had a whimsical feeling I did not want to realise it too quickly. So I went back to Peter [Bruce] and the Dôme and

Montparnasse. 'I have a home, old man,' I said. 'And now what I want is a *wife*. I am ready for the greatest of all life's adventures — Marriage.'

The ensuing chapter, entitled 'Blessed State' gives Robert's version of how he approached this particular adventure. 'Occasionally I am a man of resolution and, having conceived the idea of wedded bliss, behold me three months later nailed to the Cross of Matrimony.' As Robert took the plunge in mid-June 1913, it would place the purchase of Dream Haven impossibly in mid-March; but as he never furnished dates for his narrative he was never confronted by such glaring discrepancies. The story of the gamble taken in the purchase of the house may well have elements of truth in it, but the timing was wrong, as will become apparent later on. Briefly, the purchase of the holiday home was to come *after* marriage, not before. Robert claims that his approach to marriage was peculiarly Scotch:

> I wanted a wife who would be willing to black my shoes of a morning. I remembered how my dear mother shone the boots of myself and four brothers before we went to school, spitting on them to make the blacking go further. Scotch girls would do that especially if they were humbly born. They had 'siller sense'. I dreaded a wasteful woman. Yes, I wanted a wee Scotch lassie who would respect the bawbees.
>
> Well, if I couldn't have a Scotch mate a French one might do. It was claimed they made the best wives in the world — canny and *sou-conscious*. She must belong to the small *bourgeoisie*; better if she had known poverty, for then she would appreciate all I could give her. A Cinderella marriage — that was the stuff for me. But once I had made my choice I would abide by it. There has never been a divorce in our family. Such a horror would have made my Covenanting ancestors turn in their graves.

Robert admitted that, at heart, he was a prig. He might mock morality and scoff at respectability, but, deep down, he wished to conform. He was disgusted by the licentiousness he found in the Quarter, but nice girls in that circle were rare and he did not know any. 'So I put myself in the hands of Fate' as he had done so often in earlier life. One day, while crossing the Place de la Madeleine, his passage was blocked by a milling mob intent on watching a military parade. At first he hoped to get to a café where, standing on a chair, he might get a good view; but the throng was denser than he imagined. Then, in the crush, he spotted a hand-cart; an enterprising hawker was charging a franc to let people stand on top for a grandstand view. 'Instantly I was up, looking with pity on the serried bodies and thinking how one little franc can relieve an awkward situation.'

Presently he became conscious of two young girls in the crowd, having a tough time. Perhaps if they had not been pretty he might not have noticed them, but dolled up in dainty finery they made an attractive couple. They were in danger of being trampled when the gallant Robert came to the rescue and paid a couple of francs so that they could escape the crush. To his surprise, the younger girl spoke to him in his own tongue, having spent several months in England. According to Robert, this chance encounter led to a hesitant invitation home for tea, which he accepted even more hesitantly. According to Germaine (the younger girl), after the military parade Robert had given her his card and invited both girls to join him for tea at a café in the Place de la Madeleine. Afterwards he expressed a wish to see her again. 'I told him to come first to our home to see my mother.' The sisters were convent-educated and belonged to the *petite bourgeoisie* that Robert so much admired. At their humble apartment the tea might be tepid but the cakes were delicious and Robert enjoyed himself more than he had done since his arrival in Paris — which was saying a good deal. The girls' mother liked him at once and a second invitation to tea came soon afterwards, followed by little Sunday afternoon outings to Versailles and St Cloud. It was a trip to Fontainebleau, however, that clinched matters.

> I visioned the younger sister in the frame of DREAM HAVEN, and thought I could not do better. I wanted a home, a settled life, respectability, convention. I viewed the Quarter with growing disgust. A bunch of lousy libertines laughing all day long! . . . I had enough of that. I was due to play a new part. Why not a Benedict?

In real life, Robert had always hated sentimentality. By this he meant the expression of finer feelings, and he carried this mental block over into his novels. In one of them occur the memorable words, as the hero and heroine finally recognise their love for each other, 'As I have little taste for depicting scenes of sentiment, the ten minutes that followed will remain undescribed'.[9] Now, in *Harper of Heaven*, he drew a heavy curtain over his private life. 'Had I been writing the story of another man I might have revelled in details of his domestic life, but as I am telling the history of my own I feel a certain restraint.' There were matters too sacred to be revealed even to the most sympathetic reader. 'Let the biographer chronicle them when one is dead.' His marriage, 'so experimentally taken', turned out to be a huge success, although it speaks volumes for the equable temperament of the lady he married. Writing in 1946 he reflected:

> After thirty-three years of self-consideration, I still have the same wife.
> In all that term of matrimony I do not remember receiving a single

black eye. Of course, every marriage is a compromise, and to make it successful the female must be a champion compromiser. She must learn to get her own way by letting the man have his. There's an art in handling the male brute and lucky is the wench who has it.

After he had been seeing her for a few weeks Robert took the bull by the horns:

Say, why don't we take a chance? Columbus took a chance . . . Let's get hitched. I'm only a poet and as you know poets don't make money, but I guess we can manage to rub along. If you're not scared at the prospect of marrying a poor man let's live in a garret with a loaf of bread and a jug of wine, and we'll sing under the tiles.' . . . And to my amazement she accepted.

Klinck felt that this showed that Mademoiselle had a sense of humour. In fact, she was more hard-headed than even Robert realised. In 1960,[10] not long after Robert's death, Germaine wrote some notes, setting straight what little record of their marriage had appeared in *Harper of Heaven*. The salient details of their first meeting were confirmed, she being accompanied by her sister Hélène; but Germaine was quite clear that it was Robert who made the first move. During their brief courtship he did not mention anything about being a poet. He told her mother that he was a journalist working for a Toronto newspaper, but a girlfriend of Germaine's recognised his name and told her that he was a famous poet and had written a celebrated ballad about the *incinération* of Sam McGee. It was during the outing to Fontainebleau that Robert introduced her to Frank Dodd, his New York publisher. Dodd, in fact, was to be Robert's best man at the wedding.

True to form, Robert had wanted only the simplest of ceremonies, and would have preferred to grab Germaine and a valise and take the ferry to Dover for a registry office quickie in England. But Germaine insisted on the proprieties being maintained. She was convent-bred and a devout Catholic; she had to get an interview with the bishop, and the price of dispensation to marry a Protestant, even one as tepid as Robert, was a promise from him that all the children of the marriage would be raised in the Catholic faith. Robert accepted her terms with equanimity. He told Archie Bruce that he had had 'to promise my progeny would be little Papists. If one has to accept religion I reckon one might as well go the whole hog, and the Catholic brand has its good points.'

The records show that Robert William Service, *journaliste* by profession, married Germaine Bourgoin, *vendeuse*, on Thursday, 12 June 1913. Robert apparently wished to get wed the following day, tempting superstition; but civil marriages were not permitted on Fridays (or Friday the thirteenth at any rate). Germaine was thirteen years younger than her husband, having been born at St Maur des Fosses, in the *département* of Seine on 22 September 1887. In 1913 she was living with her mother and two sisters at 16 rue des Boulets. She was the youngest daughter of Constant Bourgoin, who had inherited, and then mismanaged, a distillery at Brie-Comte-Robert on the outskirts of the city. Eventually his wife was obliged to leave him for a time and raise her three daughters single-handed, something virtually unheard of in those days. Germaine's mother was Marie Emélie Klein, of Alsatian stock.[11]

After both civil and religious ceremonies there was a celebratory lunch for Germaine's family and four of Robert's friends (the Armingtons, Archie Bruce and Frank Dodd), followed by a few photographs in the nearby Jardin du Luxembourg, and then it was time to catch the boat-train to England.

Harper of Heaven, not the most organised of autobiographies at the best of times, is positively muddled over the sequence of events in the summer of 1913. Robert conveys an impression of setting up house with his bride, and going to England at a much later date, but Germaine's own memoir indicates that this is where they spent their honeymoon. Their visit to London, at any rate, was a huge success. They did the sights like any other tourists, although Robert confesses that 'with my interest in people and my indifference to historic sights I gravitated slumward. Pubs, not palaces, were what intrigued me; costermongers, not countesses.' The main purpose of the trip was to negotiate royalty terms for *The Pretender* with Fisher Unwin, 'a dignified man with a beard and frock coat', whose office was an Adam room in the Adelphi. The royalties on the English editions of Robert's novels were paltry compared with the money which the New York editions brought in, but they were by no means negligible. In fact, the first royalty cheque from Fisher Unwin for the second novel amounted to over two thousand pounds.

One evening Robert and Germaine looked up Jimmy Bone. 'In place of the black-haired boy with twinkling eyes I now saw a little man with a big bald head and an air of authority. Yet his eyes still twinkled and his wit was apt.' Bone had been appointed London Editor of the Manchester *Guardian* only the previous year. At Bone's home the newly-weds were introduced to the Anglo-American poet Christopher Morley, who obviously expected the progenitor of Dan and Sam to be a real roughneck, though all he said was 'You're different from what I thought you would be'. As usual I was *not my type*, mused Robert.

According to *Harper of Heaven* the Services spent two weeks in London before returning straight to Paris. Things were going very well for Robert.

But as I basked in the sunny smile of fortune I had one dreadful fear. I
was living far below my means. If I went on I would be spending only
the interest of my interest. Even a Scotsman would revolt at that. I
must do something about it. So I bought the wife a bicycle, polished
up my own and we started on a tour of Touraine. After doing the
Château country we moved by easy stages to Brittany and at last came
to the little fishing village where I had passed such a happy holiday.
That evening we sat on the same rabbity hill on which I had spent so
many hours of reverie.

There across the golden cove was the house I had bought — DREAM
HAVEN. It looked lovelier than ever, but very lonely too. It seemed to
reproach me; so I said to the wife: 'There's a cute cottage.' And she
said: 'It's beautiful, but so sad. People should be living in it and how
happy it would be!' And though we spoke of other things our eyes
always returned to the little house with the red roof; so presently I
said: 'Let's go over and have a look.'[12]

Robert would have us believe that they went up to the cottage, unlatched the
garden gate and went up the path to take a look. Germaine allegedly protested
that the owner would not welcome their intrusion, but Robert turned the
handle and, on finding the door unlocked, suggested that as there was no one
around they might as well take a look. Again Germaine demurred but he
pressed on. To their surprise they found the dining-table freshly laid. Then the
kitchen door opened and out popped Anastasia, the cook-housekeeper, to
welcome them. Tasie Pezeron had prepared supper and aired the beds, having
been forewarned of their arrival. Then Robert confessed to Germaine that he
had deceived her. 'This house is mine, furnished complete to the car in the
garage.'

What Germaine is supposed to have made of this, after having to put up
with a push-bike for several weeks, is not recorded. Anastasia, incidentally, was
the name of the heroine of *The Pretender*, a poor French girl whom Madden
rescues from suicide. In Robert's existence at this time, fact and fiction were so
inextricably interwoven that, thirty years later, he had difficulty in disentan-
gling them. Germaine's account, however, is much more prosaic. They stayed
only one week in London, but Robert was anxious to get back to France, so
they took the steamer to Jersey and from there crossed to St Malo, 'looking for
a small place' as a holiday home. They explored the Emerald Coast, but felt
that Dinard, Saint Lunaire and Saint Briac were too civilised. Leaving Saint
Briac, they crossed the Frémur estuary 'in a very small boat at high tide'
though they could wade across at low water. Nowadays a road bridge over this
tidal reach links Saint Briac sur Mer with Lancieux and the unspoiled hamlet,

eighty years on, has become a bustling resort of holiday homes. 'We loved it, but RW wanted to be sure that the water was very warm, so he bought two bicyclettes to make a tour to see the nicest and warmest places of all.' During this period Robert wrote at least two of the pieces subsequently published under the title 'Zig-zag of a Vagabond'. According to Germaine, 'It was after that tour we decided Lancieux was the best for us, being at the shortest distance from Paris or London.' Dream Haven, according to Germaine, was not purchased until the autumn of 1913. At first they stayed at the Hotel des Bains on the rue Nationale, but after a few days Robert rented 'Avel Brao', a house off the rue de l'Islet. It was their landlord, Monsieur Legue, who supplied Germaine with her first bicycle and actually taught her to ride it.[13] Further east along the rue de l'Islet is the street known as rue du Corps de Garde which took its name from the coastguard hut which at one time stood on a little promontory. Some time previously, the mayor of Lancieux, a Parisian businessman named Jules Jeunet, had built two villas, at either end of the village. One, named La Source, he occupied himself and the other, on the site of the coastguard hut, he put up for sale. It was the latter villa, with its red tiles and brightly painted green shutters, that caught the fancy of Robert and Germaine. They went to the estate agent in Saint Briac and enquired about various properties. Robert insisted that the estate agent take him and Germaine round the coast in a small boat so that they could view the properties from the sea. The villa, then known as Le Corps de Garde, stood out prominently on its cliff-top, surrounded by bare moorland and approached by a tortuous footpath overgrown with bramble thickets. The story about the gamble with the vendor appears to be wholly apocryphal, the negotiations to purchase being conducted through the estate agent.

On their return to Paris for the winter they took a furnished apartment at 11 rue Compagne Première, belonging to James Stephens.[14] In the same building lived the English poet and artist, Mina Loy, a close friend of Gertrude Stein, though Robert curiously forgot to mention this. His apartment was in a loft over a mechanic's workshop and when the various machines got going 'we jiggled and joggled . . . How could my landlord have written his radiant poetry in such a racket?' Cynthia Stephens, 'the most charming of women, as pretty as a picture', once said, 'The Services are the best tenants I ever had and the only ones who left the apartment as clean as they found it.' Robert promptly christened the tiny apartment the Rabbit Hutch. 'I did not insist on the garret of which I have so often sung, but I compromised on an apartment that came mighty close to it.' It was pretty spartan, comprising two rooms 'barely big enough to swing the proverbial cat' and including a 'cupboard kitchen whose sink was my bathroom'. It is surprising that such a successful writer should have been content to live with such frugality. The tiny flat was just off the

Boulevard Raspail and the rent was three hundred francs a year. 'I gave the wife a thousand francs to furnish it and she did so with taste and discretion.' Germaine was very clever with her needle and ran up curtains and cushions with her own hands. Often she would ask her husband's opinion, seeking his approval, but he would put on his wise look and just say 'Swell!' Half the time, however, he never noticed any difference. 'Details bored me. As long as I was comfortable I was more than content.'

The desire to shield his married life from the inquisitive stare of his readers was perhaps understandable, but the constant reference to Germaine simply as 'the wife' — a dreadful Scottish habit — was unpardonable. The few brief glimpses of her in the autobiography are rather patronising:

> Under her ministrations I got so fat I scarcely knew myself. She would return from market with huge baskets of provisions — chickens, grapes, rich pastry — all absurdly cheap. She tried to show me her accounts but I brushed them aside. Then once in a while she would timidly ask me for more money. Perhaps I should have taken more interest in her home-making but I was too preoccupied, for I had taken the plunge and was deep in A NEW NOVEL.

This is clearly a reference to *The Pretender*, which Robert had begun many months earlier. At one point he told Bruce that he wrote it in six months; elsewhere in *Harper of Heaven* he claimed that it took ten months, most of the travail being in the first five. He had negotiated terms with Frank Dodd and Fisher Unwin in June 1913 but the final draft was not actually completed till Christmas Eve that year. Copies of the manuscript, neatly typed on Robert's Remington, must have gone to the publishers shortly afterwards, for the British and American editions both appeared early in 1914.

Robert considered this his best work to date, and was disappointed that it failed to achieve the commercial success of his first novel, or indeed, of his volumes of verse. He put this failure down to the fact that 'if an author gets tabbed for doing a certain type of work the public won't let him do something different'. Despite this, his Latin Quarter novel would always be his favourite, 'perhaps because I was so radiant when I wrote it. And though I romped and rollicked through it, it contained passages that record my rapture.'

When the novel was finished, Robert resumed his old lazy ways. Having avoided the bohemians of the Dôme while work was in progress, he took up with Archie Bruce once more. According to *Harper of Heaven* he sprang his marriage on Bruce as a surprise, many months after the event, when in truth Archie had been one of the witnesses. This was a gross distortion which, by refraining from giving any dates, Robert never had to reconcile with the truth.

In the autobiography he speaks of a trip to London *after* the novel was completed, as 'a belated honeymoon', but there was only one such trip, and it took place the day after the wedding. So, too, he would conceal from his friend the fact that he had just written the novel which Bruce was always meaning to write. When he told Germaine that he had invited Bruce to dinner one evening he gave her twenty francs to purchase a few extras for the meal. 'Ah! those were the days. One could have a roasting chicken for seven francs and a bottle of Barsac for five. And that evening, though I was supposed to be a starving scribe, no millionaire could have fared better.' Half a page is devoted to describing in mouth-watering detail the feast that Germaine had prepared, right down to the bottle of Château Lafitte with the main course and the champagne with the dessert. Afterwards, the two gorged males smoked Egyptian cigarettes, swilled cognac and sipped coffee while the dutiful wife did the washing-up in the kitchen. When Bruce commented favourably on the pretty dress she was wearing, Robert answered airily, 'Yes. She makes all her clothes. She has fairy fingers with a needle.' He wanted to take her to the Galeries Lafayette to buy her a new gown, but she considered this too expensive. 'Oh dear! It's going to be very hard to break her of her economical habits,' he added rather smugly.

In May 1914 Germaine and Robert returned to Lancieux and spent an idyllic summer at Dream Haven. He purchased a Breton spaniel called Coco and a new canoe which he christened *Daisy*, his pet-name for his wife.[15] In this fragile craft one day he rescued a small boy from drowning, and then had to go back into the water to look for the brat's shoes. In June Archie Bruce joined them for a holiday, and there is a charming photograph of the two men, trousers rolled to the knee, shrimping with Breton fishermen. This holiday put new life in Robert's friend: 'He seemed to grow ten years younger the month he was with us.' He swam strongly, went on hazardous canoeing trips with Robert, and pottered about in the garden. The three of them would cram into Robert's new car, a De Dion Bouton open tourer, 'long and low with graceful lines, and finished in brass that gleamed like gold'. Once a week Robert and Germaine would drive into Dinard to do their shopping, ending up at the celebrated *salon de thé* of Jean Lebras. At other times, the car was used for rides through ancient Breton villages and picnics amid the ruins of medieval castles.

> When I look back on that first summer in Dream Haven it seems to me incredibly sweet. I marvel how so much joy could be compassed in a single season. I did no work, but read until the early morning hours with the waves plashing under my window. I went a three-hour walk over the sands, clad only in bathing trunks; or if the tide was high I

tramped the land far and wide. I became notorious as a solitary walker, hailed by farm and fisher folk alike. And as I walked I dreamed. I planned new books, I savoured the success of old. I was at the zenith of life, enjoying it as never before. Again and again I said: 'It's too wonderful. It cannot last. Something sinister is beneath it all.'

Germaine and Robert were walking across the fields one afternoon when they suddenly heard the bells of the village church ringing out the tocsin. A neighbour came running down the path crying, 'War. Our men will have to go. My husband . . .' Now they could see peasants leaving their fields and hurrying to the village square beside the church where the *Garde Champêtre* read the mobilisation announcement, tears streaming down his grizzled cheeks as he ended with '*Vive la France!*' Subdued, the villagers drifted back to their cottages to get their menfolk ready to depart. As Robert trudged back to Dream Haven he had a feeling that nothing would ever be the same again. 'Never again would we see that eager, care-less world; never exult in the golden present, thinking that the future would be equally serene. Never, never again . . .'

CHAPTER 10

FIRST WORLD WAR

Everywhere thrill the air
The maniac bells of War.
There will be little of sleeping to-night;
There will be wailing and weeping to-night;
Death's red sickle is reaping to-night;
War! War! War!

'The Call' in *Rhymes of a Red Cross Man* (1916)

ROBERT WAS IN HIS FORTY-FIRST YEAR WHEN THE FIRST World War erupted in August 1914. Although well past military age, he immediately thought of enlisting. A recruiting office was opened in Paris to enable British expatriates to join up. Robert darkened his hair and mentally took several years off his age. With his fresh complexion, wiry figure and boyish good looks, he felt confident that he would slip through the thirty-five-year net. He fancied the Seaforth Highlanders, though why he chose this regiment was not explained. All went well until it came to a medical examination. 'You can't wear puttees with that thing,' snapped the medical officer, indicating a varicose vein. For a man who took such an intense pride in physical fitness, the rejection on medical grounds was intolerable. That innocent bulge in his left calf probably saved his life, however, for that battalion of the Seaforths was virtually annihilated on the Somme. 'I would probably now be lying near my brother in a grave in Flanders Field. Sometimes a blemish is a blessing.' The brother was Albert, baby of the family, killed in action while serving as a lieutenant in the Canadian Infantry, in August 1916.

Having been rebuffed by the British Army, Robert seems to have idled away the autumn and winter of 1914. The next sentence in his autobiography implies that he took immediate counsel 'of my good friend John Buchan, a man whose brilliance dazzled me', but John Buchan did not actually come to Paris till the beginning of 1915. The reference to his 'good friend' was the only example of name-dropping in either autobiographical volume. As a rule, when actual names, as opposed to pseudonyms, were given, they pertained to people with whom Robert had no more than a passing acquaintance. But of John Buchan he wrote:

Had he not gone to my old University, gained a scholarship for Balliol, written a dozen books, become a Member of Parliament? He was also partner in a big publishing firm and head of a famous news agency. So young, with so many irons in the fire. Yet I do not think he dreamed of the high honours that would ultimately be his. At that moment he was a ranking Colonel and writing a history of the War.

I met him in the lounge of the Hotel Scribe. He had a slim figure and a sensitive face under a bulging brow. When I told him I wanted to join the ranks he shook his head. 'Join the Officers' Training Corps and get a commission. We want men like you.' I disagreed, for I knew myself better than that. Though I can obey ardently I cannot command. Always that inferiority complex. I am incapable of handling men, while responsibility unnerves me. All of which I tried to explain to John but left him unconvinced.[1]

John Buchan, eighteen months younger than Robert, had indeed gone to Glasgow University. Like Robert, he was not a native of the city but grew up there. While Robert lived in Hillhead close to the University, John lived in Pollokshields and almost every day walked the four miles from the South Side to Hillhead. There, it must be said, their paths diverged. In the session of 1892–93 Buchan attended the Greek class at eight in the morning, whereas Robert attended the Ordinary English class at four in the afternoon — by which time John was back home in Pollokshields, studying till midnight. Although John was an avid reader of English literature, there is no record of his attending the classes in that subject. Interestingly, he too was captivated by Kipling and emulated Austin Dobson's experiments with the French verse forms of villanelle, rondeau and ballade: 'There was no lingering value in such confections, but I have a lingering taste for them'.[2] On the other hand

Browning, who was Robert's favourite poet for a time, he never understood, and even towards the end of his life, 'still found too difficult in patches'. At Glasgow University mathematics and moral philosophy were his other consuming interests. It is improbable, though not impossible, that Buchan and Service knew each other then. Robert does not mention this brilliant younger man in the relevant chapter of *Ploughman of the Moon*, and Robert himself does not feature anywhere in Buchan's own autobiography, *Memory Hold-the-Door*. While Robert was sending in light, three-stanza verse to *Quiz*, Buchan was already contributing solemn gnomic verse to *The Yellow Book*. While Robert was serving his banking apprenticeship, the high-flying Buchan took a first and won a scholarship which took him to Brasenose College — not Balliol as Robert stated. While Robert was drifting wherever Fate might push him, Buchan was planning his future in a coldly ambitious manner, cultivating 'the right people' at Oxford. Robert was mucking out cowsheds at the Eureka Ranch when Buchan was called to the bar at the Middle Temple. While Robert was stamping the mail at Cowichan, Buchan was pulling strings to secure his appointment as Private Secretary to Lord Milner, the High Commissioner for South Africa. And about the time Robert swallowed his pride and entered the Canadian Bank of Commerce at Victoria, John Buchan was embarking on his publishing career, as a partner in the prestigious Edinburgh firm of Thomas Nelson and Sons. He had gone to Oxford in 1895 as a relatively penniless student; within a year he had published his first book, *Scholar Gipsies*, closely followed by the historical romance *John Burnet of Barns*, and by the time he graduated the royalties from his verse and prose made him arguably the wealthiest man in the Arts faculty. While Robert chose as his soul-mate the daughter of a Parisian distiller, Buchan married Susan Charlotte Grosvenor, related to the Dukes of Wellington and Westminster and half the English aristocracy beside.

The rest of Robert's comments on John Buchan in 1915 is oddly at variance with the facts, and confused chronology as usual. It is true that Buchan had dabbled in politics ever since he had stood as the Conservative candidate for Peebles and Selkirk in 1911, but he did not actually enter Parliament until 1927 when he became MP for the four Scottish universities. Thereafter he arranged his affairs so skilfully that he managed to rise to the top in both spheres of literature and politics. But in 1914–15 the careers of both men were extraordinarily similar. Far from being a 'ranking Colonel' when they met, John Buchan was just recovering from a serious illness which had confined him to bed for three months in the autumn of 1914. While in bed, he had corresponded with the War Office about joining the Army, but was told that in his present state of health it was useless to think of it. To distract himself from the boredom of confinement to bed in Broadstairs he whiled away the time by writing *The Thirty-Nine Steps*. Back in London, he was ordered a complete rest in bed and special treatment, but at the end of the year he wangled an appointment with *The Times* as their correspondent in France. His status, in fact, was very similar to that which Robert later enjoyed with the *Toronto Star*.

Years of study at Oxford and his subsequent London-based career had almost obliterated John Buchan's Scottish accent, but in 1915, with sixteen books — fiction, non-fiction, poetry, histories, a biography of Raleigh and a collection of short stories — to his credit, he was widely regarded as Scotland's outstanding literary figure, a worthy and prolific successor to Sir Walter Scott. It was for this reason that he was the principal speaker at the Burns Supper organised by the expatriate community at the Hotel Scribe near the Opéra on 25 January 1915, and this was the only occasion on which, as far as can be ascertained, the two men ever met. Probably the only thing they had in common was a passion for long walks; both thought nothing of a twenty-mile tramp. At dinner, John told Robert that he had just finished the latest of his Richard Hannay adventure yarns, *Greenmantle,* which had sold twenty thousand copies in advance. Commenting on the absence of haggis from the menu, Buchan drily observed, 'A Burns banquet without the haggis is like *Hamlet* without the Prince'.

Robert marvelled at John's facility and his success. 'For so fine a scholar he had a rich sense of humour, and it was a grievous pity a man of such grace and distinction should meet with an untimely death.' It was not, in fact, until 1916 that John Buchan managed to get into uniform, in the Intelligence Corps, but he was extremely well connected and, as an officer on the General Staff, had the ringside seat that enabled him to publish, in 1921–22, his bestselling *History of the Great War*. By the time Robert was actually part of the war effort, however, John was already being head-hunted by Prime Minister Lloyd George as his Director of Information under the War Cabinet. After that brief encounter at the Scribe, their paths never crossed again; Buchan, by that time Lord Tweedsmuir and Governor-General of Canada, died in Ontario on 11 February 1940, a few months before Robert and his family passed through on their way to wartime refuge in Vancouver.

One other point in Robert's recollection of his meeting with Buchan is worthy of comment. 'Though I can obey ardently I cannot command' is flatly contradicted by Robert's lifelong 'horror of authority' and marked aversion to taking orders as well as giving them. The youth who defied Sergeant Walker on the Hillhead playground would not have taken kindly to the discipline of the British Army of the First World War, and it is difficult to reconcile Robert's view of himself at this time with the habitual loner and stubborn maverick. No doubt his feelings in 1915 were coloured by patriotic sentiment and that lust for adventure which was never far from his mind.

Mindful of his brief, inglorious experiences in Turkey, Robert wrote to the *Toronto Star* offering to supply articles about the war. One late-August evening in the Place Clichy he rescued a drunken Tommy from a mob of derisive women, bought him a bottle of wine and got a graphic eye-witness account of the retreat from Mons from the sole survivor of one of the rearguard units which had been badly mauled at Le Cateau. After the frontier battles of August, and the retreat of the French and British forces, the Germans advanced swiftly through France. By the beginning of September, barely four weeks into the war, some German units were poised on the banks of the Seine, on the very outskirts of Paris. It seemed as if the campaign would be a re-run of the lightning war of 1870. Then, on 3 September, the German First Army wheeled to advance to the south-east, thus exposing its flank. General Galliéni, Military Governor of Paris, was the first to appreciate the opportunity which had suddenly presented itself. Mobilising all the cars and taxi-cabs in the city, he rushed every available soldier from Paris to the Marne. Robert was one of the onlookers in the Montmartre streets along which marched regiments from Niger and Senegal as well as the Foreign Legion. Seeing the Paris taxis crammed with cheering *poilus* was an inspiring sight 'and only in the dim dawn did I go home, too tired to write my story'. For an anxious week, while thousands fled in disarray from the capital, Robert and Germaine stuck it out in their new flat in the rue de Cherche-Midi, Montparnasse.

> The weather had been brooding and sinister, but the Sunday dawned bright and clear and somehow we all sensed that a miracle had happened. Apprehensively we had been waiting to hear the guns of the enemy; now all was silent. Only later did we know that one of the most glorious pages in history had just been written.

No record of Robert having written about the retreat from Mons or the first battle of the Marne has been traced, and it was not, in fact, until the middle of 1915 that he obtained accreditation as a war correspondent. At that point in the conflict there were not the organised facilities, or the military-style uniforms, which later gave correspondents a certain amount of status in the combat zones. At best, they were regarded by the High Command as a bloody nuisance; at worst, they were looked on at regimental level as potential spies for the other side. It is difficult at this remove in time to appreciate the intense paranoia that pervaded the areas in which actual fighting was taking place. At first Robert contented himself with fairly bland stories garnered in rear-area hospitals and training centres, but the best he could come up with was a graphic account of the arrival of a trainload of wounded at Rennes, not far from Lancieux where he and Germaine spent that summer.

The war of movement, which had begun with such panache in August 1914, soon ran out of momentum and both sides were bogged down along the Western Front in a system of defensive trenches that extended for a thousand miles, from the Swiss frontier to the North Sea. There seemed only two ways of breaking the deadlock that ensued when the war was barely two months old. The idea of a vehicle impervious to enemy machine-guns and capable of traversing trenches and other obstacles was conceived in Britain, eventually seeing the light of day in 1916 as the tank. The other solution to the problem was to go round the trench barrier, but opinion soon divided between those who advocated such tactics and those who took a broader view of the war and opined that an attack elsewhere, in Russia or the Balkans, would make the Germans loosen their grip in the West. With the collapse of the Gallipoli operation, however, greater attention was given to the alternatives. The British attempted a breakthrough at Neuve Chapelle, with disastrous results, while the Germans found the answer in chlorine gas, at Ypres. In both cases Canadian troops were heavily involved. The newly arrived First Canadian Division spearheaded the attack at Neuve Chapelle, and it was the heroic resistance of the Canadians on the French flank that prevented Ypres being a total disaster.

To supply the *Toronto Star* with more colourful and exciting news of the Canadian war effort, Robert moved north, to Calais, the location of the main British base camp. At the Station Hotel there, he found a brilliant band of journalists, but they depended largely on soldiers going on leave or 'Blighty victims' for their stories. Robert was not very successful. 'The regular newspaper men got tips that left me an outsider.' The general advice from the press boys was 'if you value your skin don't go near Dunkirk'. This was like a red rag to a bull, and Robert determined to get to Dunkirk by fair means or foul. Shrewdly he realised that if he took the train to Dunkirk, so close to the front line, he would promptly be arrested at the station, but there was a village a few miles from the town, and when the train stopped there Robert alighted and decided to walk the rest of the way. In the village he paused at a café, where the other drinkers eyed him distrustfully and the landlord made a bee-line for the telephone. Leaving hurriedly, Robert approached Dunkirk by a roundabout country lane and eventually reached the town centre where he ordered a meal at a café.

From here he had a marvellous vantage point and could observe all the comings and goings. All day long he wandered around, seeing a hundred things he was not supposed to see, and all the while thinking how smart he was in getting ahead of his rivals. That evening he was arrested by a truculent gendarme and hustled off to a major who was quick to note the Turkish, Bulgarian, Austrian and German visas in his passport. He was marched through the streets, hissed at by a vindictive mob, and locked in a guardroom overnight. The following day he was taken under escort to the naval authorities in charge of the port. There he was given a severe dressing-down by a British officer and ordered out of the town, with the menacing news that Dunkirk was rife with rumours of spies and that only that morning half a dozen suspects had been shot by nervous French gendarmes out of hand. Back in Calais he regaled the pressmen with his lucky escape, but they roared with laughter and thought that being shot as a spy was 'a helluva joke'.

This episode disillusioned Robert with the correspondent game, but he was still determined to have another attempt at 'a ringside seat at the Big Show'. Things gradually improved and, as a result, the *Toronto Star* accepted a number of pieces, which appeared each Saturday from 11 December 1915 until 29 January 1916. These were mainly reflective pieces that lacked the urgency and immediacy of hot news, but they provided vividly detailed descriptions which gave readers a much clearer sense of the horrors of modern warfare, and disabused them of the glamour and romance. These articles, entitled 'The Red Harvest', 'The Orchestra of War', 'Where Ruin Begins', 'The Valley of the Thousand Dead', 'In the Trenches', 'The Attack' and 'On the Inferno's Edge', were later reworked to provide much of the ninth and tenth chapters in *Harper of Heaven*.

The immediate opportunity to get closer to the action came in the autumn of 1915. The account in *Harper of Heaven* is confused and hazy, due to the lapse of thirty years between actual events and Robert setting them down in his autobiography. But in 1921 Robert published *Ballads of a Bohemian* which drew heavily on his wartime experiences. Unlike *Rhymes of a Red Cross Man*, published in 1916 and therefore even closer to events, the later volume of verse was interspersed with prose passages, written in the form of a diary or letters. Although quite fictional, they were clearly drawn on actual experiences in 1914–15; indeed, so realistically were they set out that at least one previous biographer accepted them at face value.[3] Thus Lockhart describes as 'an early note from the front' a passage dated 'The Somme Front, January 1915' which actually preceded the poem entitled 'Priscilla' which was the first in book four — 'Winter' — in *Ballads of a Bohemian*. The passage itself has the ring of truth; only the date which Robert assigned to it is impossible, for the Somme Front did not come into being until July 1916 and dragged on for half a year, the last major offensive taking place at Beaumont-Hamel on 13 November. Accepting January 1915, however, Lockhart fell into the error of assuming that Robert had embarked on his new war job by that date.

In point of fact it was in September 1915 that Robert read an announcement in a Paris newspaper concerning the raising of the American Ambulance

Unit which was recruiting drivers. Robert immediately wrote for details, and a few days later received a letter asking him to come for an interview at the Hotel Meurice. There he was casually informed that a 'bunch of the boys were whooping it up in the Ritz Bar' — sounded familiar — when someone suggested that they form an ambulance corps. 'We all had cars and were willing to turn them into ambulances and drive them ourselves, so we decided to offer our services to the French government.' The offer had been accepted and now the American volunteers were attached to the army of Marshal Foch. Robert was told that, if he joined them, he would be sent to the Front, 'only you must promise not to write a word on anything you see'.

Robert readily assented, though he had reservations about the promise not to write of his experiences. 'In the meantime I went to London, bought a uniform and felt rather a fool in it.' With a linen shirt, necktie, khaki barathea Service Dress tunic and jodhpurs, the uniform was very similar to that worn by British Army officers at the time. Indeed, the 'gentlemen drivers' of the Ambulance Corps enjoyed officer status which embarrassed Robert endlessly. 'I was not a fighting man, yet *pukka* soldiers were saluting me. I got so that when I saw a Tommy coming I would dodge round a block.' Probably if he had worn his Red Cross arm-band the confusion would have been more read-ily avoided, but Robert was ashamed of his non-combatant role. Photographs of Robert in his ambulance uniform, however, not only show the distinctive red and white brassard, but shoulder straps of gold braid which were *definitely* not army pattern. 'If only I could get some *gore* on my uniform I might feel better. Anyway, I was no longer a nosy newspaper slacker . . .'

The imaginary note, though erroneous in both date and location, provides probably a reasonably accurate picture of Robert's experiences around the end of 1915 and the beginning of 1916:

> There is an avenue of noble beeches leading to the Château, and in the shadow of each glimmers the pale oblong of an ambulance. We have to keep them thus concealed, for only yesterday morning a Taube flew over. The Rumpler Taube (Dove) belied its name, as it was a very effi-cient and rather deadly fighter aircraft. The beggars are rather partial to Red Cross cars. One of our chaps, taking in a load of wounded, was chased and pelted the other day.
>
> The Château seems all spires and towers, the glorified dream of a Parisian pastrycook. On its terrace figures in khaki are lounging. They are the volunteers, the owner-drivers of the Corps, many of them men of wealth and title. Curious to see one who owns all the coal in two counties proudly signing for his *sou* a day; or another, who lives in a Fifth Avenue palace, contentedly sleeping on the straw-strewn floor of a hovel.

Other prose entries are headed 'In Picardy, January 1915', 'Near Albert, February 1915' and 'The American Hospital, Neuilly, January 1919'. When they were published in 1921, readers might be forgiven for thinking that they were wholly genuine. I might add that, when I read *Ballads of a Bohemian* as a small boy, I was convinced that Robert had lost his left arm in the Argonne in 1917, from the very convincing account given in the last of these extracts, and it was only on seeing photographs of him many years later that I was disabused of this fancy. There is a danger, therefore, in investing these prose passages in this book with too much authenticity, or in relying on them for hard facts about Robert's wartime career. Here and there, however, there is a grain of verifiable truth. In the prelude to the ballads entitled 'The Three Tommies', for example, there is the laconic entry,

> We have just had one of our men killed, a young sculptor of immense promise. When one thinks of all the the fine work he might have accomplished it seems a shame. But, after all, to-morrow it may be the turn of any of us. If it should be mine, my chief regret will be for work undone.

At the end of the ballad there is another prose passage beginning 'Daventry, the sculptor, is buried in a little graveyard near one of our posts.' There was no British or American sculptor of that name, nor, indeed, any young sculptor fitting this description. On the other hand, Robert's unit was in the vicinity of Neuville St Vaast where, at the beginning of June 1915, the French army launched a furious assault on the German lines. In that action fell Henri Gaudier-Brzeska, who was dead on arrival at the field hospital. It may well be that the prose passage was inspired by the death of the young French sculptor, barely twenty-three years of age. His career had scarcely begun, yet the work he produced in the short period from 1912 to 1915 was of such a calibre as to set him apart from the run-of-the-mill young artists struggling to make a living in Montmartre at that time. Robert, on his own admission, often studied the makeshift tombstones and grave-markers which he so frequently encountered on his solitary walks and speculated on the waste of human life. It may be that he chanced upon Gaudier-Brzeska's grave.

For a more factual account one has to turn to *Harper of Heaven*, even though Robert was recalling events thirty years afterwards. He may have had a casual attitude towards dates, but the impressions left by his experiences on the Western Front were starkly etched in his memory. Within a week of recruitment he was driving an ambulance under enemy gunfire.

> It was on a long stretch of Flanders road, and I had five wounded in my car. This road was raked by a German battery as I hurried over it.

Suddenly I heard a shell burst. I saw a cloud of black smoke, while gravel and stones spattered the car. I hesitated to dash on or to stop; but my orders had been to do the latter, so I put on the brakes. A good job too, for ahead there was another explosion with a mushroom of evil black smoke. I had three walking wounded and two stretcher cases, so with the aid of the first, I got the stretchers into the ditch and there we waited till dusk. I had felt no fear, only a thrill that had something of pleasure in it. I had been under fire. I could go back to Chelsea now and take a salute.[4]

There was a certain incongruity in life at the château, where the gentlemen drivers slept on the floor but supplemented their French Army rations with extras that compared favourably with the best officers' mess. 'Dinner every evening was a scene of hilarity. Wine flowed freely and everyone was in high spirits.' This frenetic gaiety was induced by the scenes of carnage all around, and the constant fear of sudden death. As if they needed a reminder, the castle would occasionally be rocked by gunfire. Robert likened his job to driving a taxi. Whenever he felt like a soldier he reminded himself that he was only a phoney one. Off duty, he went for long walks through the fields of Picardy. Often he would gain a knoll from which he could see spires of villages in enemy hands, and would wonder wistfully what was happening there. There was also the diversion of enemy aircraft, the Fokker Eindecker or perhaps a Rumpler Taube, 'dodging between silver puffs of shell-burst'; he watched them, often hoping to see one brought down, 'but they seemed to enjoy a miraculous safety'.

Seeking something more exciting, Robert volunteered for outpost duty. There were ambulance posts close to the First Aid Stations, with cars manned day and night in readiness. There were two drivers to each car, relieved every ten days. Life was rough, for they had to sleep in their clothes on the floor of a ruined cottage, a tent or a dug-out, constantly exposed to shellfire. Robert put his life in the hands of Providence: 'Usually we resigned ourselves on a bad night of bombing, thinking that if a shell did get us we would never be any the wiser.' Night driving was the worst, as they could not show the faintest light and the roads were pitted with shell holes. 'It was nerve-racking, crawling on low speed, with a badly wounded man along those coal-black devastated roads.' On one occasion Robert had a man die in his car, an incident which he passed over swiftly in horror. He also took his stint with the stretcher-parties that went into the firing trenches and even out into the wastes of No Man's Land. 'The danger enhanced the heartening feeling of saving life.' These hazards gave Robert and his companions a pride in their job. 'We felt a certain shame that we were not fighting men.' Most of the British volunteers were, like Robert, over military age, while the younger men were American citizens whose country was still neutral. One of the most hair-raising trips, which Robert performed regularly, was along the sardonically named Sacred Way, a little roadway only seven yards wide, running along the track of a disused railway, which maintained contact with the French front-line at Verdun. In one twenty-four hour period at the end of February 1916 no fewer than 6,000 vehicles passed along this narrow lane — one every fourteen seconds — in a frantic bid to keep the Twentieth Corps supplied. Real danger was ever-present, but in the makeshift mess of the Ambulance Corps there was an *esprit* which must have reminded Robert of his days with the carefree roisterers of the bank mess in Dawson.

One morning he noticed on his leg a tiny black speck which was sore to the touch. At first he dismissed it as an insect bite, but the following day it had swollen alarmingly. It was the first of what turned out to be a veritable plague of boils. In the course of the ensuing eight months Robert counted ninety-nine. 'I was only sorry I had not one more for I have a preference for round figures.' Sometimes he had three at once, sometimes 'just a super-one'. He was pronounced to be badly run down and was invalided out. He returned to Paris, 'quite unfit for war work' which worried him more than all his other miseries. In June 1916 he and Germaine went to Dream Haven and there, with sea bathing and rest, Robert's old spirit returned. The boils continued unabated, despite a rigorous diet and much time spent in the warm sea. Then, just as suddenly as they had come, his boils disappeared. 'The last of them healed and I waited in vain for its successor. It was really incredible that there should be no more, for I had the habit of them and life seemed lonely without them'.

As he convalesced, the idea came to him to record his impressions of the Front in verse, just as he had done in the Yukon and the Arctic. He had not kept a diary, but those long months so close to the carnage were terribly vivid in his mind. All at once he felt excited, even exhilarated. He dragged out his Remington and pounded out the verse as fast as he could. Ideas for story poems came surging at him — the man with no legs, the man with no arms, the blind man, the faceless man now took the place of those immortal characters from the High North. He began with a list of themes, adding to them from time to time. He was so eager to begin that he could not sleep that night. Next morning he took the first item from the list and inserted a blank sheet in the typewriter. 'Inspiration was not long in coming. By night I had written the first poem.' In five months he had fifty-three poems for *Rhymes of a Red Cross Man* which he posted to Fisher Unwin. Before the year was out, Robert's fourth volume of verse had been published by Barse and Hopkins of New York and William Briggs in Toronto, as well as the English edition. Fisher

Unwin was quietly optimistic, but the New York publishers were wildly enthusiastic. The United States had not yet entered the war but public opinion was solidly behind the Anglo-French effort, and Robert's war poems hit the bookstands at the right time. For nine months this volume headed the list of best-sellers in *The Bookman* and, in so doing, gave his earlier works considerable stimulus.

Hitherto the serious poetry critics had largely ignored Robert's work or, at best, treated it with levity. Now, however, reviewers in the heavyweight broadsheets were hailing his latest volume as containing some of the finest poetry to come out of the war. In perspective, Robert's verses did not come up to the standards of Rupert Brooke and Robert Graves, but they enjoyed an immense vogue on both sides of the Atlantic. Because he was a popular versifier rather than a poet, Robert got across to a mass audience who never heard of Brooke or Graves. Unlike Robert's early verse written at the time of the Boer War, there is very little jingoism in the Red Cross rhymes, but a great deal of cynicism and disillusionment tempered by compassion for the sufferings of the ordinary Joes, the *poilus* and the Tommies. The volume does not deal with the deeper issues of the period, the 'war aims' or the politics. Indeed, Robert's ambiguous position was reflected in the singular absence of the officer class in his poems. On the other hand, he did not flinch from writing movingly about the victims of the conflict, including German wounded or prisoners. For Trail of Ninety-Eight, substitute Western Front. It is a chronicle of man facing mortal danger with dour resilience, of romantic impulses inspired now by loyalty and comradeship and not the sordid scramble for yellow metal. Unconsciously the mood of the ballads is akin to that of Burns, certainly uncoloured by the refinement to be found in the war poems of Colonel John McCrae, the Canadian poet best remembered nowadays for his imperishable lines 'In Flanders Fields'. McCrae, two years older than Robert, was killed in action in one of the final campaigns of the war.

In this collection Robert fully exploited the dramatic monologue, with a good ear for the cockney speech and the jargon of the infantryman. In *Songs of a Sourdough* and its sequel, Robert had so often been the detached reporter, the outsider observing the miners and trappers of the North, but not actually one of their kind, never forgetting his class or his profession. In this latest volume, however, the ambulance-driver was one of *them* for he had shared all but the very worst of the horrors of trench warfare. He did not present a detached, far less a superior, view of life — and death — at the Front. Readers were confronted with vivid sensations of soldiers marching gaily 'up the line' and their rapid sense of shock and disillusionment when coming under the withering hail of machine-guns or the incessant bombardment of artillery. There is the gut-wrenching wait for the signal 'to go over the top', the grim realities of

No Man's Land, the pathos and poignancy, the humanity amid so much inhumanity, the loss of comrades, the sardonic gallows humour and the futility of the murderous onslaughts that won barely a yard or two. There is the pain and the suffering, the nostalgia for home and loved ones, and the longing not for victory but merely an end to it all. Gone are the absurdities of 'Dan McGrew' and 'Sam McGee'. Here is the anguish of a sensitive writer who had been through it all; the volume was poignantly dedicated to his brother Albert, one of the countless victims of the slaughter known as the Somme.

Germaine and Robert were back in Paris during the winter, but were now living at Neuilly-sur-Seine five miles north of Notre Dame; it was a small town, still semi-rural but rapidly being absorbed by the sprawling city. It was here, on 28 January 1917, that Germaine gave birth to twin daughters, Doris and Iris, an event which presumably brought great joy, although there is absolutely no mention of it in *Harper of Heaven*.[5]

Robert was pronounced fit for service in April 1917, but as he was preparing to rejoin his ambulance unit the United States entered the conflict. The Ambulance Corps was promptly disbanded and its mainly American element absorbed into Pershing's expeditionary force.

All those young Americans who talked with an Oxford accent and wore handkerchiefs in their sleeve had joined the regulars. Our Chief refused to take a minor position and died soon afterwards. I think his heart was broken to see his beloved work disregarded, but he will always be remembered with affection by those who served him.[6]

Here the chronology becomes confused again. The very next sentence reads, 'Having now disposed of my book and my boils I felt free to listen to the voice of conscience which again adjured me to join the army'. This implies an event in the spring of 1917 but in fact, as the next sentence reveals, Robert is talking of exactly a year later. 'But at that moment we in Paris were right in the firing line, for the Big Bertha was bombarding us daily.'

The original Big Berthas were 42cm howitzers produced at the Skoda Works in Bohemia (now the Czech Republic) and used by the Germans to batter the forts of Liège and Namur in 1914. It was erroneously assumed at the time that the guns had come from the Krupp factories in Germany, hence the nickname after Frau Bertha von Bohlen, matriarch of the Krupp family. In 1918, however, Krupp did indeed produce a super-gun with an eight-inch calibre and a barrel 110 feet in length, capable of lobbing a shell weighing 264 pounds. This frightening high-velocity weapon was sited in the forest of Coucy, seventy-six miles from Paris, and began shelling the French capital on 23 March 1918. In the ensuing passage, describing what it was like to be on the receiving end of this terror weapon, Robert unconsciously reveals a tiny fragment of his personal life.

> At regular intervals we heard the boom as another shell crashed on the city. As I sat on a bench on the Boul' Mich' one fell nearby. A bearded Frenchman sitting alongside me went on reading his paper calmly, but I felt very jumpy. I went up to the Rabbit Hutch to reassure my family.
>
> Suddenly there was a blast in the area across the way and a shell fragment smashed our window. I was holding my little daughter who began to howl. Then another crash behind us which destroyed the entire basement of a neighbouring house. We were due for the next, because they were bracketing the fire. However, there was nothing I could do about it: with Big Bertha one was helpless. So, holding my bawling infant in my arms, I tried to soothe her, and with a sense of fate we waited for the next shell-burst that we were sure would destroy us. Bertha was regular in her visitations and we counted the minutes as we watched the clock. How slowly the time passed! Now she was due . . . Now she was dubious . . . Could it be she had knocked off for lunch? Breathless we waited, but the minutes passed and no doom dropped from the skies. Satisfied with her triumph — a church and two hundred victims — she was through for the day.[7]

Dramatic stuff, indeed, but this was stretching poetic licence to the limit. In the first place, Robert and his family were not living at the tiny flat in the rue Compagne Première which he had dubbed the Rabbit Hutch. At this time they had a fine apartment on the Boulevard Jourdain, near the Parc Montsouris on the southern outskirts of the city. The impression given is of incessant bombardment, but firing was sporadic, a giant shell being fired about every third day, in a random fashion calculated to inspire the maximum terror for the minimum effort. In fact, although the bombardment lasted 140 days, the total fatalities in almost five months amounted to only 256. The most serious loss occurred on Good Friday, 29 March 1918, when the church of St Gervais took a direct hit, killing or wounding 156 Easter worshippers. No doubt Robert exaggerated the frequency and deadly impact of the shelling to heighten the dramatic effect, but the reference to a daughter, in the singular, concealed a very real personal tragedy.

Over the winter of 1917–18 Robert took Germaine and the twins to the Riviera. It was at Menton that Doris caught scarlet fever and died on 25 February 1918. She was only thirteen months old and the stronger of the two babies. Fearful that they might lose Iris as well, her parents became overprotective for a time, but she survived the tragedy. The loss of Doris deeply affected Robert who assuaged his profound grief by writing a poem, in English and French, ending with the poignant lines:

You've taught me Grief, wee piteous face!
And boundless pity too;
You're taking to your resting place
Part of my heart with you.

My little girl whose smile so right,
I'll see while sight endures!
This life of mine I'd give to-night
Could I but ransom yours.[8]

This poem, whose tenderness and pathos were never surpassed in any of Robert's vast output, was never published. Writing to a friend in July 1918, the man who had witnessed appalling suffering on the Western Front confessed that he could not think of his loss without bursting into tears.

After the Good Friday massacre at St Gervais, Robert decided to evacuate Germaine and Iris to the safety of Lancieux — 'a good job too, for the very day we left the Zeps came over and gave us a proper pasting'. In the 'blessed tranquillity' of Dream Haven Robert was assailed by guilt at having escaped from the war. In the end he offered his services to the Canadian government and in due course was attached to the Canadian Expeditionary Force with a commission to tour France, reporting on the activities of the troops.

I was to have a Cadillac, a chauffeur, an officer guide and freedom to choose and plan my itinerary. So, buying a new uniform, I fastened on it the green band of 'Intelligence' and very proud I was of it. 'Intelligence' sounded armyish and implied a modicum of mentality. But one of the official war correspondents sneered. On his shoulder straps he had a nickel badge with the letters 'W.C.'. 'Why don't you get one of these,' he said, 'instead of that green abomination?' 'I would, only I don't want to pass myself off as a fighting man,' I answered. As he was of military age he gave me a nasty look.[9]

This was one of the high points of Robert's life. He toured Canadian Army camps, especially the forestry camps located in the beechwoods of the Channel area and the gummy pine groves of the Landes and the Vosges. 'In this way I covered much of the country, so that apart from my work it was an educative experience.' He inspected airfields, hospitals, field kitchens and ordnance depots. He visited the Canadian infantry and artillery in the front line, and one day ate lunch in a crumbling cottage with the commanding general. As the brass-hat chewed his pork chops a stream of wounded were passing and he watched it serenely. 'No, I do not think I lost too many men in our last battle,' he remarked with an aloofness which Robert says he envied, although his true feelings were left unexpressed.

In the closing phase of the war Robert also met up with Joe Boyle whom he had known in Dawson. Boyle was one of the new breed of mining engineers who profited when the pattern of mining shifted to the big operations. At the beginning of the war, however, he had left Dawson, raised a company of troops for active service, and gone off to Europe. Colonel Boyle DSO OBE headed the Allied military mission to Romania and saved that country from annihilation, for which he was made Duke of Jassy. He was a close friend of the royal family and infected them with his fervent love of Robert's ballads.[10] Queen Marie (whose photograph Robert had used in his vain subterfuge to ward off predatory ladies in Bucharest), Crown Prince (later King) Carol, Princess Marie (later Queen of Yugoslavia) and especially young Prince Nicholas became ardent Service fans. When Joe Boyle died in 1923 Queen Marie paid for his elaborate tombstone on which she inscribed Robert's words, from 'The Law of the Yukon':

> A man with the heart of a Viking
> And the simple faith of a child.

With the Royal Engineers Robert travelled on narrow-gauge electric railways that criss-crossed the battle zone, often linking up with the light railway network of the enemy. They zigzagged through ruined villages and toured old battlefields. And in a corner of the Ypres salient he visited the grave of his brother Albert, killed two years previously. He also visited many of the camps of the Labour Battalions, one of which was commanded by 'Peace River Jim' Cornwall, another old buddy from the High North, who took him on a terrifying tour of the battlefront somewhere in southern Belgium. In a hamlet from which the enemy had just withdrawn, they found the bodies of dead Germans everywhere. Robert retrieved a Luger pistol from one of the corpses and was ferreting around for other trophies when three Germans emerged from a ruined house and surrendered themselves. 'Gravely and bravely I marched them to the nearest Tommy. Life seemed to have no value just then: if I had potted the poor devils no one would have objected but themselves.' Thus Robert realised the 'primitive irresponsibility' of the battlefield, where the only law was that of survival.

Soon sated with terrifying experiences, Robert ceased taking notes and his diary was unwritten. 'I have no record of this period but my memories are too many to put on paper.' There was Le Cateau with its reek of mustard gas and its streets strewn with civilian corpses. In one house that he peered into he saw 'five wax-like women lying on their beds as if sleeping peacefully'. In one open space a Belgian machine-gunner lay sprawled over his *mitrailleuse* surrounded by seven dead Germans. 'Everywhere were macabre scenes like the chamber of horrors of some super Madame Tussaud.'

He recoiled with disgust at the charnel-house that was the battlefield. Many of the dead had been robbed; even their boots had been taken. 'Rifling the dead was almost invariable,' he noted laconically.

> Heaps of bodies littered the ground. Some were headless, others mere torsos, like butcher-meat fresh from the slaughter-house. Dead, dead everywhere — so many of them. One hoped they would be buried before they had time to putrefy. But the burial parties were working night and day . . .

In one village, which the Canadians entered hard on the heels of the retreating Germans, they found every house looted and vandalised in an orgy of wanton destruction. On one occasion in late autumn Robert, accompanied by a Canadian major, took the car to a point at which their driver announced he was unwilling to go farther. They were within sight of the German troops 'flying as if they were being swept forward by a giant besom'. Consulting their map, they saw that they were in the coal-mining district around Denain, and had unwittingly come much farther than the Allied front-line. As they drove through seemingly deserted villages, people suddenly emerged from cellars and ruined cottages to greet them with cries of joy. They decided to press on, and at the end of a dusty road came to the outskirts of Lille. The city was supposed to be still in enemy hands, but there was no sign of the Germans. Everywhere Robert and his companions were cheered on, with the comforting news that the *Boches* had run away. Festooned with garlands, they entered by the Cambrai gate, dismounting to avoid a huge crater and going ahead on foot where they were 'tossed in a tempest of osculatory enthusiasm'. Robert made an extempore speech in French when the mayor invited them to the town hall, but beat a hasty retreat when a staff car full of the top brass suddenly appeared.

Lockhart, commenting on Robert's war service, draws attention to the fact that the entry under his name in *The Canadian Who's Who* 'indicates he was decorated three times, facts he does not include in his autobiography'.[11] This implies the award of decorations for bravery in the field or gallant conduct; but the reason Robert never mentioned his medals was because they were the standard trio of campaign medals, the 1914–15 Star, the British War Medal and the Victory Medal, or 'Pip, Squeak and Wilfred' as the Tommies derisively named them.[12]

Back in Paris a few days after the Lille escapade, Robert worked like a man possessed. He would produce a book entitled *War Winners* and, with Germaine and Iris away at Lancieux, he had the peace and quiet to get on with it, pounding his Remington morning, noon and night. The theme of the book was the effort of those who worked without glory to win glory for others. He was warming to his theme when, one morning about eleven, he was disturbed by a clanging and ringing as every bell in Paris began pealing. The war was over.

Returning to his apartment after a day-long celebration, he was suddenly filled with loathing for the war and all that it represented. Taking up the manuscript, he tore it in tatters. 'No more war. Not in my lifetime. Curse the memory of it. Now I will rest and forget. Now I will enjoy the peace and sweetness of Dream Haven.'

CHAPTER 11

HOLLYWOOD AND THE SOUTH SEAS

So I'll enjoy my dividends and live my life with zest,
And bless the mighty men who first — *invented interest*

'Five-Per-Cent' in *Bar-Room Ballads* (1940)

CHAPTER ELEVEN OF ROBERT'S SECOND VOLUME OF autobiography begins with his return to Paris. Living at Lancieux beside the sea had given him 'spacious ideas that needed fuller expression' and 'it was evident that the Rabbit Hutch was no longer big enough for me'. Doubtless in order to simplify matters for his readers, he was maintaining the fiction that he and his family were still living in James Stephens's little flat above the machine-shop, when, in fact, the Services had been accustomed to rent different apartments each winter when they moved back to the city. After spending the worst of the winter of 1917–18 in Menton, however, they decided to celebrate the end of the war by wintering in Monte Carlo.

This was the first of two seasons spent in the pint-sized principality of Monaco which derived most of its revenue from the world-famous Casino. Although not a betting man himself, Robert was fascinated by the high-rollers and made a detailed study of gambling methods, gathering material which he was later to use in his third novel *Poisoned Paradise*. Poetry was momentarily forgotten, although he did compose some verses about the Armistice. By some accident, however, he lost the manuscript and forgot all about it — until he was astounded to see the poem published anonymously in the *Daily Mail* some time later.

Now that the war was over, however, and life was getting back to normal, Robert and Germaine decided on something larger and more permanent. In the spring of 1919, however, Paris was still packed with refugees and others displaced by the recent conflict. Finding an apartment to rent was extremely difficult. Robert wished to be close to the Luxembourg Gardens and that vicinity was the most coveted of all. There was a little house at 27 rue de Fleurus near the park with which he fell in love, but it was already occupied. He would often pass it and wonder who the strange, mannish woman was who defied feminine dress conventions. Only later did he learn that she was Gertrude Stein.

'The only way to get an apartment was to make love to a *concierge*. This I did successfully, with a *billet doux* of a thousand franc bill.' Soon the Services found themselves installed in a magnificent ten-room, two-storey residence on the sixth and seventh floors of 1 Place du Panthéon, a few minutes' walk from the Jardin du Luxembourg. On the lower floor were five bedrooms while most of the upper floor was taken up by a huge studio giving on to a balcony that overlooked the dome of the Panthéon. The studio became Robert's library, one wall lined with a thousand books. He indulged in an orgy of furnishing a palatial apartment, 'until at last the place assumed the look of a setting for a plutocratic poet'. As he stood on his balcony Robert savoured the view:

> I could look over the pigeon-mottled roof of the Pantheon to the dark grey tiles of the University. How I loved my view! Notre Dame, the Sainte Chapelle, Sacré Coeur. There in my spacious solitude I realised how dear Paris was to me.

Although the great pile dedicated to the heroes of France was just across the square, Robert confessed that never in ten years did he cross its threshold. 'If it had been at the other end of Paris no doubt I would have paid homage at the shrine of its Great. But here across the street — well, I could drop in any old time.'

In the immediate post-war period he resumed contact with Archie Bruce, still referred to by the pseudonym of Peter McQuattie. In *Ballads of a Bohemian* Archie provided Robert with the inspiration for a mythical character called McBean, 'a Scotsman with the soul of an Irishman', who recurs in the prose passages until his supposed death in action. In the same pages occurs a poet named Saxon Dane, clearly modelled on James Stephens. Both of these pre-war buddies were still living in Paris in 1919, though Bruce was a changed man, even better dressed than the dapper Robert, as befitted his position as the head of Reuter's and a man destined to marry an heiress. Stephens, 'a brave wee man stepping stoutly with the valour of a big fellow', was a frequent companion, 'but as he stalked the Boul' Mich' I did not butt in on him, for I feared he might be in the throes of poetic parturition — as indeed I was myself.' So they tramped along the street, side by side, 'a poet and a rhymester, each in his fashion lambasting his soul for the glory of his Maker'.

Robert, in fact, was now hard at work on his fifth volume of verse, although two years were to elapse before it appeared in print. *Ballads of a Bohemian* was, in many respects, more ambitious than the previous volumes, and unusual in that it contained 'patches of prose' to link the ballads.

> I liked the prose better than the verse and still think a few words of commentary on a poem enhances its interest. But most people don't feel that way, and when I came to publish this volume it was the least successful of all my work.

It was also more artfully constructed, being divided into four books, each devoted to a season of the year. It purported to be the work of one Stephen Poore, an American bohemian poet living in a garret in Montparnasse before the war who joins the American Ambulance Corps, is wounded at Verdun, joins the American Army in 1917 and loses his arm in the Argonne and is still in the American hospital at Neuilly in January 1919. The curious seasonal arrangement therefore covered spring in Montparnasse (April and May 1914) and early summer, with references to the parks, such as the Luxembourg (always Robert's favourite) and the Montsouris (which was close to the flat on the Boulevard Jourdain), and the cafés (the Deux Magots and the Closerie de Lilas) that Robert frequented. The third book, entitled 'Late Summer' was allegedly set in July and August 1914, with references to the Dôme Café, the Café de la Source and the Café de la Paix. The momentous days at the beginning of August even find the poet in Brittany, where the mood of the peasants on the day war broke out is beautifully captured. The last book, headed 'Winter', bears dates and places in January and February 1915 which proved so confusing to Lockhart in tracing Robert's own movements. The final part, headed January 1919, explains the lapse of time with the fictional letter from the American hospital.

Each season was divided into sections numbered in roman numerals, and thus grouping the verses according to themes. In producing a book in such an elaborately contrived manner Robert sacrificed some of the natural inspiration that was the hallmark of *Rhymes of a Red Cross Man*, but there was a new maturity and sensitivity in these verses, tempered by Robert's wartime experiences and personal loss. The ballads belonging to the halcyon days before August 1914 are of additional interest, forming a link between two of Robert's novels, *The Pretender* and *The Master of the Microbe*, both of which were rich in local colour. By contrast, the ballads of 'Winter' dealt with the war and formed, in essence, a supplement to *Rhymes of a Red Cross Man*. The final section was particularly poignant, with poems about *les Grands Mutilés* of the war: 'The Sightless Man', 'The Legless Man' and 'The Faceless Man'. This book was finished at Dream Haven in December 1919, whither Robert had gone, 'working alone far into the winter and coupling up my final rhymes as I stalked the rain-soaked fields'. With a supreme effort he finished it in time for Christmas, and then returned to Paris, 'weary but happy for the usual family reunion'. Robert played hide-and-seek with Iris in the ten-room flat and reduced his plump mother-in-law to tears of laughter with his antics. 'In the midst of the gaiety I put away my precious manuscript in the bottom of a trunk — and there it remained for over a year — neglected, forgotten.' The making of it had taken so much out of him that he hated it. 'I could not bear to re-read the manuscript. I was sick of the literary game. Poetry was a disease. I had broken out into a rash of it and now all I asked was to be cured.' This explains why it was not until 1921 that *Ballads of a Bohemian* was published. Barse and Hopkins produced it in New York and Fisher Unwin in London, but the Canadian edition appeared under the imprint of G.J. McLeod of Toronto. Typical of the reviews was that in the *Montreal Star* which found the latest volume of verse disappointing: 'Although it contains a few lyrics of superior quality, the ballads and narrative verse lack the fire, the roll and the intriguing rhythm of his earlier days'.

After Christmas Robert took Germaine and Iris back to the Riviera. They made a poignant pilgrimage to the grave of their baby daughter in the beautiful cemetery of Menton, where she lay near the mortal remains of Aubrey Beardsley. Through the early months of 1920 they wintered in Monte Carlo, as they had done the previous year.

Back in Paris by April, Robert began to play another role, that of the 'plutocratic poet'. Having opulently furnished his large apartment, he dressed the part. He began by getting a new wardrobe expensively tailored at Poole's. As a finishing touch he now sported a monocle which he bought from a pawn-broker for ten francs. He bluffed his way with it for ten years. 'People in Paris accepted it without derision and I made an effort to live up to it.' Behind it he concealed his inferiority complex: 'Screwing it in my eye I looked supercil-iously at the world'. This affectation was picked up from James Stephens and, in due course, it was copied by Archie Bruce, 'though his black ribband was broader than mine'.

The frugal habits of a lifetime were hard to break. All this time fresh editions of his verses continued to pour forth from the presses of three countries, and the royalties mounted up. Robert had little interest in money matters, being content to invest in bank stock. Although he was aware of a stock market boom he did not realise what he was worth until he happened to see *The Times* one day and cast an eye over the market prices. When he thought he was worth fifty thousand dollars, it turned out that his investments were worth twice as much. Briefly he flirted with the notion of buying an estate below Grasse, but almost as quickly he dismissed it. 'Property was a bit of a burden. It would worry me, weigh on me. Better cash in the bank.' Apart from his holiday home at Lancieux, Robert was quite content to rent apartments wherever he lived. Perhaps the thought of property, which might have rooted him to a particular place, offended his vagabond propensities.

The Left Bank of the 1920s was subtly different from the pre-war period. Many of the young Americans who had arrived with the Expeditionary Force stayed behind, drawn to the free and easy lifestyle of the Latin Quarter. This was to become a golden age of great literary movements and high artistic endeavour. Many of the artists and writers who are household names to this day lived there at this period. The names of those who frequented the bistros and cafés of Montparnasse read like the roll-call of twentieth-century culture. Robert was aware of this exhilarating atmosphere:

> Literary movements were being born. In the Quarter small magazines were being produced, each with its mission of modernity. Blocking the doorway of Sylvia Beach's Bookshop one could see the portly form of Ford Madox Ford, accompanied by the vivacious Violet Hunt. In the shop with its Shakespearean sign one would run into James Joyce peering short-sightedly at the shelves, or Antheil the composer, buzzing with enthusiasm. In the Quarter were many who afterwards became famous — Giants in Gestation.

It is debatable to what extent Robert was touched by this ferment of creativity. In *Ballads of a Bohemian* there is an amusing series of couplets entitled 'The Philistine and the Bohemian' which reveals an intimate knowledge of the buzzwords of the immediate postwar era, and the lines are studded with the names of the painters, poets and philosophers who were the height of fashion. But the poem ends on an acerbic note, with the moral punch-line 'Don't try to be what you are not'. It is doubtful whether Robert seriously considered breaking into the circle of contributors to the *Little Review* or Ford Madox Ford's *Transatlantic Review*. He was content to be the detached observer, the outsider looking in. Some of his comments betray, if not a philistinism, at least a puritanical streak:

One day I was walking down a leafy road when I met a youth with a maid. She was admiring the chestnut trees in bloom, so I handed the lad my cane and told him to reach down one of the flowers for her. Soon we got into conversation which turned to books. For a stripling he spoke with some authority, turning into ridicule the pretentious scribes of the Quarter and their freak magazines. 'There's only one of them,' he said, 'that I can see getting anywhere, and he may go pretty far. Keep your eyes on a man called Hemingway.' He spoke of Joyce and made the following pronouncement: 'I believe everything that can be thought can be said, and everything that can be said can be written.' Then he told me his name was Henry Miller.

He was a slim youth of medium height, and at that time I do not think he had published any of his notorious books. His name meant nothing to me and I did not see him again. But something of destiny seemed to brood in his eyes and I never forgot him. So when someone handed me a copy of *Tropic of Capricorn* the author's name struck a chord of memory. Of course the book shocked me but I could not deny a strange flicker of genius in its wildest flights. Though I have read many pornographic books from Cleland to Frank Harris, Miller outvies them all. You can purge most authors but if you expurgated *Tropic of Cancer* there would be little left. His books are prohibited and probably you will never see a copy, but if you do you will realise that freedom of expression has its limits and even hatred of hypocrisy cannot condone the frankness of the tenderloin.[1]

It is interesting to speculate on whether Service and Hemingway met. If they did, then both kept silent on the matter. They had a great deal in common: both had a restless, nomadic streak, unlikely to knuckle under to conventional domesticity; both rejoiced in their manliness, with a penchant for outdoor pursuits, boxing and physical fitness. Moreover, they had belonged to the same outfit during the war, although Robert had been in France and Flanders in 1915–16 and Hemingway in Italy in 1918. In the immediate post-war period, however, Hemingway was actually in Toronto. When he returned to Paris late in 1921 Robert had already left the city for the United States. In the later 1920s, when Hemingway's star was in the ascendant, Robert was gradually withdrawing from the world into a reclusive carapace. Ironically, it was as foreign correspondent for the *Toronto Star* that Hemingway returned to Europe in 1921, and that ought to have been some sort of bond. But Hemingway belonged to a different generation (he was twenty-five years younger than Robert) and in temperament and outlook he differed radically from the quiet little Canadian-Scot. His first published works were *Three Stories and Ten Poems* (1923) and *In*

Robert at Selig's studios, Hollywood, 1922

Robert in a sailing dinghy,
Moorea, 1922

Robert Service

The Services' studio flat on the sixth and seventh floors of No. 1,
Place du Pantheon, Paris

Robert flexing his muscles on the beach; this photograph illustrated the jacket of *Why Not Grow Young?* (1928)

Cutting hay at Lancieux, 1938

On the beach at Nice, *c.*1930

Robert with H.G. Wells at Lou Pidou,
Wells's villa at Grasse, 1930s

With his motorbike, Lancieux, 1939

At his desk with his Corona typewriter, Nice, 1935

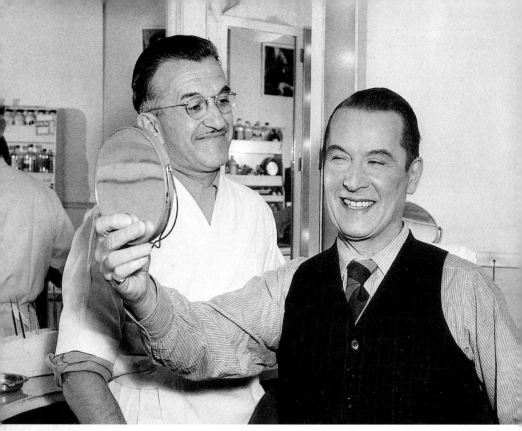

Jack Pierce making Robert
look forty years younger for
his part in *The Spoilers*,
1942 (Universal Pictures)

The bar-room scene
(Universal Pictures)

Robert with Marlene Dietrich as Cherry Malotte on the set of *The Spoilers*, 1942
(Universal Pictures)

Robert, Iris and Germaine at Jasper in the Canadian Rockies, 1940

Hollywood literati, with Robert in the centre, 1943

Our Time (1924), both acclaimed by Gertrude Stein and Ezra Pound but apparently unnoticed by Robert Service at the time.

Robert gradually recovered his old equanimity as memories of the war receded. At first there was a post-war boom in which his bank stock rose sharply but, unbeknown to him, economic conditions were exceedingly chaotic in Canada where the bulk of his investments lay. By 1920 the inevitable slump had set in. Food products, which had brought famine prices during the war, were almost unsaleable, wheat falling from its 1919 level of $2.15 a bushel to sixty cents a year later. To be engaged in profitably, wheat-farming had to be conducted on a large-scale basis, using expensive machinery. This necessitated an enormous capital outlay which was usually found in the form of bank loans. When many prairie farmers went bust in the autumn of 1920 bank stocks plummetted. Robert, far away in Paris, got wind of a rumour and checked the market prices anxiously. 'Sure enough they had nose-dived. My brave bank stock had gone from three hundred and fifty dollars to two hundred and was still dropping. I was quite vexed. To win may be swell; to lose is hell.' On paper he had been worth over $600,000 — well on the way to becoming the first poet-millionaire. Now his net worth had been slashed by 50 per cent. Robert decided to cut his losses by selling his bank stocks and purchasing a life annuity. From four of the biggest insurance companies he took out enough to keep him in solid comfort to the end of his days.

> Now I could thumb my nose at misfortune. For all time I was free
> from financial worry. Best of all was the incentive to longevity. I must
> guard my health more jealously than ever. In short, I must live so long
> I could get ahead of the goddam Companies.

Robert's life proceeded in its customary fashion, the summers at Lancieux alternating with winter in Paris. But in the autumn of 1921 he was considerably bucked by getting a cheque for five thousand dollars for the film rights, not to one of his novels but to 'The Shooting of Dan McGrew'. With reckless bravado he broke the habit of a lifetime and decided to blow the lot on a trip to Hollywood. From the Boulevard St Michel to Hollywood Boulevard was a quantum leap — 'characteristic of my passion for violent contrasts'. It seemed a good idea at the time; a signature on a cheque would assure the gigantic jump. The reality, however, was not quite so magical. The ship was filled to capacity, so the Services slept in a dark cabin three decks down, 'hot as hell and crawling with cockroaches'. There were four sittings for meals, while the decks were too jammed for exercise.

Even New York failed to enchant Germaine and Iris, who spent most of their time there in Central Park or at the zoo, hardly daring to venture into the bustling canyons of mid-town. Robert realised that he would have to adjust to new conditions, and promptly got rid of his monocle. After years on the Continent, he found the brashness and boorishness of the New Yorkers hard to take. In vain he tried to explain to Germaine that this was democracy, American-style. 'Instead of being arrogant and regarding the working people as beneath us let us regard them as superiors, because they earn money while we merely spend it.' Shedding his Britishness, Robert did his best to fit into his new frame. On the transcontinental train they had further examples of 'democracy'. Although they had a private sitting-room, other passengers insisted on using their toilet, elderly women would 'visit' with them and call Germaine 'honey'. Only Iris seems to have enjoyed the four-day journey, falling 'in love with the genial Negro who changed our ice water'.

As they passed through the desert Robert began to cheer up, and as they crossed the state line into California his heart sang. 'How I loved it! How I will always love it!' It was more than twenty years since he had last been in Los Angeles, and the city had changed out of all recognition. The old frame building where he had bunked for two bits a night had been replaced by a skyscraper, and where he had once picked oranges for a dollar a day was now part of the bustling commercial district. He could hardly wait to get out to Hollywood, a land of make-believe that had not existed in his day. 'Now it was world-famed, and the very name brought light to tired eyes.'

At the station Robert left Germaine with Iris while he went off to reconnoitre. He boarded a street-car, intent on heading out to Santa Monica, but after riding 'through miles of low frame houses, market centres and corner drug stores' of sprawling suburban Los Angeles, he alighted on impulse on seeing the Hollywood Hotel, 'famed Inn of the Stars'. Hoping for a glimpse of Elinor Glyn or perhaps Douglas Fairbanks, he witnessed instead the Keystone Cops filming on the street. He thrilled at the sight of John Bunny and Flora Finch, big names at the time but almost forgotten nowadays. Strolling along the boulevard he ran into Charlie Chaplin and Lila Lee (who was brushing dandruff off the great star's collar). As Robert stared at the great comic actor 'Charlie turned on me a blazing regard and I wilted'. But it was otherwise a wonderful day.

That very afternoon Robert rented a bungalow for six months and then retrieved his wife and daughter from downtown Los Angeles. The house was on the hillside, with a fine panorama of Hollywood and Beverly Hills.

> The thought that it was to be ours after so much travelling filled us with gladness. We went down to the grocery at the corner and purchased a plentiful supply of provisions, amazed to find we could

buy almost anything there. Fascinated, too, for the articles were so strange to us. Laden with packets we mounted to the bungalow which already seemed to welcome us like a friend. We made such a jolly supper, laughed over it and were very happy. Then while my wife washed the dishes I sat at the piano and sang *The End of a Perfect Day*, which was most appropriate, for the bungalow belonged to Carrie Jacobs Bond. She became my friend and still calls me Buddy.[2]

Robert was fascinated by the film-making which seemed to be going on all around. 'There were few mornings on which one could not see companies working on Hollywood Boulevard.' Robert visited all the studios, being impressed most by Fox and Universal. 'I also interviewed old Selig in his zoo, and Louis Mayer on his lot.' William N. Selig (1864–1948) had made the first film in California — *Power of the Sultan* (1907) — and produced the first version of *The Spoilers* (1914); but he is best remembered for his animal pictures, and his zoo was almost as well known as his studios. Louis Burt Mayer, eleven years younger than Robert, had been born in Minsk but as a child had been brought to Canada before drifting to New England in his late teens where he entered the film industry. Mayer was 'dapper and affable and spent an hour with me' and Robert had his photograph taken, arm in arm with the great movie mogul who had purchased the rights to Robert's most famous poem. Twenty years later, when Robert was back in Hollywood, things had changed: 'today he is as unapproachable as Royalty itself'. Robert met, and was photographed with, such stars of the period as Marie Prevost, Priscilla Dean and William 'Big Bill' Russell. A photograph of Robert and the last-named was to be captioned in the family album 'Big Bill and Wee Willie'. (Throughout life Robert was known by various names: to Germaine he was always Robert, pronounced in the French manner; to his friends and younger brothers he was more familiarly known as Bob; but to his mother — the Parkers had a penchant for using middle names — he was always Willie; and referring to himself in the third person he was invariably Wee Willie, unconsciously underscoring his innate inferiority complex.)

Russell and Robert became good friends, and through him the poet was introduced to Noah Beery who was making a film about the Far North at the time. Robert also lunched with the producer Robert Hughes and his star Colleen Moore. Through Russell, however, Robert was able to get a glimpse of the downside of the film business. Big Bill hoped to get the leading role in Nazimova's production of *The Doll's House* but was turned down because he was overweight. In vain he dieted drastically; the more he fasted the more he shed the pounds from his body, but his face was as chubby as ever. Then he went on a binge over Christmas and put all the lost pounds back. When he failed to get comic parts more suited to his chubby countenance he fell on hard times. One day he confessed to Robert that he had sold his car. To a cinema actor that was the last straw; without his car he was as helpless as a blind man without his dog. 'I realised my poor friend couldn't make the grade and soon after he disappeared.'[3]

In December 1921 Robert invited his mother down from Alberta to spend Christmas with his family. Robert had not seen her for ten years and, as he waited for her to arrive on the Oregon Express, he was not sure that he would recognise her. Twice he accosted an elderly lady with a 'Howdy, Ma!' by mistake; but then Emily appeared. This was Germaine's first meeting with her mother-in-law and no doubt she was feeling rather apprehensive, but she need not have worried.

> She looked so calm and casual she put us at our ease. She had rosy cheeks, blue eyes and a look of determination to make the best of being seventy. I was favourably impressed as I introduced her to my family, who were a little awed by her dignity and poise. After that, our home life took on a more pleasant pattern than ever. The old lady fell in love with Hollywood; she had preserved her youthfulness of spirit and was thrilled by all she saw. No more jolly household could be imagined.

For all the tinsel show of Hollywood, Robert's lifestyle in this period was characteristically canny. The family lunched out — on hamburgers and apple pie — at the Sunset Cafeteria on the Boulevard, but invariably dined at home in the evenings. Robert was not his father's son for nothing: to feed the roaring open fire he would gather up the empty crates from a vacant lot where they were dumped by shopkeepers, and break them up for firewood. Returning one winter's evening from one of these foraging jaunts he happened to look through the living-room window.

> My wife and my mother sat on either side of the brick fire-place with a fire alight. My daughter squatted on a rug playing with a doll, while in the background sparkled a Christmas tree. I thought it was one of the nicest domestic pictures I have ever seen.

It is significant that one of Robert's sweetest memories should be of a scene in which he was not a participant, but the observer, the outsider looking in. Even when he was ensconced on his Morris recliner under a reading lamp, 'with a movie mag in one hand and a butter cream in the other', he was subconsciously detached from the womenfolk. One evening he had a bright idea. 'Mother and the Missus seemed so pally, playing double solitaire. Shrieks of laughter came from them, while my daughter prattled on the floor with her dolls. We were an ideal household; but surely, I thought, they would not miss me if I left them for a while.' Loafing on a *chaise-longue*, stuffing himself with chocolates and chain-smoking cigarettes, Robert had let himself go. In disgust, when donning his evening dress for a Wampus Ball and finding that there was a six-inch gap between the buttons and the buttonholes, Robert was assailed by a sense of guilt. This, coupled with the vagabondism in his veins, gave him the urge to be off on his own. Reading Louis Beck's *White Shadows in the South Seas* rekindled an interest in the Pacific which, decades earlier, had been roused by Robert Louis Stevenson.

Hesitantly he broached the subject. 'Look here, you folks seem to hit it off pretty well. Do you think you would tear each other's hair if I quit you for a while?' This was greeted in silence, so he continued quickly, saying it was the duty of every novelist to write a romance of the South Seas. 'I don't want to lag behind de Vere Stacpoole, so if you can spare me a couple of months to get my dope I'll go there. How about it?' It was Emily who broke the silence. 'By all means go, Willie, and write your book. Oh, these men! They give me a pain in the neck — they think they're so darned indispensable.'

What Germaine made of this is not recorded in her own memoir; she merely noted that Robert's sudden decision came just after Iris's fifth birthday, late in January 1922. Germaine, who had a very equable temperament, got on well with Emily whom she described as 'very agreeable to live with'. Three days later, Robert set sail on the SS *Rarotonga* bound for Tahiti. He had little to say of the voyage across the Pacific, though 'it was notable enough', mentioning only that the passengers included 'a Duke, a Duchess and a French Count'. What made the biggest impression, however, was the death of a young girl on board and he recalled how the ship stopped in the early dawn and the poor girl was lowered into her ocean grave. 'I was the only one who saw, for the death was kept quiet so as not to disturb the other passengers.' On the two-week passage to Papeete, Robert whiled away the time by reading the extensive literature on the South Seas in the ship's library. His head seething with *Faery Lands* and *The Moon and Sixpence*, he felt well primed to meet the real thing.

> It may seem presumptuous to attempt a novel with two months knowledge of its locale, but I knew the value of first impressions. I would make notes of all I saw, so that when I came to write everything would come back to me vividly. And after all, is not the story the thing, the setting secondary? . . . When I went to Tahiti it was really with a spirit of adventure and romance.

Eight weeks in French Oceania, as it was then known, provided Robert with three chapters in his autobiography, headed 'Beachcomber De Luxe', 'Tramping Round Tahiti' and 'Moorean Idyll'. He rented a bungalow with a trellised balcony and idled his time away in a hammock caressed by the gentle Pacific breezes. Memories of his cabin in Dawson must have come into his mind. Once again, he had the solitude which he craved, and he savoured every moment of it. Every evening he dined at one or other of the two hotels which Papeete then boasted, the Diadem and the Tiare. 'In both I got the same tough chicken and about the same number of ants in the soup.' But Robert enjoyed the pleasant meals on the veranda under 'the stars scintillating in a sky of velvet'. Even the huge cockroaches did not disturb his equanimity. The twenty-five pages devoted to the Tahitian interlude are among the most lyrical that Robert ever wrote. Undoubtedly, by concentrating on novels, he missed his true metier as a travel writer. Had he developed his talent in this direction he would assuredly have risen to the front rank.

Significantly it was not so much the lush tropical vegetation, the beautiful beaches of the Baie de Matarau and the scenic splendours of Moorea which evoked the best writing; it was, as ever, the people, from the first impression on the dockside of the women in their muu-muus to the bronzed fishermen in their scarlet and gold pareus. And, inevitably, it was the seamier sides of life that fascinated him most of all. One day he visited a 'dream valley, full of peace and innocent joy' and stumbled upon a crystal stream on whose banks stood dainty huts of bamboo, As he approached, the valley awakened, 'curtains of tappa were lifted, screens of fibre pushed away'. And then, to his horror, Robert discovered that he had strayed into the island's leper colony. Surrounded by emaciated people with fingerless hands and gargoyle faces, he encountered a one-legged, one-eyed skeleton who jabbed a monocle into a scabrous eye slit and addressed him in an upper-class English drawl: 'Hello, old chap, you seem to have lost your way.'

> 'Who are you?' I asked, and he answered: 'One who has already dug his own grave and waits to fill it. Who *was* I? That doesn't matter. In Piccadilly many knew me once. Fair ladies, God bless 'em, have loved me, but of the man I was this is all that remains . . .' He took the glittering glass from his eye and dangled it foppishly. 'Nothing left but a monocle.'
>
> 'Can I do nothing for you?' I faltered. 'Your friends . . .' But he shook his head and there was something bitterly brilliant in his smile. Tapping the breast of his tunic with the glittering object he drawled: 'Nothing, old chap. I'm dead. officially dead. Good-bye.' He finished in the same mocking voice, and his grey form melted into the lush scenery.

On another occasion Robert was accosted by a man whom he took to be 'a low type native', his legs covered with horrific sores; but as soon as he opened his mouth Robert realised that he was American:

'I gotta hut out there on the point. Rented a bit of land and hoped to make a grub-stake when this *fay-fay* got me. Both legs swelled, so I laid up and a *vahini* brought me my eats. It went away but I'm scared it'll come back. Guess I'll have to get out. I hate to do that, for this country's cured me of lung trouble. Tough, ain't it? You go to a hot country because you're a lunger and you gotta go back to a cold to be cured of *fay-fay*. Life's a picnic on this island. But *fay-fay*! . . . Oh hell! Guess I'll pull out.'

Over a period of several weeks Robert tramped all over Tahiti, exploring picturesque valleys, climbing the mountains, treading warily on narrow cliff paths, wading through innumerable streams, often waist-deep. Although he noted that the women often followed him with frankly lascivious eyes, he was touched by the innate good manners and unfailing courtesy of the islanders, often being invited into their huts to share their meals. Their gracefulness charmed him, and he regretted the ways in which the coming of the white man were spoiling this earthly paradise. Then, as he was revelling in the sheer beauty of the land and its inhabitants, he would be brought up short by some other ghastly scene. At one village where he paused in the hope of getting a cool drink of lime squash he met a woman whose face and body were emaciated, though her legs were elephantine. She obligingly knocked down a couple of coconuts for him and cut their tops. 'Then I thanked the woman, who beamed with pleasure and gave me the impression that it was she who was grateful.' Later, drying his feet after sloshing through a stream, Robert was disconcerted to find that they had a parboiled look and his ankles swelled visibly. For a horrible moment he thought he had caught the dreaded *fay-fay*, the scourge of the islands. 'I loved that word; such a frivolous way to describe a repellent disease.' (*Fay-fay*, or filariasis, is a tropical disease caused by a blood parasite, which results in painful and grotesque swellings of the legs and genitalia.) His mental equilibrium was further disturbed on meeting the skeletal figure of a man with monstrously swollen legs, who fed him bananas, oranges and coconuts. 'He was all courtesy, a natural gentleman, and to have offered him payment would have marred the graciousness of his gesture. For the joy of giving seems precious to these people, and if kindness be — as I think it — the greatest of the virtues, they atone by it for their laxity in other ways.'

Robert was not the only literary figure in Tahiti at the time. In the lobby of the Tiare Hotel he ran into Charles Bernard Nordhoff, 'a handsome young fellow, blond and brimming with vitality', who begged Robert to visit his co-author James Norman Hall who was in the Papeete hospital. He went the following day and found Hall, a long, lean and dark fellow who reminded him of Stevenson. Hall was very ill but received him with smiling charm. 'A rare personality and a writer born', he had a power of evoking atmosphere. This was years before Nordhoff and Hall shot to international fame with their books about the *Bounty* mutiny.

The last part of Robert's sojourn in the South Pacific was spent on Moorea, a rugged island whose majestic grey outline, between an azure sky and a deep-blue sea, rounds off the beauty of Papeete's waterfront spectacularly. The harbour of Papeete always looks deceptively calm, but once one gets beyond the protection of the coral reef the stiff breeze between the islands whips up the waves. The ninety-minute voyage to Moorea is bad enough nowadays on the *bac* car-transporter *Tamarii Moorea 2* but, back in the pre-ferryboat days of 1922, Robert hired 'an old pirate of a fisherman' to sail him over. This 'big, hulking Rarotongan, only half-sober' insisted on leaving Papeete at sunset in order to take advantage of a favourable wind. Even so, the crossing took an entire night and it was still dark when the hills of Moorea loomed up more blackly against the sky. There was a fearful moment while the sailing-boat plunged through the gigantic combers that crashed on the coral reef, ringing the island about two hundred metres from the shore. 'There was a crash that flung me off my feet, a hideous grinding, then smooth serenity. We had made it. We were safe.' Even then, the choppy waters of Moorea's wide-curving bay left Robert feeling very queasy, and not inclined to join the drunken, one-eyed skipper for a breakfast of roast pig. Before they made it to the shore Robert was violently sea-sick. In the lee of the island, however, the sea turned to a vitreous blue that magically changed shade, from sapphire to deepest indigo.

Like every other visitor who comes this way, the fantastical shapes of the great, jagged mountains are what impressed Robert most. 'They were like medieval ruins, here a cathedral spire, there a Norman keep, yonder the ramparts of a citadel; the verdure covered them with a semblance of ivy that completed the illusion.' The boat tied up at a rickety pier and here Robert was escorted to his host's bungalow by Mara, the lissom daughter of the housekeeper. At a banquet in Papeete Robert had met Major Brandish, an Englishman who had been gassed on the Western Front and who had gone to the South Seas to recuperate. He had a house 'half hidden in a tangle of greenery' on the edge of the bay. In Papeete he had been clad in evening dress; here on his own territory, he wore only a native pareu and a gold wrist-watch. For dinner that evening they were joined by an American writer named Bean who arrived in white dinner-jacket, in a pirogue paddled by a Japanese. There was a surreal quality to the scene, especially the feast served on a table covered with snowy napery, 'the silver of exquisite design, the wine glasses like gleaming bubbles'. Later, Brandish took Robert on a tour of his vanilla plantation. The poet was much taken by the beautiful plants with their long, waxy, exquisite leaves and elegant beans. 'If I were a poet and had to toil, I would be a vanilla planter,' he thought. The side-trip to Moorea was the highlight of the South Seas sojourn; days were idled away on rum punch and roast sucking-pig. How unreal the rest of the world seemed. Even Hollywood seemed a world away, while Dream Haven and the Place du Panthéon were distant memories. 'Decidedly a dangerous place, this Moorea, vamping one from the world.' Momentarily he was tempted to chuck everything and remain in that land of lotus-eaters, but he was hard-headed enough to realise that it was too cloying. His companions ultimately deserted the island. 'Brandish came into a title and went back to England; Bean wrote a Tahitian novel that was a best-seller and went to live in Laguna.' The pull of civilisation was too strong.

After two months of idleness and self-indulgence, Robert sailed back to Los Angeles, 'disgustingly curve conscious'. His family laughed to see how his waistline had expanded in the time he had been away. Matters were not improved when Emily told him that he reminded her of his poor dear father. This horrified Robert, remembering that Papa was corpulence personified. He was appalled to discover that he was twenty-five pounds overweight and immediately embarked on a crash diet. As his family tucked into their meat-balls and spaghetti at the Sunset Cafeteria, Robert stuck to spinach and dry toast. 'This too, too solid flesh is going to melt pretty quick if there's any will in little Willie.' Nothing less than a five-day fast, however, made any impression on his girth. In three months he succeeded in losing twenty pounds and indulged his *Schadenfreude* at the sight of his obese Hollywood friends.

In May 1922 the six-months' lease of the bungalow expired and it was time to head back to France. The family went to the station to see off Emily. 'With regret we watched the Old Lady leave for the north. She glided from the scene like a Duchess.' The ensuing half-page provided a brief pen-portrait of Emily.

> With her black silk dresses, her gold chain and her cameo brooch she took with her an atmosphere almost Victorian. She only wanted a lace cap and mittens to complete the picture, but when I suggested them she said: 'Nonsense, Willie, you want to make your Mother an old woman.'

Emily was actually only sixty-seven at the time, and younger than her years in many respects, enjoying the company of young people. Her diversions were cards and crime, the first in the form of solitaire, the second in detective fiction. 'She liked gangster films, dime novels and banana ice-cream.' Even today, Iris remembers the lady with pink cheeks, shining blue eyes and the laughing smile with great affection. It was Emily who unwittingly gave Robert's career a change of direction. 'I never read your poetry,' she said, 'but a new volume from you solves the Christmas present problem.' This jocular put-down provoked the riposte that there would be no new volume. The material garnered in Tahiti just would not gel. 'Too scenic and virtuous. I should have gone to French Guiana. Misery is my meat.' But Robert was still smarting over the disappointing sales of *Ballads of a Bohemian*. Even his earlier volumes of verse were beginning to flag. In Hollywood, however, his brief flirtation with the film world stimulated his ambition to write more novels, with one eye on the possibility of their translation to the screen. Emily might disparage his poetry, but she was always on at him to write the kind of books she liked, and he promised that he would try.

Robert and his family were back in Paris by the autumn of 1922, and he soon settled back into his old ways. 'I don't care where home is, it is always the dearest spot on earth, for it enshrines the treasures chosen so lovingly through the years.' He caressed his books, fondled his furniture and feasted his eyes on his pictures. Hollywood and Tahiti had been exciting diversions, but back in his princely apartment opposite the Pantheon, he was in his true milieu. Iris started school that autumn and Robert discovered a new pleasure as he trudged across the Jardin du Luxembourg every morning on the way to the Ecole Dalton, holding the hand of his little daughter.

> How eager she was to get to school so that she could play till the bell rang. She would drag me forward, prattling till we reached the gates, and there her little playmates would welcome her with joyful cries. As she rushed to join them she never looked back, for she plunged into another world in which I had no part. With the release of her hand I lost her till the moment I waited at the gate again; then, school over, she trotted by my side telling me of her day's doing. And for seven years I did this, seeing her grow in grace and charm. Ah, the childhood of our children — will anything in life ever be so precious?

The first of several films based on Robert's work was made by the Metro studio in 1923 and had its world première at Jury's Tivoli Cinema in the Strand, London, on 13 May 1924. Entitled *The Shooting of Dan McGrew*, it was directed by Clarence Badger and starred Lew Cody as the eponymous hero, Barbara La Marr as the Lady known as Lou and Percy Marchmont as the Piano-playing Stranger. Mae Busch, who later achieved fame as the sharp-tongued virago in the Laurel and Hardy films, also had a part in this film. A month later it came to the Capitol Theatre in New York but was panned by the *New York Times* whose reviewer dismissed it as tame and amateurish. It was a strange concoction that ranged from the South Seas to New York before heading for the real action in the Yukon. There was little suggestion of the Far North, and the film was not redeemed by the charismatic beauty of Miss La Marr who was pronounced to be unimpressive: 'Her overdoctored lips glisten in the glare of the Kleig lights and she indulges in her usual conception of excitement by panting.'[4]

CHAPTER 12

PARIS, 1922-29

Oh, it's pleasant sitting here,
Seeing all the people pass;
You beside your *bock* of beer,
I behind my *demi-tasse*.

'On the Boulevard' in *Ballads of a Bohemian* (1921)

A THIRD OF THE WAY THROUGH, *Harper of Heaven* CEASES TO
be autobiographical in the strict sense, and becomes instead a sequence of
cameos derived from some of Robert's travels in the interwar years. In addition, a score of pages are devoted to his exploration of the Parisian slums, but
frustratingly there is hardly any mention of his literary endeavours. In fact, no
sooner had the Services returned from Hollywood than Robert returned to his
Remington. But instead of rendering his experiences in California and Tahiti
in verse or prose he picked up a project which had been germinating for
several years. In the article entitled 'Baedekering in Brittany' which appeared
in the *Toronto Star* on 3 January 1914, Robert told his readers of visiting the
casino at Dinard near St Malo where he successfully played the tables for thirty
francs a day, using a system of his own devising. Klinck[1] speculates that Robert
may have had his initiation in the art of roulette in the gaming saloons of
Whitehorse and Dawson, although this seems extremely unlikely, in view of
his professional position and professed parsimony. In the winters of 1917–18

and the immediate post-war years, however, Robert had stayed at Menton and later in Vence with Archie and Lizzie Bruce. These extended sojourns gave him ample opportunity to visit Monte Carlo and study the world's most famous casino and its habitués at first hand.

The principality of Monaco, little more than half a square mile in extent, is a remarkable survival from the Middle Ages. The Greeks had a temple on the rocky headland, dedicated to Herakles Monoikos. More than a thousand years later, in 1297, Francesco Grimaldi from Genoa and a band of desperadoes disguised as Franciscan monks seized the rock and carved out a fief which maintained a precarious alliance with its powerful neighbours, France or the Holy Roman Empire. In 1793 the French National Convention annexed the principality and dispossessed the Grimaldis, but they were restored by the Treaty of Paris in 1814. The Treaty of Vienna a year later placed Monaco under the protection of Sardinia. In 1848, when revolution swept through Europe like wildfire, tiny Monaco was not immune. There were uprisings in Mentone and Roccabruna which were promptly occupied by Piedmontese troops. In 1860 the price paid to Napoleon III for assisting in the unification of Italy was the cession of the county of Nice to France and the following year Monaco passed under French protection, Mentone (Menton) and Roccabruna (Rocquebrune) being sold to France separately for 400,000 francs. Nowadays, as one drives along the coast road from Nice, it is impossible to tell where Cap d'Ail ends and Monaco begins, the only indication being the orange rather than yellow posting boxes at the roadside.

Today Monaco derives its wealth from its position as one of Europe's principal tax havens, but a century ago the chief source of revenue was the Casino. Although there appear to have been gaming tables at Monte Carlo in 1856, gambling did not develop into a major enterprise until some years later. In 1861 the entrepreneur François Blanc, recently deported from Homburg, obtained a fifty-year concession from Prince Charles III. This later passed into the hands of the Monaco Sea Bathing Society and Foreigners Association which paid an annual rent of two million francs in the early 1920s, as well as a generous slice of the takings. The Monegasques themselves were forbidden access to the Casino but were exempt from taxation and derived immense profits from the visitors who flocked there in the season. Robert's opinion of this strange situation does not appear anywhere in his autobiography, which is hardly surprising as he was actually residing in Monte Carlo by the time *Harper of Heaven* was in gestation. But his early views were expressed mordantly enough in his novel *Poisoned Paradise*, which was published late in 1922 by Dodd Mead and Fisher Unwin. Not surprisingly, there is no mention of this novel in the autobiography either.

This is a much better book than his previous novels, what would nowadays be called 'docudrama' with its detailed descriptions, extremely technical at times, of gambling techniques and the various systems devised by hopeful punters in order to break the bank. This is the chief interest of the book, but it is also shot through with early post-war cynicism. Superficially, Monaco, with its beautiful climate and breathtaking scenery, was a little paradise; but not far below the surface lay the disillusionment of the addicts who gambled everything away and then starved to death or committed suicide. There were hints of the corruption and absolutism of the princely administration. The descriptive writing showed a new maturity and the plotting was much more deftly handled than in the previous books. Only the romantic aspects were dealt with in Robert's usual perfunctory fashion, and the passages, where Hugh, the hero, and Margot, the heroine, live together as master and housekeeper or brother and sister do not ring true. But what this novel lacked in passionate embraces and torrid lovemaking it more than made up in the vividness with which Robert brought to life the atmosphere of Monte Carlo and its denizens. The characterisation was much better; even minor players were more fully rounded and convincingly delineated.

Although the chief value of this novel nowadays is sociological, with its portrait of a largely vanished way of life, it was given commercial immediacy by elements of the ripping yarn which doubtless is what made it so appealing to the film-makers. To be sure, there are occasional *longueurs* when the novel reads more like a travelogue. Hugh is given a trip to Corsica, probably because Robert and Germaine made two trips to that Mediterranean island just after the war. There were elaborate details of travel, lodgings and especially meals, reflecting elements which would later be found in the two autobiographies. The cynicism of the author at the foibles of human nature contrasted sharply with his undisguised rapture for the scenery of the Riviera:

> The scenery was as lovely as a painted panel. Between umbrella pines he saw the majestic sway of the sea. Snowy villas peeped from sombre cyprus groves. The palms were pale gold in the wistful sunshine. Magic names glorified the common-looking stations — San Raphael, Agay, Nice. In the setting sun the way seemed to be growing more and more wonderful, as if working up to a climax of beauty . . . And to think that this loveliness had been here all the time, and he had not known![2]

Poisoned Paradise was well received by the critics at the time, and the film rights were sold almost immediately to the newly formed Metro-Goldwyn-Mayer. It was filmed under the direction of L. Gasnier, with Kenneth Harlan as Hugh and none other than Clara Bow as Margot. Carmel Myers also had a major role, playing the ghastly Mrs Bellmire. Unlike the previous film, *Poisoned Paradise* the movie closely followed Robert's story. Like the novel itself, the film was generally well received, though the *New York Times* reviewer considered that it deserved something better than 'a dime-novel title'. He found in it 'a great deal of truth interspersed with impossible fiction', and he regretted that the director had not made it a more important picture with closer attention to Monte Carlo and the sociological aspects which Robert had highlighted in the text:

> He could have shown the losers applying for enough money to return home, the men who were saved from misfortune by having a train to catch at the height of their good luck, the women who faint and vanish through mirrored doors and the old women who beg for money in the perfumed atmosphere of the roulette room.[3]

Despite niggles like this, the film was a box-office hit, and helped to sustain the novel as a best-seller. Robert was evidently surprised, though pleasantly so, at the public response to his latest book. Perhaps his mother had been right after all. Henceforward he would devote his creative talents to prose. For fifteen years he turned his back on verse. Instead he concentrated on producing the kind of thrillers which Emily craved for. He could not write the sort of detective fiction she enjoyed best for 'the cold logic' of them bored him. But he could make up 'stories that leaped from one lurid situation to another' and his fertile imagination did the rest.

Before the end of 1922 Robert started work on a new book entitled *The Roughneck*. Despite his reservations about writing a novel on the strength of two months' first-hand experience of life in Tahiti, the strength of this book lay in its marvellous descriptive passages. What Gauguin immortalised on canvas, Robert painted rhapsodically in prose which had a fine lyrical quality. Thus he described the first impression of Papeete, as seen from the deck of the approaching ship:

> Then from the roaring whiteness of the reef they turned to look at the land. It seemed to leap at them in the eager appeal of its beauty. Through the crystal clearness the velvety shores were radiant with joy and colour. Those pale groves must be coconut palms. Down to the beach they thronged, leaning over the water and fluttering a frivolous welcome. Behind them were tenebrous mountains matted with jungle. It was a steep land, smothered in greenery. Its violent verdure cataracted down the flanks of the hills, and petered out in those pale flirtatious palms.[4]

Throughout this novel there are many passages of a similar quality. Nothing was too trivial to excite Robert's interest and delight his eye. Thus, even the simple matter of fording a stream was transformed:

> There were good-sized pools and the water had an opal tint, like soapy water. In the depths were giant black shrimps. The rocks were covered with russet-coloured lizards, and mosquitoes rose in clouds. How fortunate there were no snakes.[5]

Robert was obviously pleased with these word-paintings for he used several of them, almost word for word, in the relevant chapters of *Harper of Heaven* a quarter of a century later.[6] Indeed, even more than *Poisoned Paradise*, this novel reads like a travelogue. Its strength lay in rhetorical descriptions of Tahiti and Moorea, and had he published his descriptions and his anecdotes in a straightforward travel book he would have produced an infinitely better book. But by placing them in the framework of a thriller Robert made a grave error of judgment. The plotting on this occasion was far-fetched and obviously contrived, while the characterisation was two-dimensional. Robert himself was aware of the book's shortcomings, for he later described it as 'a series of dramatic situations linked up to form a story. When the hero was not rescuing the heroine from dire peril the heroine was saving the hero from imminent danger.'

It was written at Lancieux over a period of nine months, Robert remaining at the seaside long after Germaine and Iris had returned to Paris. 'I got a lot of fun with this book,' he wrote. 'I associate it with long tramps through the fenceless fields of early winter with a bracing wind, and my dog crazy with joy as he accompanied me.' Robert, too, was full of happiness. The work went without a hitch. His hero and heroine became so real to him 'that they did things of their own accord'. He ended the book one evening at tea-time, 'wrote the lovely word FINIS and sat there quiet, tranquil, content'. Craftsmanship rather than artistry was involved, evident in the sigh of relief as Robert thought, 'Another job done, another book in the bag.' It was dismissed in a brief paragraph:

> My book was a success. It was a best seller and was sold to the Cinema people. They made an entirely different story of it and even wanted to change the title. So what remained? I wondered. And why that five thousand dollar cheque they paid me? What a crazy world where one gets something for nothing.[7]

The novel was published by Barse and Hopkins in 1923 and was transformed into a film the following year — the third of Robert's works to hit the screen that memorable year. In the celluloid version George O'Brien played the hero, Jerry Delane, while Billy Dove played Felicity. Despite Robert's dismissive comment, the story-line was more or less faithful to the book, although the script-writers wrought radical improvements on the plotting. In the book there are scenes in Brittany which in the film were more logically set in the South Seas. The film was premièred in New York early in December 1924 and the review published the following day summed it up as 'a boy's idea of adventure'.[8] The anonymous film critic devoted several lines to the powerful physique of George O'Brien, drawing attention to his deep chest, brawny arms, the strength of an ox, the ankles of a Mercury and an artistic waistline — the model of Robert's own ideal of physical perfection.

A fascination which became, for a time, an almost total obsession, was the slums of Paris. In *Harper of Heaven* one is left with the impression that this developed after the return from California, but here and there Robert lets slip incidental details which place the nocturnal jaunts in the Marais in an earlier period. In fact these plunges 'into the purlieus of poverty' were already evident in the pre-war period and provided some rich colour for *The Pretender*. In 1919–21, however, they became such a regular habit, night after night, that Germaine began to complain. Robert was deaf to her *petite bourgeoise* entreaties as he donned his oldest clothes and jammed a cloth cap or a stained beret on his head. By night he explored the bistros and bal-musettes and mingled with 'putrid humanity'. Then, in the wee small hours, he would return to his princely apartment, strip and have a good hot bath before climbing into a soft and friendly bed. This wealth of material was to provide three chapters in the autobiography: 'Obscene Scene', 'The Lower Depths' and 'Caught in the Criminal Net' as well as the background for his thriller *The Master of the Microbe*. Indeed, with commendable economy, many of the descriptive passages in the autobiography were lifted verbatim from the novel.

That this preoccupation with the lower depths belonged to 1919–21 rather than to 1922–24 is borne out by the fact that, on one memorable occasion, Robert was accompanied by Archie Bruce on a visit to a disreputable dive aptly named the Auberge des Assassins. Bruce was still Reuter's chief in Paris in 1919 and, as such, frequented the deliberations going on at Versailles which culminated in the signing of the peace treaty between Germany and the Allied powers on 28 June. It must therefore have been around that date that Robert, dressed as an *apache*, ran into his old friend in the Boul' Mich'. Robert's memory was faulty when he later wrote: 'I had not seen him since I had made my sudden trip to the States.' In fact Archie was resplendent in evening dress and was on his way to a banquet at the British Embassy to celebrate the signing of the treaty. 'He was so pompous now, with his talk of the Peace Conference, Lloyd George and Clémenceau.' This brought out Robert's sense of inferiority again, but he determined to put his old friend in his place, and persuaded him to accompany him. He hailed a taxi and off they went to the notorious Auberge.

'Of all the black and bitter boulevards that encircle Paris the one called Macdonald is the most discouraging,' he wrote. 'Why it should have a Scotch name I never discovered.' Robert had little interest in history, else he would soon have learned that the boulevard was named after Etienne Macdonald, kinsman of the redoubtable Flora and one of Napoleon's marshals. At any rate, the Scottish name reassured Archie, although the press chief had misgivings when they entered the sink of iniquity. Robert played a little joke on his finely attired friend, whispering to the *patron* that his companion was none other than David Lloyd George, then Prime Minister. Lloyd George was in Paris from the middle of January till the end of June 1919 and, with Woodrow Wilson and Georges Clémenceau, his photograph was constantly splashed across the front pages of the tabloid newspapers. It so happened that Archie Bruce bore a striking resemblance to the Prime Minister, with the same large white moustache and long flowing white hair, so the *clochards* in the bar were convinced and regarded him with awe. Archie played up to the charade, ordering bottles of pinard for the assembled drinkers and packets of cigarettes all round as he left. Fortunately for his peace of mind, Archie thought the whole thing had been set up, and that this was merely a show. As they parted, he told Robert, 'These boys played their parts well, but it's too realistic to be real. It's a great set-up. I must give it a boost in the Press and put the tourists on to it.'

In January 1924 Robert celebrated his fiftieth birthday. The twenty-five pounds which he had put on during his trip to America and the South Pacific had been whittled away, but not without cost. Drastic dieting had been accompanied by rigorous exercises of a type which was then fashionable in the United States and involved weight-lifting and the use of extensors and expanders to build up the chest and arm muscles. Shortly after his birthday Robert contemplated entering a boxing tournament but wisely decided to have a medical check beforehand.

'Whatever have you being doing?' demanded his doctor. 'Keeping fit,' replied Robert, proudly bunching his biceps and cording his stomach muscles in the approved washing-board fashion. At fifty, he had the rippling physique of a man half his age. He expanded his chest muscles and looked 'like a picture postcard of Gene Tunney', but the doctor was far from impressed. He asked Robert what sort of exercise he was taking. Proudly Robert recited the strenuous daily programme. 'Yesterday, for instance, I worked two hours in the gym. Then I had a swim in the pool before lunch. In the afternoon I did a three hours' hike. In the evening I put on the gloves . . .' The doctor reached for an apple and snapped it in two, revealing it to be rotten at the core. In this graphic manner he broke the news that Robert's heart was enlarged and racing out of control. If he kept up this punishing regime he would he dead before he was sixty. By developing his muscles he had damaged the most important muscle of them all. The walls of his heart were dilated; there was regurgitation, perhaps a lesion. He was, in fact, in bad shape despite his appearance.

By way of advice the doctor suggested a natural cure. Robert had to give up alcohol, tobacco, red meat, coffee 'and every form of exciting food'. He was to eat very little in the evening, walk a great deal but never hurry, keep cheerful and calm and practise placidity. Robert had marched into that consulting-room feeling like a million dollars; now he slunk out looking like thirty cents. Even then, he was unconsciously playing a role. 'I walked wearily with what I thought was a look of pathetic resignation. I even imagined that the passers-by were regarding me with pity.' From being a fitness freak Robert plunged immediately into hypochondria; the state of his heart obsessed him. The nights were the worst, when he had panic attacks and palpitations. His 'pet hobby was the consultation of doctors'. They all told him the same thing: he had a defective heart, hypertrophy and abnormally high blood pressure. It was a timely warning, and with luck and a drastic change in lifestyle he might live to a ripe old age. For a year he worried excessively about his health, his fertile imagination working overtime. Then he gradually settled down again. By 1925 he was less conscious of the beating of his heart and ceased to listen for the hiccup at every tenth beat which betrayed syncope. 'The least worry gave me a setback and its stutter persisted.'

In 1926 Robert was advised by one of his doctors to go to the health resort of Royat in the Auvergne. 'It was not until the third year of my heart experience that I achieved a return to normal.' The chapter entitled 'Confessions of a Cardiac' described in great detail the thermal station whose waters were 'the nearest thing to the fountain of eternal youth'. Even after his first immersion in the rusty water Robert felt better. He had gone there 'sceptical, discouraged and neurasthenic'. His heart was 'depressingly irregular' and he had little hope of beneficent results. But the atmosphere was tonic in its purity, and the surrounding countryside so beautiful, that, from the outset, Robert felt invigo-rated. He was greatly reassured by one of the specialists there, a 'little, round, rosy professor of Clermont University' — actually the renowned Gabriel Perrin[9] — who brought the comforting news that there was no lesion. Robert, he concluded, had strained his heart by some prodigious effort. His heart was dilated and its rhythm affected, but he was confident that he could cure these problems. After a week of bathing in the rich, brown waters, Robert's blood pressure dropped from 220 to 150; while that hiccup which had irritated and worried him so much disappeared and never came back. Baths were alternated with ten-mile tramps through the woods, and Robert rigorously turned his back on the epicurean dainties, sticking to steamed potatoes and stewed prunes.

For three seasons (1926–28) Robert went to Royat and placed himself in Perrin's hands. During the first period he was alone, and to this belongs one of the few extant letters to his wife. It is on a plain sheet of quarto typing paper, and is handwritten. Addressed to 'My dear Daisy' and headed 'Thursday', he told her that 'the country is lovely, prettier than Brittany even'. At 'the succursal of Raoul in Clermont' he bought a pair of strong shoes 'with soles of crepe caoutouchou (*sic*) because I walk so much'. Then he continued:

> I am feeling awfully well and looking well too. I have not yet worn my Poole suits as there are practically no visitors yet. We are only 6 at my hotel. I am enclosing menu. As I eat chicken every day you might stand yourselves one occasionally. I eat so carefully I am sure the others look on me as a model. The fat lady has bought a box of *pain régime* instead of bread but she still piles into the spaghetti. I am losing weight a little in spite of our fine food. I have just been to see the doctor who is greatly pleased with the progress I have made. My blood pressure was 18½ only. He put me through some pretty severe tests and was more than satisfied. Well I must keep it up.
>
> Tell old Muggsums [Iris] to do well her lessons. You might send me another packet of bran by the post.
>
> With best love to you both.
>   Your affectionate Robert

During the second and third seasons Robert was accompanied by his family. Iris recalls these sojourns at Royat as rather boring. Her father went off on his daily jaunts leaving her and her mother to amuse themselves as best they could.

Robert also spent some time on his own at Lancieux, probably in autumn, after Germaine and Iris had returned to Paris for the latter to go to school. From this period have survived three letters. Robert was now getting on with some work, which would account for the fact that these letters were typewritten. The first one, simply headed 'Thursday', answered one of Germaine's in which she had told him that she had had an alveolar abscess requiring a tooth extraction. This provoked the response, 'I am surprised about your douleurs. And the weather so fine too. You have to go to Hollywood to be well.' Domestic matters were discussed: Germaine had taken a new servant who was giving her satisfaction. Robert approved, saying 'By all means hold on to her. Pay her as mich (*sic*) as you want. Wages will probably rise to the 500 francs mark', but he added cannily, 'by that time I hope we will have discovered a way of doing without them'. Then he went on:

The young wolloper [Iris] must be getting very important with her twenty books. I am afraid she won't take much notice of her poor old decrepid (*sic*) daddy. You should have seen little Willy this evening sipping his Campbells soup and shouting Its a poor heart, etc. I have discovered a most charming bakers at St Briac where I get heavenly bran bread. I toast it for supper every evening.

This letter was written about October, for Robert remarked that the weather had changed that day and was now cold and misty. 'My work is getting on nicely. I never fail to do the quantity I plan. My liver and heart are behaving well. Altogether my stay down here this time is much pleasanter than I expected.'

The next letter, headed 'Wednesday morning', was probably written a week or two later, for Robert begins with an apology for his failure to return to Paris on Sunday as planned. This sheds a brief light on his prolific output when the mood was upon him, for he explained that he still had some eight chapters to do.

However I hope to catch the train on this day week, so that I will be home for the Thursday. I am getting pretty tired, and could not stand it very much longer. Two days ago while wee Willie was tapping furiously on his typewriter, two enormous gendarmes came again and asked him all kinds of questions. They wanted my *permit de sejour*. When I told them I had sent it away, they asked for my *recipisse*. Of course I had none, so they got very excited and talked about a *procès verbal* and began to shout at me. They also asked a lot of questions about you which I could not answer. When they heard you had travelled to Paris without a *pièce d'identité* they nearly had a fit. I almost thought they were going to suggest the guillotine for you, and I carefully concealed the fact that I had done so too. Really, it's very annoying. It's bad enough working thirty hours a day without having two gendarmes as big as the house camped in the garden all the time. If people here bother me much more I shall have to go and live in another country.

The rest of the letter was taken up with gossip. The girl who had got Anna's brother into trouble was called Boissac 'or a name like that'. She was a little blonde about eighteen and lived at the *prevauté*. 'His wife is getting a divorce.' The *cousine* of Dangou was starting an *épicerie* and Madame Merdrinac was furious. Robert's dog Coco had been suffering from eczema and the bare patch on his back had not improved. 'I wash it and keep it clean, but don't see the hair growing yet. However he seems awfully well, and apart from that is quite beautiful.' The weather was milder again and Robert was feeling well, 'except that I am tired of this continuel (*sic*) work, and need a change. I haven't had a single day's rest since I came down.' This letter departed from his usual formal salutation, with the typewritten 'Affectionately, The pepere of Cocumsky'. The last letter in the series was headed 'Monday' and showed Robert's customary exuberance:

> Just one more letter and I will be finished. I have only three more chapters of my book to write. It has gone fine and not given me much trouble.
>
> I am still having wonderful health. I feel very gay, enjoying everything. I usually walk about between the bedroom and the kitchen as I do my writing. I generally keep on working as I eat my lunch and finish up about four o' clock. Then I have my bath, exercise and walk. I enjoy putting on my old military coat and big boots and going for a walk on a rough day. If you were here I think I could enjoy staying here the most of the Winter, but it would be rotten for the kid.
>
> This will be my regime when I come back: Morning, a medium-sized cup of tea. Lunch, a small portion of meat or fish, some potatoes or green vegetable, but not both, and some bran and jam. Supper, soup, pudding or compote and bread and butter. Postum. I hope you approve of this. I also want to drink a bottle of Vichy Hôpital a day, so you might order a dozen. If I can only keep up this marvellous spell of good health in Paris I will be pleased. For the last three nights I haven't heard my heart at all. I believe its (*sic*) getting gradually all right again. Nothing like taking care.
>
> Well, I shall be counting the days till I see you both again. With love and kisses to you both,
>
> Robert

Robert's *renaissance* came about as a result of the long walks after lunch when he roamed the high hills of the Auvergne. In Lancieux he kept up the same rigorous regime, going for brisk walks along the Grande Plage towards Beaussais, doing physical jerks as he strode out along the sand. To the Lancieutins Monsieur Service, the only man in the village to own a motor-car, seemed an eccentric millionaire, well known to everyone for his strange habits of exercise.

It was, indeed, a rebirth, for the combination of diet, bathing and hiking gave Robert a new lease of life. No born-again Christian was ever more fanatically devoted to his new-found cause; Robert became a positive zealot for healthy living which was eventually to find expression in a book rhetorically entitled *Why Not Grow Young?*. With the subtitle *Keeping Fit at Fifty*, it was published in 1928 and, although Robert was disappointed with poor sales at the time, it eventually ran to a second edition, in 1952, with the subtitle *Living for Longevity*. It was written at Dream Haven, probably in the early summer of 1928 before Robert returned to Royat for the third season, for he was 'still suffering from an athlete's heart' when he wrote it, and aimed 'to prevent other fools of fifty from acquiring one'.

> My book was to present myself as a painful example of vanity and ignorance. Nevertheless, I was enthusiastic in my worship of health, and determined to be an apostle of radiant well-being. Crank though I might be I was on the side of the angels.

Significantly, this was the only book which Robert actually identified by name when writing his autobiographies. It was the one dearest to his heart.

> The others do not matter much, but to me this one does; for I wrote it, not for gain nor glory, but to do good. I read a hundred books to post me, and I filled it with quips. I wrote it in one adorable summer of dream-drugged mornings, when I sprawled half-naked on the sand and looked with rapture at the lazy, laughing sea. I remember I got sun-stroke working without a hat and had to lay off for two weeks. During that time a motor hummed in my head and I could not even think of thinking. Neither could I sleep for that infernal buzzing in my brain, and spent the night pacing the garden in distracted impotence. I also had strange spells of loss of identity, in which I could not remember my own name. It amused me a lot as I struggled to think of who I was and how much money I had in the bank. For a Scotsman the last was a radical test of amnesia.[10]

The manual that emerged from Robert's ordeal was a curious amalgam of health hints and homespun philosophy. More importantly, however, it revealed for the first time the self-deprecating candour which was to be the hallmark of *Ploughman of the Moon* and *Harper of Heaven*. It opened with a lengthy autobiographical section going back to the days of Robert's boyhood and adolescence, dealing fairly cursorily with aspects which were to be more fully examined in the two autobiographical volumes. It sketched his fondness for solitary walks and reading books, his unrealised ambition to go to sea, his lack of nerve as a ladies' man, his insatiable wanderlust, his bondage as a wage-slave, his perfect health and temperate habits in the Yukon, contrasting with the decline into gluttony which came with prosperity. A sardonic catalogue of dos and don'ts dressed up as sermons and homilies, briskly summed up at the end of each section, was rounded off with a chapter entitled 'The Religion of a Man of Fifty' in which Robert expounded his philosophy, addressed to 'the Philosopher in Every Man', in practical and materialistic terms:

> I realize that I am a fool and that I know nothing. But I do not see that others are much wiser or know a great deal more. Baffled by the mystery that surrounds me, I cease to puzzle over it. Having satisfied my lust for reality I am willing to return to illusion again. Unable to understand life, I accept it as it presents itself, seeking to get all the enjoyment out of it I can. Thrown back on life itself in its concrete and actual presentment I become resigned to a destiny I cannot fathom. I make the best of my circumstances, try to put myself in harmony with them. I develop my capacity for the enjoyment of surface values such as form and colour; I accept emotions and sentiments at their *face* value. I cease trying to probe the depths, and without question take my happiness as it comes . . . As to the existence of a God, I know nothing. But I maintain that nobody does know anything. And this is just as it should be, for whatever the nature of supreme reality, it is inconceivable that it should be conceivable . . . Kindness and sympathy is the best religion of all.[11]

Commenting on this book, of which he was inordinately fond, Robert added that it had 'a sorry sale'. For the first time in his literary career he had to admit failure, attributing it to the old trouble: 'Once a man gets tagged for doing a certain type of work the public are loath to accept anything else from him. From Yukon ballads to health homilies was too rude a break even for my most devoted fans and my book fell flat.' It was published by Barse of New York but Fisher Unwin rejected it, and thus brought to an end Robert's lucrative association with that firm. Instead, it was accepted by Ernest Benn of London, a company which was to publish the prolific output of his later years. Robert remained adamant that this was 'a brave wee book' and it must have given him some comfort when Dodd Mead brought out the second edition in 1952. In his second volume of autobiography Robert, then in his mid-seventies, proposed that some day he would write a book entitled *Ninety Not Out* in which he would describe 'my conflict with the calendar and my triumph over time'.

The keep-fit book had, by way of frontispiece, a photograph of Robert in bathing trunks, 'the costume in which he wrote this book' according to the publisher's blurb. This was a full-length, side view of the author, showing the proud profile of a middle-aged man who had won the fight against flab, a vivid encouragement to his readers.

The book on which Robert was so frenetically engaged when writing to Germaine from Lancieux was one or other of two thrillers which were in more or less simultaneous gestation. In *Harper of Heaven*, Robert with his usual casualness, implies that work on both took place after he had moved to the South of France, but in fact they were both written in the latter part of the Paris period and published in 1926 and 1927. Despite the faulty chronology, however, Robert's account of the circumstances in which they came to be written is probably accurate enough. He was in a dilemma; he had promised two different publishers his next book.

> How to satisfy them? By writing two, of course. And that is what I did.
> I began on my Paris underworld book, finished it that winter, and the
> day I wrote *The End* I began the first chapter of another. This time the
> scene was laid in the country around my beloved Dream Haven, but
> with my *penchant* for the *macabre* a gruesome book I made of it. Its
> preparation accounted for another year, then I handed over both
> manuscripts to their respective publishers.[12]

The first of these novels, *The Master of the Microbe*, was published in New York by Barse and Hopkins. It will be recalled that Robert's first three novels were brought out by Dodd Mead, but for the fourth (*The Roughneck*) he had reverted to the firm that had published his verse. It would appear, therefore, that Barse and Hopkins had taken out some form of contractual option on his next novel. At some point, however, Dodd Mead, who had published nothing new from Robert's pen since 1922, got a similar option, and it was in fulfilment of this obligation that Robert wrote *The House of Fear*. As Barse and Hopkins published their book in 1926 and Dodd Mead theirs a year later, it seems improbable that the manuscripts of the two novels went to their respective publishers simultaneously as Robert maintained. Moreover, both books had the same English publisher, Fisher Unwin, who brought them out synchronously with the American editions, in 1926 and 1927.

In *The Master of the Microbe* Robert distilled the material he had gathered on his 'noctambule' descents into the Parisian slums. Once more, a series of dramatic scenes was woven around extensive descriptive passages; one is reminded, in the latter, of Victor Hugo in *Les Misérables*, but there unfortunately the similarity ends. The plot is unbelievably convoluted, the coincidences stretching the credulity of the reader to the limit. None of the principal characters turns out to be quite what he or she appears, and sometimes not one mask but several layers have to be peeled away before we get at the truth. Even the hero, obviously modelled on Robert himself, is a throw-back to James Madden in *The Pretender*. He is Harley Quin, and just in case the reader is too dim to get the point, he is often facetiously addressed by one of the other characters as *Harlequin*, the pantomime character who traditionally conceals his identity behind a mask. The chief supporting role is taken by an *apache* named Julot (a character who appears in *Ballads of a Bohemian*) who turns out to be . . . but that would be revealing one of the more startling (and improbable) of this book's many *denouements*. Harley, like Robert, has an apartment near the Pantheon; and like Robert, he disguises himself in order to make frequent forays into the slums, each one more ghastly than the one before.

And this is where Robert's powerful descriptive passages take over. Many years later he was to repeat entire chunks of them in the respective chapters of *Harper of Heaven*. The Paris Robert was describing was rapidly disappearing, for in the immediate aftermath of the First World War the fortifications erected in the 1840s were dismantled and the city became inextricably linked to the outer suburbs. What Napoleon III and Haussmann had failed to complete in the 1860s was accomplished more than half a century later. In the 1920s, however, the Marais and the Zone still remained, the congested slums into which the dregs of France had sunk. Harley Quin, a young superman endowed with immense physical strength (like all Robert's heroes) and detective powers of genius, is embroiled in the plans of the aptly named Sinistra to hold the world to ransom by the use of a powerful virus. Much of the plot centres on the virus and the attempts of the criminal gang to locate the magic serum which forms the antidote. Whoever finds this serum will become, indeed, the Master of the Microbe. In evading the unwelcome attention of the police, who suspect his complicity in the murder of an eminent immunologist, not to mention the devilish machinations of Sinistra and his cohorts, Quin lurches from one hiding place to another, the medium for Robert's exhaustive descriptions of the slums.

These sordid milieux were not hard to find. Close by the Pantheon, for example, lies the rue Mouffetard, today a respectable street of antique shops and smart restaurants but then, 'the juiciest slum in all the city'. As one saunters along this quaint old thoroughfare today it is hard to visualise what it must have been like before inner-urban decay was reversed.

> The rue Mouffetard is a steep, unsavoury street that seethes with sordid humanity. The houses are mouldering with age, the doors dark tunnels burrowing into decrepitude. In an evil half-light sinister shadows haunt it. Every second entry is a bar and in its dim depths men with faces entirely evil foregather. Near it is the rue St Medard, frequented by the garbage-rakers and close by the Flea Market, where they sell their finds. Round the Place Maubert radiate poisonous alleys and close by is the

Café des Clochards, refuge of those homeless outcasts who sleep under the bridges of the Seine.

Robert prowled through this 'furtive region' clad in a turtle-necked sweater, a cloth cap and old flannel trousers. It was quite a trick to get away from his posh apartment block without shocking the other tenants, 'but I was aided by my concierge, an ex-policeman, who understood my motive'. The concierge would take Robert's raincoat, with which he had concealed his slum disguise, so that no one would recognise 'the tough-looking bum as the mono-cled individual who stared arrogantly at them in the elevator'. Robert became almost a split personality, by day the respectable *littérateur*, by night the *apache*. Germaine objected to his nightly excursions not so much on account of the danger to which he was exposing himself — he was always careful to play down this aspect — but on the more practical grounds that he might come back with fleas or lice.

Although this book is a cinematic sequence of melodramatic incidents it was not, *pace* Lockhart,[13] made into a film. Nor was his sixth and last novel, which incidentally, he dedicated to 'My Mother, Who in spite of her seventy-odd years, can still enjoy a Tale of Mystery and Crime'. The hero on this occasion was the Hon. Peter MacBeth, perhaps an amalgam of Peter McQuattie in the autobiography and McBean of *Ballads of a Bohemian*, although in no respect similar in appearance or character to the real-life Archie Bruce. In effect, the Hon. Peter was, again, Robert himself, and suffers from the same cardiac condition as his creator, even practising the same natural remedies to effect a cure. All Robert's novels began with the hero meeting a girl who looked inter-esting, and this one was no exception. The opening scene is set in Belleville, east of Montmartre, which was also the locale for *The Master of the Microbe*; but the action then moves swiftly to Brittany where the hero enjoys the rugged scenery not far from Lancieux. Peter purchases a villa, the White House (Dream Haven) near the village of Auberon (Lancieux). These places, idyllic and tranquil in real life, become the settings for a sequence of the most grue-some incidents that Robert could conjure up. Every device imaginable is brought into play, from gothic mansions with secret chambers and under-ground passages to strange burials, werewolves, bestial smells and grotesque masks. Toss in a rich assortment of shady characters and the entire gamut of wickedness, stir thoroughly, and *voilà* one has the recipe for a thriller which, for nimble plotting and rapid movement, left all of Robert's previous prose writings far behind. The dialogue was still rather stilted and inclined to the mawkish in the love scenes, and the conversation of the Frenchmen and Bretons is often stereotypical and perfunctory; but, on the whole, this book showed a newly found mastery of dialogue which considerably enlivened the text. It was almost as if Robert was envisaging the cinematic quality of the book, bearing in mind that he must have been writing it at a time when talking pictures were just coming in.[14] And, despite the melodramatic tricks, the plotting was also greatly improved, giving the book a cracking pace which made it hard to put down until the last page. With a good story-line and the back-drop of the Breton landscape, it would have made an excellent film. Given the commercial success of *The Pretender,* which came to the screen in 1928, *The House of Fear* ought also to have been a box-office hit. But negotiations to film it were abruptly broken off.

The answer to this mystery may lie in the fact that, in 1929, Robert found himself on the receiving end of a libel writ. Lightheartedly he dealt with the matter in his autobiography, without, of course, naming names:

> Having rid my system of lurid literature I thought a spell of rest was indicated, and I was beginning to enjoy it when one day I received a lawyer's letter. Up to now lawyers had played no part in my existence and I disliked them as much as I did doctors. And now this letter left me paralysed with horror. With heart thumping I read it over and over, scarce believing my eyes. For it accused me of libel most foul and reptilian. It seemed I was a slanderer, a base-minded bespatterer of the reputation of a certain member of a well-known family. In my latest book I had maligned his family in the most insidious and evil way, and it was going to cost me dear.
>
> No one could have been more innocent than I, and it still seems to me that no inference could have been more far fetched. But there you are. Writers are a race to be reprobated, and I was told that if I defended my case it would cost me thousands of pounds and I might lose in the end. It was not the money that mattered but the horror of appearing in court. Then again so many other innocents were involved — even the printer; so I said I would agree to pay up.[15]

The only time that Robert ever alluded to this unpleasant incident again was in August 1940 when Thelma Craig of the Toronto *Globe and Mail* interviewed him on his way westwards after the fall of France. When she queried why he had published nothing for ten years, Robert told her ruefully that he had spent five of the ten trying to pay off a libel suit. In fact, as his autobiography stated, it never got as far as a lawsuit, for Robert preferred to pay the outrageous sum demanded in order to avoid the unwelcome publicity of litigation. To Miss Craig he admitted: 'I used what turned out to be the nickname of an English Peer in one of my writings that had a Wodehousian flavour, and I had to pay . . . and pay . . . and pay'. Then he went on bitterly, 'The publishers just leave it to the poor author in such cases. So I said what was the use of trying to write?'

The threat of a libel action frightened Robert. Never in his wildest nightmares had he imagined that such a thing could be possible. Even when he blithely harnessed the name of one of the bank's respected clients for 'The Cremation of Sam McGee', he probably never gave a thought to the long-term repercussions. Poor McGee, a copper-mining engineer from Ontario, took a dim view of the ballad that used his name and suffered till the end of his life from tired jokes about whether he was warm enough yet; but back in 1907 all he did by way of retaliation had been to transfer his account from the Bank of Commerce to the Bank of British North America.

In fact, neither in *The House of Fear*, nor in any of his other novels, did Robert give a character a nickname of any sort, far less one that might be associated with an English peer, despite a discussion with H.G. Wells over a hypothetical case where someone called Buggins might have sued had he used his nickname of Buggsy. In *The House of Fear* the hero, the Hon. Peter MacBeth, has certainly some Wodehousian elements in his character, but there was no one of that name, or anything remotely like it, associated with a peer of the realm. In the book, however, Robert stated that Peter was the younger brother of 'Lord Strathbogie', a peer who is described on page 58 as 'sanctimonious'. Apart from a later reference to 'the illustrious house of Strathbogie' the name does not recur in the novel, nor does Peter's brother make any actual appearance.

As grounds for a libel suit, this was extremely flimsy. It is probable that the London lawyer who wrote to Robert via Fisher Unwin was merely trying it on, and there was a very fine line between the preliminary threat of litigation and flagrant extortion. Had Robert himself consulted a lawyer the libel threat would have been quite properly exposed for what it was and the matter dismissed out of hand; but he panicked and agreed to pay up the ten thousand pounds demanded by way of settlement out of court. Robert says that he was still paying up five years later, but the litigant's death in February 1934 probably brought this disgraceful episode to an end.

The English peer who instigated this action had been born plain Cuthbert Matthias Kenworthy, son of the Revd Joseph Kenworthy, rector of Ackworth near Pontefract. An interest in genealogy led him, at the age of sixty-three, to petition the House of Lords for the revival of a barony which had been in abeyance since 1369. In May 1916 he took his seat as the ninth Baron Strabolgi. What this had to do with Strathbogie may not be readily apparent, but the first baron, David de Strabolgi, was also tenth Earl of Atholl and derived his name from the vale or strath of the Bogie, a river on the borders of Aberdeenshire and Banffshire. Indeed, in some thirteenth-century documents his name was spelled Strathbogie, although his ennobled descendant preferred the medieval version. Being charitable about this unfortunate matter, one can only suppose that the novelty of the title had not worn off and that the ninth baron was unduly sensitive to any slur, real or imagined. Perhaps the sanctimonious epithet struck a raw nerve. The noble lord's entry in *Who's Who* gave as his sole achievement the fact that he had travelled round the world, while his recreations were listed as 'hunting, golf and fishing'.

John Strathbogie, ninth Earl of Atholl, was beheaded by Edward I in 1306, and thus had the dubious distinction of being the first nobleman of his rank to be executed for treason since Waltheof was beheaded by order of William the Conqueror in 1086. His son David, the tenth Earl, submitted to Edward in 1307 and was regranted his earldom. In 1312 he joined Robert the Bruce but quarrelled with him two years later and forfeited his Scottish estates. In October 1314 he fled to England where Edward II granted him land in Yorkshire. Three years later he sided with Thomas of Lancaster against Edward but was pardoned for his treason in 1318 and then rewarded with the barony of Strabolgi which, though derived from an obscure Scottish river valley, was an English peerage. Perhaps if Robert Service had a keener sense of history he might have seen the irony of the libel action.

CHAPTER 13

THE RIVIERA, 1929-39

O Land of Song! O golden clime!
O happy me, whose work is play!

'Dedication to Provence' in *Songs of a Sun-Lover* (1949)

IN 1929 THE OWNERSHIP OF 1 PLACE DU PANTHÉON CHANGED and the new owner decided to sell the apartments to their tenants. Robert was offered his palatial flat for two hundred thousand francs (then about £8,300). Within twenty years that apartment was to be worth ten times as much, and today such flats are approaching the million-pound mark. Although he could see, at the time, that the offer was a very fair one, Robert turned it down and consequently was forced to move out. This was probably the stimulus he needed to make a move that he had been contemplating for some time. 'For even Paris may pall after fifteen years and though I knew it like the inside of my pocket I did not want to be a boulevard barnacle.'

Several visits to the Riviera from 1917 onwards had convinced Robert that *there* was the earthly paradise. 'California may run it close, but for lovely, irresponsible living give me the Riviera.' In the autumn of 1929, therefore, the Service family moved south, taking an apartment at 4 rue Dante in Nice.

Despite its poetical name it had a slummy suggestion; for it was a working-class quarter and the house was old. The rooms had high ceilings painted after the beautiful Italian fashion. What joy to live under such lovely ceilings! We had seven rooms, but . . . no bathroom. The rent came to two hundred dollars a year and we paid our maid ten dollars a month. Indeed, with the popular market at our door life was incredibly cheap. No matter how lavishly we spent we could not help saving money — a very sad state of affairs. However, there were people we could help and that consoled us for our budgetary surplus.[1]

Who precisely Robert helped financially was never specified, but no doubt the mothers of Robert and Germaine received money from time to time and he certainly paid the costs of putting his brother Stanley through medical school. Strangely enough, after leaving Paris, Robert did nothing about finding a school for Iris who, ever afterwards, would bitterly regret that her schooling effectively ended at the age of twelve — not so much on account of the education she lacked but the loss of opportunity to make friends of her own age. At the age of sixteen Iris, on her own initiative, obtained a job in the English Library at Nice, but when she came home and told her parents Robert vehemently put his foot down. Why did she need a job? If she needed money, did he not give it to her? He failed to see that the girl needed a measure of independence; and Iris, kept so close to her mother's apron-strings, gave in. Something of Robert's attitude towards his daughter may be gained from the curious fact that he never called her by her name. We have already seen, in the few extant family letters, how he referred to her by a variety of nicknames; but to her face she was always 'Sis' or 'Old Girl'. Iris resented this, but characteristically never complained.

If he could afford something better, why did Robert choose such a mean street as the rue Dante? The probable and simple answer is that it suited him. Just as he felt comfortable lounging around in old clothes, like the frayed tweed jacket he affectionately nicknamed Old Whiskers, so also he preferred living in a working-class community. It fitted in nicely with his bohemian temperament.

Nowadays, the rue Dante has moved upmarket and the apartments have been thoroughly modernised without sacrificing their Italianate charm, dating back before 1860 when Nice, the birthplace of Garibaldi, was still an Italian city. It runs parallel to the celebrated Promenade des Anglais, and is therefore only a block or two north of the seafront where Robert went to bathe every day till the end of October, long after the summer visitors had gone and even the hardy residents found the sea too cold. One day, while walking along the promenade, Robert saw a figure in the raging surf and plunged in. He managed to grab hold of the drowning man just as he was being swept into deep water. 'I hung on and a huge breaker crashed us up on to the cobbles. Resisting the back surge I let the next comber wash us to safety.' The man he had rescued turned out to be an Italian youth who, crossed in love, had tried to take his own life. He almost succeeded, for it was hours before he regained consciousness. Somehow, the young man imagined that Robert, having saved his life, was now responsible for him and sought financial assistance. 'Perhaps he was right. Having restored him to the misery of life it was up to me to alleviate it. However, confronted with a severe cold and a ruined suit I hardened my heart.'

Robert's description of the flat revealed, for the first time, the semi-detached nature of his marriage. There was never any reference to the sleeping arrangements at Place du Panthéon but a ten-roomed apartment housing two adults, a maid-servant and a child probably indicated separate bedrooms all round, and Robert's nocturnal peregrinations tend to reinforce that view. At the rue Dante, however, there was no doubt:

> I loved my neat bedroom for I made of it a combined den, library and workroom. My books lined the wall, while above them hung my collection of guitars. In a corner was my roll-top desk, a typewriter and easy chair. Best of all, I had the most wonderful bed, an old-fashioned four-poster, covered with gay chintz, with beautiful carved woodwork. I had special mattresses made for it and wedge-shaped cushions that tilted it up, so that it was like a trough. Instead of supporting a quarter of my body it sustained one half. As I advanced in life I decided my bed was my best friend, and all money spent on it was wisely spent. I relaxed in it with a sigh of content, never ceasing to be grateful for its comfort. I have now enjoyed it for twenty-five years and cheerfully hope to die in it.

From the window Robert had a fine view of the street 'with its scrabble of sordid humanity' that he always found so fascinating. That first winter in Nice was delightful. While Germaine and Iris worked hard to make the flat habitable Robert gave them his moral support. As he strummed one of his guitars and watched the passing throng he felt little moved to get back to his typewriter. 'My poor Remington! Sometimes it would be merry for a month, then lapse into disuse.' Robert imagined the typewriter saying to itself:

> That lazy devil! Neglecting me for his idle strumming. thinks he can sing, the silly mutt; making cheap melodies and putting idiotic words to them. He's just as phoney at that as he is at everything else. His job with me is the only one he *can* do; yet he fritters away his time in futilities, when he might be making my keys tap out Eternal Truth.

Robert was quite content to idle away his time. There was a new town to be explored, and he revelled in the delights of discovery. In place of the winter gloom which he found all too often in Paris, he found sunshine, flowers and gaiety and the people were as joyous as their abode. Everything was within walking distance — 'no more tedious hours wasted in taxis and the Metro'. The Services had the best of both worlds, spending their winters in the Riviera sunshine, and then moving north to Brittany in the summer to avoid the unbearable heat. The trip north and south between their two homes was accomplished in a leisurely fashion, usually taking five days by road. In the twenty years that Robert drove between Brittany and the Riviera (from that first winter at Menton onwards) he had three cars — first a De Dion Bouton, then a Renault and latterly a Lancia. The journey was infinitely varied, and Robert never took the same route twice, preferring the country lanes to the major motor roads. Although he listed it in *Who's Who* as one of his recreations, he did not enjoy motoring. 'It was always an adventure, but for a nervous chap like me, something of a strain; and the joy of arriving at my destination gave me a sense of achievement quite out of proportion to my deserts.' He confessed to being 'an oldish fellow with a natural loathing of machinery, and haunted by the horror of a breakdown'. He was 'a pusillanimous driver' who should have been arrested for slow driving. 'I was rather a nuisance as I crawled along at forty kilometres an hour.' He had the Renault painted bright red so that its accentuated visibility might suggest danger and prevent other cars from crashing into it. 'However, in a million miles of driving I never had an accident,' he boasted.

In Nice Robert resumed contact with the Bruces who lived at Vence, only a few miles away. Through Archie Bruce, Robert was introduced to H.G. Wells, who had taken a villa at Malagnou near Grasse after the death of his wife Catherine in 1927. In the early 1930s Robert was a frequent visitor to Lou Pidou, and he and Wells became close friends. They had the same strength of personal convictions which, fortunately, seem to have been largely in accord. Wells's rapidity of judgment implied impatience of those who did not share his political or philosophical outlook, but in Robert he found a kindred spirit. If Robert was chagrined at the poor response to *Why Not Grow Young* it was Wells who consoled him with his kind remarks, telling him that he practised the special exercises which Robert had recommended for middle-aged fitness. As Wells was eight years older than Robert, and of a more sedentary way of life, it is to be hoped that he did profit from Robert's advice. At any rate, despite kidney disease, tuberculosis and diabetes, he lived to the age of eighty. Wells also strongly urged Robert to fight the libel case, exclaiming indignantly, 'We must stop that sort of thing. No author is safe these days. Writing is becoming one of the dangerous occupations.' Wells observed that, even if Robert were pilloried in court, the case would be a good advertisement for his book. But Robert's inferiority complex made him shrink from litigation. 'I would cut a pitiable figure. Though innocent as a lamb I would give the impression of a sinister criminal. No, I'll let it go.'

Robert described a lunch at Lou Pidou:

> Sitting on a high seat at the head of the table Wells was wonderful in an Olympian way. He ate very little but emitted sparks of wit and wisdom at frequent intervals. He was rather unique with his high-pitched voice and esoteric eyes. I had known him for thirty years but he had not changed much. He brimmed with vitality and was quite disappointed that I refused to play Badminton with him, the result of which would have been my humiliation. From his terrace the perfumed valley sloped gently to the sea. It was so peaceful I did not wonder he chose to write his books there.[2]

It was here, too, that Robert met 'the brilliant Odette, the most coruscating creature imaginable. Indeed she stands in my memory as the cleverest woman I have ever known.' Robert only met her twice, but she created a profound impression of wit, vivacity and charm. Characteristically, however, by the time he came to write his second volume of autobiography, he had either forgotten her real name or confused her with Odette Hallowes, the celebrated heroine of the Resistance. The 'most coruscating creature imaginable' was, in fact, none other than Colette. Sidonie Gabrielle Colette was born in Burgundy in 1873 and was therefore a few months older than Robert. By the 1930s she had become France's most famous woman of letters. Shortly before she died in 1954 she paid a last visit to Monte Carlo and a vivid description of the octogenarian flirting sensuously with Willy Maugham was given by James Lees-Milne. Twenty years earlier, her personal magnetism must have been electrifying. At that time she habitually spent the winter months in St Tropez, but on several occasions she was a house-guest of the Prince and Princess de Polignac at Grasse, and it was probably during these visits that Robert encountered her at Lou Pidou.

The reference to having known Wells for thirty years is puzzling. If Robert implied a friendship dating back from the time of his first visit to Lou Pidou, this would place their first meeting in 1899 or 1900, which is impossible. It is more likely that Robert, writing this passage in 1947, was thinking back to the winter of 1917–18 when he first visited the Riviera, but in that context to say that Wells had not changed much in thirty years is also nonsense, for he died in 1946. This may be no more than Robert's casual approach to chronology playing havoc with the truth.

Through Archie Bruce, Robert also met an old music-hall star, on whom he bestowed the pseudonym of Byron Binns in *Harper of Heaven*. This vaudeville artiste was supposed to be Robert's double, though this was, according to Robert, only remotely true. They both sported monocles, were about the same height, had ruddy faces of an open type and greyish hair.

> But there the likeness ended, and I never could understand why unknown females should bow graciously to me. It annoyed me because I was slim where he was stocky, I was prim while he was cocky. He loved society while I shied away from it. He was lethargic while I was all vitality. Although ten years my junior he seemed that much older than I.[3]

Byron Binns was, in fact, Milton Hays, a Lancashire music-hall artiste turned poet and novelist. Even if Robert could not see the similarity, other people often remarked on their striking resemblance to one another. One anonymous correspondent to a Los Angeles newspaper, writing about 1942, commented that Hays and Robert Service could have passed for twins.

> I used to see both of them a lot on the Riviera and never knew which was which. I remember Hays once saying to Service, 'I suppose you and I have written more of Kipling's bad verse than any two copyists alive'.
>
> Service smiled his shy smile and said, 'Whenever I see him I sneak down an alley.'
>
> More recently I ran into one of them in Hollywood and had to stall for ten minutes to find out which one it was.[4]

Hays died in Nice in 1940, shortly before the fall of France. Despite religious differences — Hays was a fanatical Christian Scientist while Robert was now a professed agnostic — the two became great friends. The son of a textile worker from Wigan, Hays gravitated to show business by way of a minstrel group on the sands of Blackpool. Later he busked to theatre audiences queuing for admission and eventually got an opening in a Manchester music-hall, but overnight became a successful comedian. Then he developed a series of humorous monologues and always finished his act with a song of his own composition or a recitation of his latest poem. He wrote over a hundred songs, composing the music as well. He could write a song in a night and sing it the next day. He made a fortune from the sales of his sheet music and gramophone records. One of his comic monologues was quoted by Kipling and recorded by Charles Laughton. He also published two humorous novels which enjoyed a measure of success in the interwar period.

Hays abandoned his vaudeville career when he was at the height of his fame, and retired to the Riviera with his French wife. He and Robert could often be seen on the Promenade des Anglais, arguing or upstaging each other. 'Carried away by his own verbosity he would stop and go into a song or dance,' wrote Robert. Through Hays, Robert met many of the other expatriates who had settled in Nice. One of these was Rex Ingram, the sculptor, painter, writer, film director, art connoisseur and authority on Arabian art and culture. 'He had an imperious quality that made it difficult to bear patiently with vulgarians.'

One day Hays halted Robert in front of a burly, bearded figure. He was always forcing introductions on Robert who groaned inwardly, wondering who this imitation of a Corsican bandit might be. The bearded man turned out to be the actor George Robey who, having recited some of Robert's monologues on stage, was glad to meet the originator of Dan McGrew in the flesh. At the time, George Robey was making a film version of *Don Quixote* and was playing Sancho Panza, hence the beard. The film was not a box-office success; it did not give Robey the opportunity to display his comic talent to the full, while Feodor Chaliapin, playing the Don, was miscast and apparently intoxicated most of the time, for he kept falling off his horse. Robert's view was that if the out-takes of Chaliapin had been retained and the rest scrapped, the film would have been very funny. Robey, on the other hand, was a teetotaller. He exercised regularly and took care of his health — qualities which Robert admired.

Another actor he got to know well in this period was Laddie Cliff. One night at the Casino he sang one of Robert's songs entitled 'Lipstick Lou', to the consternation of the croupiers in the roulette room. A dapper little man, as neat as a jockey, he had a hoarse voice that hinted at the cancer which would end his brilliant career. He went around with one of the Lupinos, a famous theatrical family, and in front of the Negresco bar they would do an impromptu tap-dance — 'A gay little bird, dancing in the shadow of doom'.

There were many literary personalities on the Riviera at this period, such as the novelist Phillips Oppenheim, the novelist and playwright William Locke, H.G. Wells and W. Somerset Maugham, but they were not obtrusive to the public gaze. Robert met Willie Maugham on a number of occasions, especially in the late 1940s and early 1950s when the latter lived at Cap Ferrat, but in 1929–30 the man who seems to have impressed Robert most was Frank Harris, then at the end of his career and almost at the end of his life, for he died in 1931 in his seventy-fifth year. Harris was a flamboyant figure who had made his reputation as a journalist before turning to more literary endeavours. A friend of Oscar Wilde, he produced a biography of him in 1920. Another of his books was *The Women of Shakespeare* which he subsequently turned into a stage play. There was something *louche* about Harris, confirmed by his remarkable autobiography *My Life and Loves*. Robert's pen-picture shows what a vivid impression he made, even in old age:

Frank hit the eye. He had his *apéritif* on the terrace of the Mediterranée, where he would sit with fiery face and blazing blue eyes. He was naturally arrogant and had none of the bland geniality one associates with age. He wore a white hat with a rakish tilt, white flannel trousers and very fancy waistcoats. Some said he dressed like a Jewish pawnbroker, some like a drummer for perfumery. He had a dark moustache, fiercely uptwisted, and coal-black hair which Wells told me was dyed. He had a deep voice which he cultivated, because being small he sought to impress people by the power of his vocal delivery. He had a big nose that suggested the Jew, though he was aggressively Irish. He walked along the promenade, seemingly absorbed in memories of which he had a rich store. His stare was discouraging, but let a pretty woman pass and how his eyes lighted up.[5]

Robert knew the ageing roué by sight, years before he was actually introduced to him by a fellow Irishman, Frank Scully, who was then the Riviera correspondent for *Variety*. Scully had a gift for original phrasing and a sardonic style. He sustained a serious leg wound during the First World War and suffered a great deal of pain for years before the leg was amputated. When Robert knew him he would often describe himself as having one leg, one lung, one wife and one son. 'A gay stoic, his life is a triumph over obstacles that would have discouraged most men.' Actually, when Robert first met Scully just after the war his wife Alice was expecting their first child; Scully would make her get on a weighing machine, proudly pointing to the pound increase. Twenty years later, Robert renewed the friendship in Hollywood, and found that that unborn child was taller than his father.

The occasion of Robert's introduction to Frank Harris was the latter's seventy-third birthday, which occurred not long after the Services settled in Nice. His wife Nellie, whom Wells called Frank's 'one hold on respectability',[6] gave a cocktail party in his honour, and Frank Scully, who was then ghosting Harris's biography of George Bernard Shaw, gave Robert an invitation. Shaw, incidentally, once said of Harris, 'He is neither first-rate, nor second-rate, nor tenth-rate. He is just his horrible, unique self'. Interestingly, Robert went alone, and for someone as shy as he was, the riotous party on the fourth floor of an apartment block was both intimidating and irritating. One man, on being introduced, told Robert that he had often recited his 'Shooting of Sam McGee'.

Emma Goldman, the international anarchist, was also at the party. She had been born in Kaunas, Lithuania, the daughter of the manager of the Russian state theatre in that city. In 1886, at the age of seventeen, she emigrated to the United States where she worked in a factory in Rochester, New York, and later in New Haven, Connecticut, where she became associated with anarchists. Two years later she went to New York City and formed a liaison with Alexander Berkman, who tried to assassinate the industrialist Henry Frick in Pittsburgh during the Homestead steel strike of 1892. After Berkman served a fourteen-year sentence she resumed the relationship. She herself was sent to prison in 1893 for inciting a riot. During the First World War she and Berkman were convicted of interfering with war preparations and sent to prison. Later they were deported to Russia, but disapproving of the Soviet system they moved to Western Europe. Emma edited various anarchist periodicals and had recently published her autobiography when Robert met her. 'She bubbled with vitality, yet I could not reconcile her with the firebrand of my imagination.' When introduced to Robert, she said, 'You're the man who makes poetry pay,' to which he riposted, 'I make rhyming remunerative.' Strangely enough, Emma subsequently moved to Canada, where she died in May 1940.

Frank Harris held a cocktail in one hand and asked Robert why he was not drinking. He appeared to resent it, so Robert explained, 'My heart. If I drank that I would hear it beating in bed all night long'. Harris grunted, 'When I go to bed it's to hear somebody else's heart beating.' Harris's conversation was completely in an erotic vein, and all the while his blazing eyes were darting round the room appraising the pretty women. On being introduced to Robert, Harris professed never to have heard of him. But his sweet little wife begged Robert to write something in her album, so he obliged with an extempore quatrain:

Frank Harris, let me greet with glee
Your birthday seventy and three;
And say, old buddy, I'll be vexed
If you don't ask me to your next.

'How he must have snorted with disgust if ever he read the doggerel,' added Robert, 'but he never did ask me, for by his next birthday he was eating his salad by the roots.' This is inaccurate, for Frank was well on his way to his seventy-fifth birthday when he died. Harris was a prolific and industrious writer, and Robert had the greatest admiration for his works on Shakespeare and Wilde, but disliked his pornography. As for Harris, 'he was a highbrow and would consequently despise my work'. In 1929–30, when Robert knew him, Harris was very hard up. On one occasion he told Robert that he had asked George Bernard Shaw for the loan of several thousand pounds and Shaw told him that he could not afford it. Frank was peeved about it, evidently regarding Shaw as a multi-millionaire. Harris had made a lot of money by his pen, but his extravagant lifestyle reduced him to penury, and only his biography of

Shaw, mainly written by Frank Scully, saved him from destitution. When he died, Nellie begged the Services to take over the apartment but the thought of sleeping in the room in which Frank Harris had died repelled Robert, mindful of a curious experience which he had had in Paris, while sleeping in the seedy Hotel d'Alsace in the very bed in which Oscar Wilde had died in November 1900. Robert had passed a sleepless night, racked with the tragic horror of his thoughts, compounded by the fact that he passed the time by reading Wilde's powerful and moving 'Ballad of Reading Gaol'. In the morning he thought of writing a poem on the death of Oscar Wilde, but the subject was too painful.

Archie Bruce lived in some opulence at Vence and cultivated the great and good of the literary world. On one occasion James Joyce was a house guest, 'suffering from sick eyes' and working on a new book. D.H. Lawrence was dying of tuberculosis in the hospital at Vence, a stone's throw from the Bruce villa, when Robert came to Nice, but he never had the opportunity to meet him, which was perhaps just as well. The puritanical streak in Robert was revolted by writings on sex, and latterly Lawrence was constantly analysing the sex motive in his prolific writings. On the other hand, Lawrence's widow, Frieda von Richthofen, was a frequent guest of the Bruces. Idly, Robert speculated how Joyce and Lawrence, the respective authors of *Ulysses* and *Lady Chatterley's Lover* — two of the most widely discussed, banned books of the twentieth century — would have reacted to each other, but added characteristically 'I dreaded these literary big shots and shrank from meeting them'.

After the move to the Riviera the Service family settled into a regular routine. In the late spring they would load up the car and drive north. Now the journey was expanded from five days to over a month, most of which would be spent at Royat where Robert took his annual cure. Gabriel Perrin continued as his physician, regaling Robert with irreverent anecdotes about another distinguished literary patient, Maurice Maeterlinck, the Belgian writer, who also lived on the Riviera. Robert never met Maeterlinck at Royat because their seasons did not coincide, but in the late 1930s their paths crossed on a number of social occasions.

At Royat, however, Robert's best friend, taking his annual cure at the same time, was 'a French statesman called Cailloux (*sic*), who sported a monocle like myself and was hated for his arrogance'. The statesman was actually Joseph Marie Auguste Caillaux, eleven years older than Robert. He was the scion of a political family and had had a brilliant academic career. About the time that Robert began his banking apprenticeship Caillaux entered the Ministry of Finance, later becoming a lecturer at the École des Sciences Politiques in Paris. While Robert was a cow-juice jerker in Cowichan, Caillaux was the member for Mamers in the Chamber of Deputies. In the year that Robert was elevated to storekeeper and sub-postmaster, Caillaux became

Minister of Finance and during his three years in office wrought enormous reforms in the complex tax system. In 1911–12 he was Prime Minister, and again Finance Minister in 1913–14. When *Le Figaro*, as part of a virulent press campaign against Caillaux, published intimate letters between the politician and his wife before their marriage, Madame Caillaux shot the editor, Calmette. At her trial, Caillaux defended his wife with such passionate eloquence that she was acquitted. During the war he was entrusted with a delicate economic mission to South America, but during his absence the slanderers and rumour-mongers got to work and accused him of negotiating secretly with the Germans. When Clémenceau came to power in 1917 his one great rival was Caillaux. Clémenceau revived the innuendoes and demanded the suspension of his rival's parliamentary immunity. Caillaux proclaimed his innocence in one of the finest speeches ever made in the Chamber, and demanded to be heard in the courts. His parliamentary immunity was suspended, and in January 1918 he was arrested on a charge of high treason.

It was not until February 1920 that he was brought before the Senate, sitting as the High Court of Justice, and indicted for plotting against the security of the state abroad. After a lengthy debate, the accusations collapsed one by one. By 213 votes to 28 the arguments of the Procureur-Générale were refuted. Nevertheless, Caillaux was not completely exonerated. He was condemned to three years' imprisonment, the loss of his civic rights and five years' internal exile and ordered to pay the costs of the case, amounting to 53,000 francs. In vain did Démange, the senior advocate of the court, remind the Senate that they were condemning a man on a count on which he had not been defended. As he had already spent more than two years in prison, Caillaux was set free the following day. He returned to Mamers and devoted himself to writing books of memoirs and political thought. The amnesty of 1924 restored his political and civic rights and the following year he was invited to join the Painlevé ministry as the only man who could reduce France's chaotic finances to order. When his measures appeared too stringent he was dropped, but became a Senator. In 1926, after another cabinet crisis, he was again Minister of Finance but his tenure was brief for his recipe of more work, increased production, colonial development and reduced expenditure did not suit the government. Caillaux was perceived as too dictatorial, and there is no doubt that the measures he advocated roused considerable resentment. He was again Minister of Finance in the shortlived Bouisson cabinet of June 1935.

This, then, was Robert's friend at Royat. Wallowing naked together in the medicinal waters, the politician and the poet had much in common, apart from their 'conky hearts'. In Robert, Caillaux found a rugged individualist, a maverick, a man who walked alone and did not suffer fools lightly — qualities which he himself possessed in abundance.

The return to Lancieux was always an event. From his reference to Coco 'ready to tear me to bits with joy' it is evident that the dog remained at Dream Haven and never accompanied the family back to their Riviera flat. At Lancieux Robert could look forward to 'five months of radiant living and divine loafing'.

In January 1934 Robert celebrated his sixtieth birthday, but apart from his grey hair he would easily have passed for a man fifteen years younger. Strong, wiry, tanned and muscular, he was the epitome of robust good health. Having been an obsessive fitness freak, however, it was difficult for him to shake off the habit of excessive exercise, despite his doctor's warnings. At Dream Haven he indulged his passion for long walks and physical culture. These were passions which he enjoyed on his own. Neither Germaine nor Iris joined him on his strenuous walks, although he insisted that his daughter have a swim each day, regardless of the weather.

On the beach, before each swim, Robert practised his own system of exercises, including one in which he pivoted on his back on the beach. By grinding round on the small of his back, however, he picked up some infection which, in due course, developed into a carbuncle.

It will be remembered that, during the First World War, Robert had been prey to a series of boils. Now he was afflicted with a painful swelling the size of a dinner plate which infected his entire back. What started as a 'rubicund convexity' gradually developed into a cluster of about twenty huge boils. When he finally got around to visiting a doctor he was told that it would require an immediate operation. In those pre-antibiotic times, septicaemia would have ensued within days, and death would have been inevitable. The operation to remove this suppurating mess was only partially successful, for Robert now had a high fever, and for several days he hovered between life and death. After the fever abated there was the torture of daily dressings and then, some time later, a second operation to remove recurrent infection. Robert would never forget the look of horror on the face of the hospital matron when she removed the dressings for the first time. This reaction, from a woman seasoned to gruesome sights, filled Robert with despair. Later on, when the surgeon asked him to take a look at his back in a double mirror, Robert refused. 'I never dared look at that mutilated torso. Even today I have never seen the huge scar it has left me for life.'

For a man who had worshipped physical perfection, it was a cruel blow. Thinking of how his back had become 'a bunch of putridity' Robert — who had written in *Why Not Grow Young?* 'To make myself a temple pure wherein I live serene' — was mortified. It had taken the surgeon's knife to purify him. The great carbuncle almost unnerved Robert; certainly it affected him much more gravely than his heart trouble. Heart weakness was often a symbol of long life, for it tended to make people more careful. But the carbuncle was a poisonous corruption which had polluted his body, and but for the skill of the surgeon and devoted nursing care Robert would have succumbed. It saddened him to learn later that the nurse who had looked after him with such care was herself dying of consumption. The director of the clinic in Nice where Robert went to have the wound dressed likewise turned ill suddenly and died soon afterwards. The deaths of these two relatively young people affected Robert greatly.

During the Nice period Robert wrote little of any consequence. He neglected his typewriter for the guitar, the accordion and the piano. Singing and accompanying himself gave him a lot of pleasure, 'however painful it sounded to others'. Over the years Robert composed many songs for the guitar, where words and tune seemed to click, and later he arranged them for the piano. Eventually he sorted out the best twenty of his songs, complete with musical settings for the piano, guitar, ukulele and accordion, and in 1939 the volume entitled *Twenty Bath-Tub Ballads* was published by Francis, Day and Hunter of London. It has to be said, however, that the title was only too well-chosen.

> I had my book sent to many well-known cabaret singers, but no one, as far as I knew, ever sang my songs. They were a colossal flop. My friends did not compliment me, while musicians were strangely silent. I had not expected such ignominious failure and for a while I was crushed. But . . . they still sound good to me. For I still sing them to imaginary applause and still I go on making others.[7]

Robert had played the ukulele, guitar and piano for years, but in the late 1930s he took up the piano accordion, purchasing a magnificent instrument, 'with a hundred and twenty bass chords and a range of three octaves'. On this instrument he laboured diligently for four years and eventually had a large repertoire of songs. In the cafés around the rue Dante were many Italian accordionists, 'shabby fellows who, with a glass of beer and a cigarette dangling from their lips, would play with nonchalance music that had a splendid swing and a wealth of floriture'. Robert admired them greatly and would have given thousands of francs to perform with such virtuosity. Something of the old Parisian habits lingered on: 'Often I went to shady dance halls to listen to the rhythm of the accordion'. Sometimes he persuaded one of the players to lend him his instrument for a java or a tango, but Robert found it difficult to play to the steps of the dancers, instead making them keep time with him.

The second autobiographical volume is remarkably silent on other personal details. There is hardly any mention of Germaine or Iris, nor is there any mention of travels with them to Spain and North Africa. These were merely tourist jaunts *en famille* and if Robert made any notes of these journeys he never utilised them in any of his writings. So, too, he often paid lightning visits to London, mainly to see his publishers. In 1930 the seal was set on his poetic career when Ernest Benn brought out *The Collected Verse of Robert Service* and three years later Dodd Mead published the same volume under the title of *The Complete Poems of Robert Service*. In the summer of 1930 Robert, on his own, even made a sentimental trip to Scotland, revisiting the scenes of his early childhood and erecting a tombstone to his family in Kilwinning.

So the 1930s passed in almost total idleness, when long walks, physical culture and music-making were Robert's chief pursuits. He never thought of writing. He would survey the bookshelf on which his books were arrayed, but somehow it seemed as if they had been written by someone else. 'Yet there they were, the concrete result of my dreams and the source of the comparative luxury in which I lived.' But the fellow who had written them was not the fellow who now pumped an accordion and looked at them with indifference. 'I felt as if that other fellow had died, and one day I had evidence that others thought so too.'

Reading *The Times*, Robert came upon an article entitled 'Heritors of Unfulfilled Renown', enumerating the poets who had been killed in the First World War, and there, to his astonishment, was his own name. On this occasion Robert surmised that the writer had confused him with his brother Albert who had been killed in the trenches before Ypres in 1916. But throughout the late 1930s Robert often encountered people who thought that he was dead. This was partly explained because Robert had not published any new verse since 1921. The fans of his ballads did not associate him with 'the books of machine-made fiction' and had never heard of his book on healthy living. Even his own brothers, apparently, thought he had passed away and were astonished when he turned up on their doorstep in Vancouver in 1940. Apart from the article in *The Times*, however, an obituary notice, first published in the *Christian Century* of 14 October 1935, noted that:

> Robert R. Service, for 29 years a secretary of the international committee of the YMCA, died suddenly in Shanghai, China, Sept. 29. Mr Service went out to China in 1906, and after 18 years of service in Chengtu and Chungking, he was called to Shanghai to become a member of the national staff, and to serve as regional secretary for western China.

This was picked up by other papers, and reprinted in a garbled form, jumping to the conclusion that the decedent was the bard of the Yukon. Robert's reaction to this was mixed. 'They thought me dead, so I never bothered to deny it; for I savoured a kind word, even if I had to pass on to win it.' On the other hand, it rather pleased him that his efforts at 'self-obliteration' had succeeded so well.

> Here in a slum of Nice no one had ever heard of me. I cultivated obscurity as assiduously as others strive for publicity. Very few of my neighbours knew that I wrote. I was just one of them, content to go on like that to the end. I loved the casual, easy-going Riviera with its wealth of amusement and its sunny charm. I enjoyed the irresponsibility of living in a foreign land where one is an onlooker, and cares nothing for the way things are run as long as one's own comfort is assured.[8]

Unfortunately for Robert, the outsider and onlooker, the political situation in France was rapidly deteriorating. Post-war France had witnessed numerous changes of government, some lasting only a few months, as the moderate National Union and the Cartel of the Left see-sawed in power. In 1936, however, France voted in a government of the extreme Left. The Popular Front was an alliance of socialists, radical socialists and communists, opposed by extreme right-wing groups. The elections of that year marked the eclipse of liberal sentiment and a return to authoritarian tendencies. Politics rapidly polarised as the economic situation worsened. Attempts to stabilise the currency and institute a sweeping programme of industrial legislation merely stoked the fires of unrest. This, in turn, led to a panic flight of capital from the country which triggered off the financial crisis of 1936–37. In March 1937 the Blum government tried to return to traditional fiscal policies and financial sanity. When the Bill passed in the Assembly, the communist-led trade unions tried to force the government back to a revolutionary policy and orchestrated the Clichy riots of 16 March. These had the opposite effect; confronted by a dictatorship of the proletariat, the general public backed the government. There was mounting irritation by the delay in opening the Paris Exhibition, a great world fair, due to the workers' strikes and go-slows. The rest of 1937 was marked by continuing instability, riots, industrial disputes, strikes and short-lived ministries. The franc was devalued by 33 per cent, followed nine months later by a further devaluation of fourteen per cent. There was a massive deficit in the trade balance and production sank to an all-time low. Public morale was lower than at any time since 1914. The Popular Front collapsed on 10 March 1938 (the very day that Hitler annexed Austria) when the extreme socialists and communists withdrew their support from the government. France began to swing to the right during the summer of 1938, but this provoked a communist back-lash that manifested itself in strikes and riots.

At first Robert was unconcerned by these political upheavals, though he observed cynically, 'What a lovely land France would be if it were not for twenty million Frenchmen.' Robert the agnostic was apolitical as well. He was proud of the fact that he had never voted in all his life. Although outwardly detached, however, inwardly he seethed with disgust at the antics of the extreme Left and was afraid of the fascists and their leader Doriot. The Spanish Civil War was then raging, and the struggle between Franco's Nationalists and the republican regime was closely followed across the frontier. This was also a year in which anti-French demonstrations were orchestrated throughout Italy, mainly to further Il Duce's ambitions in North Africa, but also to recover the Mediterranean territory (including Nice) which had been lost to France in 1860.

Robert was both repelled and fascinated by the political extremists around him. Of the communists he wrote, 'They were so violent and unrestrained. I went to their meetings and got a great thrill out of the fighting and rioting that ensued.' He also attended a Doriot meeting and hated the fascist audience. 'But all around the hall were a mob of communists who tried to prevent me entering and even threatened me with violence.' Robert felt that he had a right to hear both sides and was incensed by these attempts to intimidate him. 'The rabid, riotous mob who called themselves the proletariat were just as disgusting to me as the sly and secret supporters of Mussolini.' He was acutely aware that communist influence, even in the sunny South of France, was all-pervasive. Archie Bruce's chauffeur and gardener were both communists, though their employer was blissfully unaware of the fact. True to the dictum 'know thine enemy', Robert 'went to communist conventions, read Red papers and joined the clamouring crowds outside the newspaper offices'. He witnessed police charges, saw windows smashed and wanton damage done. 'No one took any notice of me,' he added naively, 'for I was obviously an innocent bystander.'

In the midst of all this turmoil he conceived the idea of going to Russia to see for himself whether it was an earthly paradise as the communists maintained, or the antechamber of hell. 'Perhaps a visit to the land of the Soviets might convert me to communism.' Robert had always felt a sneaking sympathy for the down-and-out, so it was logical that he should extend it to the up-and-coming. 'I would go to Russia with an open mind, observe dispassionately and form my own conclusions'. He contacted Intourist in Paris and booked a tour. In July 1938 he left Germaine and Iris in Lancieux while he travelled overland to Copenhagen, Stockholm and Finland, and then took the train from Helsinki to Leningrad. His first tour was spent in Leningrad and Moscow. The Soviet Union was very much a closed society in the late 1930s and Stalinism was at its height, following the series of purges and state trials that culminated in March 1938. Most of the foreign travellers were communists or at least sympathisers, and certainly the majority of the tourists in Robert's group fell into this category, although there were exceptions, such as 'Mrs Tacoma' (a lecturer on the women's club circuit), 'Mr Missouri' (a retired shopkeeper) and 'the Drummer', a young man who exercised his charm on blonde Russian girls while Robert was content to look on.

The tour was well organised by Intourist, probably over-organised, for the group was carefully shielded from the real Russia. They were kept well away from the slums and shown only the showpieces of the Soviet state, yet Robert was quick to observe the general air of dilapidation everywhere, the potholed roads, the broken paving, the peeling paintwork, the rotting timbers and crumbling façades of the once-prosperous shops along the Nevsky Prospect. The tourists were shepherded by hand-picked girls — 'silk-stocking socialists' — who were well trained, intelligent and obliging but incessantly propagandist about communist superiority and for ever parroting a tirade condemning capitalist crimes against humanity. But now and again Robert and the Drummer managed to sneak away from the organised party and mingle with the crowds. Robert was left with an impression of people with lots of paper roubles, thanks to full employment, but with precious little in the way of consumer goods on which to spend their money. Robert meticulously recorded his impressions; as usual, it was his descriptions of people rather than places which came across most vividly. 'I like Russians but I dislike communists,' he wrote. Comparing Russia and France he observed that in both countries the women were more capable than the men. He was repelled by the seediness and poverty everywhere. Even the hotels where he stayed, once the show-pieces of the Tsarist regime, were badly run-down, although he invariably had an enormous, over-furnished room with *en suite* bathroom. The food was excellent on the whole, and meals were described in great detail. Everywhere Robert noted vestiges of the old regime and made the happy discovery that, although tipping was officially banned, the occasional rouble worked wonders in improving the otherwise indifferent service in hotels and restaurants.

The Bolshevik Revolution was little more than twenty years old at the time of his first visit, and Robert detected many dogged survivors from the past. At the Hotel Astoria in Leningrad, for example, he nicknamed his elderly waiter 'the Prince' on account of his aristocratic bearing despite his shabby appearance. There was an encounter in the street with a smooth young man brandishing a fistful of rouble notes who was anxious to purchase Robert's western-style clothing, despite its shabby condition. Prudently Robert declined and was promptly treated to a display of bad manners which, he noted sadly, were all too common in the younger generation that had grown up under communism. Both in Leningrad and Moscow, however, Robert resumed his habit of nocturnal perambulation and noted that he was never once importuned as he would have been in Piccadilly Circus or the Place de l'Opéra. An Intourist guide had told him that there were no prostitutes in the Soviet Union, and he was inclined to take her word for it, though mainly on the practical grounds that the cramped housing conditions made prostitution difficult. Later he realised that prostitution had only been driven out of sight and that high-class hookers plied their trade in the lobby of the hotel — as the Drummer learned to his cost.

Dutifully Robert visited the approved attractions, such as the Black Catheral of Kazan, which had been converted into a museum ridiculing religion, and the Palace of Pushkin, honouring the great Russian poet. Seeing the relics of the old order produced mixed feelings. 'I have only to think of the old Czarist regime to feel as ruthless a communist as the best.' But seeing the private apartments of the imperial family at the Winter Palace Robert felt 'a sincere pity' for the human beings who had lived there.

In Moscow Robert stayed at the Metropole. One of the highlights of this part of the tour was a visit to the Park of Culture and Rest, to which Robert devoted an entire chapter of his autobiography. All too often, however, the tours were to dreary places such as the Dental Department of the Hospital of the Truck Trust and projects associated with one or other of the Five-Year Plans. Robert's descriptions of these and other 'Soviet side-shows' were, on the whole, graphic and captured the atmosphere of Stalinist Russia superbly. Only occasionally, however, did his political naivety show through. Politics was a matter that had left him cold since the days of his proletarian priggishness back in Glasgow. Although he had no illusions about the sorry state of the USSR he had a characteristically ambivalent attitude towards the regimentation which was apparently putting Russia back on its feet after centuries of corruption.

> That part of me which is logical believes in a scientific organization of
> Society, in economic planning, in classless co-operation — all that stuff
> that sounds like claptrap. My mind approves of it but my heart hates it.
> I would loathe to be regimented and restricted. I only admire reform
> in other people.

One of the most vivid impressions he had was of meeting a crop-headed youth who addressed him and the Drummer in fluent New York English. He had come over from Trenton, New Jersey, a red-hot communist who rapidly became disillusioned and then made the cardinal mistake of shooting off his mouth about the regime. Arrested on a charge of sabotage, he was thrown into prison for six months and his papers confiscated. Now he was anxious to get out of the country but lacked both the means and the passport to do so. He gave the Drummer his brother's name and address in Trenton and begged him to do something that might save his life. Something of the atmosphere of paranoia and suspicion rubbed off on the Drummer, usually an easy-going fellow. Suspecting that the youth was an *agent provocateur* for the OGPU, he brushed him off, but Robert could not so easily forget the look of terror in the boy's haggard expression. The OGPU was the Soviet secret police organisation charged with eliminating 'political and economic counter-revolution'. In other words, the Stalinist equivalent of the Gestapo. Their departure from Moscow was delayed by two days and they were confined to their hotel because of an OGPU investigation into two of the party. But the enforced delay enabled them to watch a communist youth parade from the bay window of Mrs Tacoma's bedroom. The enormous parade marched down an otherwise empty street. 'The public did not matter. All that counted was the Party; so relentlessly they came on, exultant in the bright sunshine. To me there was something terrible, even frightening about it all.' The parade lasted all of four hours.

With the menace of young communism on the march, Robert was heartily sick of Moscow and longed to escape, but inexplicably their tickets were denied them. Then, the following evening, their tickets just as suddenly materialised and they had a frantic moment packing and rushing off to catch the train to the West. This turned out to be a very pleasant surprise, for the train was extremely luxurious, with ample two-berth sleeping compartments, hot running water and cushioned seats. Moreover, the tour group appeared to be the only passengers, so that the journey was accomplished without the customary crowding.

The homeward journey was marred, however, by the Customs examination at the frontier. Leaving the Soviet Union turned out to be much worse than entering, and they were held up for two hours while their luggage was microscopically examined and items, such as furs, confiscated. Armed guards searched compartments and under the carriages for would-be escapers before the train was allowed to pass through barbed-wire entanglements into Poland. By contrast, here was a country where the peasants were gay and smiling, their clothing was cleaner and more colourful. The Polish Customs officers were well groomed, polite and complacent and, in his exuberance at escaping from Russia, Robert could have embraced them.

The rest of the journey lay through Germany and Robert spent several days in Berlin. Here he felt 'disliked and tolerated'. At the hotel he had no blankets on his bed, 'only a chunky feather quilt that was too warm and half covered me'. The maids mocked him, the waiters were sour, the concierge contemptuous. It was a horrid hotel, just off the Friedrichstrasse. Robert stuck it out for a week, wandering all over the city and failing to appreciate its Teutonic charm. Throughout his Berlin sojourn Robert spoke English only once, when cashing a cheque at the American Express Office. Fortunately he had not forgotten his schoolboy German and got by. 'Feeling no end of an alien I sought the Tiergarten and the friendliness of trees, while I watched innocent children play military games.'

It has to be said that Robert's impressions of Berlin were largely subjective, coloured by a deeply engrained dislike of Germans which went back at least as far as his first voyage from New York to Europe. This set him to reminiscing about the only German he had ever liked. Apparently Frieda was a girl whom he had known in Glasgow for she had taken up with a pal who had enlisted in the Volunteers, the forerunner of the Territorial Army. Frieda later returned to Germany; as she was Jewish, Robert fervently hoped that she had died before the Nazis came to power. On the train from Berlin to Paris he had a horrifying first-hand experience of what life was like in Hitler's Third Reich. Seated opposite Robert in the compartment was a youth, garishly but expensively dressed. He discovered that the lad was Jewish and was being sent to New York where he had wealthy relatives. His health was delicate and his family were anxious to get him to a place of safety, and he had a passage booked the very next day on the liner *Ile de France*.

At Aachen, however, the green-uniformed Grenzpolizei pounced on the luckless Jew and seized his luggage, minutely searching the compartment in case he had concealed anything. As the train departed from Aachen without the boy, the courier smugly confided to Robert that his last sight of him had been in one of the interrogation rooms where he had been stripped and was enduring an anal examination for concealed jewels. It was with a sense of foreboding and menace to come, that Robert returned to Paris and went straight to Dream Haven. He had been away for two months, the Munich Crisis was at its height, and Germaine and Iris were understandably worried for his safety. Soon afterwards they returned to Nice for the winter. Robert's sojourn in the Soviet Union and Nazi Germany made him appreciate his good fortune all the more. He could look forward to six months of happiness, 'to my walks in the high hills, my talks with Byron on café terraces, my visits to Peter in his swank villa; with just enough work to make me enjoy the careless rapture of the south'.

Then, one day, he found himself sitting before his typewriter staring at a blank page. Eventually he tapped out FOUR BLIND MICE . . . *Chapter One*.

There! I had started a novel. It was to be an Escape Story and to have a Russian setting. But by the time I had done ten thousand words I realised I did not know enough about the country to write a hundred thousand. Nothing for it but to return. So I wrote to Intourist and was inscribed for their most elaborate voyage. There! Again I was booked for Muscovy, but this time it was to be more Oppenheimish. Well, so much the better. Vive the Adventure Trail.'[9]

On this second journey, at the beginning of July 1939, Robert travelled from Paris via Aachen and Berlin. At the Polish frontier he had a very bad time with the Nazi Customs officials — 'green toads' Robert dismissed them contemptuously — but was then hauled off to an interrogation cell under the railway station for a grilling by a youngish man who spoke English. Robert's heart thudded as he realised that he was in the grip of the Gestapo who wanted to know why Robert had in his luggage the Jewish writer Max Nordau's *Conventional Lies of Civilisation*. 'It wasn't so much what they did as the nasty way they did it. In that bare vault the air was charged with hostility.' Robert had never felt so relieved as when he was finally released and allowed to reboard the train. In less than a year the atmosphere in Germany had changed radically. Everywhere were men and women in militaristic uniforms. Even the children were regimented into the Hitler Youth and gave the stiff-armed salute with shrill cries of 'Heil Hitler'. The air was heavy with menace and Robert felt that war was just around the corner.

By contrast Poland was friendly and welcoming. On this journey Robert travelled second class and shared a crowded compartment with a Pittsburgh Jew named Bronsky, a communist couple, Louis and Myra Gutzmann from New York, a foxy-faced army cadet (whom he later suspected of stealing his money) and a friendly mouse-like girl called Rosebud who bestowed on him the nickname of Bobsky. She confided to Robert that she planned to assassinate Stalin and tried to recruit him in this crazy enterprise. Later he speculated about this strange girl, and some three years later came across her photograph in a Los Angeles newspaper which identified her as 'a fairly well-known short story writer'.

On this momentous journey history repeated itself when Robert suddenly discovered that the cash he was carrying, some twenty thousand-franc notes, had vanished from his wallet. He was seized with panic and his heart thumped uncontrollably. Beads of cold sweat formed on his furrowed brow. Immediately, paranoia set in and his suspicions fell on his travelling companions. Gradually he eliminated them in his mind, except for Rosebud and the young officer cadet. In the end Robert's suspicions centred entirely on this young man, solely because he seemed to have narrow, shifty eyes. Strangely, however, Robert did not enlist the aid of the railway guard, nor did he actually confront the suspect outright. When the cadet left the train, Robert sank back timorously in a mixture of resignation and relief. Although devastated at the loss of his money, Robert consoled himself with the fact that the entire trip had been paid for in advance, so he could get by without cash. In Moscow he checked in at the Hotel National, more modern than the Metropole. There he spent two weeks in atrocious summer heat and trudged round the fifty-three pavilions of the Great Russian Exhibition. Then on to Gorky (now Nizhni-Novgorod once more) and a boat-ride down the Volga where the party was joined by the Buntings from Brooklyn: Pop 'a regular Babbit', Ma 'a matronly Daughter of the Revolution' and Wilbur, whom Robert promptly nicknamed Babe, 'a big gangling boy majoring in Political Economy' — ready-made characters for a novel. With amused detachment Robert looked on as Babe and Lydia, the Intourist guide, developed a relationship which, absorbing while it lasted, was doomed to failure. The antics of his fellow-passengers tended to distract Robert from his avowed intention of studying the Soviet people, although he made strenuous efforts to chronicle the women railway-workers, the toiling peasants, the Russian *bourgeoisie* and even the gypsies who travelled steerage on the river steamer. All of this was lovingly and lengthily set out in *Harper of Heaven* which devoted a hundred and eighty pages — two-fifths of the total — to the two Russian trips. This material would have been far better hived off into a separate travel book, for it gives a lopsided appearance to what purported to be an autobiography. It could also have been pruned profitably, and the rather long-winded disquisitions on every meal expunged. The details of the hotel bedrooms and the disgusting lavatory facilities he found everywhere except in the top hotels would also have had more impact had they not been repeated *ad nauseam*.

The dreadful Gutzmanns were on this trip, and they were rapidly becoming disenchanted with the workers' paradise. Membership of the American Communist Party had not saved them from the indignities of a thorough hour-long search at the Soviet frontier; in fact, if anything, their Party cards had excited even more suspicion on the part of the Customs officials. They were an odd couple, both clad in corduroy trousers. Tall Myra looked mannish while her short, slight husband looked positively girlish. On the Volga Myra had her nose stuck in a book which absorbed her totally. Later Robert discovered that it was *Confessions of a Nymphomaniac* and when he dipped into it he was appalled 'for it was a pool of sheer filth . . . Every page was packed with prurience, presented in the language of the gutter'. He was about to throw it down in disgust when Myra suddenly appeared and grabbed it from his hand. 'Her face was suffused by either anger or shame, and as she flounced away I knew she was my enemy.' At the end of the trip, when Myra presented the book to Lydia in the fervent hope that she would get it translated for Russian publication, Robert snatched the book and chucked it overboard.

On the fifth day they anchored off a town which had formerly been called Samara but which had now been renamed by the communist authorities. Robert remarked that it was now called something else, but failed to note that it was Kuibyshev. Its main claim on Robert's attention was the fact that Pop Bunting spent much of his time in a fruitless search for 'a Service Station with a retiring room for males'. On the seventh day they arrived at Stalingrad, formerly Tsaritsyn and, since 1961, Volgograd, where the cruise ended. From Stalingrad Robert took a night train to Rostov, sharing a sleeper with a peasant farmer and his small son. Saratov was 'listless and forlorn' but Rostov-on-Don was 'gay and pleasant' and 'the pick of Soviet cities'. His Intourist guide here was the most glamorous woman he had seen in Russia, for whom he felt 'it must have been rather a nuisance to have to waste her sweetness on my silver hair'. She spent half a day droning on about the city, but what it amounted to could have been written on the back of a postage stamp.

Robert's tour became much more interesting, the farther he penetrated into the heart of the Soviet Union. The descriptions were as meticulous as ever, although Robert tended to have a casual approach to placenames. 'Orginikidzi. Why did these silly Sovietists curse a town with such a name?' he asked rhetorically, oblivious to the fact that the key to the Caucasus, formerly Vladikavkaz, had been named Ordzhonikidze after the Soviet leader of that name. 'Well, it was a miserable place, hardly worthy of better.' For a guide he now had an argumentative boy of sixteen whom he called Boris, a student from Leningrad working in the summer vacation. Robert and Boris engaged in long political discussions, faithfully recorded in the diary and later transcribed verbatim in the chapter entitled 'Georgian Highway'. Boris tried to convert Robert to communism, but only increased his loathing of it. The boy wrote poetry, and Robert promised to send him one of his books.

Although Robert's detestation for the Soviet system increased, his admiration for the Soviet peoples grew day by day. He was immensely impressed by their stoicism and the almost lyrical quality which shone through, even in the most poverty-stricken areas. On one occasion he encountered a company of Red Army soldiers singing lustily as they marched down the street. On another he saw a band of proletarians, also singing. 'They were poor, ugly, shabby, but they were equally inspiring . . . A people who can sing exultantly, despite poverty and sordid surroundings, are to be reckoned with.'

From Ordzhonikidze Robert was driven over the mountain passes to Tiflis, now Tbilisi, the capital of Georgia. His chauffeur had 'deep-set eyes with a humorous mouth' which inspired confidence. 'If anyone could coax this old buggy over the Caucasus Mountains I reckoned he could.' Going on by train to Batum, he reached the eastern shores of the Black Sea where he went swimming and was surprised to find a party of fifty female bathers, all in the nude. 'Of course the sight of so much naked pulchritude shocked me, and I would have retreated had I not forced myself to look at it from an *aesthetic* angle. Indeed, had not the boat sailed that afternoon, I think I might have continued my studies.'

Although by now Robert was becoming used to Russian trains and steamers loaded to three times their capacity, the overcrowding on the Black Sea steamer stunned him. 'The passengers seemed piled in layers on its decks. In spite of this, a black mob on the wharf still clamoured to go on board.' Robert could not help noting that, thanks to Intourist, he was able to sail through this dense, seething mass, 'to be assured of space and comfort where all was crowded confusion; in a classless society to be assured of the privilege of class.' He had a 'dainty and spacious' cabin all to himself. There were two berths, but the occupier of the lower one preferred to remain with his wife and daughter in their cabin. He was a Polish prince, the military attaché of his embassy in Moscow, 'a slender, fastidious man, stemming from the old aristocracy and proud of his patrician birth'. His wife was very stout, but Robert won her affections by presenting her with a box of digestion pills. 'I always assume that fat, middle-aged women who complain of heart trouble are really suffering from flatulence, and they readily respond to my understanding sympathy. Some say it with flowers, some with music; I say it with gas tablets.'

The Polish military attaché in Moscow on the eve of the Second World War was Colonel Romuald Wolikowski. Remarkably, he managed to survive the vicissitudes which overtook the Polish officer corps interned after the partition of Poland and massacred at Katyn, for he was later promoted to major-general and headed the Polish Military Mission established in Moscow after the Nazi invasion of the Soviet Union in 1941.

The Polish diplomat was pessimistic about the condition of eastern Europe. He told Robert about the latest purges in the Soviet Union which had all but eliminated the bourgeois class. He feared a war was imminent, but was confident that the superb Polish cavalry would be more than a match for the Russians. Although the latter had tanks, Wolikowski considered the Red Army badly trained. Indeed, since the execution of the brilliant Marshal Tukhachevsky and seven top generals in 1937, and the murder or dismissal of most officers above the rank of major in the course of the following year, the Soviet armed forces were in considerable disarray. Robert's comments on this, of course, had the benefit of hindsight. The Pole should have realised that the very Russians he hated so virulently were his source of safety. 'It seemed certain that Russia feared Germany and would never allow Poland to be taken by the Huns . . .'

The ship called briefly at Theodosia and then sailed on to Yalta where Robert put up at the best hotel. There, to his unpleasant surprise, he ran into

Louis and Myra Gutzmann who had now gone native, sporting knitted skull-caps and peasant blouses. Later he saw them amid hundreds of other nude bathers on the beach. He had to admit that Myra Gutzmann had a superb figure. Unfortunately she was disconcerted by his frankly lascivious gaze and hastily took refuge in a bathing hut from which she would not emerge. Robert dined that evening with the Polish family, but the diplomat seemed withdrawn and worried. He had tried to book seats on the plane back to Moscow but found his transportation blocked unaccountably. He was worried about reports coming in regarding Danzig (now Gdansk), then a Free City but under rabid Nazi control.

On arrival at Odessa Robert checked in at the Hotel de Londres, 'a fine old place of five stories, dating from the old regime'. Everything beautiful in Russia seemed to be a relic of Tsarist times and this hotel, with its tapestried walls and carved oak chairs, was a prime example. Robert's insouciance was rattled on discovering that the OGPU officer, to whom Myra Gutzmann had complained of Robert's conduct on the Volga steamer, was sitting in the lounge. His mental equilibrium was further disturbed, however, on running into Louis Gutzmann that afternoon.

> He approached me with a grin you could see a block away. 'You've heard the news?' he yelled. 'It's wonderful! It's grand! Gosh! I feel bucked about it. Hitler and Stalin have shaken hands. Ribbentrop and Molotov have signed a peace pact and sworn eternal friendship. The Germans and the Russians have teamed up, and Oh, what a team! Now we'll see something doing!'
>
> As a German-American communist I could see his point. It jarred me horribly. For a moment I stood gasping and staring at him, then I began to curse. Oaths I had not used for years ripped out of me. I cursed Hitler and Stalin and their pact of iniquity. I cursed the Soviets as double-crossing bastards. I cursed the communists with all their works. Louey got furious and he began to befoul Britain. We had a row right there and I nearly slammed the little runt down the grand stair-way. As we raged, people stared at us curiously and I realised I had better break away or I would get into trouble. So abruptly I left him in the middle of a tirade against British Imperialism.[10]

This places Robert's visit to Odessa precisely, for the Non-Aggression Pact was signed on 23 August 1939. Now it dawned on Robert why his Polish friends had been stranded in Yalta. With the threat of Soviet retaliation removed, it seemed that Poland would be doomed to German attack. In fact events moved with startling rapidity. As a portent of things to come, Odessa was now blacked out after dark, the night sky stabbed by searchlights, and air-raid precautions were stepped up; but in Kiev, whither Robert went by train the following day, life was going on as normal. This was a much happier city than Odessa, and Robert almost felt at home when he ran into a party of a hundred and fifty Parisians. Many of them were communists, prepared to enthuse over everything Soviet, but at least a third of them were *bourgeois* tourists and there were at least half a dozen honeymoon couples. Robert was roped in as interpreter, as the Intourist guide spoke only English, and he joined the Parisians on their sight-seeing tour. At dinner that evening he was invited to join the honeymoon table, and marvelled at the chic of the young French brides, who made their Russian counterparts look so lumpen. Robert spent several days in Kiev and enjoyed himself more than at any other time on this trip, but his pleasure evaporated one day on finding the young OGPU officer from the Volga and Yalta ensconced in the lobby of the hotel.

Convinced that the secret policeman was trailing him, Robert panicked and made a beeline for the Intourist office to see whether he could get a reservation on the night train to Warsaw. There was a nervous moment when the Intourist clerk could not find his passport among the pile lodged at the office. In any case, the train was fully booked. It was suggested that he remain in Kiev for the rest of the time as his railway passage was booked for that time. Had Robert not panicked, and remained in Kiev till 2 September as originally planned, he might have been spared a very harrowing and dangerous journey home. He would have been diverted through neutral Romania, Yugoslavia and Italy. But in his desire to leave Russia as soon as possible, he refused to take no for an answer.

In the end a compromise was reached. The girl at Intourist promised to make a further search for the missing passport and suggested that he should return to the office the next day. The next twenty-four hours were a nightmare, as Robert's paranoia gripped him. But after a sleepless night and a hasty breakfast he returned to the Intourist office and was mightily relieved to learn that his passport had turned up. There was now nothing to prevent his departure on the midday train.

Warsaw, Berlin, Paris, Brittany — in three days he would be back at Dream Haven and cavorting in the sea. He was so elated that he returned to his hotel for a second, and much more sumptuous, breakfast. Then he packed his bags and headed for the railway station. Leaving Russia! Again he experienced the euphoria of escape. His last impression of Kiev was picking his way through the ragged bundles and bodies cluttering the station concourse. 'Only in the Proletariat Paradise could one witness such dumb acceptance of poverty.'

In the dining-car of the train Robert met a Canadian professor, whom he called Mrs Moosejaw, from the town where she resided, and a Clydeside communist whom he dubbed Donald Duck because he 'had a swagger and a blah-blah voice that made me think of this famous creation'. Robert was travelling first class, because the trip had been pre-booked, but his lack of cash (which had not been a problem on the package trip) now presented itself. Reminiscent of his experience years earlier on the train to Chicago, he grabbed as much food as the Soviet dining-car would permit and resolved to live on that over the next two days. He might be rather hungry by the time he got to Paris, but there his in-laws would be able to succour him.

After a series of unaccountable delays the train reached the Polish frontier on Sunday morning, 1 September. There Robert changed from the sordid Soviet train into the spick-and-span Polish carriage. They were just about to depart when a Polish officer boarded the train and dropped the bombshell. The German border was closed. 'We are now in armed conflict with the Reich. It is war, war, WAR.' There was immediate consternation, and anger that the Soviet authorities had let them come this far when they must have known that war was imminent. Robert decided to press on to Warsaw. On this leg of the journey the train was crowded with Polish reservists rejoining their regiments and Robert encountered an officer who reminded him of the cadet he had suspected of stealing his money. Seeing this officer, however, jogged Robert's memory. He had meant to divide his cash into two, but could not remember whether he had actually done so, Now he searched inside his old, worn jacket and there, stuck down in the lining, he found a small package — a wad of ten *mille* notes. Gloatingly he counted the francs. Now he could pay his way home in comfort.

At the terminus in Warsaw Robert, Mrs Moosejaw and Donald Duck were met by the British Consul who advised them to leave Poland as quickly as possible and suggested that they make for Riga in Latvia by the evening train. Everywhere there were signs of preparations for all-out war; buildings had been sand-bagged and trenches dug amid the flowerbeds in front of the Hotel Bristol. Yet in the dining-room of the Hotel Polonia, where Robert freshened up, the silver and napery were set as if for a banquet. That afternoon Robert saw his first Luftwaffe squadron, coming across the cloudless sky in a perfect V formation. Everyone gazed up at the aircraft open-mouthed as they waited tensely for the bombs. But none fell. The bombers passed overhead and then, from an eastern suburb, came the sound of blasts. The enemy was pounding the industrial district of Praga. No Polish fighters rose to intercept the German aircraft. Robert experienced a strange sense of elation at this dramatic scene. 'Here was a book, a big book, for my making — one of the documents of the war. If only I had been an American I would have taken the chance and stayed on, but I was a belligerent (or supposed I was) and it was up to me to get away as fast as possible.'

The journey from Warsaw was singularly unpleasant. Robert and the others travelled in an uncomfortable third-class compartment, crammed with young soldiers, most of them 'uncouth country clowns and nearly all drunk'. They sang and swapped bottles, till one after the other they passed out. 'Then down they slumped on the floor and lay in heaps, making me think of dead on a battle-field. And in the midst of that inert huddle of humanity I sat on my up-ended valise like Rodin's *Penseur* and dodged the vomit that sprayed from all sides . . .'

The following afternoon they pulled into Wilno, then a Polish city. Robert, writing his second volume of autobiography almost nine years later, may be pardoned for stating that he was now on Lithuanian soil. In fact, this district was seized by Russian troops about two weeks later and then handed over to Lithuania on 10 October 1939, as an inducement to the Lithuanians to permit Soviet garrisons on their territory. But the facts make a nonsense of Robert's description:

> What a comfort to stroll on the sunshiny platform and to breathe fresh air! We were on Lithuanian soil, free of the war zone. In the station restaurant we had supped at my expense, though I was forced to pay twice the tariff because I only had Polish *zlotys*. My trouble was that in every small country they despised the currency of the previous one; and in Vilna it was only by telling them that I had nothing else that they took what remained of my Polish bills. Later on, in Riga, they would have spat on them.[11]

In October Wilno became Vilnius, but after the Soviet annexation of Lithuania in 1940 it became Vilna, and only reverted to Vilnius after the break-up of the Soviet Union in 1990. From Wilno Robert and his companions travelled by a Latvian train north to Riga where they arrived late in the evening. Because he spoke French, and also had a comparatively large sum of money, Robert assumed command of the British party; though he was accustomed to follow others, he now found leadership thrust upon him. Trying to find a hotel for the night, he unwittingly led his fellow travellers to a brothel where they secured three small rooms. Riga appealed to Robert: it was 'a likeable old city, with quaint houses and cobbled streets'. The following day they left for Tallinn in Estonia, whose 'bleakness matched my own mood'. They had to hang around the dock for hours waiting to board a Baltic steamer which would carry them to Stockholm. The night was spent on deck and Robert watched a myriad grey islands pass like ghosts. 'In the moonlight they came up like bubbles, thousands of them, so wild and clean and free.' When Robert ran out of cash, Donald Duck, who had been sponging on him, cheerfully scrounged a huge meal of *smorgasbord* off a couple of Swedish girls. This Scottish free-loader disgusted Robert, who felt that his communism was of the 'what's yours is mine' variety. On the boat, however, Robert met a young Swedish lawyer who was reading a volume of Galsworthy and they discussed literature. When Robert casually mentioned that he had not eaten for two days the young man marched him off to the dining saloon and insisted on plying him with bread, cheese and coffee. Robert was not quite as hard up as he appeared; it was just that he had no desire to change any of his precious thousand-franc notes into Estonian currency, and he was also increasingly irritated at the way Donald Duck expected him to pay for everything.

In Stockholm they checked in at the Eden Hotel and it annoyed Robert that Donald Duck should have a room at his expense. 'At dinner that night, as I watched him guzzling rich food with that take-it-for-granted manner, he gave me a dose of socialist doctrine for which I suppose I should have been devoutly grateful.' In fact, Robert had the feeling that in letting him pay, Donald was Robert's benefactor. 'He was so patronising he ended by making me feel in his debt.' Robert spent most of his time in Stockholm camped out in the office of the Norwegian consul who was doing his best to refuse visas to everyone. Among the stranded travellers was a touring company of English magicians. In this manner Robert spent three very anxious days, but eventually the visas were granted enabling him and the other Britons to travel by train to Bergen. Robert and Mrs Moosejaw gave Donald Duck the slip, though Robert paid for his room and left him a thousand-franc note for travelling expenses. Donald Duck was incensed when he discovered that they had booked seats on the train without him and sulked all the way to the station. Robert told him coolly that he could follow on the next train, but he never saw him again. Afterwards his conscience troubled him; perhaps he should have given the Clydesider two thousand francs. 'If he had shown any appreciation of my help I would have taken a chance. As it was, he seemed to think I was a bloated capitalist there to look after him'.

The overnight journey, sitting bolt upright on wooden seats in a cramped third-class compartment, denied Robert sleep and he envied the lucky ones who snoozed and snored triumphantly. In the morning they pulled into Oslo and they had a struggle to get aboard the crowded train bound for Bergen. The seats were just as hard, but the magnificent scenery was a compensation. This produced one of those lyrical passages which echoed Robert's description of that first train ride through the Rockies more than forty years earlier.

Bergen was wreathed in drizzle when they arrived. Robert had a good hotel and an excellent meal, but he would have enjoyed Bergen more had he not been so worried about getting away. Most of the time was spent haunting the shipping office, where he was told that the next sailing was booked to capacity and that there would not be another for ten days. Mrs Moosejaw now came to the rescue. She had a Canadian Pacific return ticket and there happened to be a CPR agent in Bergen. This personable young man went to the shipping company and pleaded their cause so eloquently that the captain and chief engineer of the steamer gave up their cabins to Robert and Mrs Moosejaw. They had only minutes to pack up and board ship before she weighed anchor. Klinck[12] mistakenly says that the ship was a Canadian Pacific boat, on a misreading of the passage in *Harper of Heaven*, but the ship then on the Bergen-Newcastle run was the SS *Venus*.

Now, for the first time in a fortnight, Robert could relax. He had a comfortable cabin and he could loll in the saloon, order tea, and talk with Englishmen fresh from their salmon fishing. 'Now they were hurrying home to join up and cheerfully get themselves killed.' Yet the voyage was not free from danger. Already German submarines were hunting in packs in the North Sea, so the steamer took a detour far to the north and the crossing took two days. At Thomas Cook's in Newcastle Robert changed his last thousand-franc note and checked in at a family hotel opposite the railway station. The following morning he took leave of Mrs Moosejaw. 'She had been a gallant sport, never once showing discouragement, or pessimism — an example to Donald Duck and this Old Codger.'

The train to London was packed with troops but Robert, inured to the slow trains of Russia, found that it went at a thrilling pace. In London he blew his last coins on the taxi fare to his bank where he withdrew a hundred pounds, mostly in one-pound notes 'for it was unbelievably comforting to have lots of money again'. Even now, however, he was not home and dry. The French Consulate had suspended the issue of visas. It was to take him three weeks to get the necessary travel documents. During this enforced delay Robert stayed at the Imperial Hotel in Russell Square, from where he wrote to Germaine on Sunday, 17 September:

> Dear Family:
> You see I am writing every day because there is not much else to do. I am hanging round waiting for a permit to go home and feeling quite cheerful about it as I am at this moment gorged with a huge hotel breakfast. I am living like a prince with a pocketful of money. So it all seems like Heaven after all I went through to get here. I have a lovely room and am being well looked after. Tomorrow I will have some shirts washed and a suit pressed. They need it.
>
> London looks very funny. 9 out of 10 people carry gas masks on the street. I went to get one but they had not my size so I am going again tomorrow. The shops have all sand bags piled up in front and their

windows crossed with adhesive tape. But there are very few uniforms to be seen and everyone seems cheerful. The hotel is quite empty.

If you go away before I get over get Poulard to fix up my motor as usual. I still think it would be better to take the train to Nice. It does not seem right to use petrol at this moment even if one can get it. Above all guard preciously my manuscript of verse. It is to be published in Febry. I am starting a novel right away to be published in August. I saw my publishers and they are keen about it. Well I'll finish my Sunday papers and go for a walk to Shaftesbury Avenue. Expect my daily bulletin tomorrow. Besto — Bobovich.

This letter, posted two days later, did not reach Lancieux until 26 September. Early in October Robert was granted a visa and set off for home. At Folkestone all his books were confiscated and he was lucky to retain his diary of the Russian trip. At Boulogne there was a further delay for trains were now only running at night. It was two in the morning before he got to Paris and checked in at the Terminus Hotel by the Gare du Nord. He awoke to a Paris that was strangely empty. His in-laws had fled and Robert was alone in a city 'that was carrying on in a strange atmosphere of apprehension and fatality'. At the Commissariat of Police he was told that Nice was now in the war zone, and travel there was strictly forbidden. This was the last straw. In desperation he packed his bags and went over to the Gare de Lyon and calmly demanded a ticket for Nice. Amazingly, he was handed one immediately and shortly afterwards he boarded the train, spending a comfortable night in a *wagon-lit*. After a comfortable night 'the prodigal father arrived in the forenoon and surprised his family sitting down to lunch'.

CHAPTER 14

PHONEY WAR

'Courage, my comrades, war is near.'
I hear afar its hateful drums;
Its horrid din assails my ear:
I hope I die before it comes . . .
Yet as into the town I go,
And listen to the rabble cheer,
I think with heart of weary woe:
War is not coming — WAR IS HERE.

'Portent' in *Songs of a Sun-Lover* (1949)

BY THE TIME ROBERT RETURNED TO NICE, POLAND HAD
ceased to exist, partitioned between Germany and Russia whose troops had
crossed the Dwina and Dniestr at dawn on 17 September. Three days later units
of the Wehrmacht and the Red Army met on the upper Dniestr. There was one
minor hiccup when German infantry fired on a Soviet cavalry column, killing
three men; the Russians charged, and despatched fifteen of the Germans with
their sabres before the misunderstanding was sorted out. Thereafter the
dismemberment of Poland by the two great totatilitarian powers began. Polish
troops under General Kutrzeba continued to hold out in Warsaw till 27
September. Fighting on the Baltic coast ended on 1 October, when the last
remnants of the Polish Navy surrendered. In a lightning campaign lasting four

weeks the Germans had sustained fewer than 10,000 casualties and taken over 700,000 prisoners. These were the lucky ones, for most of the officers of the Polish Army who fell into Soviet hands were massacred at Katyn a few months later.

The dramatic collapse of Poland, a country with an army of three million men, should have galvanised the western Allies into action. In Britain air defences were considerably expanded, so that when the Battle of Britain started the Royal Air Force was a match for the much-vaunted Luftwaffe. But in France little or nothing was done to prepare for the German onslaught. The French took comfort in the Maginot Line, the chain of forts and defences which had replaced the trench systems of the First World War from the Swiss frontier to the North Sea. If the Germans were rash enough to launch an attack on this impregnable ring of steel it would be the worse for them. Otherwise life in the autumn and winter of 1939 went on much as usual, though had Robert gone to Lancieux instead of straight to Nice he might have been surprised to find that, all along the Breton coast, humble cottages had been bought up at greatly enhanced prices as the prudent but wealthy of Paris sought bolt-holes from the coming storm.

The American Senator William Borah coined the term 'Phoney War' which was snappier than Churchill's 'twilight war', and easier to pronounce than *Sitzkrieg* (sitting war) which was the German counterpart. It described a seven-month period in which adversaries glowered at each other across Europe, wondering what the other intended to do; a period of belligerent attitudes, of lassitude, apathy and slackness, of little real action. The RAF refrained from bombing Germany in support of hard-pressed Poland, for fear of alienating public opinion in the United States; instead of high explosives, bombers dropped leaflets informing the German people of their leaders' wickedness. When Hugh Dalton, a Labour politician with many friends in Poland, urged the bombing of the tinder-dry Black Forest before the coming of the autumn rains, Sir Kingsley Wood, the Air Minister, told him, 'You can't do that. That's private property. You'll be asking me to bomb the Ruhr next.' Britain's reaction to Nazi Germany was thus curiously unwarlike at this time.

On the Continent, the war had assumed the same, unreal, defensive quality. By 27 September some 152,000 soldiers and almost 10,000 RAF personnel of the British Expeditionary Force under Viscount Gort had crossed the Channel without the loss of a single man. Anglo-French forces amounted to seventy-six divisions, facing thirty-two German divisions, so that an attack in support of the Poles would have been feasible. The excuse for inaction was that the Siegfried Line (Germany's answer to Maginot) was immensely strong. The French raised the doctrine of 'strategic waiting' to a fine art. The delay was fatal, for it enabled Field Marshal Brauchitsch to raise the strength of the

Wehrmacht in the west to a hundred divisions, mainly seasoned veterans of the Polish campaign. Prior to October 1939 the Siegfried Line had been manned by ersatz battalions, poorly equipped and inadequately trained, while the defences were far from being as impregnable as Nazi propaganda maintained.

Of course, there was a much-publicised invasion of the Saarland by French cavalry units early in September, amounting to a number of timid and half-hearted probes of the German defences, but by October, as German forces began to build up and the worst winter in recent years set in, the French retreated with due prudence to the comfort and seclusion of their defences. In the first three months of the First World War the Old Contemptibles had lost over 50,000 men. By contrast, the first British casualty of the Second World War on the new Western Front was Corporal T.W. Priday, killed early in December when his patrol unexpectedly ran into a German scouting party.

While the British and French troops settled down to sit out the intense cold and the boredom, their politicians speculated on Hitler's intentions and the prospect of bringing hostilities to a conclusion without firing too many shots. After all, the business over Austria and Czechoslovakia had been settled without resorting to war; and now that Poland had disappeared the immediate cause of the conflict had been removed. The British and French governments regarded as encouraging Hitler's 'peace offensive'. On 6 October the Führer addressed the Reichstag, proposing a comprehensive agreement that would give everyone a feeling of security and peace. This bit of kite-flying was dismissed by Daladier five days later, and by Chamberlain on 12 October, both sceptical of Hitler's promises. Ribbentrop (24 October) attacked Britain for being so unconciliatory. Meanwhile peace gestures were being made by others. King Leopold of the Belgians conferred with Queen Wilhelmina of the Netherlands early in November and they offered to act as intermediaries between the belligerents. Germany rejected this well-meaning proposal on 15 November. With the onset of the bitter winter weather the Phoney War stagnated even further. This produced a false optimism in Britain. Even Churchill, in a broadcast of 12 November reviewing the first ten weeks of the war, considered that 'time is on our side'. He went so far as to suggest that if Britain came through the winter without any large or important event occurring 'we shall in fact have gained the first campaign of the war . . .'

While Sweden, Switzerland and the Vatican introduced strict rationing between September 1939 and March 1940, France was enjoying the antithesis; under the new Family Code, introduced to increase the birth rate, a bonus of up to eighteen pounds was granted for the first-born child. When Churchill raised the international temperature on 20 January with an inflammatory broadcast castigating neutral countries and extolling the merits of the gallant Finns who had shown up the incapacity of the Red Army in the Winter War, he was immediately howled down, both at home and abroad, and provoked severe criticism in the parliaments and press of Belgium, Holland, Denmark, Norway, Sweden and Switzerland. When James Cromwell, Canadian Minister to the United States, gave warning of Nazi intentions on 19 March he was publicly reprimanded by Cordell Hull, the American Secretary of State, on the grounds that such a statement was 'likely to disturb the relations between this and other governments'.

So the dithering and bickering continued, and the peoples of Europe, both belligerent and neutral, tried to get on with their lives as best they could despite the blackout and rationing and increased taxation. In Nice that winter Robert strutted round in his new Savile Row suits and went for long walks among the high hills. His reveries under the sunlit elms, however, were not unproductive, for he was hard at work on the new volume of verse hinted at in his letter to Germaine from London. In the spring of 1940, when the Phoney War was at its height, *Bar-Room Ballads* was published in London by Ernest Benn, in New York by Dodd Mead and in Canada by Saunders of Toronto. Later this would form book six of the *Collected Poems of Robert Service* published in 1952, but not surprisingly the *Twenty Bath-Tub Ballads* were then omitted.

Of *Bar-Room Ballads*, Robert's first book of verse for nineteen years, he wrote, 'It was neither better nor worse than any of my previous volumes and was received with the same gentle tolerance.' Typical of the reviews that greeted this book was that published in the *Toronto Globe and Mail*:

> Mr Service's new book of poems . . . is packed with lore gathered during that Yukon exposure, together with other nostalgic pieces; of which perhaps the sourdough stuff is preferable. Mr Service cannily disavows any profound poetic ardor: he'd rather be jester than minstrel, rather 'pipe a pot-house ditty' than 'touch the heart to pity': he confesses he's 'a graceless hobo in the Land of Letters' and admits rhymes of 'booze' with 'Muse'. All of which his admirers acknowledge — and love him just the same. These poems will go over big in this dark hour when a bit of levity is needed to cheer a man.

The heavyweight newspapers and literary periodicals in England, however, appear to have ignored it altogether. This book of a hundred and twenty-eight pages reverted to the style and pattern of the earliest volumes, abandoning the elaborate prose and verse structure of *Ballads of a Bohemian*. It consisted of forty-six pieces and five 'frivolous songs' (the quintessence of the bath-tub ballads). About half of the ballads harked back to days in the Yukon: 'The Ballad of Salvation Bill', 'The Ballad of How MacPherson Held the Floor', 'The Ballad of Hank the Finn', 'A Sourdough Story' and 'The Ballad of the Leather Medal' were in the same genre, and inspired by the same characters and situations, as the Sourdough songs. 'The Ballad of the Ice-Worm Cocktail' had, in fact, been composed by Robert during his Arctic trip by canoe and taught by him to the crew of the Mackenzie River steamer. It had thus passed into the oral tradition of the Far North and even been published anonymously in several anthologies, before the identity of its author was established in *Bar-Room Ballads*.

In this volume Robert experienced a recrudescence of spirit, and completely recaptured the reckless inspiration which had made the best of his Sourdough songs so memorable. In colour, atmosphere and melodramatic force, in graphic and picturesque simile, in vivid and sharply etched vignettes, in the startling and, at times, disturbing phraseology, these ballads stood up to anything he had previously written. Highlander or Sassenach, one cannot read 'The Ballad of How MacPherson Held the Floor' without chuckling at every stanza; and the double rhymes and the gory melodrama of Hank the Finn lingers in the memory long after reading the tremendous last line. The ballad had been inspired by the public hanging at Dawson in 1908, a spectacle that had seared itself into Robert's soul. 'The Ballad of Touch-the-Button Nell' had much of the old rumbustiousness, from the opening lines:

> They gave a dance in Lousetown, and the Tenderloin was there,
> The girls were fresh and frolicsome, and nearly all were fair,

to the closing stanza, with its tragic lament:

> They gathered up the broken bones and sadly, in a sack
> They bore to town the last remains of Lew Lamore, the macque.

This ballad, which Robert's publishers had rejected thirty years earlier, was just the sort of thing to delight the large and enthusiastic audience which had long revelled in 'The Shooting of Dan McGrew'.

Other ballads were inspired by more recent adventures. 'Atoll' and 'Beachcomber' recalled the Tahiti trip. In this group the outstanding pieces were 'The Ballad of Lenin's Tomb' and the stark 'Warsaw' which, in its first stanza, recalled the dramatic moment when Robert despaired of getting aboard the train leaving the doomed city, but at the magic mention of England the crowds had parted for him. Six months later, however, Robert sombrely speculated on how that word might now be greeted:

> ENGLAND! they cried for aid, and cried in vain.
> Vain was their valour, emptily they cried.
> Bleeding, they saw their City crucified . . .

O splendid soldier, by the last, lone train,
Today would you flame forth to fray my place?
Or — would you curse and spit into my face?

One curiosity was 'Little Puddleton' which, purporting to be a quiet English backwater, might well have summed up Robert's life at Dream Haven and if his vision was limited his logic was sound. In 'Bookshelf' Robert revealed his catholic and eclectic tastes in literature and confessed that he had turned his back on such early favourites as Shakespeare, Keats, Wordsworth, Tennyson and Browning. Instead, the bards in whom he found inspiration were Omar Khayyam, Oscar Wilde, Coleridge, Burns, Bret Harte, Eugene Field, Henley, Chesterton, Kipling, Masefield and Houseman:

Behold my minstrels, just eleven
For half my life I've loved them well.
And though I have no hope of Heaven,
And more than Highland fear of Hell,
May I be damned if on this shelf
Ye find a rhyme I make myself.

Arguably the best verses in this collection were not the dramatic monologues, but the lyrics and shorter poems into which Robert had crowded a more mature philosophy reaped from his rich and varied experiences in many parts of the world. These were marked by a charm of simplicity, a potency of sentiment that never degenerated into sheer sentimentality, and at times they sounded a nostalgic note that would find an echo in many hearts. 'Dolls', which was probably inspired by Iris as a little girl, was a perfect gem of retrospect. 'Each Day a Life' was a singularly apposite piece:

I count each day a little life,
With birth and death complete:
I cloister it from care and strife
And keep it sane and sweet.

★ ★ ★

Oh, that all Life were but a Day
Sunny and sweet and sane!
And, that at even I might say;
I sleep to wake again.

'Enemy Conscript' and 'Don't Cheer' ended the volume on a grimly thoughtful note. This was a more philosophical volume than its predecessors, and

there was a much greater pre-occupation with the abstract in those pieces entitled 'Courage', 'Security', 'Longevity', 'Resignation' and 'Sensibility'. Robert's
personal philosophy came across clearly in 'Laziness' and his economic mani-
festo was declared in 'Five-Per-Cent'. His self-avowed interest in the
Rabelaisian was all but absent, a notable exception being the brilliant ballad of
'Bessie's Boil' with its fine range of regional accents for good measure.

This raises an interesting question which has never been satisfactorily
answered: who wrote that most notorious parody 'Eskimo Nell'? 'The
Shooting of Dan McGrew', after the passage of three decades, had become a
classic, its author hailed alternately as the leading American or Canadian folk-
poet of the twentieth century. Typical of the tributes was that written by Simon
Strunsky in the *New York Times* in 1941: 'The trouble that beset Dan McGrew
in the Malamute saloon is now part of our folklore south of the 49th parallel',
demonstrating that this celebrated Yukon monologue was by that time as
much a part of American heritage as Canadian. Robert had taken the anapestic,
galloping verse-form popularised by Kipling, but transformed it by adding his
own syncopating and barbarous alliteration. The result out-Kiplinged Kipling
and created a style that was distinctly Service. Distinctive, but not inimitable,
for it inspired an army of parodists. In his *Collected Parodies* (1926), Louis
Untermeyer wrote a brilliant parody entitled 'Rudyard Kipling and Robert W.
Service Collaborate on a New Red-blooded Ballad' which magnificently sent
up the genre. The bawdy ballad entitled 'Dangerous Dan McGrew' has earned
a measure of immortality in its own right:

> A bunch of the boys were whoopin' it up
>   In one of the Yukon halls;
> The kid that handled the music box
>   Just sat a-scratchin' his balls.[1]

but this pales into insignificance alongside 'Eskimo Nell' which has appeared
in numerous anthologies and even been distinguished by separate publication
in various forms. Interestingly, an attempt to trace this classic cloaciniad back
to its origins points to composition somewhere in the South of France in the
1930s! One widely accepted theory is that it was penned by Noel Coward, and
certainly there is a wit and elegance shining through the extravagant depravity
which point towards the Master. More recent scholarship, however, has
suggested Graham Greene as the true author. But there is a school of thought
that believes Robert Service himself was the author, although, if he was, he
never avowed it.[2]

Bar-Room Ballads was largely composed in the new apartment which
Robert rented in the winter of 1939–40. This was at 6 Place Franklin, the

Palais d'Etoile du Nord, a few hundred yards west of rue Dante and in a much
more salubrious neighbourhood. The flat was on the ground floor and had a
terrace that gave on to a beautiful rose garden.

> Ornate and florid in style, it made one think of a château. The rooms
> had proportion, balance, spaciousness, and my bedroom was the finest
> in the house. But to me it was precious because it was the room in
> which Gaston Leroux wrote his famous novel — *The Mystery of the
> Yellow Room*. In fact it *was* the Yellow Room, as my concierge assured
> me, and described how Gaston, a fat little man, used to work there in a
> gorgeous dressing gown and skull cap, bearded and spectacled like
> another Zola.
>
> And if his style was contrastingly romantic, at least in fecundity he
> resembled the Master. A man of great imagination he aspired to be a
> French Conan Doyle, but being so much in demand for newspaper
> serials proved his undoing. Of his many works the *Yellow Room* was the
> best; in fact, it is one of the finest detective novels ever written,
> because its solution is absolutely unguessable. And here in my
> bedroom, lying in my majestic bed, I surveyed its walls papered in a
> rich design of gold, and liked to think it had been the source of his
> inspiration. Indeed, just below the balcony that gave on the pergola
> was a sculptured scroll-work up which the villain must have scaled to
> commit his crimes. In any case that was the most delightful bedroom I
> have ever known, and probably ever will know. [3]

That winter both Milton Hays and Archie Bruce died. Archie had apparently been in poor health for some time, though occasionally he would muster
the strength to descend from his sumptuous villa at Vence in his immaculate
Rolls-Royce and take Robert for a drive. On those occasions they would reminisce about their carefree bohemian days in the Latin Quarter. Robert was now
sixty-six and Archie ten years older, 'two Old Codgers living in the lap of luxury'.
Two days before his old friend died, Robert paid him a visit and dutifully admired
his roses although these flowers, in the mass, bored him. He was buried in the
cemetery at Vence, near the grave of D.H. Lawrence. Here again, Robert's
memory was faulty when he recorded this melancholy occasion in *Harper of
Heaven*, for he seems to have thought that Lawrence had died 'only some weeks
before' when in fact he had died in March 1930, a full decade previously.

Robert saw little of Milton Hays that winter. Hays was working on a play
entitled *Prevailing Wind* which the local dramatic society of the expatriate
British community had offered to stage. Hays was an ailing man by this time,
which probably explains his 'pettish and finnicky' nature. (During a prelimi-

nary reading, while Hays was declaiming the lines, the leading man began to caress a pet bulldog, whereupon Milton rose and walked out.) Hays took little exercise, and worried incessantly about the war and its restrictions. Robert referred to Milton's heart condition and breathlessness, but omitted to mention his death, which occurred soon after the fall of France, by which time Robert and his family were back in England.

The Côte d'Azur escaped the worst excesses of that savage winter, and although there were noticeably more men in uniform around the town, Nice went about its customary business as tranquilly as ever. With the turn of the year, however, things began to change, imperceptibly at first. Barbed wire entanglements appeared in the wooded hills and Robert was compelled to curtail his walks. Then tented camps sprang up all over the hillsides, but the soldiers had little to do except smoke cigarettes, drink *pinard* and play *manille* 'They got ridiculously plump and were horribly bored.' The general public shared this *ennui.* 'We had alarm rehearsals in which sirens screamed and all were supposed to go to the shelters. No one did.'

But just along the coast was the Italian frontier and a radio station that blared out constantly an ominous message from Mussolini that Nice, Corsica and Haute Savoie were Italian and must be returned to Italy. This revanchist message became more and more strident with the coming of spring. Robert decided that his family were too close to the frontier for peace of mind, so when they packed up and made ready for the annual drive back to Brittany they did so with more than usual care. As they packed away their goods and chattels for the summer months, 'some prophetic sense must have made my family more lavish with mothballs than ever before'. Pictures were covered, carpets rolled up, curtains folded away and beds dismantled. On 11 May 1940, while they were finishing these elaborate arrangements, Robert learned in the newspaper that the *Blitzkrieg* had begun the previous day.

The relevant passage in *Harper of Heaven* conveys the impression of the flight northwards as having taken place later the same day, but it was not until 20 May, more than a week later, that the Service family left Nice. By that date the military situation had deteriorated alarmingly, although no one could comprehend just how bad it really was. The Services apparently had no difficulty obtaining seats on the train to Paris. At Lyon, Robert bought another newspaper and learned to his dismay that General Gamelin had been replaced as commander-in-chief by the seventy-three-year-old Weygand, deputy to Marshal Foch in the First World War and just returned from command of the forces in Syria. Weygand's appointment was made late in the evening of 19 May, the day on which Paul Reynaud's government, now withdrawn from Paris to Tours for safety, had been reconstituted, bringing back the even more elderly Marshal Philippe Pétain from Madrid (where he had been French ambassador) to become Deputy Premier. By the time Robert and his family reached Paris they were appalled to discover that France was reeling under the German onslaught. Robert and Germaine stayed several days in the capital before they could get seats on the train to Brittany. In the meantime the news was confusing and rumours were rife. Then one day a flight of Luftwaffe aircraft swooped low over the city but dropped nothing as it was merely a reconnaissance sortie. No one took shelter; the Parisians stood in the middle of the streets staring up at the sky. That night the sirens sounded again but no one descended to the shelters.

The following day the Services boarded the train. The corridors were so jam-packed that it was impossible to get to the toilet (which was occupied anyway by a woman nursing an infant). Ten people were crammed into the Services' compartment. Many of the travellers were Belgian refugees and Robert noted the high proportion of young children, waifs who had lost their parents in the shuffle and confusion of the retreat. 'In every station were swarms of lost children, and notice-boards with their names, so that if their parents were on the train they could be claimed.' There were horrific tales of refugee columns on the crowded roads of Belgium being strafed by Stukas.

The train terminated at Rennes, and rather than wait for an indeterminate period for an onward connection with no hope of finding a hotel room for the night, Robert decided that they should press on to Lancieux if they could. Miraculously he found a taxi parked outside the railway station and asked the cabbie to drive them all the way. At first the man refused point blank, but then Robert recognised him as a man from Lancieux. As mutual recognition dawned, he changed his attitude and agreed to drive them there if Robert could scrounge sufficient petrol for the trip. Eventually they set off, 'with a song of joy in our hearts', but along the way they noticed abandoned cars which had run out of fuel. Many of them had Belgian number-plates and all had mattresses lashed to the roofs. Some had broken windows and others were riddled with bullet holes. Those still struggling to keep on the road were piled high with household goods, bedding and bicycles. Many of these cars were driven by women with broods of children. Finally they reached Lancieux and soon were ensconced in Dream Haven which seemed lovelier to them than ever.

> I never watched so eagerly for my eyes to fill with that blessed vision, the red-roofed house on the point, the sandy cove, the pines and the gorse, with beyond the green sea broken by rocky islets. And there was Tasie and her family awaiting us with hugs and kisses, and the old house all ready to welcome us as if it too were smiling joyfully.

The euphoria and relief of being back at Dream Haven were shortlived. The village was full of Belgian refugees, camping out in the school and the *mairie*. There was already some resentment of these interlopers using up all the milk, butter and eggs and leaving little for the regular residents. The refugee problem did not abate. Suddenly there were fresh waves of refugees, French people this time, from Alsace, Lorraine and other eastern districts, who painted a lurid picture of the German advance and the horrific destruction of Rethel and Sedan. Clutching at straws, people comforted themselves with the thought that a seasoned campaigner like Weygand would make a stand. There would be a second Battle of the Marne, Paris would be saved and the tide would turn. The new refugees were bedded down in barns and out-buildings on straw palliasses, but even the most basic foodstuffs had to be severely rationed. At night Robert and his family lay in bed uneasily listening to the unaccustomed drone of aircraft. Hard on the heels of the easterners came a swarm of refugees from the north, from Boulogne and Calais. They were accommodated in makeshift tents erected in the fields. Now only potatoes and turnips were available to feed the newcomers.

Eagerly Robert tuned in to the radio. The French broadcasts were incoherent and incomprehensible; those from the BBC were unbelievable. Paris was declared an open city; there was to be no stand at the Marne as in 1914. If the Germans crossed the Seine, where would they be checked? Suddenly the horrible truth dawned that there would be no hiding place from the dreaded *Boches*. Then another wave of refugees arrived. These were from Paris and central France and had no intention of battening on the Bretons for they were only pausing to draw breath before moving on. The enemy was now too close behind. The only escape was to get across the Loire to the south and head for the Pyrenees. By now the radio bulletins were barely keeping up with the rapidity of the German advance. The Panzer divisions were already in Picardy. Farther north, the tanks which had sliced through the Spahis (African cavalry) at Sedan on 10 May raced across France and reached Noyelles on the English Channel exactly ten days later — about the time that the Service family reached Paris. Then Rommel's tanks swung northwards and in another week had taken Calais. Two days later, on 28 May, King Leopold of Belgium ordered his troops to surrender. Paul Reynaud, the French Prime Minister, broadcast the news 'in a broken voice of scorn and sorrow', making a desperate appeal to Roosevelt to intervene. In Lancieux the Belgian refugees wept with shame and anger at the news. Although Leopold would later be reviled for an act of betrayal there was absolutely no other course open to him. Even before the Belgian surrender the British Expeditionary Force was in the process of extricating itself from Dunkirk. Between 24 May and 4 June a third of a million men would be evacuated in the greatest feat of military improvisation since Galliéni commandeered the Paris taxi-cabs to rush his troops to the Marne in 1914. News that the British had evacuated themselves from

Dunkirk reached Lancieux soon after Robert and his family got there. His autobiography is silent on the matter, but in several newspaper interviews which he gave in England and Canada soon afterwards Robert recalled ruefully how hostile many of his Breton neighbours were towards him at this time, as if he personally were to blame for this latest example of perfidious Albion's treachery.

After the Belgian capitulation and the British evacuation of Dunkirk the end was well-nigh inevitable. It might have been possible to fight a series of rearguard actions, as De Gaulle advocated, using the twelve hundred modern tanks of the French armoured forces to harass the enemy's extended flanks, but unfortunately the mentality of 1914 prevailed and Weygand braced himself for a fight to the death before Paris. On 9 June the Germans attacked the French Fourth Army on the Aisne, between Neufchâtel and Attigny, and met with the stiffest resistance so far. The French fought desperately before being driven back to the Marne, exhausted and greatly depleted. There, on the following day, as they dug in for the final onslaught, they heard the news that Mussolini had declared war on France. Later that day the Germans crossed the Seine and the defence of Paris became hopeless. Paris was declared an open city and the armed forces withdrew in some disorder, with no particular plan in mind. There was some vague notion of continuing the fight in the centre of the country, but at best this could only have prolonged the struggle needlessly. The Army was hopelessly encircled.

On 13 June the Germans, having crossed the Seine west of Paris, reached Évreux and pushed on to Dreux, driving before it the remnants of the French Tenth Army which withdrew into Brittany. The Germans perceived Brittany as a redoubt and prepared to assault it with an aerial bombardment. It must have been on or shortly after that day that Lancieux had its first taste of total war, when a German aircraft dropped a bomb on the village. Germaine and Iris became hysterical when the bomb exploded in a nearby field, and flight was uppermost in their minds. Robert, on the other hand, was for standing firm. He could not help seeing himself in a romantic pose. 'Let the *Boches* come. I will take to the woods, and you can steal out at night and bring me food. I will be an outlaw, a sort of Robin Hood.' But his womenfolk soon pricked this romantic bubble. 'A cave was no place anyway for an Old Codger. My idea was idiotic . . .'

This conceit was later developed in some of the newspaper interviews which Robert gave in Canada. One newspaper even ran a story with the head-line 'Faced Life as Hunted Man Deep in Woods of France So Poet Came To Canada'. What Robinson MacLean actually reported, however, was not so highly coloured, but sheds an interesting light on Robert striking a heroic pose:

His chief regret is that he was unable to stay in France, to see it win back its identity and its self-respect. He planned to stay, even when he learned that the Gestapo would probably try to hunt him down. But when he realized that he would have to hide in the woods and forage for his food from French houses where there would be little enough for those who had to stay, he left.[4]

According to the account given in *Harper of Heaven* Robert had a motor-bike in the garage and had sufficient petrol to go for a reconnaissance. He rode off to St Malo where he saw vessels loaded with troops. At first his heart leapt at the sight of reinforcements, but when the ships cast off and weighed anchor his spirits sank in despair. The British forces, and remnants of the French Army, were leaving in disarray. Shocked and saddened, he was about to head back to Lancieux when he heard the cracked and quavering voice of an old man on a radio. It was Marshal Pétain, the hero of Verdun, announcing that he had taken over from Reynaud as Premier and would be seeking an armistice. To this end, he asked his gallant countrymen to cease fighting.

Around me men were crying openly, and women were moaning and wailing. Everyone seemed crushed by this tragedy that no one had even remotely dreamed of. So I slipped away abashed by so much poignant grief.

The Reynaud ministry fell from power at 11.30 p.m. on 16 June and President Lebrun immediately asked the aged marshal, just past his eighty-fourth birthday, to form a new government. Pétain surprised the President by promptly producing a full list of his cabinet from his briefcase. The following day Pétain broadcast to the French people asking them to stop fighting. At the same time the government initiated negotiations with the Germans and Italians via Madrid and the Vatican, seeking their terms for an end to hostilities.

Not surprisingly, the chronology of Robert's account is rather confused at this point; what he later claimed was spread over several days appears to have all taken place within a few hours on 17 June, between Pétain's dramatic broadcast at 12.30 p.m. and the Services boarding an English ship at St Malo the same evening. Robert, however, stated that he returned to St Malo 'on Sunday' and found the British consulate abandoned. At dawn the following day he went down to the village where all kinds of rumours were flying around. 'The Germans had bypassed us and were in St Brieu converging on Brest.' In fact, the Wehrmacht entered Brest on 19 June, two days after the Service family had taken ship for England. On his way out of the village

Robert encountered a stream of cars coming from Rennes which had been newly bombed. 'These cars had broken windows and were pitted with bullets. They were loaded with bloody passengers who were still faint from the horror of the bombardment.' Rennes was attacked on 16 and 17 June and tanks of the V Panzer Division entered the town on the day after Robert and his family left France. To be sure, this town, which was then the headquarters of the French Tenth Army, was heavily bombed, in a massive raid which began about ten-thirty on the morning of 17 June. Unfortunately, a munitions train packed with high explosives was standing in the railway station and took a direct hit, the resultant explosion destroying two troop transports and a crowded refugee train. Although the extent of the horrific carnage was never precisely known, it has been estimated that over two thousand people were killed that day. Robert's tale that five thousand people had been slaughtered in the attack was a gross exaggeration. This was a figure which he gave repeatedly in newspaper interviews over the ensuing weeks, without actually naming the town. Only once was this queried — by Dick Sandbaum, a Winnipeg reporter — but on that occasion Robert refused to say which 'neighbouring town' had sustained such loss.

On the same afternoon of 17 June, he rode his motorbike in the direction of Dinan and witnessed the *Blitzkrieg* for himself.

> As I neared the highway linking Dinan and St Brieu some peasants ran out to warn me. 'Do not go further, Monsieur. The Boches are there on the road ahead.' But curiosity overcame me and, leaving my bike in a cottage, I crawled across some fields. There in a hayrick beside the road I was cowering when there came a swift stream of motorcycles ridden by grey-helmeted, goggled warriors armed to the teeth. France had nothing like that, I thought half admiringly, and when they had ceased to pass I crawled fearfully away.[5]

The order to take Brest and Cherbourg 'as a matter of honour' did not come from Hitler to Rommel until 17 June, and the actual advance from Rennes did not begin until 19 June, two days after Robert and his family had fled, but it is highly probable that mechanised infantry units were operating independently of the main tank forces, and roaming the countryside at will, all organised resistance having collapsed. After seeing the German motorcycles Robert returned to St Malo once more, dodging through the oncoming stream of refugees which clogged the road. Fortunately, he knew the Breton country-side like the back of his hand, and navigated along footpaths and twisting country lanes to get back to the seaport. Here he discovered four tramp steamers at the wharf evacuating wounded British troops, and enquired whether he could wangle a passage to England. He was told that there might be a chance if he were on the spot just before they sailed. Despite all this frenzied activity Robert still found time for some refreshment and conversation. In the town itself he called at a tea-room run by an elderly Irishwoman. Over a pot of tea and some scones he asked her if she intended staying on. 'Why not?' she replied. 'People will still have to drink tea and eat scones.' She was from the Irish Free State and, as a neutral subject, she was quite confident that the Germans would not molest her. But she advised Robert to go, 'for his daughter's sake'.

According to his autobiography, the old Irishwoman made up his mind for him. Later, however, he mused that if he did not get away it would definitely be death for him, 'for I was on the Black List on account of things I had written'. This romantic notion seems to have developed later on, and was frequently mentioned, with heightened dramatic effect, in newspaper interviews on the other side of the Atlantic. There is no evidence to suggest that Robert was indeed a marked man, nor indeed was there anything in his published writings that could conceivably have made him a target of Nazi animosity.

Approaching Lancieux, he ran into Germaine and Iris on the road and told them curtly, 'We're going. There's to be no snivelling. You must keep control of your nerves. You can only take one suitcase each and I give you half an hour to pack.' While the ladies packed their valises and donned three dresses apiece, Robert destroyed cheque-books, bank-books and other papers of any value. Then he fondly caressed some of the two thousand books in the library and, feeling heartbroken, took a last farewell of the home he loved best. There was a tearful goodbye from Tasie and the little maid Aline, and the aged Coco whined and whimpered, sensing that his master was leaving with undue haste. Robert loaded the Lancia and drove to St Malo by the back lanes to avoid the never-ending torrent of refugees. In the town he called at a small garage where he parked the car. The garage proprietor offered him a paltry sum for it, but Robert refused to sell, even though he doubted whether he would ever see it again. From there Robert and his family lugged their cases down to the docks and on the way fell in with an English girl. This was providential, for she accosted a British sailor who directed them to the Port Captain. Robert had an anxious moment as they encountered three naval officers. His heart was thumping as he said that they were trying to escape and asked if they might get a boat. He need not have worried. With alcoholic heartiness one of them replied, 'Why, yes. Go ahead. Take the *Hull Trader*. She leaves in half an hour. And let me tell you, you're lucky. We have to stay and blow up the Port.'

At the quayside they found two ships moored side by side, and the outer vessel was the *Hull Trader*. A kindly seaman helped them aboard and carried their bags down to the captain's cabin, which was given over to Germaine and Iris for the two-day trip to Weymouth. Robert himself secured a berth for'ard, not too reassured when he discovered that the hold was crammed with high explosives which the sudden turn of events had prevented being unloaded at St Malo. Two other ships were evacuating Army and RAF personnel, a mini re-run of Dunkirk. Fortunately, they had fighter cover from the RAF so the danger of being strafed by enemy aircraft was minimal. Shortly before they weighed anchor a column of trucks and cars arrived with a fresh batch of wounded. Robert gave up his berth to a seriously wounded soldier who died on the voyage home. In the captain's cabin he found a crush of female refugees, including five squawling babies. By now Robert was getting anxious, for soon the tide would be too low to leave the harbour, and still the truck-loads of wounded were rolling up. But as the sun set the last of the wounded were brought aboard and at last the ancient coal-carrier cast off. Gingerly they edged away from the quay and scraped through the narrow dock gates, getting a grim wave from the demolition party as they went.

Luckily they had a calm sea but there was a full moon. Under normal circumstances Robert would have found the silvery moonlight romantic and might have been inspired to compose a verse; but that night he cursed it. Twice during the night they heard the drone of aircraft overhead, and the troops were put on full alert, but the dreaded bombing never materialised. Then there were enemy submarines and mines to worry about. 'That water was just staked with disaster, and every moment of that night I lay awaiting the shock of being hurled to eternity.'

In broad daylight the following morning Robert took stock of the situation. The ship was carrying several hundred wounded, about five hundred troops and fifty refugees. It was late afternoon when they drew into Weymouth, but a further three hours passed before they were allowed to go ashore. The wounded were given priority, then the troops were marched off, and finally the refugees were allowed to disembark. Now they had to cope with British bureaucracy which tagged them, gave them a medical check-up and deloused them before they were taken to a church hall for a hearty meal followed by interrogation by the police who quizzed Robert closely about the European visas in his passport and asked him the name of the ship on which he had travelled from Bergen to Newcastle the previous autumn. Under guard, the refugees entrained late that night for London. On arriving in the metropolis in the cold grey dawn they were met by buses which took them to a police station which was swarming with refugees.

It was little consolation to Robert to find so many people with interesting tales to tell. Had he been alone he would have revelled in the situation, but the thought of Germaine and Iris having to spend the night at the police station worried him. He had a sudden panic when he realised that everyone was being minutely searched. Robert had some Reichsmarks in his wallet, but he made an excuse to visit the toilet and flushed the incriminating banknotes down the pan. After that they were again examined medically and given a hot bath. Finally they got their passports stamped and changed their French money. 'At last we were told we were free . . . Oh, that wonderful moment!' Tearing off their tags, they hailed a taxi and an hour later were eating five-bob dinners at the Imperial Hotel.

Interestingly, Maurice Maeterlinck, then aged seventy-seven, escaped from France about the same time along with his wife and two cagebirds. When the birds were threatened with quarantine, Maeterlinck grandly presented them to the ship's captain. Somerset Maugham arrived in London shortly afterwards, but by an even more roundabout route. For ten days after Mussolini stabbed the 'Latin Sister' in the back, nothing happened; but then, on 20 June, when the collapse of France was a foregone conclusion, Italian troops began their Mediterranean and Alpine offensives. While all assaults on the mountain passes failed lamentably, the attack on Nice soon ground to a halt on the coast road outside Menton where a dozen men succeeded in blocking the advance of an entire division until the Armistice was signed on 24 June. Several weeks earlier, Maugham, along with some three thousand other British citizens of the Riviera, boarded an elderly coal-carrier at Cannes and crawled down the coast to Gibraltar, a hair-raising voyage that lasted three weeks. His arrival in London was reported in *Cavalcade* on the same day as that of 'Canadian poet Robert Service, creator of Dangerous Dan McGrew and other Alaskan figures'.

CHAPTER 15

THE YEARS OF EXILE, 1940-45

I was in Warsaw when the first bomb fell;
I was in Warsaw when the Terror came —
Havoc and horror, famine, fear and flame,
Blasting from loveliness a living hell.

'Warsaw' in *Bar-Room Ballads* (1940)

LONDON DEPRESSED ROBERT; IT FILLED HIM WITH A SENSE
of doom. 'The tenebrous silence of the black-out, those weaving search-lights
affronting the stars — I felt the impending terror and wanted to escape.' After
a few days at the Imperial Hotel, he took a flat at Swan Court in Chelsea for a
month while he sorted out his plans. During this period what was later to
become known as the Battle of Britain started. Soon after the French
concluded their Armistice on 24 June, nightly air-raids on southern England
began. These were apparently random and haphazard, designed to give
Luftwaffe crews practice in night-flying and the use of new navigational aids,
as well as to keep up the pressure at little cost. A few bombs were dropped in
East Anglia and Kent, mainly on airfields, but there was no bombing of civilian
targets during the period when Hitler was putting out peace feelers. The offer
of peace terms was published on 19 July 1940, and rejected three days later.
Intensive bombing of radar stations and airfields began soon afterwards.
London itself was not attacked until the night of 24–25 August, and then only

by accident when a few jettisoned bombs fell on the city. In retaliation the RAF bombed Berlin on several consecutive nights — an occurrence which Göring had assured Hitler would never happen. The enraged Führer promptly vowed revenge and ordered bombing raids on London, which began in earnest on 7 September. The Chelsea flat where the Services lived was destroyed in the Blitz, but by that time Robert and his family were long gone.

On Friday, 19 July, the very day of Hitler's peace proposal, Robert was reported in the London press as intending to sail for Canada the following week.[1] A few days later the Services packed their suitcases and boarded a train for Liverpool where, on 26 July, they boarded the Canadian Pacific steamship *Princess Helene* heading to Montreal with a thousand evacuee children and a contingent of RAF cadets bound for flying training in Alberta. For three nerve-racking days the ship tacked and dodged enemy submarines. It was an unpleasant voyage, and Germaine later recalled that they had to wear life-jackets at all times, day and night. They took comfort from the winking lights of their destroyer escort. Then on the fourth day the destroyer turned back and they knew they had entered the safe zone. On the morning of Thursday, 1 August, they disembarked at Montreal and Robert immediately found himself besieged by reporters, eager to get a first-hand account of the fall of France. For a man who had shrunk from publicity and, in fact, had led an almost reclusive life for years, the unwelcome glare must have been almost as traumatic as the events of the past few weeks. But Robert appears to have been gratified by his new-found fame, for the headlines hailed him as the Canadian Kipling or the Bard of the Yukon, and for the first time in his life he began keeping his press-cuttings, which Germaine would dutifully paste into a handsome leather-bound album, purchased in Vancouver. Robert's arrival coincided with the release of the Canadian edition of *Bar-Room Ballads* whose sales were considerably boosted by the press publicity surrounding his return to Canada.

Robert booked into the Windsor Hotel in Montreal for several days, a fact that was widely reported in the newspapers. Sitting in the lounge of the hotel one day, he was approached cautiously by a youngish man.

He was good-looking and well built, with an air of professional prosperity. 'Do you know who I am?' he said. 'No,' I replied with polite apology, 'I'm afraid I don't.' 'I'm your brother Stanley,' he told me so persuasively that I was forced to believe him. I knew I had a brother who was a doctor in Ottawa, but when I had last seen him he had been a lad, and twenty years do make a difference. So I was introduced to his wife and he drove me to Ottawa where I had a spot of money trouble, for I found that all my funds in Canada were frozen.[2]

Stanley was then on the staff at Toronto General Hospital. Robert's cash problem was soon resolved, and the Services took palatial rooms at the Royal York in downtown Toronto. There, Saunders, the Canadian publisher of *Bar-Room Ballads*, organised a book-signing session which was well attended by the press and drew gratifyingly large crowds of fans. Among them Robert had another visitor whom he had not seen for many years. Harold Tylor, now retired, was living on the outskirts of the city at the time and, seeing a report of Robert's arrival, went along to meet his old companion from the bank in Whitehorse. Their reunion was duly photographed and appeared in a number of papers and magazines. Until this time Robert had been something of a rolling stone, never corresponding with anyone after he had moved on to pastures new; but the friendship with Harold Tylor, resumed in August 1940 and continued by correspondence, was to last until Robert's death eighteen years later.

Occupying an adjoining suite at the Royal York was Gracie Fields. When apprised of this fact by Thelma Craig, the reporter who interviewed him for the Toronto *Globe and Mail*, Robert reminisced that he had once written a poem for his fellow Lancastrian, which he had entitled 'Tripe and Trotters', but then he had changed his mind and never sent it to her.

In his autobiography, however, Robert dismissed his week in Toronto simply as 'a grand time, though I found I was too much in the spotlight for my shrinking nature. There were broadcasts, autograph parties, crowds of visitors.' Robert was always being asked for his views on the conduct of the war and its likely outcome, or a statement of his political philosophy. He reassured one Montreal reporter that 'There will always be a France because the [Vichy] government doesn't represent the people at all'; to another he declared optimistically that the war would be won in the air. 'We are getting stronger all the time and in a few more months England will be stronger. Then will be the time to send bombers over German towns night and day.' In Winnipeg he reported that he had found a wonderful sense of elation in London. 'The people are all keyed up and want nothing better than for Hitler to invade the country. They're just asking for it.' Diplomatically, he added that 'the magnificent colonial troops' from Canada, New Zealand and Australia who swarmed the streets of London were giving 'a tremendous lift' to the English people.

To Robinson MacLean he asserted, 'Capitalism is doomed. Socialism will stay in England after the war has been won. Our old world is finished.' The reporters who interviewed him were surprised to find not the boisterous roughneck they had imagined from the early Yukon ballads, but a quiet-spoken, kindly man with dancing eyes and a very mild manner. Indeed, this adjective began to irritate Robert and his interview with Thelma Craig closed with the words 'Please don't call me meek and mild.'

In the course of one of these interviews Robert told a reporter that he had decided to drop his middle initial, explaining that his rich Uncle William, after whom he had been named, had died and left him not a cent. William (1848–1925) was probably the most successful of Robert's uncles. He graduated from Glasgow University with degrees in Science (1874) and Arts (1875) and was appointed Assistant Master in Kilwinning Public School before becoming Classics Master at the exclusive girls' Park School in Glasgow and eventually Rector of Coatbridge High School.[3] When he died in March 1925, he left £17,256 — a considerable fortune for those times.[4]

Robert's reaction to being cut out of the will and his subsequent decision to drop his middle initial were pithily summed up in the poem entitled 'Uncle William', which appeared in *Songs for my Supper*:

> There was once a double-you
>   Midway in my natal name;
> Lest its loss should trouble you,
>   Let me herewith solve the same:
> It alludes to Uncle Bill,
>   Who ignored me in his Will.

In the course of the next three stanzas Robert claimed that his uncle had disapproved of him 'as a vagabond fantastic', and would have seen him 'plunge a total wreck' rather than 'throw the life-line of a cheque'. Robert, however, continued to sign his name 'Robert W. Service' — a matter alluded to in the punch-lines:

> Uncle's stingy shade to vex,
>   With his name I sign my cheques.

Following their brief pauses in the great cities, Robert was glad 'to escape to Jasper Park, the bears and the glaciers'. After a couple of days the Service family left Toronto by Canadian National Railways and went via Winnipeg and Edmonton to Jasper in the Rockies where they spent a week relaxing in a log cabin and going for long walks round Lake Beauvert and through the beautiful Maligne Canyon. Jasper was much smaller than Banff and its holiday chalets infinitely less pretentious than the great Scots baronial pile of Banff Springs. For the first time since landing in Canada Robert and his family could relax. While it was gratifying to be lionised and regarded as a celebrated poet, Robert was nevertheless thankful for the opportunity to get away from the crowds of well-wishers and the newspapermen who ambushed him at every stop in his well-publicised itinerary. By 11 August he was in Edmonton where the train stopped for about half an hour, early on a Sunday morning. An enterprising cub reporter for the local newspaper tried to obtain an interview with the great man but at that ungodly hour Robert was not prepared to co-operate. Nothing daunted, the young reporter filed some copy with the headline 'The Sourdough Poet Was Whooping It Up — In Bed':

This is the law of Service, and Sunday he made it plain.
Don't go looking for interviews when he's riding on a train.
Six-thirty was much too early, snug he was in the hay,
And the train porter told the reporter he might be there all day.
There are strange things done, ain't it so my son, by the men who moil for tales.
But this scribe did what the average kid would do when he sees and fails.
Minus ire or frown he hied downtown, careless of job or pelf,
And at ten past eight 'twas his happy fate to be back in bed himself.

On Tuesday morning, 20 October, the Service family arrived in Vancouver where they rented the Tudor Manor at Sylvia Court, overlooking the city with splendid views of the harbour and Vancouver Island. Next to the Riviera this was where Robert felt most at home. Walking around the still familiar streets or seated on a bench in Stanley Park, he could relive bittersweet memories of forty years before. Needless to say, his arrival in the chief port of British Columbia was trumpeted in the newspapers and the *Vancouver Sun* of 7 September even published a lengthy article by his old girlfriend Laura Berton, complete with five photographs (including an up-to-date portrait of the famous poet), which occupied almost two pages of the paper.

Robert seems to have made no attempt to contact his family, most of whom were living in or around the city at the time. There is no mention in *Harper of Heaven*, for example, of visiting his mother's grave; indeed, Emily's death the previous year at the age of eighty-five passed without comment in the autobiography. But in Vancouver Robert was accosted by a fine-looking woman who said, 'Do you know who I am?'

Staring blankly I admitted that I was absolutely at a loss, and she answered: 'I'm your sister Agnes.' It was very bewildering for an Old Codger, and it took me quite a time before I got used to folks coming up to me saying: 'Hullo Bob! Why, I thought you were dead.'[5]

That was Robert's sole reference to meeting any of his family in Vancouver at that time, but the newspapers reported that the highlight of his visit was a reunion with his brother Peter, who sold the poet's books at the Sourdough Bookshop on West Pender Street. Peter had not seen his eldest brother for a quarter of a century and made the mistake of greeting the wrong old codger at first; but when Robert eventually appeared he bore down on him with the sort of whoop heard in the Malamute Saloon on a brisk night. The pair exchanged a grin and a wordless handclasp. By now, however, Robert was tired of airing his views on the war and tight-lipped when the subject of Dan McGrew was raised for the umpteenth time. 'My own pet is "The Cremation of Sam McGee",' he replied in answer to the perennial question, shivering in the cold drizzle, but was quick to plug his latest efforts, 'But there's some verses I like in my last book, too.' Interestingly, Robert's age was given as sixty-four, an error which recurred in all the Canadian interviews. He was actually in his sixty-seventh year. To be fair to Robert, a great deal of the inaccurate reporting about his earlier history was derived from the press notices distributed by Dodd Mead and Saunders. Thus Robert was said to be looking forward to revisiting the house in the Duncan district 'where he lived for a few months after first coming to Canada in 1894'. This was the source of the canard, still widely believed, that he had only been seventeen when he first went to British Columbia.

Another myth, widely reported in magazine articles and emphasised in both previous biographies, is that Robert never returned to the scenes of his early poetic triumphs. Certainly this would seem to be borne out by *Harper of Heaven* which is completely silent on the matter. But in late August 1940 Robert, without wife or daughter, made his first trip in an aeroplane when he flew from Vancouver to Whitehorse aboard the *Yukon King*, a twin-engined airliner of Yukon Southern Air Transport. The Vancouver newspapers published a photograph of Robert on the tarmac in front of the aircraft, posing with the pilot, Captain Sheldon Luck, under the bold caption 'Robert Service Has First Plane Ride'. The report in the *Vancouver Daily Province* ran: 'The smoke-filled gambling rooms and hurly-burly dance-halls which provided material for Robert Service's poems on the gold rush days in the Yukon were never further from his mind than when he took his first airplane flight last Friday.' Robert was described as 'quiet and unassuming' and was questioned during the flight by the newspaper's reporter regarding the authenticity of Dan McGrew. Robert admitted that he did not know anyone named McGrew, but confessed that 'the lady known as Lou' was a real person. As for Sam McGee, well, he had known him slightly . . . Robert wearied of these incessant questions about the characters in these early ballads. Why did no one ask him about his later verse, or his novels, or his book on healthy living? But he put up with the importuning of the pressmen with quiet good humour.

Robert stayed 'only a short time' in the Yukon, according to the newspaper, and it is probable that he returned to Vancouver on the very next flight, two days later. There appears to have been no record of his flying visit in the Yukon press at the time. Furthermore, despite several press reports of an impending visit to Vancouver Island, it was to be almost twelve months later before Robert got around to going over the haunts of his early manhood.

Against his better nature, Robert was corralled into the Vancouver literary and social scene. Germaine and Iris felt at home when the family was invited to *Une Soirée Québecoise* at L'Alliance Française in Sylvia Court. At the Arts Fellowship garden party in Cypress Park, the home of Mrs F.B. Lewis, Robert was one of the guests of honour, the other being Sir Charles Roberts, a pillar of the Canadian literary establishment.

By a strange coincidence, the long-suffering Sam McGee died at his home in Beiseker, Alberta, a few days later, on 10 September 1940. After working as a mining engineer, McGee had made a fortune as a contractor building roads for the federal government. Unlike Robert, McGee had frequently returned to the Yukon and was wryly amused to note that on the Yukon River steamer *Klondike* an enterprising officer used to take the more gullible passengers aside and offer, if they would say nothing about it, to sell them a small bottle containing some of the ashes of the late Sam McGee. When the passengers reached Skagway and were on their way down the coast, they began comparing notes about their Yukon trip and would then discover that twenty or thirty of them had ashes from the cremation. That skipper, during his career on the Yukon, must have sold tons of ashes. McGee was not particularly proud of the fact that he was the real-life hero of Robert's most celebrated ballad, but was tolerant with excited tourists when he encountered them on his own frequent trips to the High North.

Inevitably, when news of Sam's demise broke, reporters badgered Robert for a personal tribute. 'A very fine type of sourdough prospector' was Robert's comment. When pressed further Robert admitted that he had only met Sam on one occasion, and that was some time after the ballad was published. 'I felt a bit embarrassed, but he did not seem resentful at all. He mumbled something and went out again.' What he muttered, however, was that he was transferring his account to another bank. Robert continued:

I didn't know the man personally. I only know that he was a very decent chap and quite well known in the north. The character was absolutely imaginary. I happened to be turning over the bank ledger and I came across the name of Sam McGee, and it seemed a good name to use. It sounded well and it rhymed well.

Sam was not from Tennessee as the poem stated, but hailed from Lindsay, Ontario, and was thus well used to harsh Canadian winters. He left the Yukon in 1909 and settled at Great Falls, Montana, only returning to Canada in 1937 at the age of seventy to live with his daughter, Mrs Ethel Gramms, in Alberta. In fact, the real Sam seems to have been rather ambivalent about his immortalisation. His daughter claims that he was rather touchy about the poem but, at the same time, a valedictory address given to him when he left the Yukon was his most prized possession. On more than one occasion, when confronted by people who doubted whether he was *the* Sam McGee of Lake Lebarge fame, he would produce the testimonial by way of proof. And just for the record, he was decently interred in Rosebud Church cemetery, Beiseker — a far cry from cremation on 'the marge of Lake Lebarge' in the midst of a Yukon winter.

Robert was faintly embarrassed by this incident, and tried to steer the interview round to the state of France. He felt that he wanted to get back over there. 'I feel almost as if I am shirking something,' he added. 'After living for a year in the war zone you get used to the atmosphere. Every moment is exciting.' By contrast, Robert found Vancouver dull and lacking in thrills. He was chafing to get back to Dream Haven and wondering what had become of it and his flat in Nice. He bitterly regretted that he had unwisely left behind a forty thousand-word manuscript of a novel about the French National Lottery, although he conceded that the subject had been overtaken by events. The magnificent panorama of Stanley Park, English Bay and the mountains of the North Shore was beginning to pall. Robert was quoted as saying, 'I can get more kick out of the slums of Nice than of the best quarter of any capital on earth'.

To this period belongs the triplet quoted in his autobiography:

Vancouver rain, Vancouver rain,
Again I heard its soft refrain
Tap-tapping on the window pane

and he longed for the Californian sunshine. It was widely reported that Robert Service was planning to take out Canadian citizenship at an early date, but he never did; and to the end of his long life he retained his British passport. Towards the end of December, immediately after celebrating Christmas with his relatives in Vancouver, Robert moved his family south to Hollywood. He took the lease of a charming little bungalow at 1346 North Orange Drive,[6] two blocks from the Hollywood High School, with a fragrant deodar in front and gum trees behind. Palms and pepper trees abounded. 'Immersed in verdure and frilled with flower beds it was a joy to the eye and a comfort to the heart.

In short, a lovely little abode, our home for five years.' Robert would never forget the evening of their return to Hollywood:

> It was late December and the length of the boulevard was ablaze with Christmas trees. Coming from the pitchy dark of London it stunned us with amazement. Indeed, the plenitude of food and the lavishness of light in this country seemed almost incredible. And now through miles of luminous lanes we drove to Hollywood Hotel where we rested till we discovered our adorable bungalow. And so we settled to a simple life in which the worries of war were for a while forgotten.

After the excitement and upheavals of the previous six months Robert was mentally drained and physically exhausted. In January 1941 he celebrated his sixty-seventh birthday quietly with Germaine and Iris. His life followed the long-established pattern, months of 'divine loafing' following a period of intense activity. 'It was a life of routine, bland and suave, and, for a year at least, of undisturbed privacy.' Robert would rise at eight, awakened by bright sunshine flooding in at the window. He would take a cold bath and spend ten minutes exercising in the bathroom. While this was taking place, he would be watching the antics of his puppy, a substitute for the much-missed Coco. Meanwhile, Iris would be preparing breakfast which Robert and Germaine took in bed. As they enjoyed their toast, marmalade and tea, Robert would read aloud from whatever 'bed book' was handy. Over that first winter in Hollywood he specialised in the works of Somerset Maugham, for whose writings Germaine was 'curiously avid'.

At ten Robert would get up and listen to the news on the radio. 'It was always interesting, sometimes thrilling, occasionally painful.' After the news he shaved, dressed and went shopping in the neighbourhood market. After near-starvation in Brittany and strict rationing in London, it was a joy to forage through the vast markets, returning to the bungalow around midday laden down with bulky bags. While the women prepared lunch Robert would take the dog for a walk. 'It was pleasant sauntering in the sunshine under the magnolias, passing a pleasant word with a neighbour.' Then home to a well-spread table and a well-cooked meal. Three times a week the Services dined out, preferring a 'rather swagger cafeteria' or a restaurant where plain home-cooking was the bill of fare and one could have a good chicken dinner for a dollar. After lunch Robert took a nap. 'A drowsiness would overcome me and I would climb into my pyjamas. No dozing in a dressing-gown for me. Bed, my best friend, was not to be treated so scurvily. Between the sheets I stretched and pounded the pillow for two solid hours.'

After tea Robert would start on his daily hike on the hills. These strenuous walks were always taken alone. 'For two hours I would be the solitary pedestrian, here in Hollywood more conspicuous than ever.' On these long tramps through the canyons and over the hills above the sprawling tinseltown Robert never encountered another pedestrian, though he was frequently importuned by passing motorists who invariably stopped to offer a lift. 'Foolish people! Why should I drive when I could enjoy the pleasure of walking?' He was filled with exultation when he reached some peak affording a panoramic view of the city of Los Angeles.

> In the gathering dusk myriad lights would bloom and waver, green lights trembling, ruby lights twinkling, golden and silver lights spangling like jewels — a garden of light outspread for the joy of my gaze. How privileged I felt, and how sorry I was for those who could not see this beauty through my adoring eyes!

From these walks Robert would return 'glad and glowing' with an eager appetite. Supper would be taken in the kitchen nook, 'a jolly little booth enamelled pale blue and cushioned with gay chintz'. Robert loved this kitchen corner and would gladly have taken all his meals there, rather than in the dining-room as Germaine insisted. The views from the picture-windows of the bungalow were enchanting, of trim lawns bordered by banks of flowers. 'Nearly every day in the year we had sunshine, with flowers smiling up at us.' After the chilling mists and soft rain of Vancouver, the perpetual sunshine of southern California was the tonic Robert needed. This was surely the only way to live, always in sunshine, 'forgetting such things as dour skies and wintry days'. Not for the first time, Robert congratulated himself on his good fortune as a writer. 'I carried my workshop around in my head and I could choose my own environment.' Here it was ideal — with the result that he did no work at all.

During the first four years of his exile Robert did not write a single line. In the evenings he strolled, or sat idly on the boulevard studying its colour and movement. 'A cheap, shoddy crowd, garish in garment, fantastic in fashion, yet so interesting.' Robert was both repelled and fascinated by this parade of eccentricity — 'mostly ugly women in ungainly slacks arrayed in all the colours of the rainbow'. When this pastime palled, Robert would retire to the corner drugstore for a tranquil coffee or an ice-cream, then back to the bungalow and a quiet evening. He replaced the accordion abandoned in the flight from France and practised till his fingers ached. Then he would settle snugly in his armchair and read till three in the morning.

Robert was always an avid reader, but here he devoured at least one book every day. Nearby was a fine public library where he could borrow ten books at a time free of charge, and had over a hundred thousand titles to choose from. Sitting in this sunny, spacious and air-conditioned building, Robert would recall the old Los Angeles public library where, as a hobo, he had browsed for many hours. That library had now grown out of all recognition and boasted a stock in excess of a million volumes, but Robert never once revisited it. The comparatively small Hollywood branch library was more to his taste and, besides, it was right on his doorstep. Robert invariably walked to and from the library, laden down with his ten books — 'books never seemed too heavy for me'.

Always a keen dog-lover, Robert acquired two in Hollywood. The first was Dinky, a black cocker spaniel which had been bought as a puppy for Iris. The second was Monee, a mongrel bitch with more than a dash of the fox terrier in her but 'the greatest coward in all Dogdom', whom Robert once saw being chased up the street by a tiny kitten. In Hollywood Robert enjoyed an idyllic life. While professing that 'we are a very close and devoted family' the impression is conveyed of someone around whom the family revolved. It is significant that the fleeting glimpses of wife or daughter were merely in subservient roles, preparing meals and home-making, but seldom participating in Robert's daily routine, far less his adventures. The quiet routine and simple lifestyle suited Robert down to the ground, though in a city where everyone drove cars, his solitary perambulations must have been regarded as wildly eccentric.

In fact, the unobtrusive routine, of long walks, dollar dinners and visits to the public library, was allegedly forced on the Services by circumstances over which they had no control. Due to wartime restrictions Robert could not get access to his fortune, the bulk of which was tied up in Britain; but it is a matter of speculation how badly off he really was:

> Our greatest worry during our stay in Hollywood was shortness of funds. Of course, it's lots of fun to be poor, but not too poor. I had plenty of money in Britain but was only allowed to take out a small sum that was soon exhausted. From then on we were thrown on our own resources. We had to pledge the family furs and jewels, so that in the first year we ate our pearls and in the second our diamonds. In the third mother's mink coat covered the meal ticket, while in the fourth daughter's sables kept the wolf from the door.
>
> It was fascinating living so near to the ragged edge, like a game, but not too anxious a one, because we knew that if it came to the worst we could always go to Canada. In Toronto I could live like a prince but I preferred to live like a pauper in Hollywood. For one thing, our penury prevented us from entertaining or accepting entertainment, so that I could enjoy the exclusive life I loved best.[7]

Once more, Robert was indulging in role-playing. The royalties from *The Complete Poems of Robert Service*, which Dodd Mead had published seven years earlier, were still rolling in, stimulated by the recent appearance of *Bar-Room Ballads*. Funds from this source alone would have enabled the Services to live in a more flamboyant style had Robert so wished, but cultivating the church-mouse persona was something he always enjoyed. 'At the worst we could always go to Canada,' he wrote, but nowhere in *Harper of Heaven* was there any mention of going there after 1940. The impression is given of the family remaining in Hollywood for the duration of the war. In fact, Robert reverted to the summer and winter routine which he had followed in France. Every spring the Service family would take the train north and settle in Vancouver, returning to Hollywood when the cold weather set in. Robert's attempts to maintain a low profile were bedevilled by the American and Canadian press which chronicled his movements as religiously as they would any other celebrity in their midst.

For example, his departure early in May 1941 merited a two-column story in the *Los Angeles Times*, with photographs by Leonardo and the bold headline 'Hollywood Too Warm for Robert W. Service, Poet'. From this we learn that, after closing their bungalow, the Service family had moved into the Hollywood Hotel for several days prior to setting off for Canada. 'Hollywood is a perfect place to hide,' explained Robert to the reporter. 'Besides, many people think I'm dead, and I rather encourage the rumour.' After stating that Mr and Mrs Service and their daughter were leaving for Canada to escape the heat but would be returning in October, the report continued:

> Service, a handsome, grey-haired man of 68, has never lived extravagantly, and is not possessed of an ambition to swell his considerable wealth (that is, if the Nazis leave him sufficient to continue his present mode of life) or to work for the sake of working.
>
> 'Work's a mug's game unless you have to do it,' was his opinion.

A Vancouver newspaper noted, on 20 August 1941, that Robert W. Service was living in seclusion in an apartment block overlooking the city. 'Seclusion is his watchword here. Desk clerks and elevator boys in the apartment house are instructed to turn away callers.' This did not prevent the United Press reporter from getting a brief interview, describing the poet as 'grey-haired, florid-faced and worried' and saying that he was a changed man from the Robert W. Service who had created Dangerous Dan McGrew. 'It seems as if [the Yukon ballads] were written by another man,' he was reported as saying. 'I remember little of the Yukon, or what I wrote there.' Robert admitted to being a lone wolf. 'I have an intense dislike of artificial society.' His favourite word was 'virile'. A story had to be virile to interest him, and he thought that the public felt the same way. And he admitted that he always saw more interest in vice than in virtue. 'The only society I like is rough and tough, and the tougher the better. That's where you get down to bedrock and meet human people.' And Robert gave some sound advice to budding poets. 'Write verse, not poetry. The public wants verse. If you have a talent for poetry, then don't by any means mother it, but try your hand at verse.'

Another Vancouver paper of the same period reported briefly that the lure of the North had proved too strong for Robert W. Service, 'famed bard of the Yukon, who has closed up his Hollywood bungalow and intends making his home in this city for some time'. Iris Kent, the editor of the Society page in the *Daily Province*, recorded that 'Mr R.W. Service, well-known author, Mrs Service and their daughter Miss Iris Service, motored to Harrison Hot Springs to spend the weekend. They were accompanied by Mr and Mrs W.J. Stevens and Mrs Celesta Hamer-Jackson. The party has returned to the city.' Among other snippets from the summer of 1941 was a quatrain which Robert sent to the *Vancouver Sun*, blaming it on Iris:

> Ye gods of plenty hear my cry
>   And bring me back, I beg,
> The happy, happy days when I
>   Put butter on an egg.

More comprehensive was the reporting of the Services' visit to Victoria where they stayed for several days at the Empress Hotel, a far cry from the seedy boarding-house where Robert had lodged almost forty years earlier. Under the headline 'Noted Writer Visits Victoria', the reporter wrote, 'The advent of fond memories brought by his tour of the city, and the effect of its charm on his family, brought about the decision by the poet to remain here for the summer if it is at all possible.' But this was just another piece of disinformation, for after several days touring Duncan and the Cowichan Valley and exploring the Butchart Gardens and other scenic delights of Victoria, the Service family took the ferry back to Vancouver. The Associated Press report mentioned that Robert was 'immersed in music and composing songs', while several other reports hinted at work on film scripts and scenarios while in Hollywood.

One of these rumours was ventilated over the airwaves. On 8 October 1941 Robert made his first broadcast, for CKWX of Vancouver, and in the course of an interview with Stuart MacKay, he confided to listeners that he was currently working on the scripts of two films. One was entitled *The Lady that's Known as Lou* and was obviously inspired by Robert's most famous ballad, while the other was provisionally entitled *Pursuit* and would be a thriller set in the High North. Judging from the radio broadcast, it appears that Robert had written another novel, or at least drafted one out, and it was this that formed the basis of the thriller movie. News of these prose endeavours was widely publicised, provoking Anton Anderson to write from Whittier on the Passage Canal, Alaska, to his local newspaper 'An Invitation to Robert W. Service' in ballad form:

> Write us another sheaf of poems
> Throbbing with dash and dare,
> Fresh as the wind from the new spruce cones,
> Under the polar glare.
> Full of the power and punch you had
> When you wrote of Dan McGrew.
> And you painted for us on your pencil pad
> The scenes that we loved and knew.

and more in the same vein, ending on a slightly sour note:

> We're sick to death of your scenes of woe
> Of the War and your Paris lot.
> We want more stills of the Arctic snow
> And the scenes that you've forgot.
> Come back, Old Bard, to the way that's hard
> And alone on the Yukon Veldt
> You can splatter a line or two of rhyme
> To the tune that we all have felt.

The Services left Vancouver for Hollywood on 9 October 1941, but before he left British Columbia for the winter Robert composed a poem for Poppy Day and sent it to the *Sun* which published it early in November.

> I had a dream: I climbed a hill alone,
> A skyey hill of secret solitude;
> In mystic isolation there I stood,
> And spelled these lines star-glimmered on a stone.

> *Here lies John Smith; a radiant lad was he:*
> *Eager to ecstasy, high-souled and brave;*
> *Yet selflessly his golden life he gave*
> *To join the shining throng that makes us free.*

> I *am* John Smith: I wear a bowler hat;
> My veins run rich with mercenary ink;

Robert playing his guitar, 1942 (*Los Angeles Times*)

Book-signing sessions at
Hollywood and, below,
Toronto, where Robert
shakes hands with Harold
Tylor, who had been a
fellow bank-clerk in
Whitehorse

Studio portrait by Charles George, Hollywood, *c.*1945

The Villa Aurora, 64 Boulevard d'Italie, Monaco

Iris and Germaine beside their car, Monaco, 1949

Inside the Villa Aurora, 1950s

Robert with *Lyrics of a Lowbrow*, 1951

Robert posing beside his bookcase, Villa Aurora

Robert in his dressing-gown at the typewriter, 1956

With his younger granddaughter, Armelle, 1956

The last photograph of Robert Service, 1958

Canadian stamp issued in 1976 honouring Robert
Service and depicting his most famous creation,
Sam McGee

My belly bulges and my jowls are fat;
Of smug respectability I stink.
I did not risk my life; I baulked at that.
My craven carcase I preferred to save . . .
O Lad I might have been, God's Grace I crave!
O Dream John Smith! I doff my bowler hat
And buy this POPPY for your ghostly grave . . .

By the time this poem appeared, Robert was back in the United States. On Wednesday, 12 November, in fact, he was experiencing yet another 'first' — his first speech in public. This was an address to the Hollywood Authors' Society. Robert W. Service, 'famous Canadian poet', was reported as nearly seventy, yet this was the first public speech he had ever made.

> The startling thing about this is that this is not his first visit to Southern California. How he escaped on previous visits would baffle any mystery story writer. All the same, Mr Service spoke delightfully and, one might say, most encouragingly for those who imagine that life ceases to be exciting for those past 60. Irvin Cobb assured Mr Service that he had been more honored in this country than any of our own literary lights, as one cannot drive out any highway without seeing numerous stations named in his honor. His only rival in that respect, Cobb said, was the late Will Levington Comfort.[8]

The manner in which Robert was brought to the attention of the Society is not untypical of the man. To give herself some outside interest and improve her English, Germaine enrolled in evening classes at Hollywood High School. One evening Robert went to collect her and, as he waited, he strolled along the corridor, finally pausing in front of a door. In the classroom a silver-haired lady was giving a lecture on poetry, and, to his amazement, Robert heard her mention his name in a highly critical manner. Intrigued, he slid into a seat at the back of the class. According to her, Robert W. Service was Public Enemy Number One, because people going into a bookshop turned away from real poets and bought his verse instead. Robert was having a silent chuckle to himself over her diatribe, when one of the students jumped to his feet and protested loudly, claiming that the customer who had bought the Service ballads would not have bought the works of true poets anyway. He would have purchased nothing, and it had to be conceded that Robert's verse was a stepping-stone to something higher. There was considerable argument as other students joined in, and all the while Robert sat quietly enjoying the spectacle.

When it was over, he rose from his seat and asked the lecturer whether he, as a stranger, might be permitted to say a few words. She smiled graciously and every eye turned to the newcomer. He began: 'I have listened with the greatest interest to your discussion, particularly as the subject of it is an old crony of mine. I have known him for years, and I assure you he would be the first to deprecate the consideration of his work on such a high level. He has always disclaimed the imputation that he was a writer of poetry, and if he has ever perpetrated a really poetic line, I know he would be the first to apologise for it.'

With that he thought he had better retire gracefully, but he had not reckoned with his champion who followed Robert to the door, saying, 'I was interested in what you had to say about your friend. Where is he living now, and how could I meet him?' Robert told him that Service was living in a tiny bungalow not two blocks away, but said that he was very shy. With some devilment, however, he added, 'If you care to come along, we'll see if we can beard the Old Codger in his den.' So they walked home together and, on arrival, Robert asked Germaine if the Old Codger was inside. 'Then gravely I introduced myself and made a new friend.' The champion was Irvin Cobb, amateur poet and founder of the Hollywood Authors' Society, and he begged Robert to come along and address the members. Robert demurred, saying that he and his family were shortly leaving for their summer in Vancouver, but Cobb would not take no for an answer, and persisted until Robert, against his better nature, agreed to address them at their annual convention the following October.

This début broke Robert's self-imposed seclusion. In *Harper of Heaven* he deliberately misled his readers by saying that 'this publicity descended on me in the third year of my Hollywood sojourn' when, in fact, press coverage reveals that it took place well within his first year. Thenceforward he was increasingly in demand as a public speaker and rose nobly to the occasion. With characteristic self-deprecation in his autobiography, Robert put a different interpretation, both on his motives and on the results, in order to maintain the fiction about living close to the bread-line.

> One day I got an offer from a cosmetic society to pay me if I would give them a forty-minute address. It was only twenty-five dollars, but I entertained them for a good hour and earned my fee. Though it was humiliating to take that sealed envelope I put my pride in my pocket. Other offers followed. I tried to put up a good show and give general satisfaction. It was an entirely new line, but my experience as a reciter helped me. I determined to develop any ability I had in this way, and memorised and studied some of my ballads. The McGrew and McGee pieces were my great stand-bys. I thought people would tire of them but they did not. It is like with old songs. Folks enjoy most what they know best.[9]

A retired Shakespearean actor 'who sometimes washed dishes in the ice-cream parlor' taught Robert how to project his voice, showing him how to use his diaphragm and nasal cavities so that every word would carry. 'In the end I could address a big audience with complete confidence, and from then on public appearances lost their terror for me.' Robert had several approaches to go on lecture tours, but he declined these lucrative offers, partly from his innate diffidence but partly also because of the physical and mental strain which the lecture circuit placed on its performers. Robert was suddenly aware that he was no longer as young, or as fit, as he used to be. On several occasions, in the throes of a dramatic recitation, he was seized by dizziness and barely got through the programme. It was even more disconcerting to discover that he could no longer rely on his memory. 'My mind had a way of going blank. I dreaded these mental black-outs more than anything else.' After one or two ghastly experiences he took the precaution of having a prepared script ready to hand, although he also practised his lines so assiduously that he could deliver a polished performance without once referring to his notes. Few people watching Robert in action could have realised what an ordeal this was for him.

> As long as I was sure of my stuff I was never nervous before an audience. I could look people straight in the face and watch their reactions. But I was sensitive to the least inattention and unless I could rivet everyone in their seats I was unhappy. A cough or a whisper made me uneasy and an entry at the back of the hall put me off my stride. I concluded that I was not a natural entertainer or I would not have let these trifles put me out. I was too old to take up the game. My voice was good for half an hour, then it became worn and tired.

So Robert reluctantly gave up the notion of making money on the lecture platform and contented himself with half-hour talks before clubs and societies. Significantly, the most tiring part came afterwards when he was besieged by fans eager to get his autograph on their copies of his verse and discuss with him their favourite pieces. 'One had to smile one's sweetest and make nice remarks to each. Then there were requests for autographs and books to sign, so that when I got home I crumpled up and had to go to bed until next day.'

Astonishingly, Robert made no mention of the sterling work he performed in this line in the early months of 1942. The Japanese attacked Pearl Harbor a couple of months after the Services returned to Hollywood and by the beginning of the new year Robert had been press-ganged, through the Hollywood Authors, into doing his bit for the war effort. There then ensued a ceaseless round of tours of army camps, USO concerts and talks to the troops.

In five months Robert travelled all over California and the south-western states where, forty-odd years earlier, he had tramped as a vagabond. Everywhere he went he recited Dan McGrew and Sam McGee and was cheered to the rafters. Treading the boards and seeing the eager, shining faces of the young soldiers Robert must sometimes have cast his mind back to the days of his youth in Glasgow when he briefly appeared in *Rob Roy*, or of the rough and ready church socials and smokers in Cowichan and Whitehorse where the desire to expand his repertoire had inadvertently led to fame and fortune.

While Robert was touring service installations and training camps, Germaine and Iris stayed behind in Hollywood. Germaine enrolled with the American Red Cross, spending two days a week knitting and caring for wounded soldiers. Another two days were spent doing voluntary work at a Catholic centre for black children, while a fifth day was invariably spent at the Alliance Française, working for the French community. As if this were not enough, Germaine was still attending her English classes at the High School.[10] Iris, now twenty-five, seems to have been content to look after the home.

The lie to Robert's assertion in his autobiography that his seclusion was broken in his third year in Hollywood was amply given by his brief flirtation with the cinema, to which he devoted an entire chapter in *Harper of Heaven*, under the intriguing title 'Not this time, Cherry'. During his second winter in Hollywood, Robert was contacted by Frank Lloyd, a fellow Scot who had produced the film version of *The Pretender* in 1928. Now Lloyd was working on the production of *The Spoilers*, a classic story of the Alaska gold rush by Rex Beach. Robert, with pardonable exaggeration, states that this was 'about the tenth' version of the film; in fact, it was the fourth since 1914 when William Farnum and Tom Santschi had made their memorable screen brawl. It was remade in 1923 with Milton Sills in the male lead, and a sound version appeared seven years later, again with Sills taking the leading role. In the fourth version, filmed by Universal under the direction of Ray Enright, the role of the dance-hall hostess Cherry Malote was taken by Marlene Dietrich, while McNamara and Glennister were played by Randolph Scott and John Wayne. Frank Lloyd, having discovered that Robert was in Hollywood, came up with the brilliant idea of getting the poet to play himself in the film, although its location was allegedly Alaska rather than the Yukon.

'I just thought it would be cute to have you appear in one of the boxes of the dance-hall, writing your immortal ballad of Dan McGrew,' said Lloyd.

'Will Marlene be in it?' asked Robert thoughtfully.

'That's the bright idea. You'll have a scene with her. Now here's my suggestion.' Lloyd outlined the scene but Robert was not impressed. In the end, however, he agreed to go along with the producer's idea. In *Harper of Heaven* Robert gives a transcript of the dialogue between himself and Marlene.

Cherry: Good evening, Mister Service. What are you writing? Something about *me*, I hope?

Myself: No, not about you *this* time, Cherry. It's about a man. His name is Dan McGrew. He's a bad actor. He gets shot.

Cherry: Oh! Sounds interesting. Well, write something about *me* some time.

Then she flits gaily away, leaving me to my scribbling.[11]

Written from memory, some five years later, it is inaccurate in almost every detail although the general sense is near enough. In the actual film Robert, made up to resemble himself forty years earlier, was shown seated at a table scribbling on a piece of paper. As Cherry Malote, the gambling queen, passed by his booth in the Great Northern saloon, she remarked: 'Ah, I see you are writing a new poem, Mr Service. About me?'

'No, not this time, Cherry. I'm writing about a lady known as Lou.'

'Is there a man in the story?'

'Yes, a fellow named Dan McGrew. He's a bad actor, though. He gets shot.'

'Ah, The Shooting of Dan McGrew, eh?'[12]

Thus Robert had twenty-seven words, not twenty-three as he stated in his autobiography. Small as this part was, it gave Robert endless trouble. At home, as he rehearsed, he muttered the words 'No, not this time, Cherry' so often that Germaine and Iris took up the line as a catch-phrase, almost driving Robert crazy with their applications of it to their daily life. He tried out the line in a dozen different intonations, practising in front of a mirror with appropriate grimaces. But try as he might, he could not get that simple phrase to sound anything but idiotic. He emphasised first one word and then another, changed his tone and modulated his voice, but the more he said, 'No, not this time, Cherry', the more difficult he found it.

Then he had a session with the dramatic coach who told him not to shake his head or make any gesture, while keeping his face expressionless. The camera distorted everything, and what Robert fondly imagined was a play of emotion on his face became a grotesque grimace. Pathos became bathos, drama was reduced to farce. In despair, Robert almost resigned, but decided to keep going. Then he had to report at the costume department to be kitted out. Robert was aghast at the rig which was considered appropriate to a poet of the High North but which he thought made him look like a slapstick comedian. In the end he chose his own outfit, which made him look like a cross between a miner, a cowboy, a rough-rider and Billy the Kid. 'It was romantic, it was reckless — in short, my idealised conception of myself if the worst had been the best.' He was so pleased with the general effect that he posed in front of a mirror till he was ashamed of his vanity.

At seven o'clock on the morning assigned to shoot this scene, Robert presented himself at the studio. He remembered the date vividly because it was immediately after the Japanese attack on Pearl Harbor and everyone was 'up in the air'. The sun shone just as peacefully as ever, but in the studio all the talk was of war. Everyone talked of joining something or everything, and it was very hard to get actors, cameramen, lighting crews and the hundred and one others involved to concentrate on the job in hand. Robert was conducted to his dressing-room where he donned stetson, knee-breeches, long boots, khaki shirt and loud check lumberjacket. Then he was called to the make-up room where

> one of the most famous men in the business was awaiting me. He sized up his Old Codger. 'Well, now, they tell me I have to make a young man of you. All right. I made up Boris Karloff for *Frankenstein*, so I reckon I can do something with you.'
>
> He did. First of all he dyed my hair black. Then he took the lines out of my face. Then he enamelled my teeth and painted my eyebrows. Then he . . . well, I don't know what else he did, but by the time he got through it was fantastic. Fifty years had dropped from my age. As I gazed incredulously into the mirror I did not recognise the dashing blade I saw there. Oh, if I could only remain that way, I thought with regret.

The make-up artist was Jack Pierce, indeed one of the acknowledged maestros of the craft. He modelled Robert's face from an actual tintype photograph which had been taken of the young bank clerk at Whitehorse thirty-seven years earlier; strangely enough, Robert ended up looking nothing like himself but rather a cut-down version of Ronald Reagan. There were half a dozen films being shot on various sets that morning and while waiting for his cue Robert wandered round the studio observing the widely differing scenes. One that intrigued him was a gigantic mock-up of the head of the Statue of Liberty in which Robert Cummings was pursuing Norman Lloyd. Robert watched as the hero was saved, while the villain plunged to his doom on a double mattress. The film was *Saboteur*, being directed by Alfred Hitchcock. On the set of *The Spoilers* the finishing touches were being put to a mock-up of a dance-hall, complete with staircase, balcony and boxes, reminding Robert of the good old Dawson days with Diamond-tooth Gertie, Touch-the-Button Nell, Jew Jessie and the Oregon Mare. 'Nostalgic memories came back, and in my make-up of a Northern Sourdough half a century seemed to drop from my shoulders.' Two pages of his autobiography were devoted to describing the set in loving detail, right down to the Tabarin pattern of frilly panties worn by the can-can girls. The shooting of Robert's brief scene occupied another page and a half.

Then from behind me a vision of sizzling beauty, the divine Dietrich. She wore a gown of gold, and as she looked at me her ice-blue eyes thrilled me to my marrow. Like music that low-pitched voice rang in my ears. You can imagine how this vision of sultry seduction threw me off my stride. She was smiling down on me, her hair a towering *casque* of gold, her ravishing lips parted so that one felt one could look on her forever . . .

Robert remembered little about delivering his lines, he was so bewitched. Afterwards the director cried, 'It's lousy, but we'll let it go.' And so ended Robert's one and only venture into pictures. He stayed on set to watch the great fight sequence, lasting all of ten minutes, with which the film climaxed. Looking on as the two leading actors — and the stuntmen made up to resemble them — knocked six bells out of each other, Robert extemporised some lines:

Johnny Wayne and Randy Scott
They fought and fought and fought and fought.
With joy they shed each other's gore,
And then they paused and shed some more.
To bust each other's blocks they strove;
They wrecked the bar and crashed the stove.
Then with a heave big Johnny Wayne
Hurled Randy through the window pane.
So in the street and down the lot
They fought and fought and fought and fought.
So fierce they mixed it up I'll bet
Them galoots might be fighting yet.

The Spoilers was premièred on 21 May 1942 and was well received by the critics, the big fight scene between Randolph Scott and John Wayne, of course, grabbing most of the attention. 'The poet-laureate of the Alaska gold rush', as Robert was inaccurately described, also came in for some favourable comments and, indeed, Robert himself was surprisingly gratified when he saw himself on the screen several months after his day at the studio, although he was appalled to discover that his accent was worthy of Harry Lauder. Later he would take elocution lessons to try to modify his Scottish brogue.

In his autobiography, Robert says that he only accepted the film part because a fee of three hundred dollars was offered and that, being hard up, he could not refuse as that meant the family's meal-ticket for two months. At the end of filming he consoled himself with the thought that, 'for three minutes' work I had earned three hundred dollars, and that's not so bad'. These passages convey a mercenary streak which could not have been further from the truth. On Monday, 14 April 1942, the Canadian Red Cross intimated that, on 11 May, it would launch a Dominion fund to raise nine million dollars, and announced that it was kicking off with a cheque for two hundred and twenty dollars which had been received the previous Friday by F.W. Tuffrey, the British Columbia commissioner for the Red Cross. The cheque had been received from Robert W. Service who said that it represented 'the token payment made to me for work done in the screen play *The Spoilers* with Marlene Dietrich'. Accompanying the cheque, which was apparently the full amount paid by Universal, Robert wrote from Hollywood:

> As play acting is not my regular line, I do not wish to earn money in this way and I am donating it to the Canadian Red Cross . . . My friends in Vancouver can see I am not unmindful of their home town.[13]

Seeking to extend his professional repertoire, Robert began taking singing lessons, a fact omitted from his autobiography but widely reported, with line drawings and photographs, in such newspapers as the *Los Angeles Times* of 21 April 1942 and the *Los Angeles Examiner* of 17 April. By now he had plans to emulate his old friend Milton Hays and cut gramophone records of some songs as well as his famous monologues. Robert's voice was described as 'a rich baritone'. As his autobiography was silent on the matter, apart from the hints about voice production from the retired Shakespearean actor and 'lessons in radio technique', it is not known when Robert cut his first disc, or whether he ever recorded any of his songs. Certainly a ten-inch record of Robert reciting his most famous ballads was cut, for it was for a number of years played regularly on the Canadian Pacific steamships to entertain passengers and get them in the right frame of mind as they approached Skagway and the High North.

Because of his USO work, Robert's return to Canada in the summer of 1942 was delayed until late July. It was then that he rented the opulent Angus Drive mansion of George St John, the society columns of the Vancouver papers noting that Mr and Mrs St John had retired to their summer residence on Gambier Island. Fatigued by the hectic round of camp concerts in the United States, Robert was content to take things easy, but Germaine and Iris decided to go to the High North and see for themselves what life in the Yukon was really like. Interviewed by the *Sun* on the eve of his wife's departure, Robert said regretfully that he would have liked to have accompanied her, but 'I can't go, as I may be called back to Hollywood at any time'. Accompanied by Mrs John Campbell of Seattle, Germaine and Iris boarded the Canadian

Pacific steamer *Princess Louise*. Celesta Hamer-Jackson, who was to have joined this party, had to cancel at the last moment when she was rushed into St Paul's Hospital.

Germaine and Iris sailed up the Inner Passage to Skagway, and then took the narrow-gauge railway to Whitehorse and completed their journey to Dawson by the paddle-steamer *Klondike*, being pleasantly surprised to discover that the ship's menu-card was embellished with a photograph of Robert's cabin near Dawson. Later Germaine would look back on this trip as 'one I had never dared hope for and one I shall never forget'. Dawson was virtually a ghost town when Germaine and Iris visited it; at the census of 1931 its population had fallen to a mere 819, a fiftieth of what it had been at the height of the gold rush. Almost a decade later, it had risen to 1,043 and was beginning to enjoy a new lease of life as a tourist attraction when war broke out. Robert's log cabin had been beautifully restored and was being maintained by the Imperial Order, Daughters of the Empire who gave the poet's wife and daughter a conducted tour. Germaine confessed to being moved when she saw the moose horns over the porch like outstretched arms. Some of the sheets of wallpaper, covered with charcoal writing, still adorned the walls, but Germaine was dismayed at the rugged, spartan nature of the hut. '*Ca m'a fait triste*,' she exclaimed at the sight of the rough, bare floorboards and the meagre furnishings.

If the world had passed Dawson by, Whitehorse was another matter altogether. In 1939 the town had a permanent population of no more than 500, but within three years it had swollen to twenty times that number. Soon after Pearl Harbor, the Japanese had invaded the Aleutians, the string of islands stretching from Alaska in a curve across the northern Pacific. Although this was their only foray against the American continent, it was sufficient to alert the US government to the threat on its northern flank. Alaska, a territory purchased from imperial Russia in 1867 but comparatively neglected since then, suddenly assumed strategic importance, but communications by sea from Seattle and San Francisco were too slow and overland communications non-existent. In the spring of 1942, therefore, the American and Canadian governments embarked on a joint venture, the Alaska Highway, which, beginning at Dawson Creek in British Columbia, ran in a north-westerly direction to Whitehorse and thence to Fairbanks in Alaska, with a southern spur to Anchorage. Even today, although the road now runs all the way to Prudhoe on the Arctic Ocean and has been given fresh importance due to the polar oil deposits, this is a rugged journey because the road is unsealed; there would be no point in giving it a tarmacadam surface for the severe frosts each winter would rip it up. In summer one has the twin hazards of fine rich brown dust and infernal mosquitoes; in winter there are blizzards that reduce visibility to nil; and in the spring thaws a viscous mud that gives motoring the quality of ploughing through porridge. Back in the autumn of 1942, when up to 15,000 cheechakos were employed on the construction of the Highway, Whitehorse was again a boom town. Germaine and Iris were unable to visit the cabin of Sam McGee which the IODE had also restored; it was then home to a dozen construction workers.

On Friday, 14 August 1942, Robert and his family went to Seattle to attend the annual three-day Sourdough Reunion at the New Washington Hotel. Ironically, while the old-timers reminisced about gold rush days in Alaska and the Yukon, their way of life was vanishing for ever, as guns, tanks and tractors took the place of mining equipment in the High North. Robert, interviewed by the *Seattle Post-Intelligencer*, was uncannily prophetic. Talking of the Alaska of the future, he envisaged a time when it would be an important staging-post on inter-continental flights from Europe to Asia, taking the shortest route across the Pole. 'Some day in the future the trips we made will seem a little odd by comparison.' The *Seattle Times* reported subsequently that demand for tickets at the Sourdoughs' Banquet was so great that in the end *two* banquets had to be staged, at the New Washington and also at the Gowman Hotel. The toastmaster, musicians and speakers had to dart from one to the other, so that the diners in both venues had identical programmes. As Robert was billed as the star of the show, the highpoint being his recitation of 'Dan McGrew', he was kept on the hop that evening.

The Services were back in Hollywood by November 1942 and spent an uneventful winter there. Robert was still a seemingly endless source of interest to the American press and he was often prevailed upon to give interviews, being photographed playing his accordion or a guitar while singing one of his own ballads. How the press kept pestering him is not revealed, for Robert refused to have a telephone installed at his ivy-covered hideaway, but they beat a path to his door all the same. In a town that bristled with celebrities, Robert Service was in constant demand. Real poets and literary highbrows might regard him with disdain, but the great public loved him. Flora McKissock, who conducted the books column in the *Vancouver Sun*, highlighted this point, drawing attention to the fact that there was more to Robert's work than Dan McGrew. He was not only 'the unchallenged Laureate of the Land of the Midnight Sun' but deserved to be more widely known as 'a poet of great songs of freedom and peace'.

For the moment, however, Robert was stuck with 'Dan McGrew'. On 21 September 1943 Whitehorse got its own radio station and, for the inauguration, Robert was roped in, pre-recording a broadcast in Vancouver which was then relayed from coast to coast over the Canadian Broadcasting Corporation network. Robert referred to this event obliquely in his autobiography:

Thus it was I made a broadcast from the Frozen North, when I was really listening in the Sunny South. It gave me quite a thrill, and indeed I know of no greater pleasure than to lounge back in one's own home and hear oneself talking on the radio.

As early as 1941 Frank Dodd had suggested to Robert that he write his autobiography.[14] Robert turned down the suggestion, roguishly remarking that he was too young to tell lies about his boyhood, and that he would rather wait until he was ninety when he might have something worth saying. Dodd was agreeably surprised, therefore, when one day, late in 1944, the postman delivered a bulky parcel to his New York office and found that it contained a manuscript of a hundred and fifty thousand words. The title *Ploughman of the Moon* was derived from a couplet of Verlaine:

Pedlar of dream-stuff, piping an empty tune;
Fisher of shadows, Ploughman of the Moon.

Robert claimed that he had changed his mind because so many people and events were crowding his agenda that he was being left with little time for loafing and lounging. He had been inveigled into a Hollywood group called the Chaparral Poets who not only made him a Life Member but created the Robert W. Service Chapter in his honour. All this was most gratifying, but rather time-consuming, and the only way that Robert could ease himself out of the hectic round of lunches, lectures, meetings, rehearsals, broadcasts and book-signing sessions was to plead that he was engaged on some project so immense that all else must be sacrificed. Thus it came to him that he must write his life story. As he did not possess a car, Robert had the garage of the bungalow converted into a work-room. There he paced up and down, cudgelling his brains to conjure up long-forgotten details from his boyhood and adolescence, before tapping them out on his new Corona typewriter. Writing his autobiography took a full year, from Hallowe'en 1943 till Hallowe'en 1944.

During a whole year I worked hard on my book. It was tough going at first, for the drag-nets of memory did not prove too rich in glittering trove. I toiled valiantly, however, and pictures of the remotest past came to reward me. Even infancy surrendered its contributions. From the murk and gloom scenes vivid and vital projected themselves, and triumphantly I pounced on them. Bit by bit I filled in the frame of my tapestry, thinking, what a marvellous thing is visual memory! How was it I could reconstruct an event of sixty years ago as clearly as if it were yesterday? Yet there it was, incredible as a photograph, preserved by some magical process of the mind.[15]

Robert wrote about two thousand words a day, using an up-ended cabin trunk as his desk. This 'adventure into memory' would keep him busy till lunchtime. In the afternoons he would go for a long walk in the hills 'doping out my stuff for the next day'. By the autumn of 1944, however, Robert found that the book was far too long, and even drastic pruning could not reduce it to more manageable proportions. Then he decided to terminate the narrative at 1912. He contradicts himself in *Harper of Heaven* by claiming that a further six months were spent revising and redrafting before the final text was ready to send off to New York, but the total time taken from the first line to the final draft was exactly twelve months. As usual, Robert was very casual about events in the real world while he was immersed in this project. A reference to the gloomy events happening while the book was in progress — 'Hong Kong, Singapore, Bataan, Corregidor' — conveys the impression of composition in the dark days of late 1941 and early 1942, but the book itself is quite explicit that it was begun on Hallowe'en 1943, a fact confirmed elsewhere in the second volume. When Robert commenced the manuscript the war was going well for the Allies, perhaps not the beginning of the end, in Churchill's famous words, but certainly the end of the beginning. North Africa had been liberated and Italy had capitulated. By the time the manuscript was completed a year later, France had been liberated and, though the Americans had been halted at Bastogne, there was an optimistic feeling that the war, in Europe at any rate, would be over within months. By the time Robert had corrected the page-proofs Hitler was dead and publication came shortly after the atomic bombs on Japan finally brought the Second World War to a victorious conclusion.

Once more Robert was plunged into a frenetic round of personal appearances, broadcast and newspaper interviews, book-signing sessions and other promotional stunts organised by Dodd Mead.

> I went to bun-feasts and baby-shows; I strutted the stage, grimaced before the mike, glad-handed club ladies with bifocals, and club men with fallen tummies. I answered fan mail, autographed in stores, spoke to societies, lectured to students. In short, in the interest of my book I made a jolly good fellow of myself, which is not my line at all.

In the spring of 1945 Robert was invited to the première of the international production of *The Belle of the Yukon* starring Gypsy Rose Lee, Randolph Scott and Dinah Shore. The star-studded gala evening was held on Stage Eight at the Goldwyn studios and some four hundred guests were in attendance.

Robert was in his element, seated between Dinah Shore and Gypsy Rose Lee, who entertained the audience with two of the musical numbers. According to all the press reports, however, *the* highlight of the evening was Robert's recital of 'Dan McGrew', his personal tribute to the frozen North.

The first volume of Robert's autobiography was published by Dodd Mead in September 1945, and the following year the British edition appeared under the imprint of Ernest Benn. Hitherto Robert's novels and verse collections had largely been ignored by the heavyweight papers and literary periodicals, but now his latest work was widely reviewed. The reviews, however, were rather mixed. Most critics agreed that the book was 'honest, forthright and likeable' but some also considered it 'long', 'windy' or even 'long-winded'. Rosemary C. Benet, reviewing the book for *Hollywood*, considered that 'He writes simply, with some humour and occasional flashes of sharpness, occasional sentimentality, notably in his postscript at the end . . . The reader will end up by liking and respecting the man.' An anonymous critic concluded that 'Mr Service's autobiography is exactly the bright and fast-moving story which is to be expected from a writer of his calibre . . . Through all of his exciting and amusing experiences there is displayed the modest, sincere and tenacious Scottish personality of the author.' But Benet also noted that 'In general, what he does not want to speak frankly about, he leaves out entirely.' And Geoffrey T. Hellman, in the *New Yorker* was much more perceptive:

> Even as an autobiographer, however, Service has a certain reticence; his recollections, for example, do not contain a single date, and it is impossible to find out from them even when the author was born. He concentrates on moods and impressions rather than on names, facts, and figures. Thus a reader of the autobiography might easily suppose that he was perusing the vague memoirs of a literary vagabond who had hit a modest jackpot once or twice between moonlight walks and skating parties in the Far North instead of those of an author whose ballads have netted him a substantial fortune and have for nearly forty years been as familiar as Shakespeare to millions of people.

Some reviews were quite critical. Stanley Walker, writing quite a long review entitled 'The Old Rollicking Rhymester' in the *New York Herald Tribune* of 7 October 1945, nevertheless dismissed it as 'not a very good book'. Noting that a great many questions had been left unanswered, he continued:

> And, despite his frequent protestations, it is clear that he regards himself as a highly romantic figure. He over-writes his tale dreadfully;

even when he has something intrinsically dramatic and or amusing to tell, he spoils it with too many words. Moreover, until some new champion comes along, he must be regarded as the world's most assiduous user of clichés. But there is no getting away from it — he hit on something that somehow struck a response among millions of rhyme-lovers, and thus became the singer of the Common Man. The secret may be that he was not kidding; he took himself pretty seriously back under the Midnight Sun, and he still does.

Following publication of the British edition, the *Times Literary Supplement* of 4 May 1946 produced a lengthy and thoughtful review, entitled 'Confessions of a Poet'. The anonymous critic asked rhetorically, 'Is he presenting himself in this autobiography as a successful salesman? Emphatically not; far from crying up his wares and capacities, he gives much of his space to belittling himself.' Robert was taken to task in this august literary journal for never claiming for his popular verses that they were poetry, shrewdly pointing out that 'poetry has had much to do with making him what he is'. The reviewer indicated that the prose of this book was evidence of Robert's fluency and control of phrase. 'There are many passages which end in an epigram, and in some of them it is of the rare unobtrusive kind that at first read as merely appropriate and inevitable summary.' In the popular press, praise was unstinting and *Ploughman of the Moon* became a best-seller, the first printing of some twenty thousand copies being sold out by the end of 1945.

Now that the war was over the Services were anxious to get back to France, but four months elapsed before the necessary documentation came through. Meanwhile Iris, now twenty-eight, had enrolled for a course in domestic science and was not so enthusiastic about returning to the Old World. Then came news from the French consul in San Francisco: their visas had been granted and would be ready for collection by the time they reached New York. It was December 1945 before the family packed up, and left their little bungalow in Hollywood for ever. Robert sold his accordion and gave away his guitar. To the Robert W. Service Chapter he donated his books, and returned his library books for the last time. The Services left Los Angeles in warm sunshine and took the train east. In Chicago they found heavy blizzards, and were glad of the welcoming warmth of the Algonquin Hotel when they got to New York.

Most days during their stay, Robert steered his womenfolk to street-corner hamburger joints but one day, as a special treat, he took Germaine and Iris to lunch at the National Arts Club in Gramercy Park, on the erroneous supposition, acquired from his stay there as a guest thirty-six years earlier, that he was an honorary member. He confided this belief, and his name, to a club factotum who turned out to be a fervent admirer of 'Dan McGrew' and suavely escorted the Services to the dining-room.[16] Robert's account of the lunch is rather different, blithely unaware of the embarrassment which his assumption might have caused. 'Only the old steward remembered me and greeted me with warmth.' He sat in the chair in the bow window where he had corrected the proofs of his first novel and talked of Hamlin Garland, Graham Phillips and George Barr McCutcheon. 'Now they were mostly forgotten, their works in the scrapheap; yet the chairs and tables were the same and the club was comfortably shabby.'

Despite dreadful snow and slush — 'New York was at its detestable worst' — Robert and his family had a great time shopping. The bitter weather sharpened their appetites, but they found 'the cafeterias and automats lots of fun'. While Germaine and Iris indulged in a spree of consumerism on Fifth Avenue, Robert haunted the shipping offices trying to get a passage home. The prospects were gloomy and it seemed as if they might be stuck in Manhattan for a month. But then one day Robert heard that there were berths available on a troopship bound for Marseilles, practically on their own Riviera doorstep. Pulling strings with senior executives of American Express, Robert managed to wangle the necessary accommodation and in something of a last-minute hurry they gathered up their luggage and packages and boarded the ship the very next morning. There was an eleventh-hour panic at the Internal Revenue office where the letter from Dodd Mead saying that tax had been paid on his royalties was deemed insufficient for the grant of clearance papers. Robert had to dash off to Dodd Mead for clarification from the firm's accountant. After spending five exhausting hours Robert secured the precious certificate — *and then no one asked to examine it*. There were hectic visits to the bank, the American Express office and the shipping office, a few hours' sleep, then up at five o'clock the following morning to finish packing, pay the bills and send off the trunks. The taxi taking them down to the Battery was driven by a cabbie who had recently been a GI stationed at Beauvais. He said he had liked it fine and would gladly go back. 'Then the wharf, and once more we were on the voyage that at long last was leading us HOME.' The liberty ship which bore them back across the Atlantic could not have been more appropriately named: it was the USS *Bardstown Victory*.

CHAPTER 16

SUNSET SONGS, 1945-58

They say that Monte Carlo is
A sunny place for shady people;
But I'm not in the gambling biz,
And sober as a parish steeple.
So though this paradisal spot
The devil's playground of the rich is,
I love it and I love it not,
As man may sometimes fall for bitches.

'The Pigeon Shooting' in *Lyrics of a Lowbrow* (1951)

THE LIBERTY SHIP CAST OFF AT FOUR IN THE AFTERNOON, slid out of the harbour and into the teeth of a growing gale. The Atlantic crossing was more comfortable than the crossing from Liverpool five years earlier, but it was not a pleasant experience. Robert and his family were among fifteen civilian passengers heading for Europe on a troopship which, three days earlier, had disgorged fifteen hundred GIs. The weather was abominable, bitterly cold and blowing a gale. 'As we huddled on the hatch under the middle deck, shivering with cold, I wondered what was in store.' Having boarded the vessel at eight o'clock that morning, Robert, Germaine and Iris were miserable with the cold and dreading the voyage before they weighed anchor. As the ship slipped stealthily into the gathering gloom they had little inclination to admire New

York's spectacular skyline or the colossal Statue of Liberty. The Services were accommodated in a four-berth cabin which turned out to be the isolation unit of the ship's hospital, but at least they had their own privacy for the other cabins were ten-berth dormitories. The passage to Marseilles cost two hundred dollars each.

Once the ship got under way, the heating was switched on, transforming the cabin from an ice-box to an oven, so that Robert had to keep the cabin door open wide at night. With the racket of the engines and the shrieking of the tempest, sleep was well-nigh impossible. And, because the ship was virtually empty on this voyage it was tossed around like a hollow shell. For two days the passengers were violently seasick, but gradually they settled down to the pitching and yawing of the ship and could begin to enjoy the lavish meals provided. Robert would wander round the ship, trying to imagine what it must look like on the America-bound trips when it was loaded down with returning troops. He shuddered when he beheld the six tiers of metallic beds on steel braces down in the bowels of the ship. The tedium of the voyage was punctuated by sumptuous meals and every evening there was a film show. One evening *The Spoilers* was screened, and Robert's scene with Marlene drew applause from the handful of GIs and the black stewards. Robert got on well with the latter, one of whom was a guitarist. The ship had quite an assortment of musical instruments, so Robert borrowed a guitar and an accordion and played continually. Then he succumbed to influenza and took to his bed, devouring paperbacks from the ship's library. Shades of the Russian trips, Robert described the toilet facilities at great length. The latrine block for the GIs astonished him, with 'its circle of a hundred toilet seats, close, naked, unadorned, with only a metal rod between them'. Although it was spotless, he felt no urge to respond to those hundred invitations. 'Maybe I am squeamish, but community commodity did not inspire me.'

On a cold but sunny morning the ship docked at Marseilles. Robert was almost seventy-two and physically feeling his age. The flu had left him weak, with a racking cough. As he crawled up on deck into the chill sunshine Robert had his first view of France in five years; if only he had not been feeling so wretched he would have thought it a great moment. The Customs and Immigration officials, 'thin and shabby but quite charming in the best French manner', were very casual with the landing formalities, making only a perfunctory examination of the cabin trunks and looking forward eagerly to the splendid meal laid on for them by the ship. 'My heart warmed to these easy-going people who refused to take life too seriously.' So Robert bade farewell 'to the hard bitterness of the boat', and with a last look at its grey hull, he turned to the amenities of the land. For five hundred francs — an unbelievable sum in pre-war terms — a taxi took the Services on a tour of the bombed districts before dropping them at the railway station where they were booked on the midnight autorail to Nice. At the station they sat on their luggage for hours, afraid to move for fear of being robbed. Marseilles in the immediate aftermath of war had a frightful reputation for robbery with violence. In the darkness, the dimly lit station took on a spectral appearance made more sinister by the swirling fog. The returned exiles cowered and shivered on the chill, bare platform. On enquiring at the ticket office Robert was astounded to learn that the autorail was full up; despite his reservations through Thomas Cook, all places were already taken. The prospect of sitting all night on that god-forsaken platform unnerved him. In his debilitated state he was convinced that it would be the death of him. Then Cook's agent turned up and assured Robert smoothly that all would be well. He had an arrangement with the *contrôlleur* and by paying him a hundred francs a time certain seats would be kept off the reservation list. 'Good old corrupt France! We were saved.'

While the four hours at the station painfully ticked away Robert and Germaine fretted about the apartment in the Place Franklin, wondering anxiously what condition it would be in. But once they were aboard the train, despite the broken window and chilling draughts, their spirits lifted. Cannes, Antibes, Juan-les-Pins — how the names on the station boards rang like sweet music. At Nice Robert was in such a hurry to get off the train that he tripped and fell full length on the platform, hurting his hip. 'But little I cared. I breathed with ecstasy that ice-cold air and proclaimed its purity. My beloved Nice!' Their luggage was loaded on a barrow and they followed the porter on foot through the familiar streets of the 'musical quarter', the rues Mozart, Rossini and Verdi, to the Place Franklin. There they had a job rousing the concierge at such an ungodly hour. Robert nicknamed her *Casque d'Or* on account of her golden wig; this was also the name of the feisty heroine in *The Master of the Microbe*. Miraculously, the Services found their apartment intact. Houses on either side had been looted but theirs had been spared. As they entered, it was almost uncanny to find everything just as they had left it, down to the smallest detail.

In the light of day, however, Robert found that Nice was still suffering the effects of war. Prices had rocketed, but the shops were miserably poor. The bread was so bad that it made everyone sick. People subsisted on grey macaroni and half-rotted cauliflowers, and dysentery was rife. A cheerless Christmas, the saddest Robert had ever spent, was celebrated with a sardine and a boiled egg apiece; Nice was enveloped in an icy Alpine wind, experiencing the coldest weather in twenty years. Food was rationed and the few luxuries available on the black market commanded obscene sums. Venturing out of doors before he was completely free of flu, Robert had a relapse and narrowly escaped pneumonia. Germaine and Iris also went down with the *grippe* and had a tough time.

Anxiously they watched for the first sign of spring, when there would be vegetables and salads again. Everyone was preoccupied by food, or the lack of it. The Services were more fortunate than most, for they had fortnightly Red Cross parcels, distributed by the British consul to needy expatriates. Then parcels of tea, coffee and sugar which the Services had posted to themselves before leaving the United States began to arrive, and later food parcels containing fruit cake, jam and candy from well-wishers in Canada and the States. Iris took charge of this largesse, building up a well-stocked pantry. Gradually the weather improved and the first green shoots in the earth and the first buds on the trees appeared. With the advent of spring life improved and people lost that mood of resignation which had depressed Robert most of all. May wrought a magical change, as the flowers came into bloom and the Niçois recovered their *joie de vivre*. In the midst of the sunshine and gaiety, however, Robert was constantly reminded of the grim times so recently past, when he saw the memorials that studded the street corners, where *maquisards* had fallen in battle or hostages had been hanged.

The Italian occupation had been easy-going, but after the capitulation of Italy in 1943 Nice had been occupied by the Germans, and an unbelievably brutal regime had descended on the city. The formidable bastion built by forced labour, along with pill-boxes and barbed wire entanglements, still lined the Promenade des Anglais. The Germans had commandeered the buildings along the seafront and evicted their occupants. One of these had been Robert's bank whose officials had forced the strong-boxes and tipped their contents into sacks before storing them in another bank. Robert was lucky, for the contents of his strong-box survived the ordeal. All his silver plate, and the manuscripts of three books, had been saved. On the other hand, he later learned that his strong-box in a Paris bank had been broken into by the Germans, but as it contained only out-of-date publishers' contracts their booty was meagre. In Dinard, too, his safety deposit box was looted, but yielded only some life annuity contracts of no interest to the enemy.

Robert contacted the garage in St Malo and learned that his Lancia had survived the occupation, though four times the Germans had tried to commandeer it. It was not until the summer of 1947 that Robert was able to return to Lancieux. Dusk had settled on the village when he arrived and a summer storm was brewing. By lightning flashes he made out the path to Dream Haven and was amazed to find that the saplings he had planted all those years before had now grown into forty-foot pines, obscuring his view of the house. For the night, he lodged in the village with Tasie Pezeron and heard grim tales of the arrival of the dreaded *Boches* and the subsequent occupation.

Allegedly they had asked Tasie where was the Englishman 'who writes bad things about our Führer' and when they learned that he had escaped they smashed the door of Dream Haven and looted the house. The truth, as far as it can now be ascertained, is that the Germans were oblivious of Robert's literary reputation, far less aware of any supposed anti-Nazi writings. The nearest thing to anti-German sentiment was the pejorative use of such words as 'Huns' and 'Boches' in some of Robert's verse of the First World War. But Dream Haven occupied a promontory and had been seized on account of its strategic value, not as a reprisal for mythical criticism of Hitler. The house was thoroughly stripped of everything of value. Even the precious piano accordion, hidden under the roof-beam, was taken, while the Steinway grand piano was shipped off to Hamburg. Robert's collection of guitars and his motorbike also vanished. For much of the war Dream Haven was home to a platoon of German infantry. The sitting-room had been converted into a *Lazarett*; even to this day the door bears the red cross painted on it more than half a century ago. After Rommel's appointment as commander-in-chief of Fortress Europe, Dream Haven was strengthened and fortified, pill-boxes were erected in the garden and a network of trenches and tunnels was dug.

Robert included a rather fanciful description of the German commandant, 'who sported a monocle just like myself' and was suave and urbane. Colonel Andreas Maria Karl von Auloch, decorated with the Knight's Cross of the Iron Cross with oak leaves for his spirited defence of St Malo after the D-Day landings in 1944, had been born at Kochelsdorf in March 1893 and died at Wiesbaden in June 1968. In the Breton campaign of 1944 he was captured by American troops.[1]

With grim satisfaction Robert chronicled the punishment meted out to the local collaborators at the war's end. The harlots who had played his accordion and drunk champagne looted from his cellar were publicly cropped and marched up and down the village street. 'Our village vamp got three years in gaol, while some of the male Hitlerites were sent to the chain gang.' Robert's views of the occupation period were simplistic, dividing the little community into the Collaborationists, who were in a minority, and the Incorruptibles 'who had refused to speak to, or even look at a Boche'.

Robert's house, though its windows were smashed, its tiles askew and the plaster peeling, was still standing. Concrete platforms for gun emplacements had been installed but the work of converting the house into a little fortress was hardly begun when the Normandy invasion took place. Sadly Robert toured the scene of pillage and devastation, but his heart almost broke when he beheld the rape of his fine library. The fine bindings and rare editions had disappeared, and even the more useful reference books were gone. About a third of the books remained, but they were in such terrible condition, their pages pulped and their covers rotten, that nothing could be salvaged. One of the casualties was the manuscript of a novel which Robert had entitled *And His Seed Forever*, but whether this was the forty-thousand word novel about the French National Lottery, or some other book, is not known.

Other villas and chalets had been destroyed, either by practice gunfire or systematic demolition for building materials, so Robert felt that he had been lucky. One of these, on the opposite promontory, was the Petit Chalet, a villa which had been occupied by a Miss Loch, descendant of an old Scottish family from which had sprung a notorious factor in the Highland Clearances and a governor of the Isle of Man. Miss Loch had indulged in some genteel espionage during the Occupation, while her nephew, Captain Hughes-Hallett, RN, had been the designer of the Mulberry floating harbours used in the D-Day invasion. What the Germans started, the Russian slave-labourers, employed by the Todt Organisation to build the defensive system, finished. Hearing that the owner of Dream Haven was an English capitalist, they took delight in ripping out the plumbing and the panelling. All in all, the house presented a sorry sight; but there and then Robert determined to restore Dream Haven to its pristine glory. In the course of the ensuing summers the house was gradually renovated and refurbished. Robert added a conservatory which ran the entire front of the house and was perched on the edge of the cliff so that, seated at its panoramic windows at high tide, one has the impression of being in a ship at sea. During the summer of 1947, while Dream Haven was being made at least weather-proof, Robert and his family rented a house in the rue Saint-Enogat, near the sea-front in Dinard.[2]

Apart from travel restrictions, what delayed Robert's return to Brittany till 1947 was the family's move from Nice to Monte Carlo in the summer of 1946. Robert's motives for this were nowhere stated in his autobiography; but in newspaper interviews some years later he said that in the principality there was a remarkable freedom from bureaucracy. Monaco was like Nice, but without the pettifogging post-war restrictions. Indeed, the final chapter of *Harper of Heaven*, entitled 'The End of the Trail', makes no mention of the move at all, despite the fact that it begins with a description of the new location, without mentioning where it was:

> I am writing this on the terrace of a big brown villa, perched amid proud palms. Below me is the sapphire sea, and afar the Isle of Corsica glows like a golden ember in the diamond dawn. Olive groves wimple to the beach, waves flash like silver sea-gulls on the shingle. Twice daily I go down to play with them; I roam for hours on the mountainside, I muse on banks of rosemary and thyme . . . A place one dreams of — Journey's End for a life-long dreamer.[3]

Robert rented the upper two floors of the Villa Aurora, at 64 Boulevard d'Italie near the northern end of Monte Carlo. This splendidly ornate building, painted a rich ochre colour and decorated with glazed tiles depicting cherubs and swans in a blend of the italianate and the baroque, was to be Robert's winter home for the last twelve years of his life, and he jocularly referred to it as Sourdough Hall, for the on-going royalties from his earliest ballads paid the rent. Several stories circulated in the American press about Robert's new home. The most popular, though least accurate, was that the Villa Aurora had been a brothel in the nineteenth century and Robert was quoted as saying that Alfred, Lord Tennyson, had died in the room which he used as a bedroom cum workroom. Although the truth of the matter – that Tennyson had actually died in his own bed at Aldworth, the villa he had built for himself near Haslemere, Surrey – was easily verifiable, this ridiculous story received widespread credence. Nearer the truth was the story which Robert gave to newspapermen in Vancouver in 1948, that he was writing his poems in the room where the former owner, a *grandson* of Lord Tennyson, had succumbed from addiction to alcohol.[4]

In Monte Carlo Robert resumed the casual lifestyle of the Nice years. The lofty hills and mountain footpaths were easily accessible on one side; on the other it was but a short scramble down to the shingle beach for the twice-daily swim. Robert, in his striped singlet, dark shorts, beret and sandals, became a familiar sight. The weight he had put on latterly in the United States had been whittled off by the food shortages of Nice and in his mid-seventies Robert had as trim a figure as ever. He had three ambitions: to write a thousand poems, make a million dollars and live to be a hundred. During 1946 and the early part of 1947 he wrote the second volume of his autobiography, which was published the following year by Dodd Mead and Ernest Benn. The manuscript was completed by midsummer, for on 15 July 1947 Robert was in London where a reception was held in his honour at the Benn premises in Bouverie House. John Benn, chairman of the publishing firm, introduced Robert by saying that he had just completed the second volume of his autobiography. After tea, Robert read a humorous chapter from his manuscript, the one about his film début with Marlene Dietrich.[5] A month previously, Robert had a half-hour programme, in the series 'Time for Verse', devoted to him on the BBC Third Programme. Listeners to the highbrow radio channel tuned in at 9.25 p.m. on 6 June and heard the bard himself reciting the two great ballads which had made him immortal.

Robert had intended to entitle the second volume of his autobiography *Blue-behinded Ape*, according to an interview he gave to the *Chicago Tribune* in April 1946. This startling phrase was taken from Robert Louis Stevenson's poem 'Portrait':

I am a kind of farthing dip,
   Unfriendly to the nose and eyes;
A blue-behinded ape, I skip
   Upon the trees of Paradise.

Saner counsels prevailed, and Robert was talked out of it. Instead he derived his title from the quatrain which he inserted on the title page:

Although my sum of years may be
Nigh seventy and seven;
With eyes of ecstasy I see
And hear the Harps of Heaven.

And the term 'harps of heaven' was to be a recurring phrase throughout the book.

After the London trip in July, Robert paid his first visit to Scotland since 1930. In Glasgow he was welcomed by Arthur H. Stewart, the principal of Skerry's College and one of Robert's most ardent devotees. About September 1940 Stewart had written to Robert, then in Vancouver. A brief note from Sylvia Court on 9 October was sent in reply, but this was the start of a correspondence which was to continue for eighteen years. In the course of the following year Stewart compiled a glossary of words and phrases used in Robert's writings and sent a typewritten copy of it to Vancouver. Robert replied on 21 August 1941:

I received your glossary and have examined it with some interest. I am now returning it and thank you for having sent it.

I am afraid I do not know myself what some of the words on your list mean, for I never read my own work once it is published; and many of the words I no doubt chose at the time in an effort to be original. 'Pranic', for instance, is a form of Yoga breathing; but I haven't the faintest idea how I used it.

However, in practically every case you seem to have hit the exact meaning, and I congratulate you on the result of your labour.

With all good wishes,
   Robert Service[6]

Stewart also compiled a twenty-eight-page booklet entitled *Servicewise and Otherwise*, produced by Glasgow University Press in 1943 for private circulation. This little book consisted of short extracts from Robert's verse and prose taken from the six verse collections, six novels and *Why Not Grow Young?* Apart from the more memorable lines from the verse, the book was studded with aphorisms, maxims and one-liners from the wit and wisdom displayed mainly in the manual for healthy living. Although this booklet bears the publication date of 1943 it was not until six years later that Stewart sent a copy to his idol. Perhaps the delay arose because Stewart was worried about breaching the poet's copyright, even though the booklet was clearly inscribed on the title page 'For Private Circulation'. From the Villa Aurora on 23 February 1949, Robert wrote:

> I have just received your interesting brochure and was surprised at the contents. You need not worry about *my* permission as long as you have that of the publisher. I do not think that as long as it is for private circulation, and that no copy is ever sold, you are contravening any law. On the other hand I may regard it as a great compliment to myself, and a possible introduction of my work to new readers. If this is so I should really be thankful to you . . .
>
> I assume that Mr John Benn has seen the book and has no objection to your publishing it. I must admit that I had no memory of most of the wise-cracks you quote, so that it seems that they were written by someone else. Perhaps they were, but I wrote them first (at least I can claim I did). Anyway they seemed fresh to me and rather stimulating. They encourage me to turn out more — not too hard a job.
>
> I am only sorry your collection was not larger, as with my new book of verse to be published this Autumn you will have sixteen books to call from. Perhaps you may get out a bigger edition some time, but in case you do you might get the permission of Mr Benn, who is a very charming man.
>
> Sincerely
> R W Service

This letter sheds an interesting light on Robert's faulty understanding of his own legal position, with regard to Ernest Benn. The copyright of all his works was retained by Robert, and Ernest Benn only held the British rights to *The Collected Verse* and the two volumes of autobiography. By constantly deferring to John Benn, Robert showed his innate diffidence.

Harper of Heaven was widely reviewed around the world but produced mixed reviews. One reviewer found it 'a tough, violent book', while the *Daily Herald* pronounced it 'tough, sadistic, startling and readable'. On the other hand, the literary critic of the *Seattle Post-Intelligencer* claimed that this book was 'one of the most inspirational' he had ever read. For him the high point — or rather, the low point — was Robert's very moving account of the shock he felt when informed of his cardiac trouble:

I found myself cast into the author's black pall of thought. I found myself climbing at his side towards the light. I had the distinct sense of losing a numbness of shock, of picking up leaden feet and heart to move on. It was one of my finest experiences in the realm of the written word.

On either side of this mid-point of the narrative, the reviewer extolled the book for 'its tightly packed anecdotes galore, recounted in the glittering language that the author has all too seldom fashioned into prose compositions'. Then he concluded:

And so, I should like to put it, this gem of reading has something in it of many things; a testimonial to the power of faith; a travelogue; the fire of a world with its house in terrible disorder; and intimate moments with an arresting array of characters, not all of them Strictly Nice People.

In Canada *Harper of Heaven* was published by McClelland & Stewart of Toronto. York Reed, writing in Robert's old newspaper, the *Toronto Star*, furnished a perceptive piece entitled 'Life After Sam'. Service fans who had shot Dan McGrew and cremated Sam McGee would find little of the Yukon spell in this volume, although they would find the same keen observation and sense of novelty which had characterised Robert's earlier work. Drawing attention to Robert's assertion that he was not a poet, only a writer of verses, Reed took him to task. He had heard him on CBC radio recently reciting 'The Spell of the Yukon' in 'his gravelly old man's voice'; it might not be poetry but it was certainly verse writing of a very high order. *Harper of Heaven*, however, left much to be desired as autobiography. It was 'rather unplanned, rambling, and certainly not introspective'. Robert's adventures around the world produced 'the type of autobiography that suits Service's style. It is that of an old-time newsman, somewhat overgrown with adjectives but none the less lively and colourful'.

Having completed what was to be his last prose work, Robert was at a loose end. When he received a telegram from the International Sourdoughs' Association, informing him of the three-day convention being planned to celebrate the golden jubilee of the Trail of Ninety-Eight, and asking him if he would be kind enough to send them a congratulatory message and be there in spirit, he cabled back, 'In spirit be damned. Why not in the ruddy flesh?' Thereupon he made arrangements to travel with Germaine and Iris seven thousand miles to the sourdoughs' reunion in Vancouver. They travelled by sea and rail and arrived in British Columbia at the end of July. Interviewed on arrival at the Hotel Vancouver, Robert admitted that he was tired out by the long journey, and delivered an emotional speech: 'All the things I am and have, I owe to the North. That far-off cold and silent land has made better men of all who have ever come out of it.' He added, however, that he was not a real sourdough, 'just a piker. I never packed a piano across the white ice, never saw the shooting of Dan McGrew or the cremation of Sam McGee.'

This was a none-too-veiled reference to Mike Mahoney, the hero of Merrill Denison's book *Klondike Mike*. A legend in his own lifetime, Mahoney is alleged to have hauled a piano over the Chilkoot Pass. After the publication of *Songs of a Sourdough* Mike widened his repertoire by reciting 'The Shooting of Dan McGrew'. The recitation was enhanced by the fact that Mahoney claimed to have witnessed the incident. At the Vancouver reunion Mike was called upon to regale the audience with the background story, but he was interrupted by another old-timer, Monte Snow, who had trailed over the Chilkoot as a teenager with his father and had arrived in Dawson in 1897. He knew very well that there had never been a Dan McGrew in Dawson and leaped to his feet to expose Mahoney. But to his chagrin he was shouted down by the other sourdoughs who gave Mike the biggest ovation of his life. *Populus vult decepisse*; people like to be deceived. This echoed an earlier confrontation. In 1937 a reporter from Portland, Oregon, had got Robert to debunk Mike. When Robert's letter, attempting to set the record straight, was read out at a sourdoughs' reunion, Robert himself came in for a great deal of opprobrium. Thereafter Robert considered it more tactful to remain tight-lipped on the subject — until apparently goaded into refuting the hoary myths at the jubilee celebration.

When asked if he planned to go back to the Klondike, Robert said that he did not have the time to get up there. 'Got to get back to Monte Carlo and the Casino,' he quipped. 'I'm a bad lot, you know.' This flippant remark was interpreted literally by another newspaperman, Toddie Beattie, who wrote earnestly, 'The truth is Mr Service just loves to gamble. He goes every day to the Casino, where, when not trying to bust the bank with his system, he's jotting down new verses amid the grandeur of white marble pillars and famous old paintings.' To a third reporter, however, Robert told the truth. 'I'm now living on borrowed time. There's no time for anything but work.'

On Saturday, 31 July, Robert, Germaine and Iris were welcomed aboard Canadian National's new Pacific luxury passenger-cargo liner *Prince George*. Captain E.B. Caldwell took the Service family on a conducted tour of the ship and got Robert to autograph copies of his poems for the ship's library. The liner also possessed a recording of Robert reciting 'The Spell of the Yukon' and other ballads, and a high point of the last evening of the return voyage from Skagway was when the hostess turned down the lights in the lounge and played the record. As the ship glided silently through the Inner Passage surrounded by the peaks which were so formidable to the men who went to the Klondike at the turn of the century, the author declaimed his favourite verses in his expressive, soft Scottish voice. There would not be a sound in the lounge when the record ended. For a moment, passengers would be transported back to the days when men in rowing-boats 'rode the White Horses' of the rapids down to the tiny settlement which is now the bustling city of Whitehorse.

Robert carried a volume of Stevenson's poetry with him and confessed that he never read modern poems. 'I can't understand them,' he was reported as saying. 'And I don't even bother to try. But then it would be silly for the highbrows to understand my poetry when I only write for the ordinary people.' The Convention itself took place on 12–14 August. About two hundred old-timers were expected to attend; but in the event more than three times that number came from all over Canada and the United States. The Sourdoughs' Convention climaxed with a grand banquet, attended by such luminaries as ninety-one-year-old Nathan Kresge who had struck it rich at Gold Hill outside Dawson, and thrice-married Mrs E.L. Van Duren, best-remembered as Klondike Kate, queen of the gambling-halls. When Robert recited 'The Spell of the Yukon' every cheechako and sourdough in the emotionally charged room was in tears.

Although he had now done with prose — none of his immediate pre-war manuscripts ever saw the light of day as published novels — Robert was, indeed, working harder than ever. By 1948 and in his seventy-fifth year, Robert had some six hundred published poems to his credit. To one reporter he confided that he was 'good for another twenty years — and there's no peace until the ideas get into words'. To another he boasted, 'I'm just a writer of verse. Can't understand how amazingly easy it is. I just go for a walk and come back with a poem in my pocket.'

On Saturday, 4 September, Robert and his family boarded the Canadian Pacific liner *Empress of Canada* at Montreal bound for Liverpool. Even this departure was widely reported in the Canadian press under headlines which included such epithets as 'Noted Yukon Poet', 'the Klondike Bard' or even 'Sourdough Service'. Most of these reports were given over to Robert and his family, adding, almost as an afterthought, that other passengers included Sir Howard Kerr, Controller of the Duke of Gloucester's Household, with Lady Kerr, Sir Bartram and Lady Rumble of London, and the Canadian delegation to the United Nations Assembly at the Palais de Chaillot in Paris. The Services were back in Monte Carlo by the end of the month, and Robert immediately got down to serious work on the poems which would see the light of day the following year, in the collection entitled *Songs of a Sun-Lover*.

The appearance of this volume heralded the beginning of the last phase of Robert's remarkable career. From then until his death a new volume of verse would appear at virtually annual intervals: *Rhymes of a Roughneck* (1950), *Lyrics of a Lowbrow* (1951), *Rhymes of a Rebel* (1952), *Songs For My Supper* (1953), *Carols of an Old Codger* (1954), *Rhymes For My Rags* (1956) and *Cosmic Carols* (1957). These eight volumes surpassed all of Robert's poetic output from 1907 to 1940. The first five of these post-war volumes were republished in 1955 as an omnibus entitled *More Collected Verse*. The three remaining volumes, together with 'Verse From Prose Writings' and 'Selections From Unpublished Verse', appeared as *Later Collected Verse*, published posthumously in 1960. Klinck[7] speculated that 'the aged minstrel had not yet given up the habit of composing several songs or ballads every week', and this was confirmed by Germaine Service who, some time after Robert's death, sent three stout notebooks to Arthur Stewart, containing a vast quantity of unpublished verse belonging to the poet's last years. Out of this Stewart distilled a volume of the more polished pieces, together with Serviceana ('a symposium of items relating to the life and works of Service') and the glossary of words which had appeared in *The Collected Verse of Robert Service* (1930). This labour of love was never commercially published, and exists solely in a bound typescript forming part of the Stewart Papers in Glasgow's Mitchell Library.

The sunset songs of the remarkable Monaco period possess considerable critical and autobiographical value, rounding out, on Robert's own terms, the story of his life and his personal philosophy. From internal evidence it seems that many of the ballads in *Songs of a Sun-Lover* were composed either before or during the Second World War, and the volume itself was dedicated to Provence: 'O Land of Song! O golden clime!' In a song celebrating his seventy-fifth birthday, on 16 January 1949, he was in a mood to whoop it up and let the world know that he was still alive. There was a defiant note in 'A Verseman's Apology' in which he reaffirmed his oft-repeated stance. He was a versifier, not a poet, and he gloried in the former: 'For God's sake don't call me a poet / For I've never been guilty of that'. In 'My Library' Robert confessed that he had not found the time to read his thousand books, preferring the daily press (and the Continental versions of the English newspapers at that). In March 1948, for example, when the House of Commons passed the first stage of a Bill to end capital punishment by a majority of twenty-three votes, Robert was inspired to write a poem entitled 'No Neck-tie Party' which was published as a letter to the editor, in the *Continental Daily Mail*, under the headline 'A famous poet on the death penalty problem'. It was written in the form of an address to 'the majority of twenty-three' by a murderer rejoicing that he would now cheat the gallows, ending with the chilling lines:

> Although I did no mercy show,
> In mercy you will bid me go . . .
> That he who kills and does not pay
> May live to kill another day.

After witnessing the hanging at Dawson in 1908, Robert had described himself as a 'fervent abolitionist', and certainly that was still his view as late as 1940 when 'The Ballad of Hank the Finn' was published. Why, or precisely when, he changed his outlook is not known, but the world had become a much more violent place in the 1940s and Robert's reactionary view might also have reflected the fears and anxieties of advancing years. Certainly many of his later poems show concern for the suffering sustained by victims of brutal crimes.

Several Yukon ballads were featured in *Songs of a Sun-Lover*, attempting to recapture the success of the Sourdough songs. These ballads were more mature, more polished, and also about as coarse as Robert dared go. Interestingly, one of these, the ballad of 'Marie Vaux of the Painted Lips', had previously appeared as 'The Last Supper' in Robert's first novel, *The Trail of Ninety-Eight*, published almost forty years earlier, where it had been claimed as the work of the 'pote', Ollie Gaboodler. Robert's sympathetic attitude towards fallen women was evinced in 'Babette', 'No Lilies for Lisette' and 'White Christmas'. To the gallery of characters created in earlier verse collections were added rhyming portraits of a failed actor, a millionaire, a little Jewish orphan, a murderer, an alcoholic, a biker and his girl, a pugilist past his prime and the girl deserted by her soldier boyfriend. Many other sympathetic character studies in verse would flow from Robert's prolific pen in the ensuing years. In the last quarter of his life (Robert was confident he would live to be a hundred) he developed a more overtly compassionate philosophy, highlighting the misfortunes of the poor, the oppressed and the under-classes in general, while savagely attacking vested interest, political tyranny and war. True to his earlier style, however, his philosophy was invariably couched in simple language and incorporated in the doings and sayings of actual men and women, often expressed in the first person.

The old wordsmith was as adept as ever at finding the right word and the most telling phrase, and using them to best effect, whether irony, humour or pathos were the required mood of the moment. There was plenty of vivid imagery, especially in those subjects that he knew best and were dearest to his heart. His Calvinist conscience occasionally pricked him for living such an easy life in the sunny Riviera, although his 'ultimate and dulcet home' was just as often described in lyrical terms. Inevitably, as he got older, he gave an increasing amount of thought to the metaphysical. As is often the case with agnostics, people who genuinely do not know whether God exists, much more time and thought were given to pondering the imponderable than by those secure in their beliefs in a Supreme Being. Robert's constant preoccupation with the problem was expressed in many of his later poems. Gradually it dawned on him that life, and all his writings about it, had a religious significance. His lifelong preoccupation with chronicling and describing the little dramas of human experience brought him to the realisation that:

> God is not outside and apart
> From Nature, but her very heart;
> No Architect (as I of verse)
> He is Himself the Universe.

In the subsequent volumes many pieces took on a more meditative character, and Robert included sections actually headed 'Rhymes for Reverence'. Actually, a thematic approach was evident in both *Songs of a Sun-Lover* and *Rhymes of a Roughneck*, verses being arranged in sections entitled 'Lowbrow Lyrics', 'Garden Glees', 'Library Lays', 'Poems of Compassion', 'Vignettes in Verse' and, by contrast, 'Ribald Rhymes', some of which verged on the outright bawdy. The essential difference between these two volumes, however, was a growing tendency to moralise in the latter. Robert also betrayed the catholicity of his literary tastes in 'God's Skallywags', where he placed François Villon, Baudelaire, Byron, Poe, Wilde, Francis Thompson and Burns high above the 'merely holy' writers. He praised Maeterlinck as 'a forgotten master', communed with the ghost of Thomas Hardy as one of the 'Great Rejected Poets' and chose Cervantes in preference to Shakespeare.

A new class of verse which appeared in the *Roughneck* volume and was developed in the later books was devoted to Robert's travels. Many of these pieces took as their inspiration places and incidents in Italy and Spain, countries which Robert and Germaine visited frequently in the late 1940s and early 1950s. *Lyrics of a Lowbrow* (1951) harked back to the Klondike days with the sequence of 'Dawson Ditties', a nostalgic look at the girls of the dance-halls and gambling saloons. In the highly evocative poem 'Two Men', he paid generous tribute to Jack London and Rex Beach who had done in prose what Robert had achieved in verse. Aside from some very trenchant comments on the political atrophy of Franco's Spain, successive sections of this volume showed Robert's continuing interest in, and observation of, every facet of life and nature. As the title suggests, *Lyrics of a Lowbrow* made a virtue of the fact that Robert was writing for the common man, and the tone was set by the prelude, 'To lure the crowd, with cap and bells I sing'. The volume was leavened with flashes of humour, showing Robert's consummate mastery of the poetic one-liner.

There was also a sense of urgency, of a race against time. In 'L'Envoi' to *Lowbrow* Robert begged, 'O God! please let me write / Just one book more'. There were to be four more in his lifetime, however, and a fifth was in production at the time of his death. Robert revealed, in correspondence, that he was now composing a fresh ballad or verse almost every day. He would amuse himself by rhyming and singing lines to himself with the accompaniment of accordion, ukulele, concertina or guitar, often singing in the dark to an imaginary audience. In *Rhymes of a Rebel* (1952) he returned with renewed sparkle and vigour to the political theme, both France and Spain being targets for sardonic rhymes. In some ballads Robert adopted the persona of a French peasant or a conscript or a 'volunteer' inveigled into enlisting. These essentially anti-war poems were composed at a time when the world was embroiled in the Korean conflict and the Cold War was at its height, when the threat of a Third World War and a nuclear holocaust was very real. Although Robert was, if not a millionaire, certainly extremely comfortably off, he never lost the common touch. Many of the *Rebel* rhymes, under the collective heading of 'Lyrics of the Lost', betrayed Robert identifying closely with the underdog, or speaking out against social and political injustice.

Although he constantly decried the epithet of 'poet' as applied to himself, he was, in essence, a poet in the literal sense (the word, in Greek, simply means a 'maker'). Indeed, the late-medieval Scots word for a poet is 'makar' and Robert Service truly lived up to this ideal — far more than many so-called poets.

Monaco, like Hollywood, was a place bristling with celebrities, where one more celebrity in their midst could sink into obscurity if he so wished. In the principality, Robert kept a very low profile, and few, if any, of his neighbours knew that he was a writer. If they gave the matter any thought at all, they probably imagined the wiry little Scotsman to be a retired bank manager which was not so wide of the mark after all.

Nevertheless, at various times articles appeared in the Monaco newspapers and magazines about the celebrated poet, illustrated with photographs showing the bard in his opulent apartment, surrounded by statuary and other valuable art objects. This, and the publication of his daily routine, may have tempted the thieves who broke into the villa one day in October 1950, between three o'clock and five-thirty, while Robert and Germaine were taking their afternoon stroll. Apparently neither the outer door, nor the inner door to the ground floor, had been locked, while the door to the Service apartment was forced by a crow-bar. When Robert and Germaine returned from their walk they found a horrifying scene of utter disorder: drawers had been pulled out and their contents spilled on to the carpet, cupboards and chests had been ransacked, chairs overturned and books pulled from their shelves. The burglars found a tidy sum in ready cash, consisting of thirty *mille-franc* notes, but they also took jewellery and works of art with an estimated value in excess of two million francs (about a quarter of a million pounds sterling). Although he disdained material possessions, Robert probably never got over the shock. To Arthur Stewart he wrote a month later, saying that the loss was irrecoverable. The sense of violation of his property was probably heightened by the feeling that the burglary might have been avoided had he not succumbed to the temptation of a little bit of the limelight in the local press. Henceforward Robert resolved to withdraw into his hermitical shell.

In March 1953, however, Guy Riffet, a feature writer for the Monegasque newspaper *L'Espoir*, discovered Robert and produced a lengthy article, under a slightly inaccurate French headline signifying 'I am a young man of 80 years, affirms Robert Service, the Canadian Kipling'. The subtitle was also not quite true: 'Retired, since 1945, to Monte Carlo, he bathes every year till November' — presumably 'in the sea' was understood. One paragraph did, indeed, claim that Robert's eightieth birthday had been celebrated the previous 16 January, when, in fact, he was only seventy-nine, but it was a minor point. Robert told the reporter, 'I no longer work for the money. I do it solely for pleasure. If I never got another sou for my work I would still be quite content.'

Robert's unvarying daily routine was described in minute detail. He rose at eight, did a rigorous work-out for an hour, then back to bed for a quick cup of coffee. From nine till noon he pounded his typewriter, then lunch, a siesta and revision of the morning's work, followed by a long walk, then dinner. He was in bed by ten-thirty but then read magazines and newspapers for an hour or two. Until 15 November last, he had also bathed every morning in the sea not far from Larvotto, and would resume this practice in May. Riffet was struck by Robert's asceticism. 'If I did not have my family,' Robert was quoted as saying, 'I would happily retire to a monastery, such as les Îles de Lérins'. In seven years in Monte Carlo Robert could count no more than seven friends, mostly his near neighbours, although he admitted that, now and again, he visited Somerset Maugham at the Villa Mauresque in Saint Jean-Cap Ferrat. 'Somerset Maugham and I love different worlds,' Robert said. 'He is much more out-going, whereas I prefer to stay at home. Socialising, for me, is rather a waste of time. It's all right for young people, perhaps, but not at my time of life.' Contrary to his earlier aversion, Robert confessed that he enjoyed a game of cards, although his main relaxation was reading. The library in his villa contained over two thousand volumes, and a similar number of books was housed at Dream Haven. The old vagabond still had the wanderlust, admitting that he would love to visit Australia, New Zealand and South America before he died. 'I would also have liked to visit China,' he said wistfully, 'but I'm afraid I've left that too late.' His only criticism of Monte Carlo was that it was too law-abiding (this in spite of the burglary); it did not produce the criminal characters and the low-life types which he found so fascinating and which provided him with material for his verse. He reminisced about the good old, bad old days in the Latin Quarter of Paris. The rest of the article roamed over Robert's early career and his wartime experiences in Hollywood. Significantly, there was no mention of having written novels, far less one about Monaco itself.

In 1952 Iris, then aged thirty-five, got married. To Arthur Stewart Robert wrote on Burns Day 1954, just after his own eightieth birthday, explaining why his projected trip to Glasgow the previous summer had been cancelled.

> I am now a grandfather and I was dedicated at that time to our little Annette. My daughter married the leading banker here and is very happy.
>
> I hope your lovely wife & yourself are keeping well despite your criminel (*sic*) weather. I will try to make Glasgow this Summer & will let you know if I do.
>
> I hope you are reading the new books I write. I sent the latest to the publisher today, & I have another practically in the bag. But I am over eighty now, & there must be a limit to productivity. However, I feel hale & hearty enough.[8]

Iris married James Llewellyn Davies whose career in Lloyd's Bank was crowned when he was appointed manager of the prestigious branch in Monte Carlo, serving the needs of the wealthy expatriates. Davies was a widower, nineteen years older than Iris, with a grown-up family by his first wife. He had seen service in the First World War as a lieutenant in the Royal Air Force shortly after it was constituted in April 1918, and had subsequently worked in various French branches of Lloyd's before going to the Riviera after the Second World War. Iris played tennis with the banker's twenty-year-old daughter and what she heard from the girl about her widowed father sounded very appealing. When the girl returned to England Iris took up golf with a view to getting to know Davies, a keen golfer, more intimately. This ruse succeeded and eventually Iris and James got married. Having got her man, however, Iris never played golf again. Anne was born on 15 October 1952, while a second daughter, Armelle, was born on 12 October 1954. Both are now married with families of their own, Anne living in Paris and Armelle in Melbourne, Australia.[9]

In his eighties Robert was more prolific than ever. It was almost as if he felt that he had to atone for the wasted years of 'divine loafing' in the 1930s.

These had not been entirely wasted, however, for they were to provide a wealth of material on which Robert drew in his last decade. The two volumes referred to in the letter of January 1954 were *Carols of an Old Codger* which appeared later that year, and probably *Rhymes For My Rags* whose publication was delayed till early in 1956, mainly because both Ernest Benn and Dodd Mead brought out *More Collected Verse* in 1955.

Although many of the verses published in these volumes were derived from the rich treasure of Robert's experiences over eight decades, he was still producing pieces with a topical theme. After *Poisoned Paradise* Robert had almost — but not quite — avoided any references to Monaco in his work. Then on 18 April 1956, at a simple civil ceremony in the throne-room of the Palace, Prince Rainier III married the film actress Grace Kelly. A star-studded public ceremony, in the Cathedral of Monaco, took place the following day. Fred Majdalany of the *Daily Mail* was one of the two thousand journalists who flocked to the tiny principality to chronicle the prenuptial brouhaha for the world's press and, having discovered that the first poet he had ever enjoyed happened to be living there, he wrote to Robert seeking an interview. In due course he received a modest note:

> I am a quiet recluse, dedicated to my work, and in my 83rd year; so really I don't think I rate interview interest. However, if it would not bore you to call on me, I will be at home on Saturday at half-past four, and maybe we could put a small one down the hatch.

The 'small one' turned out to be an excellent bottle of champagne. Majdalany described Robert as 'a short gentle man with a French wife, a ruddy face, a fuzz of grey hair, and the remains of a Scottish accent'. He was entranced by the sumptuous villa commanding a splendid view of the bay and noted that Robert 'almost casually mentioned that he thinks he may be the only living writer who has made $1,000,000 out of writing verse'. Robert was quick to correct any impression that what he produced was poetry. 'I am just a writer of verse. I write every morning. Sometimes I manage three poems in a day. I build up a stock, then I make a selection and publish a volume.' Then he conceded that he was not read as much as he once was. 'The rhyming racket is not what it was. But the old ones still sell.' The original Yukon ballads had, by that time, been on sale for forty-nine years and had never been out of print; by the mid-1950s more than three million copies of *Songs of a Sourdough* had been sold. Interestingly, Robert admitted that these days he committed his verses directly on to the typewriter. He also mentioned his plans for longevity by a special programme of diet and exercise. 'I eat no breakfast, a light lunch with very little meat, a good evening meal which usually consists of rice, porridge and potatoes. I walk hard for three hours every day and I have a daily swim for six months of the year.'

Among the royal couple's wedding presents was a specially leather-bound edition of Robert's collected works, with an illuminated manuscript of a poem dedicated to Grace Kelly inscribed on the fly-leaf. Simply entitled 'To G.K.', it read:

> Princess, what magic pen was dipped
> In radiant colours of romance
> To write the wonder of your script,
> Your fairy tale of chance?
> Bring us Beauty, Art and Grace,
> Be welcome to this land of Ours.
> And with our homage take your place
> 'Mid song and flowers.
> Long may you play your golden part,
> Not only to en-sky your name,
> But to be throned in every heart
> With hearth-fire flame.
> A people we, proud of our Past,
> From modern urgency afar
> Long have we hoped with faith steadfast
> To hail with ecstasy a Star.
> Sweet Princess, may our dream come true —
> Our Star be You.

On the day before the wedding Robert was visited by the parents of the bride, and he recited the poem to them. Mrs Kelly apparently was in tears by the end. Hungry for a story, reporters picked up the ode and 'Dan McGrew's Poet' was hailed by them as 'Poet Laureate of Monaco'.

The fifth of Robert's Monegasque volumes was *Songs For My Supper*, published in 1953 and incorporated at the end of *More Collected Verse* two years later. The travel verses drew heavily on the two visits to the Soviet Union in 1938–39, and it was interesting to note that the futile love-affair between Wilbur and 'Olga of the Volga' was here rendered as a charming ballad. 'At Lenin's Tomb' not only reflected Robert's impressions in 1938 but pointed a warning to the world during the Cold War. Hitherto the contrast between the affluent poet and the poverty of which he wrote was continually being high-lighted; but in this volume Robert dropped his millionaire persona and assumed the image of the octogenarian bard who had to work hard for a crust, because no one would buy his books. This artifice enabled him to write with greater facility of those subjects dearest to his heart, the condemned felon, the wage-slave, the unwilling conscript and the underprivileged in general, and he could draw on his rich experience, directly or indirectly. The common denominator was freedom. Robert had amassed a fortune which enabled him to do what he wished, but he was always acutely aware of others, much less fortunate than himself, who were doomed to drudgery or obliged for economic reasons to knuckle under. He was a champion of liberty but not of equality or, indeed, fraternity. He was a rugged individualist to the very end.

The last volumes, *Carols of an Old Codger* (1954), *Rhymes For My Rags* (1956) and *Cosmic Carols* (1957), maintained the fiction of the poor old bard whose books did not sell because his rhymes and rhythms were no longer fashionable. But there was still plenty of the old fire and even a reprise of the Yukon ballads, of which the song of Violet de Vere, 'strip-teaser of renown', haled before a judge for disorderly conduct, is a classic. When Judge McGraw fines her twenty dollars she ripostes:

'Judge, darlin', you've been owin' me five bucks for near a year:
Take fifteen, — there! We'll call it square,' said Violet de Vere.

In 'The Twins of Lucky Strike', Lipstick Lou dies in childbirth, but the motherless babies are immediately adopted by some of the roughnecks, Black Moran from Nome promising to be their Grandpa. 'I sink zey creep into my heart,' says Montreal Maree who looks after the infants while sixty sourdoughs donate 'solid pokes o' virgin gold' to hang on the babies' Christmas tree in the saloon. The ballad ends with the incongruous scene of Montreal Maree 'awheelin' of a double pram'. This subject, which could have become mawkish, was handled with a deftness and assuredness throughout. The theme of the elderly grandfather runs through the later volumes, reflecting the unexpected pleasures which Robert derived from playing with his own granddaughters. Germaine recalled later that his greatest delight in the last years of his life was being seated in a deep armchair, with a little girl perched on each knee, while he improvised blood-curdling stories for them. One of the most charming poems he ever wrote was entitled 'Guignol' and described taking his toddlers to a Punch and Judy show.

Guy Riffet, who had discovered Robert in 1953, returned to his theme with another long piece in *L'Espoir* on Wednesday, 16 January 1956, Robert's eighty-second birthday. This time the headline was more accurate: 'Robert Service (82 years), the Canadian Kipling bathes in winter and gives himself only one day off each year; this is his birthday'. Robert was reported to be in excellent health, despite an accident on the beach at Larvotto on 28 October last when he fell and injured his spine. 'But I am still a young man,' asserted the poet. 'I hope to live long enough to cuddle the children of my granddaughters. I want to live to be a hundred and I do everything towards that. I get such pleasure out of life. For me, breathing is a great joy!' On this, his birthday, Robert was taking the day off, the only day in the year when he would not be seated at his typewriter. His daily routine was set out once more, though nowadays he worked at the typewriter for two hours at a time — from nine till eleven in the morning, but then again, from five till seven each evening, punctuated by long walks (eleven till noon and four till five). Although he rose at eight in the morning, he habitually read in bed till at least two.

Some of the figures quoted in this article are highly suspect. No fewer than fifteen million copies of *Songs of a Sourdough* were alleged to have been sold, which was a wild exaggeration; but it was probably not far off the mark to say that Robert had now composed about two thousand verses, few of them less than twenty-four lines in length. The actual published poems amounted to about half that number but eventually yielded over two thousand printed pages in all.

Among the hitherto unpublished pieces which were incorporated in *Later Collected Verse* in 1960, the man who had so often decried true poetry recanted slightly, hoping that he had, from time to time, produced a real poem:

> For every verseman by mistake
> A bit of poetry may make.

Robert firmly believed that the 'pretentious poets' of his day were actually 'versemen ninety-five per cent'. Then what, indeed, was poetry, which would have fulfilled a lifelong ambition, so carefully concealed?

> Originality of phrase,
> Imaginately ablaze;
> The word unique, the magic fire,
> That haunt, illumine and inspire;
> Not lyric lilt, nor rhyme precision,
> Not thought, not melody — just VISION.

Robert's trouble was his fecundity and facile pen. Undoubtedly, in the early period of his poetic career, he strove to be a true poet; but when his work was patronised and put down, he consoled himself with the thought that what he wrote actually paid. It might only be 'newspaper verse' but it boosted his bank balance and ultimately gave him the freedom he so desperately craved. But in the last years of his life, when he had made his fortune and money meant nothing to him, the old hunger to write real poetry surfaced again. It is ironic that much of his best work, truly sublime poetry, should come at a time when Robert was no longer so fashionable. Sales of those first Yukon ballads continued to thrive, but the Monaco volumes seldom ran to more than one printing, and that was but a fraction of the enormous print-runs of the 1920s and '30s. It was as a versifier that he had made his name, and it was as a versifier that he would go to his grave; but he deserved much better than that.

Robert was still taking his daily dip each morning until the autumn of 1956, though Germaine chided him constantly. It was not so much the swimming that she objected to, but the long, arduous climb back from the beach to the villa, which she felt was too strenuous for him. Thereafter Robert eased up on the spartan swims, though he continued to go for long walks. In 1957 the fiftieth anniversary of his first book was celebrated by the release of a paperback edition. Interviewed by the Riviera correspondent of the *Daily Telegraph*, Robert complained, 'Nobody writes about me these days, but somebody must read the books, because they go on selling.' Looking out through the window of his white-walled apartment towards the blue Mediterranean, he said, 'I am a professional writer,' adding with a boyish grin, 'I expect I shall die with a pen in my hand, trying to describe what it feels like.' He enjoyed life in Monaco, saying that a small state suited him. 'If there were more small states, the world would be more peaceful.' But he spoke sadly about the ageing expatriate community whose average age was seventy-five. 'We are all getting old here. All my neighbours are old men,' he said. 'I fancy Willie Maugham will last the longest. He was a doctor, and knows how to look after himself.' Maugham, who was actually nine days younger than Robert, did indeed live longer, dying on 16 December 1965. On one occasion Maugham told Robert that he envied him: 'You are a poet. Your work will endure long after my novels and short stories are forgotten.'

In May 1958 Pierre Berton came to Monte Carlo with a five-man camera crew from the Canadian Broadcasting Corporation to make a documentary film in the Close-Up series, about Robert's life and work. Pierre Berton, whose own name is inextricably linked to the Klondike where he was born and raised, was realising a life's ambition. It will be remembered that Robert had escorted Pierre's mother to a dance when she was a young kindergarten teacher and had even recited his latest composition to her, about Blasphemous Bill. At school in Dawson, young Pierre had recited Robert's verses which had grown out of an experience they all shared. He remembered vividly, reading the first lines of 'The Telegraph Operator':

I will not wash my face;
I will not brush my hair;
I 'pig' around the place —
There's nobody to care.
Nothing but rock and tree;

Nothing but wood and stone;
Oh, God, it's hell to be
Alone, alone, alone!

And he remembered, at the age of six, drifting down the Yukon River with his family and encountering just such a man. Forty years later Pierre could still recall the dishevelled figure, running down from his telegraph station, pleading with them to stop, have dinner, stay overnight. And when the Bertons had to move on, running along the river-bank crying out, 'Don't go yet . . . please . . . You've only just come!'

Berton published his impressions of the interview with Robert in a Canadian newspaper. The name on the brass plate at the door of the Villa Aurora was inscribed 'Mrs Robert W. Service' and, indeed, it was Germaine who greeted the Close-Up crew. She was described as 'a handsome, white-haired Frenchwoman' who called out to her husband using the French pronunciation of his name. A few moments later there emerged from 'as steep a stairwell as I have seen, a small, wiry man with a shock of white hair and the sharp features of a Scots dominie'.

Robert had, in fact, been looking forward to the visit, ever since Berton had written to him some weeks earlier broaching the subject. Robert had even gone to the trouble of writing out two scripts for the interview in advance, and committing his own lines to memory. 'This is my interview,' he said at one point. 'I'm the big shot in this one.' At another point he said, 'This is my swan song, you know. Pretty soon the old carcass will cease to function. I want to make this a good one.' Berton and his crew were then sent off to learn their lines, and return the following day. Although Robert professed not to care about his most famous ballad, he could hardly wait to recite it on camera. 'Service is a man who understands posterity and who knows the value of getting his own work on film the way he wants it.' When Berton and the cameramen returned to the villa the second morning, Robert greeted them immediately with 'I just feel in the mood for McGrew! Let's do it right now! I mightn't feel like it tomorrow.'

And so, 'in a thick miner's dialect, not untinged with his native Scottish lilt', Robert recited again the old, old tale of the man from the creeks who spun out his song of woe on a honky-tonk piano in the Malamute Saloon. Berton discovered that Robert could not quite remember this ballad, on which so much of his reputation — and wealth — rested. He improvised a good deal during the recitation, and occasionally asked for a prompter's help. Not unnaturally, Robert preferred his contemporary verse 'which does not sell very well'. During the interview he was ebullient and loquacious. When filming was finally concluded Robert was genuinely sad. 'Is it over? Is it really over?' he kept saying. But the crew was already packing up. 'Well! I'm sorry. I should have liked to go on,' he said. He stood in the doorway of his villa and the wind, catching his silvery hair and blowing it over his face, gave him an oddly dishevelled look. 'I wish it could go on forever. You know, it's made me young again; I've loved every minute of it.' As he said this, Berton caught a brief image of the telegraph operator running along the river-bank all those years before, pleading with them to stay a little longer.

A review of the programme itself, screened in August 1958, stated that Robert was 'refreshingly frank' about the means which had brought him a good living. Robert reckoned that he was fed up with McGrew and McGee and other characters from the Klondike which had haunted him all his life. 'But they will remain as a part of his memorial, his forte to couch in swinging rhyme an era of robust adventure so closely identifed with our country's development,' added the critic who concluded:

> Robert W. Service once gave voice to the wish that he could have lived
> in the Middle Ages and become a troubadour. He had the essential
> qualifications of the Medieval romantic. He put them to good use in
> the modern age and a great many readers will continue to be thankful
> for it.

Soon afterwards Robert and Germaine packed up and went off to Lancieux for the summer months. Here Robert resumed his customary routine, and even managed to write some verse. To his American publishers, shortly before his eighty-fourth birthday, he had sent a photograph, taken at Lancieux the previous summer, showing him seated in shorts, open-necked shirt and sandals. On the back he wrote:

> Alas! My belly is concave,
> My locks no longer wavy;
> But though I've one foot in the grave
> The other's in the gravy.

A rather similar photograph, but seated sideways and stripped to the waist to show his still fine physique, went in the summer of 1958 to the International Sourdoughs' Association who had asked him for the usual message, to be read out at their annual reunion in Vancouver that August. Robert sent them the following lines:

> When I was a Klondike high-roller
> I tilted my poke with the best

And though the climate might be polar,
I'd plenty of hair on my chest.
Now while I've no trace of rheumatics,
And maybe I shouldn't complain,
I'm worried because I just ain't what I was,
And I wish I was eighty again.

I still have my love for ladies,
Chuck grand-mummies under the chin,
Yet fearing a hall of Hades
I'm kinda allergic to sin.
Aye though the hootch-bird be a-singing
I'm deaf to its dulcet refrain,
When the going gets rude you've just got to be guid,
Gee I wish I was eighty again.

Some claim that the Nineties are naughty,
Them statements I grieve in reverse.
You've got to be humble, not haughty
To jiggily-jog on the hearse.
I blink at the blonde and bikini,
I shrink from the wink of champagne.
But, reforming, by heck, was a pain in the neck,
Gosh I wish I was eighty again.

This was probably his last poem, certainly the last to appear in print in his lifetime. A few days later, on 25 August, the inhabitants of Alaska went to the polls and voted overwhelmingly in favour of statehood. Alaska was due to become the forty-ninth of the United States on 1 January 1959; anticipating the successful outcome of the referendum, Robert was approached by Waino Hendrickson, the Acting Governor, to write an ode for the forthcoming inauguration. The poem was duly written, and Hendrickson subsequently sent a copy of it to *Newsweek* wherein it appeared on 14 July 1958.

Some time in August Robert contracted a bad dose of flu and was confined to his bed for several weeks. Iris and her family had gone to Lancieux to visit him and found him in a jaunty mood. They returned to Monte Carlo on 8 September, happy in the knowledge that Grandpa was getting over his illness at last. Three days later, on a sunny Thursday morning, Robert had managed to get out of the house for a short stroll along the shore, then had a light lunch and went to bed afterwards as usual. Around three o'clock, however, he called out to the maid, Henriette Pezeron (Tasie's daughter-in-law) asking her to fetch Dr Zeghers from the village. Those were his last words, for he died almost immediately, with his beloved Germaine at his side. His 'conky heart' had finally given out. Henriette told Jean Vallée that Monsieur Service had died and he immediately went to Germaine to organise the wake in the old Breton tradition, but she was unaware of this custom and would not sanction it. In the end Jean kept an all-night vigil over the corpse at Dream Haven, Germaine having moved next door. He would later recall how spooky it was, with only the sighing of the wind through the pines and the crash of the breakers on the shore, and the plaintive cry of the seabirds for company.

In Lancieux Robert was known as a dapper individual, rather reserved, always formal but a kenspeckle figure, often seen out on his long walks or canoeing trips off the rocky coast. Although he kept a low profile, and never obtruded himself in village affairs, he performed good works in the background and helped to fund a number of improvement projects, most notably the furnishing and re-equipping of the school. The beautiful war memorial erected in the village square was largely paid for by Robert to whom was presented the maquette of the bas-relief, showing a dying *poilu* dreaming of Lancieux on the horizon. In recognition of his contribution to the town over a period of almost half a century, the street leading towards Dream Haven was named the rue Robert W. Service in his honour.

Robert had expressed a wish to be buried at Lancieux, and a few days after his death a simple but very moving funeral was held. Along with the villagers who had known him mainly as a benefactor, came relatives of the poet from Britain and Canada, representatives of the British, French and Canadian governments, and literary figures from many parts of the world. A local seamstress, hearing of Robert's death, immediately embroidered a cushion with thistles, lion rampant and saltire cross of St Andrew, that the poet might have something suitably *écossais* on which to rest in his coffin. To Jean Vallée was granted the honour of bearing the large crucifix at the head of the procession. The horse-drawn hearse, laden with floral tributes sent from all over the globe, passed slowly along the street that bore his name and took his last remains through the village. At a bistro, the hearse halted while the coachmen went inside for some liquid refreshment. A press photographer captured the incongruous moment which subsequently appeared in Canadian and American newspapers with the comment that this was appropriate to the creator of Dan McGrew and Sam McGee.

The funeral cortège moved on to the cemetery on the edge of the village where Robert was laid to rest. Here, a plain pink marble headstone, simply inscribed ROBERT SERVICE 1874–1958 in gold lettering, was erected in due course on the grave bordered with begonias. Subsequently a quotation from one of Robert's poems was engraved on the upright stone:

Reward, dear Lord
Thy weary son:
May he be blest
With peace and rest,
For (*sic*) wake again.
Amen
  R.S.

The words are the last lines of the poem 'Rhyme for My Tomb' which closed *Rhymes of a Roughneck*. It is unfortunate that the first word of the last line was mistakenly rendered as 'For' instead of 'Nor' in the printed version. On the horizontal slab Germaine added her own tribute, in French:

Fauvette
Si tu voles autour
De cette tombe
Chante
Ta plus douce
Chanson

'Warbler, if you fly back to this tomb, sing thy sweetest song.' The tomb of the Service family lies at the very centre of the cemetery, just to the right of the *Calvaire*.

For several years after Robert's death Germaine continued to live at the Villa Aurora in the winter months and spend her summers at Lancieux, but failing eyesight by 1981 induced her to move into a residential home in Monte Carlo. Subsequently the distinctive ochre-coloured villa was demolished, but the site has never been redeveloped. Germaine achieved what Robert had failed to do; she died at Monte Carlo on 26 December 1989, at the venerable age of a hundred and two. Iris herself was widowed in 1984 but continues to spend the winter months in Monte Carlo, in a magnificent apartment overlooking the Mediterranean, barely a stone's throw from the site of the Villa Aurora. Every summer, as she has done since she was a baby, she goes back to Lancieux, though sadly Dream Haven has been empty and its windows shuttered for some years now. Although many have offered to buy the house she has remained true to her father's wish that she should hang on to it. Dream Haven was actually assigned to her at the age of sixteen, Robert being anxious to avoid death duties on his French estate. On part of the land, however, he built a second house (now Ker Armelle, 13 rue Robert W. Service) and it is here that Iris and her family spend their summers.

During his lifetime Robert prudently set up a trust fund for his grand-daughters. When his will was filed for probate in May 1959 the net residue of his estate was $297,874. As the copyright on his works continues until the end of 2008, however, the money accruing from his writings will have been not insubstantial. Apart from the posthumous collection of *Later Collected Verse* (1960) there have been many new editions of earlier verse volumes, and, more recently, a much-needed and long-awaited compilation entitled *The Best of Robert Service*. In recent years there have also been videotapes and sound recordings of Robert's best-loved verses. Dodd Mead and their successors, Putnam, have estimated that they alone have received almost five hundred requests to give one or other of the Service ballads musical or dramatic settings over the thirty-five years since Robert's death. 'Dan McGrew' was not only made into a film in its own right, but it was recited by Margaret Rutherford, as Miss Marple, in *Murder Most Foul*, and it provided the subject for the first ever ballet with an original Canadian theme (1952) when the prima ballerina Eva von Gencsy shot to stardom as the Lady known as Lou. Pierre Berton once claimed that of the two thousand verses penned by Robert, four were immortal classics 'and that is not a bad record'.

It has often been stated that Robert Service is the most widely read poet of this century. In 1953 the Manchester Public Library conducted a survey of poetry reading and revealed that the Service volumes were borrowed twice as much as the volumes of Walter De La Mare, T.S. Eliot and Louis MacNiece put together, and that his works were far more popular than those of Keats, Milton, Kipling and Rupert Brooke combined.[10] No other poet, save Burns, has enjoyed such a wide appeal with the common man. Nor should it be forgotten that Robert Service was the favourite poet not only of Queen Marie of Romania, but also of Ronald Reagan and Queen Elizabeth the Queen Mother, who discovered their mutual interest at a state banquet in the 1980s and engaged in a friendly duel of quotations. Prince Philip, Duke of Edinburgh, is also a fan. As the principal guest at the annual banquet of the Institute of Mining and Metallurgy at Grosvenor House, London, on 6 May 1955, he said that his knowledge of mining was provided by the verses of Robert W. Service, and then proceeded to quote from 'The Lone Trail' and 'The Shooting of Dan McGrew' at great length. The Duke had visited the Yukon the previous year, and it may have been then that he became a Service addict.

The year after Robert died, a simple stone seat with an inset plaque was erected in the Robert Service Memorial Park at Cowichan on Vancouver Island, not far from the tennis club where he had played as a young man. The memorial looks out over farmland which Robert knew so well. On the bronze plaque appear lines from 'Heart o' the North':

I who have been life's rover
This is all I would ask my friend
A little space on a stony hill . . .
Eternity passing over.

In 1974 a handsome bronze plaque was erected on the wall of the Canadian Imperial Bank of Commerce in Dawson where Robert had been teller. This plaque bears a bas-relief portrait, based on the profile bust which appeared in his early works, and is inscribed: 'Robert W. Service, poet and author whose writing spread the fame of the Yukon, was a teller at this branch 1908–9. His first poems including The Shooting of Dan McGrew were written at our branch in Whitehorse'. On 24 September 1976 a plaque was unveiled by the poet's daughter on the wall of the former post office in Kilwinning where Robert had spent his early boyhood; and on 13 July 1990 a large plaque was unveiled by Iris Davies on the wall of the tourist building in the main square of Lancieux. The ceremony was the culmination of a musical and poetical presentation of the poet's life and works entitled *Hommage à Robert Service*, organised by Wallace Lockhart with the help of Marie Dagorne, President of the local Tourist Association, and René Vilbert, the librarian of Dinan. To this day, the British and Canadian flags fly alongside the French tricolour in the square, in recognition of Lancieux's most famous resident. Robert has no more faithful devotee than Marie Dagorne. Her uncle was the mayor of Lancieux who sold Dream Haven to the poet; she herself, a year younger than Iris, has been the latter's best friend since early childhood. When asked for her lasting impression of Robert she commented, 'His eyes were very expressive and attractive, revealing an inner luminosity.' Her grandfather had shown Robert how to set seine nets for overnight fishing, while an aunt appears in the memorable photograph of Robert and Archie Bruce with their shrimp-nets on the rocky beach.

Jean Vallée, born in the very year that Robert first came to Lancieux, was closely associated with the poet for half a century. Jean's mother was the cook to Jules Jeunet at La Source, and he remembers the poet calling at the house on a number of occasions when he was quite a small boy. Robert was perfectly at ease with small children; he would crouch down to the same level and speak to them in simple language. Near Dream Haven was a field where Jean's parents cultivated vegetables. At harvest-time when they were resting from their labours, Robert would bring sweets or chocolates for the children. Later on, Jean recalled Robert as a good man to work with, always very tactful towards his employees. At a time when there was not much work in the village and few tourists about, Robert gave plenty of work to Jean's father Francis (a slater and stonemason), who built the retaining wall round the cliff-top from stones taken from the beach. Every winter, Francis could rely on several weeks' work on repairs and maintenance round the villa and its outbuildings. Later on, Jean and Francis were employed on the lengthy work of restoring Dream Haven after the German occupation, and when Robert decided to build a second house alongside, it was men from the village who got the valuable contract.

Today there is Robert Service Court in Kilwinning and Robert Service Schools in Dawson City and Scarborough, Ontario. In 1961, through the good offices of Arthur Stewart, Germaine Service set up a fund at the University of Glasgow to endow a prize in memory of her late husband, in the Ordinary English class.[11] During the 1970s Stewart continued with his labours on the writings of the poet, and to him Germaine sent much of the manuscript material pertaining to Robert's last years. In December 1973 Stewart, then a sick man (he died a few months later) deposited all his Service papers at the Mitchell Library. Unfortunately they arrived too late for the staff to mount an exhibition the following month to mark the poet's centenary.

Although several newspapers and periodicals devoted special features to the poet's centenary in January 1974, the event passed off without more substantial celebration. Two years later, however, the late Professor Carl Klinck published *Robert Service, a Biography* and on 17 August 1976 Canada paid belated tribute to the man who had put the Yukon on the literary map by issuing a stamp in the Canadian Writers series. The eight-cent stamp bore Robert's name but did not portray the Bard of the Yukon; instead, it showed one of his most famous characters. The last laugh went to the grinning figure of Sam McGee sitting up in his funeral pyre. Somehow, one feels that Robert would have approved.

:

BIBLIOGRAPHY

(First publication only)

Songs of a Sourdough
  Toronto: William Briggs, 1907
  London: Fisher Unwin, 1907

The Spell of the Yukon
  New York: Barse and Hopkins, 1907
  Philadelphia: E. Stern and Co., 1907

Ballads of a Cheechako
  Toronto: William Briggs, 1909
  New York: Barse and Hopkins, 1909
  Philadelphia: E. Stern and Co., 1909

The Trail of Ninety-Eight, A Northland Romance
  Toronto: William Briggs, 1910
  New York: Dodd Mead, 1910
  London: Readers' Library, 1928

Guldgrävartaget Anno 98
  Stockholm: Tidens Forlag, 1925

Rhymes of a Rolling Stone
  Toronto: William Briggs, 1912
  New York: Dodd Mead, 1912
  London: Fisher Unwin, 1913

The Pretender, A Story of the Latin Quarter
  New York: Dodd Mead, 1914
  London: Fisher Unwin, 1915

Bluffmarken
  Stockholm: Tidens Forlag, 1926

Rhymes of a Red Cross Man
  Toronto: William Briggs, 1916
  New York: Barse and Hopkins, 1916
  London: Fisher Unwin, 1916

Ballads of a Bohemian
  Toronto: G. J. McLeod, 1921
  New York: Barse and Hopkins, 1921
  London: Fisher Unwin, 1921

The Poisoned Paradise
  New York: Dodd Mead, 1922
  London: Fisher Unwin, 1992

Det Förgiftade Paradiset
  Stockholm: Tidens Forlag, 1927

The Roughneck, A Tale of Tahiti
  New York: Barse and Hopkins, 1923

Jack Moon Boxaren
  Stockholm: Tidens Forlag, 1927

The Master of the Microbe
  New York: Barse and Hopkins, 1926
  London: Fisher Unwin, 1926

The House of Fear, A Novel
  New York: Dodd Mead, 1927
  London: Fisher Unwin, 1927

Why Not Grow Young? Keeping Fit At Fifty
  New York: Barse and Hopkins, 1928

London: Ernest Benn, 1928

The Collected Verse of Robert Service
London: Ernest Benn, 1930

The Complete Poems of Robert Service
New York: Dodd Mead, 1933

Twenty Bath-Tub Ballads
London: Francis, Day and Hunter, 1939

Bar-Room Ballads, A Book of Verse
Toronto: Saunders, 1940
New York: Dodd Mead, 1940
London: Ernest Benn, 1940

Servicewise and Otherwise
Compilation by Arthur H. Stewart of quotations from the prose and verse of Robert W. Service. Glasgow, 1943

Ploughman of the Moon, An Adventure Into Memory
New York: Dodd Mead, 1945
London: Ernest Benn, 1946

Harper of Heaven, A Record of Radiant Living
New York: Dodd Mead, 1948

Harper of Heaven, A Further Adventure Into Memory
London: Ernest Benn, 1948

Songs of a Sun-Lover, A Book of Light Verse
New York: Dodd Mead, 1949
London: Ernest Benn, 1949

Rhymes of a Roughneck, A Book of Verse
New York: Dodd Mead, 1950
London: Ernest Benn, 1950

Lyrics of a Lowbrow
New York: Dodd Mead, 1951
London: Ernest Benn, 1951

Why Not Grow Young? or Living for Longevity
New York: Dodd Mead, 1952

Rhymes of a Rebel, A Book of Verse
New York: Dodd Mead, 1952
London: Ernest Benn, 1952

Songs For My Supper
New York: Dodd Mead, 1953
London: Ernest Benn, 1953

Carols of an Old Codger
New York: Dodd Mead, 1954
London: Ernest Benn,1954

More Collected Verse
New York: Dodd Mead, 1955
London: Ernest Benn, 1955

Rhymes For My Rags
New York: Dodd Mead, 1956
London: Ernest Benn, 1956

Cosmic Carols
London: Ernest Benn, 1957

Songs of the Far North
London: Ernest Benn, 1958

Later Collected Verse
New York: Dodd Mead, 1960
London: Ernest Benn, 1960

The Best of Robert Service
London: Ernest Benn, 1978

SOURCES CONSULTED

Manuscripts

Letters, manuscripts, press-cuttings and family memorabilia in the possession of Madame Iris Service Davies

The Arthur H. Stewart Papers, Mitchell Library, Glasgow

Parish registers of births and marriages for Kilwinning, Preston, South Meols, Clitheroe and St Cluvias

Census returns for Preston (1861 and 1871), Kilwinning (1841–91), Glasgow (1881 and 1891)

Confirmations and Inventories, Lancashire, Ayrshire and Lanarkshire

Wills, Lancaster District Registry

Registers of shipping, Glasgow (1896)

Log-books of Church Street and Hillhead Public Schools

Register of Bar-mitzvahs, Garnethill Synagogue

Records of the Commercial Bank of Scotland

Establishment Records, Canadian Imperial Bank of Commerce

Postmaster General's Minutes

Establishment Records, Post Office Archives

Printed Material

J. Innes Addison, *Roll of Graduates of the University of Glasgow, 1727–1898* (1898)

J.J. Bell, *Do You Remember?* (1934)

Laura Berton, *I Married the Klondike* (1955)

Pierre Berton, *Klondike* (1972)
The Klondike Quest (1983)

Martha Black, *My Seventy Years* (1938)

Merrill Denison, *Klondike Mike* (1938)

George Eyre-Todd, *Leaves from the Life of a Scottish Man of Letters* (1934)

Arlen J. Hansen, *Expatriate Paris* (1990)

John Hay, *Kilwinning Parish* (1967)

Revd. William Lee Ker, *Kilwinning* (1900)

Roy Lauchlan, *Kilwinning Local History Manual* (n.d.) [*c*.1985]

Sir Robert Bruce Lockhart, *Memories of a British Agent* (1932)

P. Mannex, *Preston Directory* (1873 and 1874)

David R. Morrison, *The Politics of the Yukon Territory* (1968)

Henry Brougham Morton, *A Hillhead Album* (1973)

James Hamilton Muir, *Glasgow in 1901*

Post Office Directory of Glasgow (1878–1901)

Who Was Who, vols II to V

Newspapers and Periodicals

Glasgow Herald
Glasgow Evening News
Glasgow Evening Citizen
Glasgow Weekly Herald
Los Angeles Times
New York Times
Preston Guardian
The Times

Toronto Star
Other newspapers cited specifically in the
  Notes

Major References
Harper — *Harper of Heaven* (1948)
Klinck — Carl F. Klinck, *Robert Service, a*

Biography, McGraw Hill Ryerson,
  Toronto, 1976
Lockhart — G. Wallace Lockhart, *On the
  Trail of Robert Service*, Luath Press, Barr,
  Girvan (1991)
Ploughman — *Ploughman of the Moon*
  (1945–46)

NOTES

1. The Wrong Side of the Tracks

1. James Bryce (1868), quoted in *Vanished Dwellings* by Nigel Morgan (1990), p5.
2. 'Conditions of Our Towns', in *The Builder*, 7 Dec 1861.
3. Ibid., 14 Dec 1861.
4. Ibid.
5. *Preston Guardian*, 30 Nov 1844.
6. Clitheroe parish registers.
7. Preston parish registers.
8. *Preston Guardian*, 24 Nov 1875.
9. Ibid. The newspaper erroneously gave his age as 63.
10. Wallace Lockhart (1991) speculated that the Parkers were Scottish because that was a common surname in Ayrshire, but it was also a common name in Lancashire.
11. P. Mannex, *Preston Directory*, 1873 and 1874.
12. Parish of North Meols, register of marriages.
13. 1871 Census.
14. Parish of St Johns, Preston, register of births. Robert's birth was not registered till 25 Feb 1874.
15. Lancaster District Registry, WLa 1/26, Wills, pp 233–36, 1876.
16. *Preston Guardian*, 24 Nov 1875.
17. *Ploughman*, p60.
18. Lancaster District Registry, *op. cit.*
19. Glasgow Directory, 1878.
20. *Ploughman*, pp29–30.

2. Kilwinning, 1878–83

1. Quoted by Roy Lauchlan, *Kilwinning from Old Postcards*.
2. Ibid.
3. Robert Service, quoted in Lockhart, p8.
4. *Ploughman*, p12.
5. Lockhart, p8.
6. *Ploughman*, p15.
7. James Mackay, *Burns, a Biography* (1992), p119; the substance of this myth was also given in an address to the Mauchline Burns Club by J.W. Forsyth of the Carnegie Library, Ayr.
8. Ibid., p83, quoting from the narrative of Gilbert Burns.
9. PO Archives, establishment records, 1861.
10. *Ploughman*, p4.
11. PO Archives, PMG's Minutes, 1886.
12. Glasgow Directory (1879–80); Confirmations and Inventories (1887).
13. *Ploughman*, p11.
14. Ibid., pp14–15.
15. Ibid., pp4–5.
16. Revd William Lee Ker, *Kilwinning* (1900), and John Hay, *Kilwinning Parish* (1967).
17. Roy Lauchlan, *Kilwinning Local History Manual*, Vol. I, Sec. 5 (1990).
18. *Ploughman*, pp8–9.
19. The monument stands prominently near the south-eastern side of the churchyard. Klinck (p193) said that the dates were

only partly decipherable but they may have been restored as they are now (1994) extremely legible.

20. *Ploughman*, p9.
21. Robert Burns, Autobiographical Letter to Dr John Moore, in *Complete Letters of Robert Burns* (1987), p250.
22. *Ploughman*, pp12–13.
23. Ibid., p13.
24. Kilwinning *Manual*, Vol II, Sec. 8.3 (1990).
25. *Ploughman*, pp15–16.
26. Ibid., p16.
27. Ibid., p19.
28. Ibid., p19.
29. Ibid., p25.
30. Ibid., pp27–28.
31. Klinck, pp3–4.
32. *Ploughman*, p31.
33. 'If every male would wear the kilt' (quoted by Lockhart, p12).
34. *Ploughman*, p32.
35. Ibid., p33.
36. Confirmations and Inventories (1887).
37. Kilwinning *Manual*, Vol. II, Sec. 9.12–14 (1990).
38. Confirmations and Inventories (1913).
39. Kilwinning parish registers.
40. Robert Service also visited Kilwinning in August 1947 and was planning another visit in 1958 when death intervened.

3. Schooldays in Glasgow, 1883–88
1. *Ploughman*, pp31–32.
2. Ibid., p39.
3. Ibid., pp40–41.
4. Ibid., p41.
5. Ibid., p41.
6. Ibid., pp41–42.
7. Ibid., pp42–43.
8. Ibid., p43.
9. *Hillhead High School Jubilee Magazine* (1935), pp42–43.
10. H. Brougham Morton (ed.), *A Hillhead Album* (1973).
11. *Ploughman*, p44.
12. Ibid., p45.
13. Sir David Bone, *Landfall at Sunset*, p19.
14. *Ploughman*, p86.

15. 'Handsome Nell' was thus attributed from 1851 till 1992. Before (1828–50) and since, the heroine has been identified as Helen Blair.
16. *Ploughman*, p47.
17. Ibid., p47.
18. Ibid., p49.
19. Ibid., p50.
20. Ibid., p52.
21. Ibid., p53.
22. Glasgow Directories; 1891 Census.
23. *Ploughman*, p55.
24. *History of the Western Baths* (1976).
25. *Glasgow Herald*, 16 July 1886.
26. *Ploughman*, pp56–57.
27. W. Innes Addison, *Roll of Graduates of the University of Glasgow, 1727–1898* (1898), p547.
28. Jewish Archives, Garnethill Synagogue; Glasgow Directories; 1891 Census.
29. *Ploughman*, pp58–59.

4. Adolescence, 1888–96
1. *Ploughman*, p60.
2. Ibid., p61.
3. Ibid., p64.
4. James Hamilton Muir, *Glasgow in 1901*, William Hodge (1901), pp206–7.
5. *Ploughman*, p70.
6. Ibid., p72.
7. Ibid., p73.
8. Ibid., p74.
9. Ibid., p77.
10. *Ching Ching's Own*; this weekly paper ran from 23 June 1888 to 17 June 1893.
11. *Ploughman*, p82.
12. Glasgow Directories; 1891 Census.
13. *Ploughman*, pp81–82.
14. Ibid., p79.
15. Ibid., pp83–84.
16. The same poem, slightly emended, was published in the *Duncan Enterprise*, Vancouver Island, 5 December 1903.
17. *Ploughman*, pp85–86.
18. Ibid., p87.
19. J.J. Bell, *Do You Remember?* (1934), p252.
20. J. Innes Addison, *Roll of Graduates of the University of Glasgow* (1898), p330.
21. *Ploughman*, p88.
22. *Literary Landmarks of Glasgow*, p280.

23. *Ploughman*, p88.
24. *Who Was Who*; obituaries in *The Times* and the *Glasgow Herald*, 3 February 1918.
25. *Ploughman*, p92.
26. Ibid., p93.
27. Ibid., p95.
28. The identity of Tommy Twitchwell has not been ascertained.
29. *Ploughman*, p97.
30. 1891 Census.
31. *Ploughman*, p99.
32. Ibid., p100.
33. Ibid., p101.
34. University Court, Minute 165, 21 December 1961.
35. *Ploughman*, p105.
36. Ibid., pp101–2.
37. Ibid., p102.
38. Ibid., p106.
39. Ibid., p107.
40. Ibid., p108.
41. *Who Was Who*, volume II.
42. *Ploughman*, p109.
43. Ibid., p116.
44. Ibid., p121.
45. Cited in many Canadian reference works, though the official Guide to Vancouver Island gives 1894.
46. *Ploughman*, p121.

5. Pacific Coast Vagabond

1. *Ploughman*, p125.
2. Strathclyde Regional Archives, Register of Shipping, Clyde Port Authority, 1896; Public Archives, Ottawa, Passenger Lists, 1896.
3. *Ploughman*, p65.
4. Confirmations and Inventories (1892); Andrew Service was the chief beneficiary of his father, John Service.
5. *Ploughman*, p127.
6. Ibid., p128.
7. Ibid., p129.
8. Lockhart, p28.
9. British Columbia Archives, Victoria. MS ED Se6.
10. Glasgow Directories; 1891 Census.
11. *Ploughman*, pp132–33.
12. Ibid., p135.
13. J.F. Corfield Papers, Add.MSS 852, British Columbia Archives.
14. Lockhart, p36, from information supplied by Jack Fleetwood.
15. Ibid., confirmed by a diary begun by Robert Service in 1896 (now in the possession of his nephew Kelvin Service).
16. *Ploughman*, p138.
17. Ibid., pp140–41.
18. St Cluvias parish registers, Cornwall.
19. *Ploughman*, p152. The diary kept by Robert Service in 1896 contains the pen portraits from which this section of *Ploughman* derived.
20. Ibid., p166.
21. *Los Angeles Examiner*, 14 May 1941.
22. *Ploughman*, p192.
23. *Los Angeles Examiner*, 14 May 1941.
24. *Ploughman*, p200.
25. A reference to *Bath-tub Ballads*, published by Francis, Day and Hunter (1939).
26. *Ploughman*, p212.
27. Ibid., p221.
28. Ibid., p223.
29. Ibid., p225.
30. Ibid., p226.
31. The charge of the Rough Riders up San Juan Hill on 1 July and the surrender of Santiago de Cuba on 17 July pinpoint this decision to July 1898.
32. *Ploughman*, p233.
33. Ibid., p234.
34. Jack Fleetwood, reported by Lockhart, p35.
35. *Ploughman*, p237.
36. Charles H. Gibbons, writing in *Pacific Travel*, August 1937.
37. Aileen Campbell, 'Hundred Years of Service', *The Province*, 4 May 1974, p5.
38. See Chapter 7, note 5.

6. Bank Clerk.

1. Robert Service, 'So I Have a Mild Face', *Maclean's Magazine*, 15 January 1941, pp9–10.
2. Records of the Canadian Imperial Bank of Commerce, Toronto. Charles H. Gibbons, however, stated (1937) that Service worked for a short time at the Bank of British North America in

Vancouver before joining the Canadian Bank of Commerce.

3. Derek Low, Canadian Imperial Bank of Commerce, 1974.

4. Obituary notice of John Alexander Service, from an undated Vancouver press-cutting, *c.*1950.

5. *Ploughman*, p257.

6. Klinck (p29) misread this passage and assumed that 'one of the little juniors in the bank had actually won a sizable stake when he had been sent to the Yukon'.

7. *Ploughman*, pp257–58.

8. Fred Corfield's account, transcribed by Dr Helen Henley.

9. Interview with Iris Service Davies, April 1994.

10. *Ploughman*, p261.

11. Ibid., pp262–63.

12. Ibid., p265.

13. Ibid., p267.

14. *Ploughman*, p268.

15. Ibid., p274.

16. Ibid., p276.

17. Klinck, p33.

18. David R. Morrison, *The Politics of the Yukon Territory* (1968), pp82–86.

19. *Ploughman*, p278; the earnings of the first volume were put at $100,000 (1944) but in newspaper interviews (1940–41) Robert Service claimed to have made 'half a million dollars'.

20. Obituaries in, for example, *Egyptian Gazette*, Cairo, 24 July 1950, *Performer*, London, 27 July 1950 and *Variety*, New York, 9 August 1950.

21. From information in the files of the Royal Canadian Mounted Police HQ, Ottawa, supplied by the archivist George Hann to Arthur Stewart, April 1949.

7. First Books.

1. *Ploughman*, p278. The machine on which Robert typed out his manuscript was a tiny Bennett portable, now in the possession of his nephew Kelvin Service.

2. Klinck, p39.

3. R.B. Bond, 'I Sold Service to the Public', *The Globe Magazine*, 28 June 1958.

4. *Ploughman*, p279.

5. Klinck (p38), who deduced from this that Robert Service must have been living near Duncan in 1902, although he was unable to identify the ranch and the store.

6. *Ploughman*, pp286–87.

7. Pierre Berton, *The Klondike Quest* (1988).

8. *Ploughman*, p291.

9. Quoted by Lockhart, p52.

10. Laura Berton, *I Married the Klondike* (1955), p24.

11. *Ploughman*, p294.

12. Mrs George Black, *My Seventy Years* (1938), p200.

13. *New York Times Film Reviews, 1913–1931*, p433.

14. Sir Robert Bruce Lockhart, *Memoirs of a British Agent* (1932), pp28–29.

15. Interview in the *Toronto Star Weekly*, 1 May 1910.

16. *Ploughman*, p333.

17. *Toronto Star*, 20 September 1912.

18. Laura Berton, pp71–72.

19. Pierre Berton, *Klondike* (1960), pp442–43.

8. Balkan Interlude.

1. Communication of Ludwig Beuttenmueller to Germaine Service.

2. *Harper*, p16 footnote.

3. Klinck, p75.

9. The Latin Quarter.

1. *Harper*, p35.

2. Ibid., p37.

3. Identified by Germaine Service. Klinck (p79), citing the Art Register, Glenbow Museum, Calgary, and *150 Years of Art in Manitoba* (Winnipeg Art Gallery, 1970).

4. *Harper*, pp39–41.

5. Klinck, p84; indentified by Germaine Service.

6. *Harper*, pp43–46, 60–61, 96–97 and 181–85.

7. Klinck (p86), who devotes sixteen pages to a detailed critical analysis.

8. Ibid., p99.

9. *The Master of the Microbe* (Barse and

Hopkins, 1926), p392.

10. MS Memoir of Germaine Service, in a school exercise-book bearing the price 0.95; the heavy franc only came into use in January 1960.

11. Information supplied by Iris Service Davies, 1994.

12. *Harper*, p65.

13. Marie Dagorne, 'Robert Service, Poète du Grand Nord Canadien et de la Ruée vers l'Or', *Le Pays de Dinan*, vol. IX (1989), pp193–203. Marie Dagorne was Jeunet's niece.

14. Arlen J. Hansen, *Expatriate Paris* (1990).

15. The few extant letters from Robert to Germaine are thus addressed.

10. First World War.

1. *Harper*, p72.

2. John Buchan, *Memory Hold the Door* (1940), p203.

3. Lockhart (pp93–94) quotes them without acknowledging their source.

4. *Harper*, p78.

5. Registers of births, Neuilly-sur-Seine.

6. *Harper*, p85; Charles Fenton, *The Apprenticeship of Ernest Hemingway,* sheds interesting light on the operation of this ambulance unit.

7. *Harper*, pp85–86.

8. The text here is taken from the manuscript, by courtesy of Iris Service Davies.

9. *Harper*, p86.

10. Laura Berton, pp149–51; Martha Black, pp258–69 .

11. Lockhart, p94.

12. Two letters, both dated 11 March 1920, from the British Red Cross Society to Robert Service, care of Fisher Unwin, announced his entitlement. The medals themselves were forwarded some months later.

11. Hollywood and the South Seas

1. *Harper*, pp100–1.

2. Ibid., p105.

3. Ibid., p107.

4. *New York Times*, 9 June 1924.

12. Paris, 1922–29

1. Klinck, p130.

2. *The Poisoned Paradise* (1922), p95.

3. *New York Times*, 11 August 1924.

4. *The Roughneck*, p27.

5. Ibid., p149.

6. cf. *Harper*, p115 for the description of the stream crossing.

7. *Harper*, p159.

8. *New York Times*, 3 December 1924.

9. Klinck, p141, identified for him by Germaine Service.

10. *Harper*, p179.

11. *Why Not Grow Young?* (1928).

12. *Harper*, p193.

13. Lockhart, p107.

14. *Don Juan* (1926) and *The Jazz Singer* 1927).

13. The Riviera, 1929–39

1. *Harper*, p176.

2. Ibid., p196.

3. Ibid., p185.

4. Undated fragment in Robert Service's cuttings scrapbook.

5. *Harper*, p188.

6. She was Helen O'Hara, with whom Frank Harris had eloped in 1894.

7. Ibid., p196.

8. Ibid., p203.

9. Ibid., p287.

10. Ibid., p361.

11. Ibid., p375.

12. Klinck, p159.

14. Phoney War

1. Harold H. Hart (ed.), *The Bawdy Bedside Reader* (1971).

2. Dr Helen Henley, on origins of 'Eskimo Nell', in correspondence with James Mackay, 1994. Ross Roy, however, considers that 'Eskimo Nell' was in print in North America by the late 1920s, pointing back to Robert Service himself as the author.

3. *Harper*, pp384–85.

4. From an undated and unidentified Canadian newspaper cutting, probably Toronto.

5. *Harper*, p395.

15. The Years of Exile, 1940–45
1. *London Evening News*, 19 July 1940.
2. *Harper*, p403.
3. Ibid., pp403–4 .
4. W. Innes Addison, *Roll of Graduates of the University of Glasgow, 1727–1898*, p330.
5. Confirmations and Inventories (1925).
6. Letter from Iris Service Davies, 19 May 1994.
7. *Harper*, p407.
8. *Los Angeles Times*, 19 November 1941.
9. *Harper*, pp407–8.
10. Memoir of Germaine Service, *op. cit.*
11. *Harper*, p411.
12. Transcript from the dialogue in the film itself.
13. Quoted in many Canadian news-papers, 15 May 1942, under such headlines as 'Robert Service Gives His Movie Earnings to the Red Cross'.
14. Geoffrey T. Hellman, 'Whooping it up', *The New Yorker*, 30 March 1946.
15. *Harper*, p421.
16. Hellman, *op. cit.*

16. Sunset Songs, 1945–58
1. Information supplied by Colonel von Auloch's niece, Inge Meredith.
2. Information supplied by Iris Service Davies.
3. *Harper*, p448.
4. *Vancouver Sun*, 11 August 1948.
5. *Publishers' Circular*, 26 July 1948.
6. Stewart Papers, Mitchell Library, Glasgow.
7. Klinck, p172.
8. Stewart Papers, *op. cit.*
9. Information supplied by Iris Service Davies.
10. *Co-operative News*, 14 November 1953.
11. Minute 165, Glasgow University Court, 16 December 1961.

INDEX